Offshoring and Employment

TRENDS AND IMPACTS

OECD

ORGANISATION FOR ECONOMIC CO-OPERATION AND DEVELOPMENT

ORGANISATION FOR ECONOMIC CO-OPERATION AND DEVELOPMENT

The OECD is a unique forum where the governments of 30 democracies work together to address the economic, social and environmental challenges of globalisation. The OECD is also at the forefront of efforts to understand and to help governments respond to new developments and concerns, such as corporate governance, the information economy and the challenges of an ageing population. The Organisation provides a setting where governments can compare policy experiences, seek answers to common problems, identify good practice and work to co-ordinate domestic and international policies.

The OECD member countries are: Australia, Austria, Belgium, Canada, the Czech Republic, Denmark, Finland, France, Germany, Greece, Hungary, Iceland, Ireland, Italy, Japan, Korea, Luxembourg, Mexico, the Netherlands, New Zealand, Norway, Poland, Portugal, the Slovak Republic, Spain, Sweden, Switzerland, Turkey, the United Kingdom and the United States. The Commission of the European Communities takes part in the work of the OECD.

OECD Publishing disseminates widely the results of the Organisation's statistics gathering and research on economic, social and environmental issues, as well as the conventions, guidelines and standards agreed by its members.

Also available in French under the title:
Les délocalisations et l'emploi
TENDANCES ET IMPACTS

Foreword

As part of its work on globalisation, and more specifically on global value chains, the Committee on Industry, Innovation and Entrepreneurship (CIIE) has included in its programme of work an analysis of the employment impact of international outsourcing and relocation of the business operations of multinational enterprises. The Committee has asked its Working Party on Globalisation of Industry to carry out this analysis.

The purpose of this report is to provide an objective response to the concerns that offshoring has raised in a large segment of public opinion. It aims to quantify the positive and negative effects of offshoring as much as possible, and to propose solutions that might be able to limit the downsides.

The report was prepared by Thomas Hatzichronoglou of the Directorate for Science, Technology and Industry. Other members of the Secretariat also made useful comments and contributions, among them Raymond Torres, Paul Swain, Alexander Hijzen, Marcos Bonturi, Norihiko Yamano, Pierre Poret, Christopher Heady and Marie-France Houde.

The OECD Secretariat would like to express its appreciation to all of the experts who helped prepare and discuss this report, with special thanks to Ken Warwick, Chairman of the Working Party on Globalisation of Industry. In addition, significant input was provided by Obie Whichard, Lionel Fontagné, Torbjörn Fredriksson, Michel Di Pietro and Mary Amiti.

Isabelle Desnoyers-James and Laurent Moussiegt of the Secretariat furnished statistical assistance, while Beatrice Jeffries, Julie Branco-Marinho, Paula Venditti, Florence Hourtouat and Sarah Ferguson provided secretarial services. Joseph Loux supervised the publication process.

Table of Contents

Executive Summary

This report does not look at the employment consequences of globalisation, but it examines one particular aspect of globalisation, which is offshoring. In Chapter 1, offshoring is defined as the total or partial transfer of an industrial activity (manufacturing or services) abroad, either to an existing or new affiliate, or through subcontracting to non-affiliated companies. The portion of the activity sent offshore that had been intended for the domestic market is then imported.

The main reasons that prompt firms to transfer activities abroad depend essentially on the nature of the activity concerned (production, research and development, decision centres, and so on). In the case of production of goods or services, the primary motivation emerging from opinion surveys is to cut costs, but not labour costs alone.

The report highlights the great complexity of the offshoring phenomenon and the many difficulties involved in measuring its consequences for employment. These can be negative or positive, depending on whether the frame of reference is short-term or medium-term, and whether the consequences are direct or indirect.

Skilled jobs are no longer safe from being sent offshore. Moreover, as offshoring is no longer limited to traditional sectors alone but is increasingly spreading to technology-intensive industries as well, including services, the emergence of two major Asian economies – China and India – that have partially closed their technology gaps and offer a large and increasingly skilled labour force increases the need for adjustment by more developed economies.

The authorities of some countries have launched initiatives to gauge the scope of the phenomenon, and, at the same time, universities and advisory institutes have conducted numerous evaluations. This research is done on the basis of either data at the firm level or macroeconomic aggregates using econometric techniques. Insofar, however, no country has yet instituted regular surveys in the area of offshoring.

The most relevant findings of this research show that all sectors are affected, but that the industrial sectors that have most downsized their workforce are not the ones that have most engaged in offshoring. Offshoring does not therefore emerge as a major cause of job losses. In most countries, only textiles, apparel and footwear would seem to be among the sectors that have both offshored the most and recorded the steepest job losses.

A substantial share of the jobs sent offshore is transferred to countries with lower labour costs. Here, offshoring is more commonplace in low-tech sectors that tend to employ relatively low-skilled labour. Gradually, however, it is also moving towards sectors ranked as medium or high-technology, especially in the case of services (software, computer services and other information technology services). Most of the offshoring to developed countries involves group restructuring and refocusing in capital-intensive sectors such as aerospace, pharmaceuticals or automobiles. Offshoring to developed countries also tends to be done through affiliated companies. In contrast, when the destination is a less developed country, subcontracting is then just as common a channel.

The Secretariat's calculations (Chapter 4) show that the offshoring of goods by the manufacturing sector is the most prevalent type of outsourcing abroad. What is faster-growing, however, is the offshoring of both goods and services by the service sector. As a rule, the short-term employment effects of offshoring are more important for manufacturing than for services. Thus, for a 1% increase in the proportion of imported intermediate manufactured goods, sectoral employment in the country of origin contracts by 0.15%, as opposed to roughly 0.08% in the case of services. However, the impact on employment could vary from a sector to another (Figure 4) and from country to country (table 8), as well as according to the reference period.

In the medium term, the effects of offshoring are positive for a country but fairly difficult to quantify in terms of jobs (from the macroeconomics point of view). Countries can benefit from higher consumer incomes because of the low prices of imported offshored goods (Section 4.7.1), the improved productivity of firms that engage in offshoring (Section 4.7.2), better control over inflation thanks to the impact of low import prices (Section 4.7.3) and enhanced export capacity (Section 4.7.4).

At the same time, the improved competitiveness of companies thanks to offshoring allows them to expand their market shares, profits and capital spending, which can feed through to new job creation in their home countries. The data available shows that in the service sector new job creation offsets job destruction from all causes combined, including offshoring. However, the manufacturing sector, which in the vast majority of OECD countries is losing workers primarily because of technological change, is a net creator of essentially skilled jobs. This phenomenon is even more pronounced in the sectors that resort most to offshoring. These sectors are net creators of skilled jobs.

Most of research to date shows that jobs lost to offshoring account for only a small percentage of aggregate job losses. According to the European Monitoring Centre on Change (EMCC) in Dublin, offshoring by European firms is responsible for less than 5% of total job losses in Europe – far behind bankruptcies, shut-downs and restructuring. It could then seem paradoxical that offshoring gives rise to so much discussion and fear. Chapter 5 of the report presents various explanations. It can be seen, first, that concerns are most acute in countries with high and long-term unemployment. A second explanation is that the research findings probably underestimate the employment effects of offshoring insofar as not all existing studies factor in indirect effects (Box 12, Section 5.1), including the impact of offshoring on firms that do not engage in it, on affiliates, on subcontractors and on suppliers.

Despite these problems, the importance attached to the negative consequences of offshoring stems from the fact that the job losses are known and visible immediately, whereas most of the benefits appear only after a certain time and are not perceived as direct consequences of offshoring. Annex 5 presents the results of a Secretariat questionnaire that was sent out to the national authorities of the member countries to ascertain whether they had an overall policy on offshoring and if measures were taken to try to prevent offshoring, foster innovation and re-invigorate the economy. Governments' responses to the questionnaire show that, in spite of certain proposals, no country has taken concrete coercive measures against offshoring.

This attitude may be explained by the fact that some of the measures under consideration run counter to international treaties signed by the countries. But there is also a risk, if measures to impede offshoring were put into effect, that the offshoring movement would gather pace, with firms feeling compelled to create all of their new jobs abroad, lest they become less competitive and more vulnerable in international competition.

It is probably necessary, then, to acknowledge that offshoring is a fact of life for businesses and that it would be counterproductive to throw up obstacles to prevent it. It should also be admitted that protectionism cannot be even a short-term response to the problem of offshoring.

Apart from the need for better measurement of offshoring's effects on employment and economic activity, so as to fine-tune policy action, it will be important to lay the groundwork for an economy that can adapt and specialise naturally in high-end, high-tech activities. This will entail, *inter alia*, substantial and ongoing research and development and innovation, as well as restoring the appeal of a science and technology culture.

Education and further training throughout workers' careers should be the main priority for governments and business enterprises. Without neglecting the need for social policy to help persons who lose their jobs because of offshoring, appropriate training would enable them to be hired for the new jobs created by the very companies that have shifted some of their activities offshore.

INTRODUCTION

The impact of offshoring on the labour market has become one of the major issues of concern to policymakers and public opinion. The phenomenon of offshoring as such is not really new, but it still arouses just as much debate and concern, essentially for three reasons.

Firstly, in many countries, offshoring had long affected only traditional sectors of the manufacturing industry, which would transfer the most low-skilled-labour-intensive portions of their production to countries having lower labour costs. This phenomenon sparked debate on the dangers of de-industrialisation and loss of know-how, especially on the technological level, yet the argument was often won by those pointing to the vitality of the service sector, and more specifically the role of exports in creating jobs in the sector. Today, one of the reasons that explains the new worries is the fact that offshoring is no longer confined to the manufacturing industry but also increasingly concerns services themselves. The rapid development of information technology means that different categories of services, and especially services to business, can now be imported.

Secondly, the jobs that used to be affected by traditional offshoring were in the main low-skilled jobs. On the other hand, the jobs affected by recent offshoring also involve more-highly skilled jobs.

Lastly, the third reason that causes anxiety concerns the emergence of the two great Asian economies, China and India, which have in part caught up technologically and which have a large and increasingly skilled workforce.

In this context, certain firms, including smaller ones, displace many activities to maintain their competitiveness. A short-term consequence of this displacement may be job losses in certain countries. In the medium term, however, enhanced competitiveness will enable many of these firms to create new activities and new jobs in higher-labour-cost countries as well.

Another cause that contributes to the revival of concerns is the lack of quantitative information and the poor quality of the data used in public debate to grasp the consequences of offshoring. Furthermore, the public debate is all the more confused because the term "offshoring" is used without a strict and agreed definition. Thus, the term is often attributed to a variety of cases which may have a negative impact on employment but which are not directly linked to the phenomenon of offshoring (Box 6).

Despite the weakness of data, many studies have been undertaken recently to measure, even indirectly, the impact of offshoring on employment (see the bibliography at the end of the document). All these studies, despite their imperfections, conclude that, for the time being, offshoring has little impact on employment in the compiling country. Moreover, some studies show that at present the decrease in employment because of offshoring is considerably greater in manufacturing than in the service sector, which, unlike manufacturing, is a net job creator.

The debate on offshoring has aroused numerous questions, some of which could be summarised as follows:

- How can offshoring be defined?

- What is the scale of the phenomenon?

- Has the pace of offshoring accelerated in recent times?

- How many jobs are affected by offshoring?

- What is the nature of the jobs affected by offshoring in terms of skills?

- What are the chief reasons for offshoring?

- What is the relative importance of offshoring of services compared with offshoring of goods?

- Which sectors (goods and services) offshore the most?

- Is there a predominant form of offshoring (direct investment or subcontracting) which characterises each sector?

- Could offshoring constitute a threat of de-industrialisation?

- What are the compiling countries* and countries of destination of offshoring by mode and sector concerned?

- Is there a difference as regards resort to offshoring between firms controlled by residents of a country and affiliates under foreign control?

- How can the benefits of offshoring be evaluated, especially in terms of jobs?

- How are the benefits of offshoring shared between the different economic actors?

- How many jobs are created or maintained thanks to offshoring?

- What is government policy on offshoring?

- How can public concerns be allayed and confidence restored?

This report can only answer some of the above questions. It should nevertheless be explained at the outset that this version of the report focuses its attention not on all cases of offshoring of an activity abroad, but only displacements accompanied by a reduction in activity in the compiling country, usually with loss of jobs.

The first chapter is dedicated to a definition of the concept of offshoring. It distinguishes between relocation through foreign affiliates and that resulting from international subcontracting. Particular attention is also paid to the terminology used.

The second chapter deals with the effects of offshoring on employment. The interaction between production, direct investment and international trade has an impact on employment which differs in the short and medium term. The chief motivations for offshoring are briefly presented in this chapter together with the latest developments in the theoretical debate concerning trade, offshoring and employment.

---

*   Reporting or origin countries.

The third chapter concerns measurement issues. It describes all the difficulties involved in the quantitative evaluation of jobs affected by offshoring, and the reasons why there are only indirect measurements. Various indicators are suggested in the chapter to measure the impact on employment and other approaches which have been adopted together with their limitations.

The fourth chapter presents some preliminary results based on sectoral data concerning a limited number of OECD countries. The limitations of available public data are also considered in this part, first to identify cases of offshoring and then to measure their impact on employment. Two brief monographs are presented concerning the United States and France. The choice of the United States was justified by the wealth of public data available, while France was chosen because its statistical services apply a method very similar to that suggested by the Secretariat to individual data by establishment. Indicators concerning several other countries are presented in annex. The last section of the chapter presents the main positive effects of offshoring

Finally, the last chapter sets out policies or regulatory measures to offshoring, while at the end of the chapter, a section analyses the cost of not moving offshore, and various measures which could contribute to reduce adjustment costs are proposed.

Chapter 1

DEFINING OFFSHORING

> This chapter provides an in-depth definition of offshoring, outlining the many different ways that industrial activity—in either manufacturing or services—can be shifted abroad. For a given corporate group, distinction is made between the two major types of offshoring: *i)* relocation through the corporation's own affiliates; and *ii)* international subcontracting to non-affiliated enterprises. In both cases, the portion of the operations sent offshore that had previously been intended to satisfy domestic demand is subsequently imported.

Defining offshoring is a difficult but essential task in the present context where public debate is often muddled and refers to excessively broad notions which distort understanding of the phenomenon and prevent a proper evaluation of its consequences.

First of all, the term *outsourcing* is used to designate the use of goods and services produced outside the enterprise. Outsourcing can occur within the country where the enterprise is located (*domestic outsourcing*) or abroad (*outsourcing abroad*)

The term *offshoring* is used to designate outsourcing abroad. This term covers two situations:

- Production of goods or services effected or partially or totally transferred abroad within the same group of enterprises (offshore in-house sourcing). This means where an enterprise transfers some of its activities to its foreign affiliates. These affiliates may already exist or have been created from scratch (greenfield affiliates).

- The second form involves the partial or total transfer of the production of goods or services abroad to a non-affiliated enterprise (offshore outsourcing). This operation consists of subcontracting abroad. The non-affiliated foreign enterprise could be either *i)* a firm controlled by residents of the country, or *ii)* a foreign affiliate controlled by a third party, or *iii)* an affiliate of the outsourcing country controlled by another group. The following table summarises the different situations in which a good or service is produced within an enterprise (or a group of enterprises) in the same country or abroad.

Table 1. Production options for an enterprise (or group of enterprises)

Location	Internal production (*in-house*)	External production (*outsourcing*)
Within the country (*domestic*)	Production within the enterprise and the country (*domestic in-house*)	Production outside the enterprise but within the country (*domestic outsourcing*)
Abroad (*offshoring* or *cross-border*)	Production within the group to which the enterprise belongs but abroad (by its own affiliates) (*offshore in-house sourcing* in the sense of *relocation abroad*)	Production outside the enterprise (or the group) and outside the country by non-affiliated firms. This involves foreign subcontracting (*offshore outsourcing* or *subcontracting abroad*)

Source: US Government Accountability Office (GAO)/UNCTAD (2004), *World Investment Report* 2004; OECD (2004), *Information Technology Outlook.*

In other words, production abroad of an enterprise's activities could be carried on internally (*offshore in-house sourcing*), or externally (*offshore outsourcing*), which corresponds to *subcontracting abroad*. The case of transfer of production abroad to its own affiliates will be called "offshoring in the strict sense" and transfer of production abroad to non-affiliated firms will be called "offshoring in the broad sense".

1.1. Offshoring in the strict sense (offshore in-house sourcing)

This document concerns exclusively cases where there is a partial or total cessation of an activity within an enterprise in the compiling country involving the transfer of that activity to one of its existing foreign affiliates or one specially formed for the purpose (*relocation abroad*). This operation comprises three characteristics which are summarised in Box 1.

Box 1. Characteristics of offshoring in the strict sense (offshore in-house sourcing)

Offshoring through affiliates in the same group must satisfy the following characteristics:

- Total or partial closure of the enterprise's production units in the compiling country with workforce reductions.

- Opening of affiliates abroad (or production units) which produce the same goods and services. These goods and services could also be produced by existing affiliates.

- In the compiling country, the enterprise which has offshored its production imports goods and services from its own affiliates abroad which had previously been consumed in that country, while exports could decline due to the fact that they are partially or totally supplied from abroad and destined for the same markets as the exports from the compiling country.

In the case of offshoring in the strict sense (*offshore in-house sourcing*), the three preceding conditions are necessary and exclusively concern multinational firms to the extent that they involve direct investment. The multinational firms involved in this category of offshoring may be either *(a)* parent companies controlled in principle by residents of the compiling country, or *(b)* affiliates under foreign control. It will be seen later in the report whether foreign affiliates in a compiling country tend to offshore more than parent companies.

1.2. Offshoring in the broad sense (offshore outsourcing or subcontracting abroad)

Offshoring in the broad sense involves resort to international subcontracting without direct investment.

While subcontracting essentially concerns multinational firms, it may also concern SME which do not have activities abroad. Depending on the nature of the subcontracting, prime contractors may abolish jobs in the compiling country and only create jobs abroad, or else create jobs abroad without abolishing jobs in the compiling country. Subcontracting takes place between non-affiliated firms but often in a relationship of cooperation or partnership. When the production subcontracted abroad was previously undertaken within the enterprise in the compiling country, it implies a reduction in the number of employees responsible for that production. This project is exclusively concerned with subcontracting of a *permanent* and *regular* character. Ad hoc subcontracting can be justified either by a temporary lack of capacity to meet additional demand within the deadlines imposed by the order, or to accomplish an occasional task which requires skills not available within the enterprise and the compiling country.

Box 2. Subcontracting defined

Subcontracting occurs when one firm, the prime manufacturer or contractor ("principal"), contracts with another firm, the subcontractor or "supplier", for a given production cycle, one or more aspects of product design, processing or manufacture, or construction or maintenance work.

The output is generally incorporated into the principal's final products. Subcontracting can also involve services, particularly studies, accounting, engineering, R&D, advertising, computer services or legal advice. Most of these services are of the kind that can be subcontracted abroad (international subcontracting).

The "supplying" firm must adhere strictly to the "principal's" technical or commercial specifications for the products or services in question.

Source: OECD (2005), OECD Handbook on Economic Globalisation Indicators, Section 5.4.2, Chapter 5.

An important distinction concerns the difference between subcontracting and cooperation or partnership. To grasp the difference, it is useful to distinguish two categories of subcontracting. The *first* concerns relatively commonplace goods and services with a low technological content (*e.g.* call centres, accounting, spare parts, etc.). Goods and services in the second category have a high technological content and are generally the subject of constant innovation.

Relations between prime contractors and suppliers are not the same in the two categories. Prime contractors in the first category, having a wide choice, very often exert very strong pressure on prices and delivery times and can replace their subcontractors relatively easily.

On the other hand, suppliers in the second category are more closely associated with the design of the products and thus assume a partnership role. This type of subcontracting could be called *partnership subcontracting*.

As a typical example of this type of subcontracting, relations between automobile or aircraft manufactures and their respective parts suppliers might be mentioned, (providing landing gear, instrument panels, etc.).

Both these cases generally involve high tech goods for which the suppliers cannot be mere executing agents. They must also participate in the design of products and monitoring technological developments, sometimes even imposing certain innovations on the prime contractors. The latter are much more dependent on their subcontractors than prime contractors in the first category. It would be difficult, however, to liken these arrangements generally to cooperation agreements.

In cooperation agreements, the partners often establish financial links between them (mutual capital investment) and seek through their cooperation to share costs and risks, notably in research and development, or they undertake to jointly develop a new technology.

Figure 1 presents a classification of the different forms of international subcontracting.

The presentation in Figure 1 makes a distinction not only between ad hoc and permanent subcontracting, but also between goods and services. However, in the context of this document, it must be emphasised that both for goods and services, it is the permanent as opposed to the ad hoc character of subcontracting which is of interest. Furthermore, it must be considered even more restrictively to the extent that it must be associated with a reduction on production capacity in the compiling country. In other words, subcontracting in this report means the outsourcing abroad of an activity which previously was partially or totally integrated in the enterprise in the compiling country.

As in the case of relocation in the strict sense (Box 1), Box 3 summarises the three conditions which characterise relocation in the broad sense.

Figure 1. International subcontracting typology of a compiling country

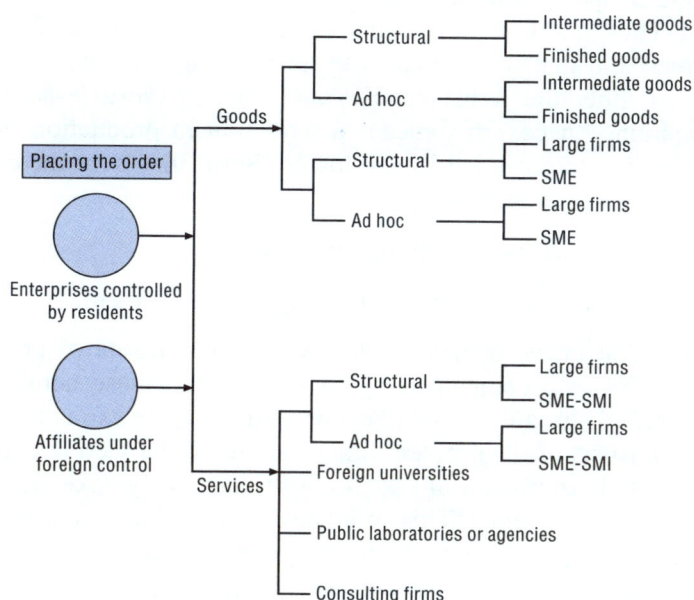

Source: OECD (2005), *OECD Handbook of Economic Globalisation Indicators.*

Box 3. Characteristics of offshoring in the broad sense (offshore outsourcing)

This category of offshoring concerns non-affiliated firms (international subcontracting).

- Partial or total cessation of an activity of production of goods or services in the compiling country with a reduction in the workforce.

- The same activity which was partially or totally ceased is subcontracted on a regular basis with another non-affiliated firm or another institution abroad.

- The enterprise which gave the order and subcontracts goods and services abroad then imports these goods and services previously produced within the enterprise to satisfy domestic demand in the compiling country (country of the prime contractor).

- In the case of subcontracting abroad, it is possible that a firm may offshore some of its activities by means of a process of outsourcing on the domestic market. The domestic firm receiving the order to subcontract the activities in question may then subcontract abroad and itself import the subcontracted goods and services, subsequently delivering them to the firm which first gave the order.La même activité arrêtée partiellement ou totalement sera sous-traitée de manière régulière auprès d'une autre entreprise non affiliée ou d'une autre institution à l'étranger.

The conditions shown in Boxes 1 and 3 are of great importance because they can be used to define the scope of this analysis. They do not flow automatically from the terminology used. Thus, the term "*offshoring*" is used to indicate that a domestic activity is carried on abroad and that it is replaced by imports of goods and services produced abroad. However, neither the terms "*offshoring*" nor "*offshore in-house sourcing*" or "offshoring outsourcing" necessarily means a reduction in production in the compiling country whether or not accompanied by job losses. But if that were the case, it would be necessary to analyse much more broadly:

- The impact of direct investment on employment.

- The impact of international subcontracting on employment.

It is considered that in the present context where the closure of production units in many OECD countries is accompanied by job losses and these activities, for various reasons, are then shifted abroad, it would be a necessity, before expanding the analysis, to address this priority aspect of the problem first of all. It will be seen later that the majority of the studies devoted to offshoring do not simultaneously take account of all the conditions set out in Boxes 1 and 3. This could be explained by the extreme difficulty, not to say impossibility, of quantifying all the proposed conditions, even with access to individual firms' data.

1.3. Particular forms of offshoring

Certain forms of offshoring are of particular interest and are worth examining separately:

1.3.1. Offshoring abroad of research and development laboratories (R&D)

Bearing in mind the importance of R&D for technological innovation and competitiveness in enterprises, offshoring of research laboratories could have much greater effects on the economies of the compiling countries than mere loss of jobs. It would therefore be useful if the analysis of offshoring of research laboratories were not confined to counting the number of researchers and technicians affected by offshoring but took a broader approach to the question, measuring the consequences for the techno-logical potential of the country concerned.

1.3.2. Offshoring of parent companies or decision making centres

As a particular case of offshoring in the strict sense, it would be interesting to examine the offshoring of parent companies or head offices of multinationals. As in the case of research laboratories, the jobs concerned are likely to represent only a very small percentage of the total employment involved in relocation. However, this phenomenon is more revealing of a country's power to attract decision-making centres than to maintain employment.

1.3.3. Migration abroad of scientific staff for an indefinite period

All the cases mentioned above concern offshoring relating to the activities of the enterprise.

The migration abroad of scientific staff is a very special form of offshoring which does not concern enterprises but personal choice. When the migration is temporary, it could be beneficial for the persons concerned and indirectly their compiling country, to the extent that such persons could acquire new knowledge and skills. If, on the other hand, it is permanent, it could have a relatively high social cost. This phenomenon, which is marginal to the problem of offshoring, is studied separately by "brain drain" specialists. It again shows the problem of attractiveness of countries for highly qualified persons.

1.3.4. Repatriation of activities to the compiling country

Repatriation of activities to the compiling country is the opposite phenomenon to offshoring. It is not particularly unusual for some activities which had been offshored to return to their compiling country. Most often, this occurs when offshoring has not delivered the expected returns to the enterprises concerned, or because the framework of conditions for the offshoring activities has considerably improved in the compiling country or deteriorated in the country of relocation. In almost all countries, governments seek the repatriation of offshoring activities, especially in the case of job creating activities or those with high added value. This question will be examined in the last part of this document.

1.4. Terminology issues

Before examining the impact on employment of activities carried on abroad, it is worth recalling the terms that will be used throughout the report. This is all the more necessary because often different terms are used to describe the same phenomenon.

If the title of the report reflects only certain aspects of activities carried on abroad (*offshoring*), that is because of the constraints set out in Boxes 1 and 3.

Externalisation abroad (*outsourcing abroad*) can be either through direct investment, *i.e.* in its own affiliates (*offshore in-house sourcing* or *cross-border outsourcing to its own affiliates*) or through foreign subcontracting (*offshore outsourcing* or *outsourcing abroad* or *subcontracting abroad* or *cross-border outsourcing to non-affiliates*). The first form of externalisation has been termed "offshoring in the strict sense" and the second "offshoring in the broad sense". Table 2 summarises the terms used.

Table 2. Summary of terms used

• **Domestic outsourcing**	=	Externalisation within a country
• **Outsourcing abroad**	=	Externalisation abroad
• **Offshoring**	=	Activity carried on abroad, relocated abroad
• **Offshoring in the strict sense**	=	Offshore in-house sourcing or cross-border outsourcing to its own affiliates. (Partial or complete closure of production unit in the home country and relocation of the same production to its own affiliates abroad)
• **Offshoring in the broad sense**	=	Offshore outsourcing or outsourcing abroad or subcontracting abroad or cross-border outsourcing to non-affiliates. (Partial or complete closure of production unit in the home country and transfer of the same production to a subcontractor abroad)

Chapter 2

HOW OFFSHORING AFFECTS EMPLOYMENT

This chapter considers the major variables that determine how offshoring affects domestic employment, and it distinguishes between the short-term and medium-term effects on employment. While the short-term effects of offshoring are often negative, in the longer-term the effects can be positive, depending on the interaction between production, direct investment and international trade flows. The chief motivations for offshoring are also briefly presented along with the latest developments in the theoretical debate regarding trade, offshoring and employment.

The phenomenon of offshoring is the result of interaction between direct investment, subcontracting with non-affiliated firms and international trade. In general, both direct investment and the use of subcontracting abroad involve trade flows, notably imports into the compiling country but also exports. The dynamic of these interactions can have positive or negative effects on employment, both directly and indirectly, and depending on whether it is short or long term.

2.1. Short-term negative effects on employment

- Company X may reduce certain of its activities in a country for various reasons (*e.g.* insufficient demand, loss of competitiveness, technological change, etc.) without necessarily relocating its activities abroad. That may translate into job losses which are not linked to relocation.

- What happens less often is the relocation abroad of the activities of Company X, a large part of which were intended to satisfy domestic demand. In that case, the part destined for the domestic market of the compiling country will be imported (intra-firm imports) while the part destined for export will be exported directly to those markets from the affiliates of Company X. There would thus be a *direct effect* and an *indirect effect* on employment.

  In certain extreme cases where all the activity of Company X is relocated abroad, the impact on employment could be greater, especially as some subcontractors might find themselves obliged to follow Company X abroad. More specific situations can arise when the imports of Company X from its affiliates partially or wholly concern intermediate goods. Then, after processing, one part of the finished goods will be sold in the domestic market and another exported.

- Company X may, however, relocate certain activities abroad which were intended solely for exports. If this relocation takes place through its foreign affiliates, employment in the compiling country may be directly or indirectly influenced. The *direct effect* would be the reduction in employment involved in the export-related activities which are transferred to affiliates abroad. The *indirect effect* might concern jobs in other subcontractors in the compiling country which contract production for exports by the firm in question. To the extent that foreign affiliates are going to export directly to the countries for which these exports are intended, jobs in other domestic firms could be affected if those firms exported similar goods to the same markets and which will now be in competition with the countries in which the affiliates of Company X which relocated its production are established.

- Company X, without ceasing any of its operations in the home country, may step up capital investment in its affiliates abroad so as to export from those affiliates to third countries to which Company X had not been exporting before.

- Now suppose that Company X ceases some of its activities and subcontracts them to non-affiliated firms abroad. In principle, these activities do not, at least directly, concern export markets in the sense that the subcontractors do not send the goods and services concerned to the export markets of Company X. On the other hand, Company X will import the subcontracted goods and services. For the compiling country, the negative impact on employment will be proportional to the number and nature of goods and services ceased and subcontracted abroad.

- Company X may also decide from the outset to create new activities or expand existing activities directly in its foreign affiliates and then import part of the goods and services and products. In that case, it does not stop its activities and destroy jobs in the compiling country, but simply creates new jobs exclusively abroad but not in the compiling country.

- Similarly, Company X may decide from the outset to subcontract certain activities to subcontractors abroad without reducing the same activities and without job losses in the compiling country.

- A final case could be envisaged where Company X totally ceases its activities in the compiling country for various reasons which are unrelated to relocation – when, for example, there is a recession or its products are no longer in demand on the domestic market – and relocates its activities abroad.

Figure 2 summarises the different situations described above concerning the interactions between domestic production, foreign direct investment and imports. The impact on employment here concerns only the *short term*, and may be negative or neutral. The negative effects on employment come from situations A, B, C and G while the effects of situations D, E and F are neutral.

Figure 2. Activities carried on abroad by country Y and short-term impact on employment

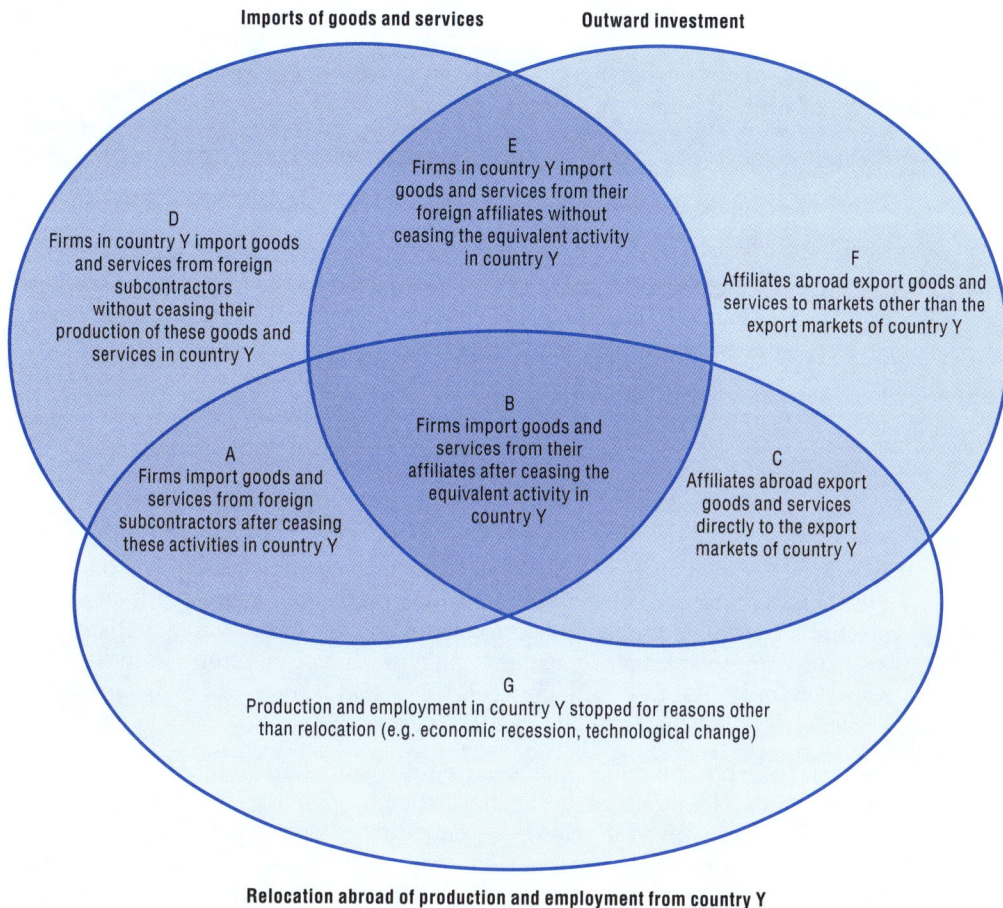

Imports of goods and services   Outward investment

E
Firms in country Y import
goods and services from their
foreign affiliates without
ceasing the equivalent activity
in country Y

D
Firms in country Y import goods
and services from foreign
subcontractors
without ceasing their
production of these goods and
services in country Y

F
Affiliates abroad export goods and
services to markets other than the
export markets of country Y

B
Firms import goods and
services from their
affiliates after ceasing the
equivalent activity in
country Y

A
Firms import goods and
services from foreign
subcontractors after ceasing
these activities in country Y

C
Affiliates abroad export
goods and services
directly to the export
markets of country Y

G
Production and employment in country Y stopped for reasons other
than relocation (e.g. economic recession, technological change)

Relocation abroad of production and employment from country Y

Source: US Government Accountability Office.

The situations directly linked to offshoring are those in A, B and C. Situations B and C are described in Box 1, while situation A is described in Box 3. Some authors consider that the fact of creating jobs abroad in affiliates, even if it does not reduce employment and activities in the same activities in the compiling country, is itself negative for employment. That could be wrong for two reasons. Firstly, there is no guarantee that an activity which was not developed abroad would necessarily be developed in the compiling country. Secondly, in macro-economic terms, the relationships between direct investment and exports are too complex, but often when the direct investment is within a framework of vertical integration, these relationships are mostly complementary.

Box 4. Firms concerned by offshoring

Compiling countries which offshore their activities

- The relocation characterised by situations B and C in Figure 2 may concern two categories of firms in country Y.

  - Parent companies controlled by residents of country Y.

  - Affiliates under foreign control established in country Y (some may also be parent companies).

- Conversely, all the companies in country Y are affected by the relocation characterised by situation A in Figure 2, including companies which are not multinationals (which do not have affiliates abroad).

Countries where activities are offshored

- Companies affected by countries of destination of relocation abroad, in situations B and C of Figure 2 will be:

  - Affiliates directly or indirectly controlled by parent companies in country Y.

    It will be recalled that in accordance with the recommendations of the *OECD Handbook of Economic Globalisation Indicators*, indirect affiliates are firms controlled by parent companies in country Y but through other affiliates whose parent companies exercise direct control (majority shareholding) [OECD (2005), *OECD Handbook of Economic Globalisation Indicators,* Section 3.3.1.2, Chapter 3.]

- In the case of subcontracting characterised by situation A in Figure 2, all the companies in the countries of destination of relocation may be affected with the exception of firms involved in trade between parent companies in country Y and their foreign affiliates (intra-firm trade). Conversely, affiliates of parent companies in country Y must be taken into account when the prime contractors in subcontracting concerning these affiliates are companies other than their own parent companies in country Y.

Another point which needs to be emphasised is the fact that offshoring is when the same goods and services are concerned as those for which production has been stopped or reduced in the compiling country and which are then imported. In other words, if the activity transferred either to the enterprise's own affiliates abroad or subcontracted to foreign producers is not the same as that which was stopped or reduced in the compiling country, then that is not a case of offshoring.

2. HOW OFFSHORING AFFECTS EMPLOYMENT – **27**

2.1.1. Offshoring and restructuring

Multinational groups distribute their activities in many countries. Given that each group has other secondary activities in addition to its principal activity, it operates a constant redeployment of its activities in the countries where it is established. Thus, it can concentrate certain activities in a few countries where it can achieve economies of scale and reduce them in others. At the same time, in countries where certain activities have been reduced or relocated to other countries, the group can create new activities, assigning to them a large proportion of its workers previously employed in the relocated activities. If these movements are very frequent, the enterprise could find itself unable to identify the number of employees affected by offshoring.

2.2. Prime motivation for offshoring

The reasons which lead firms to relocate abroad may vary depending on the sector and the form of relocation (to affiliates or through subcontracting to non-affiliated firms). Up to now, only consulting firms have questioned enterprises on this question. While for the choice of location of direct investment, the chief criterion seems to be the need for local presence in growing markets, as regards relocation of production, all the surveys show that the prime motivation is reduction of costs.

The criterion concerning reduction of costs does not concern labour costs exclusively but all costs involved in the production process (wages, financial costs, management, advertising, communication, transport, etc.). The vertical investment corresponds to the search for cost differentials and reflects the traditional comparative advantage approach. However, horizontal investment is motivated more by reasons of market access.

Figure 3 illustrates the chief reasons why enterprises go offshore, according to a survey by the consulting firm A.T. Kearney. It could be inferred that the need for market access and the need to reduce costs make the distinction between horizontal and vertical investment less relevant.

While Figure 3 shows the motivation of large firms, other surveys have been carried out in SME. KPMG carried out such a survey in France among 212 firms with a turnover of between 7 and 25 million euros. While some enterprises sometimes confuse offshoring and foreign investment, the results of the survey more or less confirm the reasons given by the enterprises as a whole (see Figure 4). It is important to emphasise that, according to that survey, the number of enterprises who said that they did not expect any gains from a possible relocation was 51% in 2003 but only 33% in 2004.

OFFSHORING AND EMPLOYMENT: TRENDS AND IMPACTS – ISBN-978-92-64-03092-3 – © OECD 2007

Figure 3. Motivations for offshoring

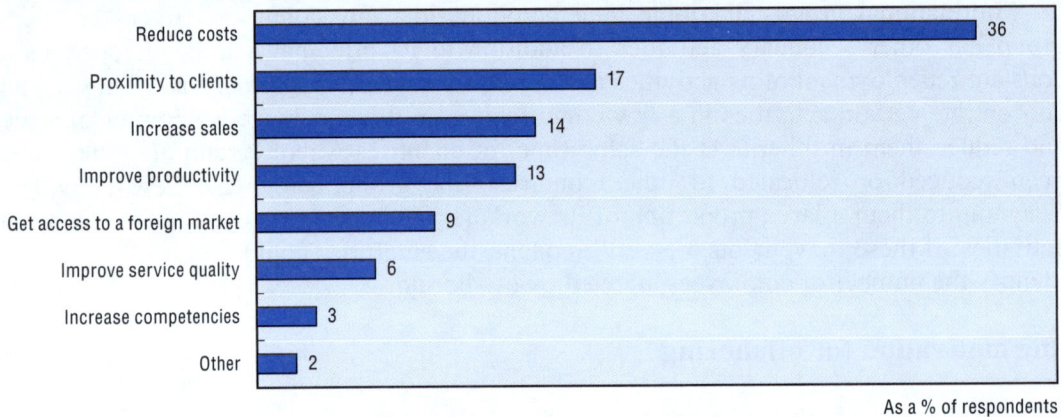

Source: A.T. Kearney (2003).

Figure 4. Motivation for SMEs to go offshore

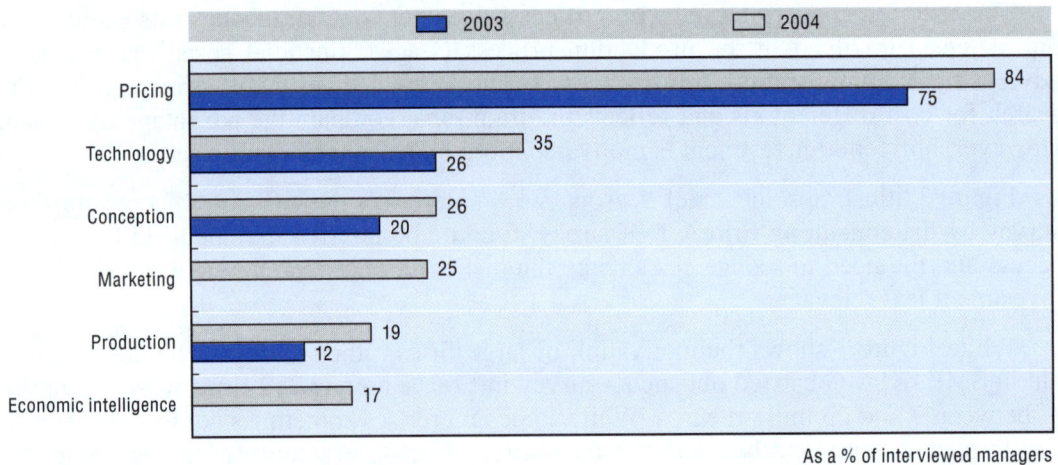

Source: KPMG.

While tax does not seem to be a major cause of relocation of production, it becomes the chief motivation when it comes to relocation of decision-making centres (headquarters). Figure 5 presents a list of criteria given by a large number of European multinationals surveyed by the consulting firm, Arthur D. Little. The figures correspond to the number of times a criterion was mentioned. KPMG consulting firm calculated the number of relocations of headquarters of multinationals in Europe, and listed countries in terms of their attractiveness (percentage of headquarters relocated) (Figure 6).

Figure 5. Specific criteria involved in the evaluation of relocation of a headquarter

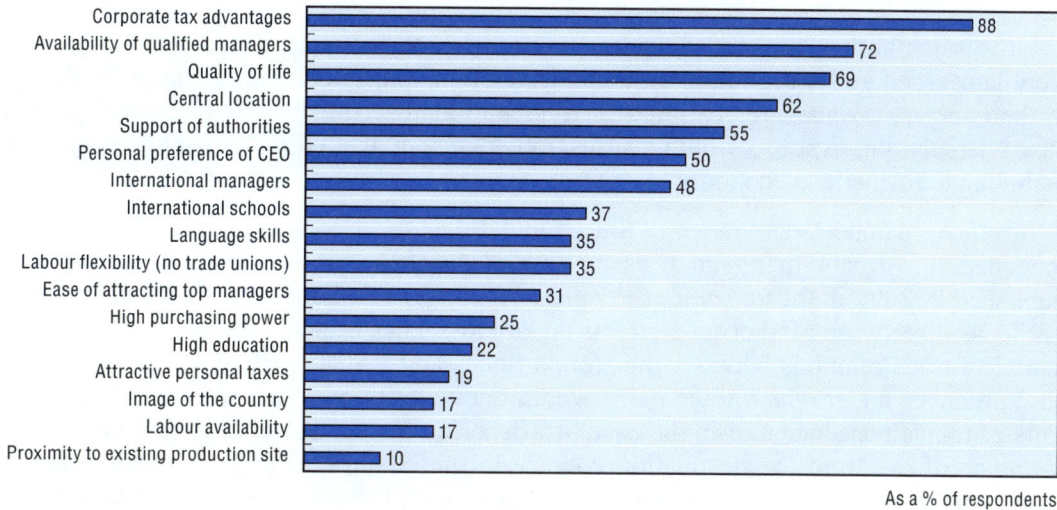

Corporate tax advantages	88
Availability of qualified managers	72
Quality of life	69
Central location	62
Support of authorities	55
Personal preference of CEO	50
International managers	48
International schools	37
Language skills	35
Labour flexibility (no trade unions)	35
Ease of attracting top managers	31
High purchasing power	25
High education	22
Attractive personal taxes	19
Image of the country	17
Labour availability	17
Proximity to existing production site	10

As a % of respondents

Source: Arthur D. Little (desk research).

Figure 6. Relocation of headquarters in Europe by country (as percentage of total)

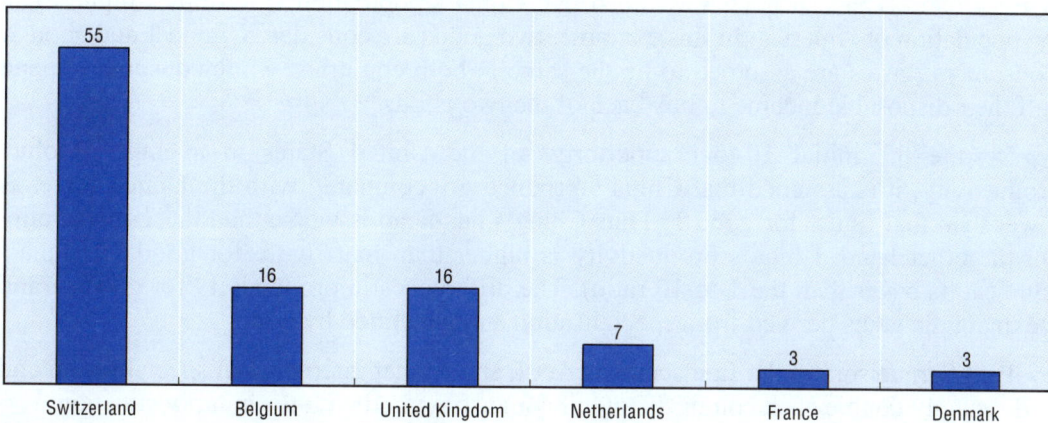

Switzerland	55
Belgium	16
United Kingdom	16
Netherlands	7
France	3
Denmark	3

Source: KPMG.

The number of jobs affected by the relocation of headquarters is very low compared with the relocation of production units. However, bearing in mind the fact that many decisions concerning the distribution of activities in different countries where the firms are established are taken by headquarters, it is difficult to evaluate the potential impact on employment.

2.3. The theoretical debate

It was emphasised in the introduction that some economists, as well as public opinion, were concerned at the economic awakening of China and India. These countries, thanks to their very low wages, relocation of activities to their territory and exceptional growth based largely on exports, would causes job losses in the OECD member countries, including the American economy.

Paul A. Samuelson, winner of the Nobel Prize for Economics in 1970, recently reopened the debate in an analysis of several scenarios of Sino-American relations published in 2005 in the *Journal of Economic Perspectives*. Samuelson's reasoning does not focus directly on offshoring's effects on employment. Rather, he seeks to analyse the nature of trade relations between the United States and China, identifying the particular circumstances under which trade gains would not benefit both countries simultaneously. This can have consequences in the case of offshoring insofar as offshoring always leads to import flows from the destination country to the country of origin. In this context, Paul Samuelson tries to gauge the impact on per-capita income in the United States, but there could be indirect effects on employment as well. He envisages two acts, the first of which has two scenes. In Act I, Scene 1, the two countries are winners and in Act II, only China is a winner.

The *first scene of Act I* analyses the consequences of the following scenario. In the absence of international trade (autarky), China's real income per capita is one tenth that of the United States. It is also assumed that China's population is ten times higher than the population of America. In this example, two goods are considered, good 1 and good 2. Consumers' tastes are assumed to be the same in both countries, while consumers spend half their disposable income to buy each of the two goods.

Despite the initial 10-to-1 superiority of the United States in average absolute productivity, it is assumed that China's productivity compared with the United States is lower than that figure for good 1. Thus China's handicap is worse than the 1-to-10 ratio. On the other hand, China's productivity is higher than that figure for good 2 (China's handicap is better than the 1-to-10 ratio). The differences in productivity for goods 1 and 2 explain the gains derived from specialisation and generated by trade.

Paul Samuelson, in the first scene of Act I, shows that international specialisation and trade exactly double each country's total income compared with the autarky situation.

The second scene of Act I describes the situation of the two countries when labour productivity has quadrupled in China for the production of good 2 thanks to Schumpeterian technical improvement (exogenous shock from technical improvement). The Ricardian comparative advantages continue to force the United States to specialise exclusively in the production of good 1 and China in the production of good 2. When 100 American workers are engaged in the production of good 1, they produce no more than before, *i.e.* 200 units. On the other hand, if 1000 Chinese workers produce good 2, thanks to their productivity gains, they can achieve production of 800 units. Global production increases thanks to the improvement in China's productivity.

The United States keep part of the gain related to the increase in global output following the liberalisation of trade. This is because the new abundance of goods produced in China (Q_2) compared with the unchanging quantity of goods produced in the United States (Q_1) reduces the price ratio P_2/P_1 of goods 1 and 2 for American consumers. The quadrupling of supply of good 2 in China may considerably worsen the terms of trade for China (P_2/P_1) and this deterioration can cause per capita income to fall as a result of the exogenous shock from technological improvement well below the per capita income before the shock. After the shock, China's share of global net output cannot be maintained at 50% but slumps to 20%. Thus, in this second scene, the United States wins because international trade allows it to benefit from China's productivity gains.

Act II begins with the same productivities as Act I (labour productivity in the United States $\pi_1 = 2$, and $\pi_2 = \frac{1}{2}$ and in China $\pi_1 = \frac{1}{20}$ and $\pi_2 = \frac{1}{5}$) but now expanding China's labour productivity for good 1 of $\pi = \frac{1}{20}$ to $\pi_1' = \frac{8}{10}$. Despite the great increase in China's labour productivity for good 1, with China becoming more productive than the United States in good 1, China still has a lower average real wage and still remains poorer in autarky than the United States.

Before the invention, just as in Act I, the United States produces only 200 units of good 1 and China 200 units of good 2. After the introduction of the invention, world output potential has markedly grown. However, all the comparative advantages have disappeared. In this situation, each country can do as well under autarky as it can if it engages in trade.

American welfare can be judged after the Chinese invention by comparing the real income under autarky (measured by the geometric mean of the number of units of each good) after the invention in an autarky situation to that before the invention with international trade.

International trade results in the production of 200 units of good 1 by the United States and 2000 units of good 2 by China. These figures show that the two countries share world income equally measured by the geometric mean $\sqrt{200 \times 200} = 200$. This means that when trade is possible, per capita welfare in the United States before the invention is $\frac{1}{2} \times \frac{200}{100} = 1$.[1] Forced to return to autarky by China's invention, the United States with its unchanging technology again divides its 100 workers evenly between producing goods 1 and 2.

Producing $50 \times 1/2 = 25$ units of good 2, real per capita income can be measured by the geometric mean $\sqrt{100 \times 25/100} = 50/100 = 0.5$. There is thus a fall in the national per capita income of Americans, since before the invention and thanks to international trade it was equal to 1.

According to P. Samuelson, it can be envisaged that such inventions in a foreign country can reduce in absolute and structural terms the per capita profits that the United States gains from international trade and globalisation. On the other hand, he concludes

---

1.   Per capita income in the United States under autarky is 0.5,

$$i.e. \ 0.5 = \sqrt{(W/P_1) \bullet (W/P_2)} = 0.5\sqrt{\pi_1 \ \pi_2} = 0.5\sqrt{2 \bullet 1/2} = 0.5.$$

that it is unlikely that this would be as dramatic for the American economy as in the foregoing example.

Pursuing the debate opened by P. Samuelson, Jagdish Bhagwati, A. Panagariya and T. Srinivasan in the *Journal of Economic Perspectives* focus their analysis on problems of relocation. The authors reject the fears formulated in respect of relocation and show not only that the total number of American jobs "relocated" is very low but the United States has no need to fear significant loss of skilled jobs. Bhagwati and his collaborators develop three alternative models referring to the trade in services to illustrate their case.

Figure 7. Benefits of relocation abroad in a single good model

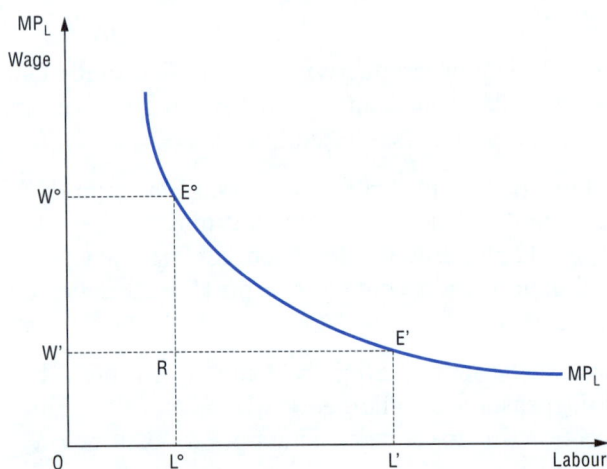

The *first model* has only one good and two factors of production, labour and capital. It is assumed that these factors have diminishing returns and that the capital endowment in the economy is fixed. The fact that there is only one good excludes the need for trade from the outset. In Figure 7, the curve MP_L represents the marginal product of labour. If $L°$ is the endowment of labour and $W°$ represents wages, the wage bill will be the area formed by the rectangle $OW°E°L°$. Suppose that an innovation allows the economy to buy the services of labour abroad electronically at the fixed wage W'. The economy continues to hire the same endowment of domestic labour but now paying the lower wage. In this case, the economy buys $L°L'$ abroad paying the sum corresponding to the rectangle $L°L'E'R$ for it. Domestic labour receives the sum corresponding to $OL°RW'$ and capital the area under the MP_L curve above the horizontal line $W'E'$. The following economic effects result. The country's total income rises by the triangular area $E°RE'$, which is the net gain from relocation of activities. The income of labour, the "import competing" factor, declines by area $W°E°RW'$ and is redistributed to capital. Thus, the owners of capital make a gain corresponding to $W°E°RW'$. This model captures the essence of the popular rhetoric that expresses doubts about relocation of activities. It shows, however, that it may be of benefit for the economy as a whole. But in the absence of a method allowing some of the social benefits received by capital to be transferred to workers, it is firms and the owners of capital who receive more than 100% of the social benefits of relocation, while workers experience only losses.

The *second model* has two goods and three factors. The country takes part in world trade where technological innovation allows relocation of activities. The two goods each use a sector-specific factor and another factor that is common to both goods. It is assumed that the import-competing good uses unskilled labour as its specific factor and the exportable good uses capital as its specific factor, the common factor of production of both goods being skilled labour. Now imagine that a technological change makes it possible for skilled labour to be outsourced.

Suppose, indeed, that an innovation allows the country to purchase the services of skilled labour abroad at a lower wage. The figure for the second model is not reproduced in this report. By successive relocation of sector 1 then sector 2, the authors show that relocation increases national income. However, the distributional issues become more complex. Assuming diminishing returns to all factors of production, the increase in quantity used of skilled labour and a decline in the skilled wage will cause the unskilled wage and the rental on capital to rise. The relocation here remains of benefit provided that it concerns a small country with fixed terms of trade and there are no other prior distortions in the form of tariffs or distorting taxes.

In the case of a large country, however, the introduction of a process of relocation will not necessarily lead to a welfare gain because it may modify the terms of trade. Initially, relocation leads to greater expansion of production of the exportable good than demand for it, which raises the possibility that the terms of trade in the goods market will deteriorate. In other words, it will cost a country more in terms of exports to purchase a fixed quantity of imports. This deterioration may more than offset the direct benefits of relocation. Alternatively, if relocation of activities causes a considerable expansion in the output of the import-competing good, the demand for imports will decline, which will lower the price of imported goods and improve the terms of trade. In this case, the direct gains from relocation of activities will be reinforced by the improvement in the terms of trade.

In the *third model,* there are three goods and two factors where goods 1 and 2 are traded internationally, while good 3 is initially a non-traded service. Assume that due to an innovation, the formerly non-traded service becomes tradable and is available from abroad at a lower price than the price in the domestic market. This means that the domestic supply of the service disappears, and the resources thus released will be absorbed by production of goods 1 and 2. As long as both of these goods continue to be produced, the factor prices measured in terms of those goods will remain the same. But since the price of the service, good 3, has declined, the buying power of the two factors in terms of that good rises. Thus, the relocation of activities will end up making the owners of both factors better off.

These three models can be thought of as describing several possible outcomes of a technological improvement that allowing intensified relocation. The first model involves benefits for society, but in the form of higher returns to capital and lower wages. In the second, with multiple factors of production and fixed prices of goods, relocation of activities again provides benefits, but some categories of workers gain and others lose. In the third, relocation of activities is beneficial by increasing real incomes of all workers, at least after they have made the transition to other sectors of activity.

Box 5. The new theoretical debate
(summary of the principal arguments)

Paul Samuelson[1]

Samuelson examines three scenarios of trade between the United States and China.

- In the first scenario, the United States has an initial 10-to-1 superiority over China in average absolute labour productivity. Two goods are considered. For good 1, China's productivity is worse than this 10-to-1 ratio. On the other hand, it is better for good 2. Paul Samuelson shows that trade leads to a doubling of income in each country compared with an autarky situation.

- In a second scenario, China's labour productivity for good 2 has quadrupled thanks to an exogenous shock from technological improvement. The United States continues to specialise in producing good 1 exclusively and China in producing good 2. The quadrupling of the supply of good 2 in China worsens the terms of trade for China whose per capita income falls. Conversely, the United States wins because international trade allows it to benefit from China's productivity gains.

- In the third scenario, thanks to special technical progress, China's productivity for good 1 becomes higher than that of the United States. In this situation, Samuelson shows that the United States, with unchanging technology for good 1, experiences a decline in per capita income as a result of deterioration of terms of trade. According to him, it can be envisaged that such inventions in a foreign country can structurally reduce the per capita profits that the United States derive from international trade. He concludes, however, that it would not have serious consequences for the American economy.

J. Bhagwati, A. Panagariya and T. Srinivasan[2]

These three authors reject the fears expressed by Samuelson and focus their work on the impact of offshoring. They develop three models.

- The first model has only one good and two factors of higher production: labour and capital. Offshoring can be beneficial for the economy as a whole, but in the form of higher returns on capital and lower wages.

- The second model has two goods and three factors (capital, skilled labour and unskilled labour). In this model, offshoring also brings benefits, but to the detriment of certain categories of worker (notably skilled workers related to exportable goods).

- In the third model, there are three goods and two factors. Here the third good concerns services which were not previously traded. If the third good (service) can be obtained abroad at a lower price than in the domestic market, offshoring through subcontracting will increase the real incomes of all workers, at least after those who have lost their jobs have made the transition to other sectors of activity.

1. *Journal of Economic Perspectives - Volume 18, Number 3 - Summer 2004*, "Where Ricardo and Mill Rebut and Confirm Arguments of Mainstream Economists Supporting Globalization".

2. *Journal of Economic Perspectives - Volume 18, Number 4 - Fall 2004*, "The Muddles over Outsourcing".

Concerning the three models developed by Bhagwati, Panagariya and Srinivasan, we would suggest stressing their limitations and underlying strong assumptions. For example, the first and third models make the assumption that labour supply is fixed and independent of the wage rate. This means that there is no unemployment and that (third model) all workers of the outsourced service sector can be absorbed by sectors one and two without any real effects on factor prices (assumption of non-decreasing returns to scale). Additionally, the third model applies to a small economy which cannot influence its terms of trade despite increasing production of goods 1 and 2. In the second model, it is insufficiently explained what happens to the skilled workers once skilled labour is outsourced. Do they continue to work at a lower wage (using the same assumption as for models one and three that there is no unemployment in the economy) or do they drift into unemployment? Another remark must be made regarding the very nature of the models presented: all are static models. The gain in labour productivity (Samuelson's model) or the abrupt availability of cheaper production models (models one and two) or cheaper services (model three) is an exogenous shock which happens all of a sudden. However, in reality such changes come slowly, and the decision to outsource is not determined exogenously but endogenously. Neglecting the dynamics of relocation reduces offshoring analysis to comparative statistics and may lead us to miss the impact of gradual adaptations of relative production, relative economic weight and relative prices.

Further, all the models presented focus on national welfare and distributional effects of relocation in order to assess whether a country wins or loses with relocation and how welfare gains (or losses) are experienced by different groups of people in the economy. But what we are really looking for in the context of this report is a theoretical model that deals with the impact of relocation on employment as such.

2.4. Macroeconomic impacts on employment

The recent theoretical debate on offshoring shows that whether it is a question of goods or services, it is the structure of the economy which determines the benefits of offshoring activities.

If offshoring of an activity essentially involves an intermediate good used to produce other goods, it acts like a technical improvement allowing savings on this input, which will increase productivity.

If offshoring involves finished goods offered to the final consumer at a lower price, it will increase real incomes.

In all cases, in the short term, there are risks of job losses, but the gains from offshoring could lead to the creation of new jobs.

The chief difference between the effects of offshoring on employment in the short and medium term is that that short-term effects are mostly direct and negative while the medium-term effects are indirect and mostly positive.

The gains from offshoring do not appear immediately and do not directly concern the people whose jobs have been affected. In consequence, the majority of positive effects are not seen as being in any way related to offshoring and only the negative affects are directly associated with it.

The complexity of the phenomenon and the difficulty of identifying the scale of offshoring other than approximately are certainly considerable obstacles to quantifying the gains and establishing cause and effect.

This section briefly presents the principal macro-economic effects of offshoring.

2.4.1. Positive effects

Growth in consumers' incomes

The importing of relocated goods and services at a price lower than the one which would have been applied if the same goods and services had been produced in the compiling country increases consumers' incomes in that country.

The growth in incomes will increase consumption and possibly saving. The growth in consumption will have a favourable impact on employment if it is mainly oriented towards demand for goods and services produced in the domestic market rather than imported. On the other hand, jobs which might be created due to additional consumption may concern sectors and jobs very different from those lost due to offshoring.

Improved competitiveness and productivity in enterprises

The improvement in the competitiveness of enterprises is reflected first in the improvement of price competitiveness. If changes in the exchange rate do not limit the decline in the cost of imported goods and services, the enterprise can either increase its margins without a significant reduction in price or pass on the full reduction in import prices to the sales price and increase its market share and indirectly its profits.

The impact on employment will depend largely on the strategy adopted by the enterprise and also the macro-economic environment. If domestic demand is growing, the enterprise will be encouraged to invest and produce more, and will indirectly create new jobs. If domestic demand is weak but export markets are expanding, it will depend on the choice made by the enterprise: either to export or to establish new production units in foreign markets.

Another important effect that offshoring may have on the activity of firms is improved productivity. Although this improvement may not necessarily have an immediate favourable impact on employment, it encourages investment in new technology and indirectly the creation of higher skilled jobs.

Export growth

Offshoring of certain activities could influence exports in two ways. Empirical studies show that at macro-economic level, foreign investment often complements trade and generates additional exports, and indirectly job creation. Moreover, the growth in incomes in the countries of relocation which are increasingly integrated in the world economy creates additional demand which could be satisfied by new exports from the countries behind the relocations.

Control of inflation

Reducing costs is one of the chief justifications for offshoring. This reduction will contribute to better control of inflation and a slowdown in consumer price rises. This will encourage a flexible monetary policy and keeping real interest rates fairly low. Indirectly, low interest rates will stimulate investment and thus job creation.

Better returns on capital

One of the causes of offshoring rarely mentioned explicitly is that in the destination countries of relocation, the wage bill is relatively low compared with the gross operating surplus. In other words, there is a higher return on investment. Thus repatriated dividends and profits, the level of which also depends on enterprises' strategies, mean better remuneration of owners of capital (see also Chapter 2, theoretical debate). Based on these results, it is nevertheless very difficult to predict the probable impact on employment.

2.4.2. Negative effects

Fall in real wages of certain categories of workers

Depending on the nature of offshoring, the importing of goods and services at lower prices will result in lower wages for workers who produce these goods and services. In the initial phase when offshoring involved mostly goods and services with low added value, it was low-skilled workers who were concerned. The real relative wages of those workers fell markedly and unemployment among them rose. It is likely that this phenomenon led certain countries to introduce minimum wages. However, the increase in cheaper skilled labour abroad, combined with offshoring of goods and services that needed that labour, also resulted in a fall in the real wages of skilled workers in the countries where activities are offshored.

Deterioration in the terms of trade

Offshoring of activities is generally advantageous for a country to the extent that it leads to a further fall in the price of imported goods and services. However, that could cause a deterioration of that country's terms of trade, especially if the exported goods and services are in a similar range. The chief cause will be inflation of the world supply at low prices of the goods and services normally exported by the country in question.

Possible decline in capacity for innovation

This applies essentially in the case of offshoring of research and development laboratories. Such relocation occurs most often in the context of group restructuring, or following a merger, and most often concerns enterprises under foreign control. The scale of this effect depends on the nature of the research carried on by the laboratories. If the research is done for foreign affiliates or enterprises, the impact will be more modest and would be limited mainly to "spill over" effects.

Loss of tax revenues

Loss of tax revenues can occur in the context of relocation of parent companies or head offices of multinationals, to the extent that a large part of the profits of the groups concerned will be transferred and taxed in other countries.

Regional effects

The closure of a factory and its relocation abroad might only have relatively minor consequences at national level, but the consequences for a particular region can be serious, especially when unemployment in the region is high and the factory was the chief centre of economic activity in the region.

2.5. Principal factors unfavourable to offshoring

Although according to recent surveys, a great many enterprises do not exclude resorting to offshore in the near future, it should be emphasised that offshoring of certain activities also involves risks which enterprises should not underestimate. The most important are briefly described below.

2.5.1. Inadequate quality of goods and services supplied

Sometimes the quality of relocated goods and services, especially when subcontracted and then imported, does not meet all the criteria to satisfy consumers in the compiling country. A strict quality control system must be established, which can sometimes mean a complex and costly organisation.

However, apart from consumer satisfaction, two other problems can have serious consequences, especially in the case of subcontracting:

- Defective spare parts which can cause safety problems, especially in transport (aeroplanes, automobiles, etc.);

- Medicines which do not comply with all the standards and may raise health problems.

2.5.2. Failure to meet delivery times

Any delays in delivery of goods and services, especially in a "just-in-time" production system, can halt production and cause enterprises to lose sales.

2.5.3. Higher costs than anticipated

Apart from the extra costs that could arise from better quality control, there could also be higher transport costs (*e.g.* fuel, insurance, etc.), adverse movements in the exchange rate, or, more rarely, new regulations in the compiling country with respect to offshoring. In addition, wages in the country where activities are offshored may also rise faster than expected, which forces some enterprises to seek another country to which it can offshore its activities once again.

2.5.4. Failure to respect intellectual property

In a country where intellectual property is not respected, enterprises run the risk of being copied and of experiencing unfair competition as a result of counterfeiting. In such countries, high tech enterprises avoid forming affiliates and certain activities relocated to those countries are repatriated to the compiling country.

2.5.5. Technological change

Technological change can influence offshored activities in different ways. Firstly, technological change can make certain production obsolete, whether relocated or not. But some changes require fairly skilled personnel to put them in place. This assumes that the local workforce in the country of relocation will have the skill needed to meet the changes. Finally, innovation in the manufacturing process can automate production to the maximum, increase labour productivity and reduce the labour needed to the minimum. That could raise questions of profitability for the relocated activity.

2.5.6. Management difficulties

Sometimes difficulties arise in the field of management, related to language, cultural and communication problems. The problems could be more acute in the case of sub-contracting, especially in services where the need for permanent communication between the local workforce and the home enterprise (prime contractor) assumes greater importance.

Chapter 3

PROBLEMS OF MEASUREMENT

This chapter explains the difficulties encountered in quantifying the impact of offshoring on employment, and why there are no direct measurements. Numerous indicators are presented that can be used to indirectly measure the impact on employment, as well as alternative approaches used in the past and their primary limitations.

Up to now, in few OECD countries have the national authorities undertaken public surveys concerning the phenomenon of offshoring. Given the importance of the fears aroused by offshoring in public debate, that might seem paradoxical.

One explanation might be the absence of a precise definition of the phenomenon and its complexity. A second reason will be the difficulty and sometimes the impossibility of enterprises providing certain information from their accounting systems.

In this context, it is not surprising to find that the bulk of the work done in this field comes from private sources, notably consulting firms.

Having defined the concept of offshoring, the OECD Secretariat, in the autumn of 2004, suggested certain indicators to measure the scale of the phenomenon. These were indirect indicators involving assumptions of offshoring in the absence of direct measurement.

3.1. Types of firms affected by offshoring

Before describing the indicators that could identify instances of offshoring, at both the sectoral level and the level of individual firms, we should look at what such indicators can measure. This is because the offshoring of a company's operations can affect employment at many other firms, including the company's own affiliates, its suppliers and its subcontractors.

The indicators suggested here exclusively concern identification of jobs lost because of offshoring in accordance with the definitions set out in chapter one.

The example shown in Figure 8 will make it possible, in the context of offshoring, firstly *(a)* to ascertain better those transactions which have a direct or indirect effect on employment, and *(b)* secondly, to identify the data which can be used to quantify that impact. The example in Figure 8 is confined to the case where an enterprise in a country relocates certain of its activities to another country. It is assumed that in Country 1, company A is a parent company, which means that it is a case of a group of enterprises, and that the parent company is controlled by residents of Country 1 (the most frequent case). Parent company A decides to scale down certain of its activities (goods and services) in Country 1 and transfer them to its affiliate B in Country 2. The transfer of these activities will involve a direct investment flow from company A to its affiliate B. Part of the new production in affiliate B will then be imported by parent company A (intra-firm imports) to satisfy domestic demand in Country 1, the same as before the relocation. A second part of the new production of affiliate B could be exported directly to countries 3, 4, ..., n, which are trading partners of Country 1. These exports will replace the exports which had previously been made directly by parent company A to those countries. Consequently, for a constant demand for imports by countries 3, 4, ..., n, exports from parent company A to those countries are initially likely to diminish. In addition, affiliate B in Country 2 will be in competition on the markets of countries 3, 4, ..., n, with all the other firms in Country 1 which export the same goods and services as affiliate B to those countries.

Figure 8. Simplified case of offshoring of goods and services

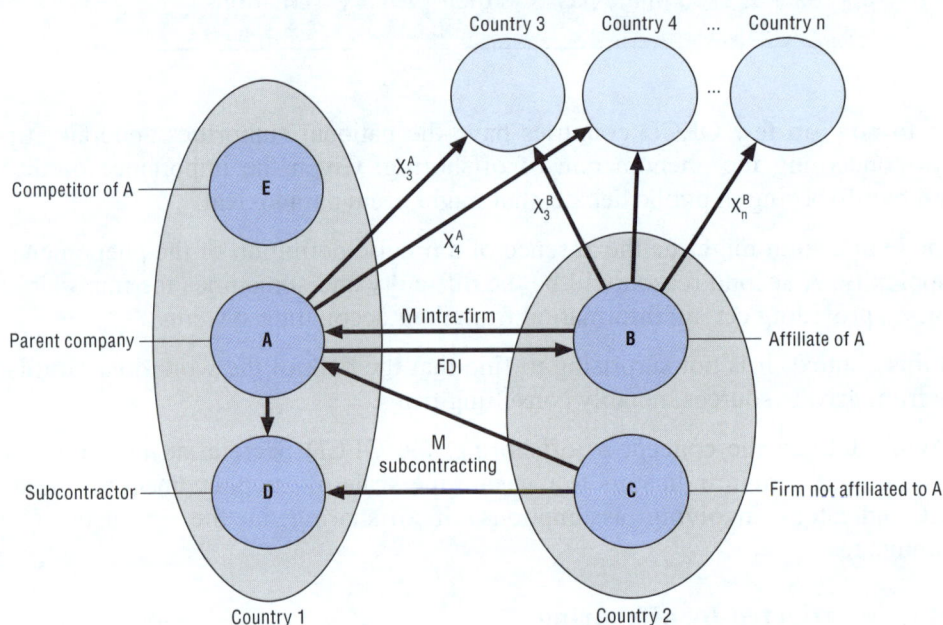

Parent company A can at the same time conclude subcontracting contracts with firm C in Country 2 which is not an affiliate of A. Thus, the goods and services subcontracted by firm C will then be imported by parent company A in Country 1.

Firm E located in Country 1 may be in competition with parent company A. To the extent that firm E does not relocate any activity abroad, it may find itself obliged to reduce those of its activities that have been rendered unprofitable by parent company A, whose relocated and subsequently imported goods and services are more competitive. As was pointed out in Box 3, parent company A may discontinue certain activities by outsourcing them to firm D inside Country 1. In this event, firm D can in turn subcontract abroad - for example to firm C in Country 2 – the activities in Country 2 for which it received the order from parent company A, and then import the said subcontracted goods and services for delivery to parent company A.

The example shown in Figure 8 is simplified to the extent that not all the firms concerned are taken into account. In reality, if the compiling country is Country 1 whose firms relocate their activities to Country 2, it would be necessary to take account of other categories of firms concerned by offshoring. They are shown in Figure 9.

Figure 9. Categories of firms to be considered in a case of offshoring

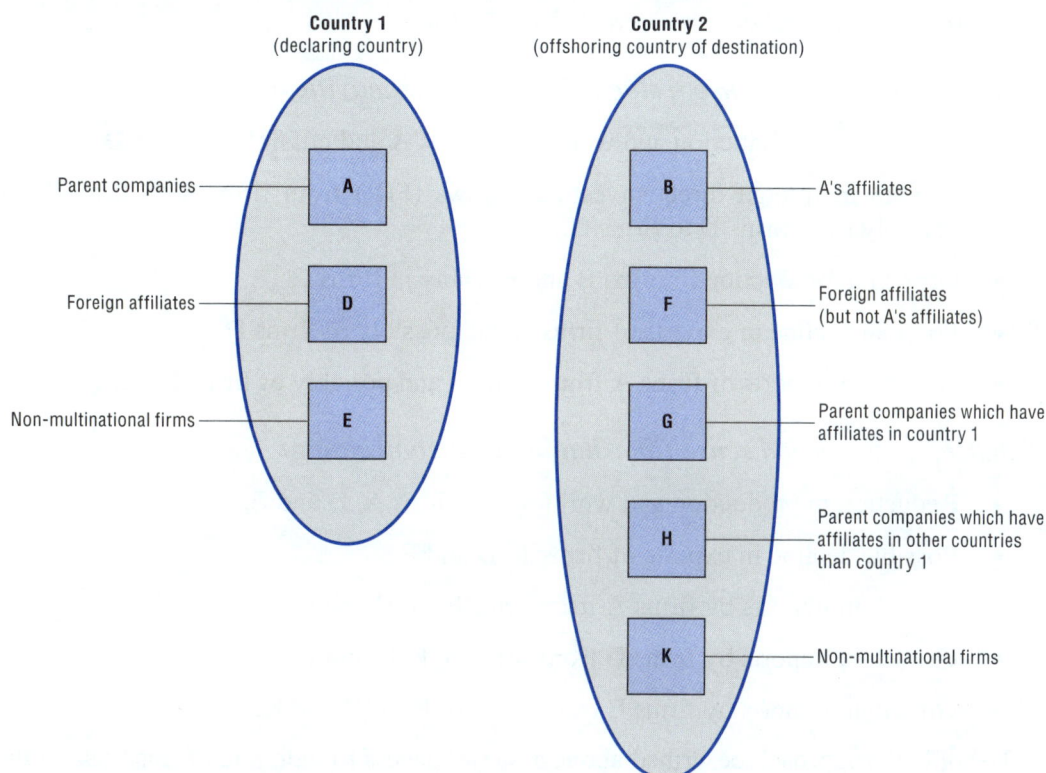

The different categories of firms taken into account in Figure 9 show the multiple aspects that need to be considered:

- The foreign affiliates D in Country 1 can relocate certain of their activities to their parent companies G in Country 2.

- The same foreign affiliates D can subcontract activities to firms B (affiliates of A) but also to the other categories F, H, and K with the exception of their parent companies G.

- The firms E in Country 1 have the possibility of subcontracting certain of their activities to firms in all the categories in Country 2.

- Certain foreign affiliates D in Country 1 can disappear and be relocated in Country 2. If the group to which they belong does not have any other affiliates in Country 1, the goods and services which formerly were consumed in Country 1 will be imported by other firms located in Country 1. In that case, these imports will not be intra-firm imports.

3.2. Proposed indicators

The changes concerning the transactions described above for the firms in Figure 9 could be summarised in two ways. A first approach can be taken using data from individual firms, while a second could be a more macro-economic approach.

3.2.1. Indicators based on individual firms' data

Offshoring in the strict sense (relocation abroad of activities)

- Reduction in production and workers in firms A and possibly in firms D.

- Growth in foreign direct investment flows (FDI) from firms A to firms B and possibly from firms D to firms G.

- Growth in production in firms B and possibly in firms G.

- Possible decline in exports of firms A and possibly of firms D.

- Growth in imports of firms A from firms B and possibly of firms D from firms E.

Offshoring in the broad sense (international subcontracting)

- Reduction in production and workforce in firms A, D and E.

- Possible decline in exports of firms A, D and E.

- Growth in imports by firms A from firms F, G, H and K.

- Growth in imports by firms D from firms B, F, H and K.

- Growth in imports by firms E from firms B, F, G, H and K.

To apply the approach described above assumes access to individual firms' data in the relocating country, information on the activities of their own foreign affiliates and the status of foreign firms which are the source of the imports.

It should, however, be emphasised that only the approach which gives access to the individual firms' data could give slightly more tangible results for presumptions of relocation. Moreover, when the approach based on individual firms' data is adopted, it should be applied at "establishment" level, but without losing sight of the ownership links between these establishments and enterprises and groups of enterprises.

3.2.2. Indicators based on sectoral data

Offshoring in the strict sense (relocation abroad of activities)

Between period t and period $t + i$, $i = 1, ...n$ and for a particular sector k

- Decline in production P^k in sector k

$$\Delta P^k = P^k_{t+i} - P^k_t < 0 \tag{1}$$

- Decline in number of employees L^k in sector K

$$\Delta L^k = L^k_{t+i} - L^k_t < 0 \tag{2}$$

- Possible decline in exports X^k in sector k

$$\Delta X^k = X^k_{t+i} - X^k_t < 0 \qquad (3)$$

- Growth in direct investment flows concerning sector k

$$\Delta FDI = FDI^k_{t+i} - FDI^k_t > 0 \qquad (4)$$

- Growth in production of affiliates PF^k in Country 1, in the countries of relocation and in sector k

$$\Delta PF^k = PF^k_{t+i} - PF^k_i > 0 \qquad (5)$$

- Growth in exports of affiliates PF^k in Country 1, in the countries of relocation and in sector k

$$\Delta XF^k = XF^k_{t+i} - XF^k_t > 0 \qquad (6)$$

- Growth in imports M^k of Country 1 from affiliates located in the countries of relocation and concerning sector k

$$\Delta M^k = M^k_{t+i} - M^k_i > 0 \qquad (7)$$

(essentially intra-firm imports)

Offshoring in the broad sense (international subcontracting)

Between period t and period $t+i$, $i=1,...n$ and for sector m:

- Decline in production P^k in the sector m

$$\Delta P^m = P^m_{t+i} - P^m_i < 0 \qquad (8)$$

- Decline in the number of employees L^k in the sector m

$$\Delta L^m = L^m_{t+i} - L^m_i < 0 \qquad (9)$$

- Growth in total imports M^m of Country 1 concerning sector m less intra-firm imports for the same sector (M^m, intra)

$$\Delta M^m = \left(M^m_{t+i} - M^{m,\text{int ra}}_{t+i} \right) - \left(M^m_t - M^{m,\text{int ra}}_t \right) > 0 \qquad (10)$$

When all the indicators suggested for a given sector pertain, it can be concluded that there is a strong presumption of offshoring

However, even in an unarguable case of offshoring, for various reasons it is highly unlikely that all the indicators suggested above will converge. The reasons why they can give divergent results will be examined later. In principle, the suggested indicators are valid both for goods and services. However, while on a conceptual plane there is no difference, because the sources of the data used are not the same, the evaluation methods for services could be different (see also Section 3.4.2).

3.3. Relevance and limitations of the suggested indicators

Assuming that the data needed is available, the question arises as to whether the suggested indicators can measure the impact of offshoring on employment. Before proceeding to an evaluation and certain additional propositions, it is worth recalling here certain cases which do not constitute offshoring.

Box 6. Cases that do not constitute offshoring

- Creation of a new production unit abroad without reducing activity and the domestic workforce.

- Growth of imports from foreign affiliates to satisfy additional domestic demand without a reduction in the domestic workforce.

- Imports from affiliates and subcontractors of products which are not identical to those no longer produced in the compiling country.

- Subcontracting abroad without reducing domestic production and workforce, on condition that what is involved is not second-tier subcontracting ordered by another firm which has stopped these activities in order to outsource them on the domestic market.

- Closure of production units due to poor competitiveness which is not a result of competition from other domestic firms which for their part have relocated.

- Reduced production and workforce in the compiling country and opening abroad by the same enterprise of activities different from those reduced in the compiling country.

- Temporary subcontracting abroad.

It has already been emphasised that the results which are most reliable and closest to the real situation concerning relocation can only be obtained at enterprise level. For that purpose the following is required:

- A list of establishments and enterprises.

- Customs and balance of payments data to provide information on the value of imports and exports according to the nature of goods and services and their origin and destination.

- Data from the business registers on employment trends.

- Sources constituted over time by groups and independent enterprises.

Box 7. Links between employment and imports based on sectoral data

a) **Reductions in the number of workers without a growth in imports**

    i) *In the case of offshoring:*

- The reduction in numbers of workers solely concerns exports which are relocated.

- The number of workers declines in a secondary activity while imports are recorded in the principal activity or another secondary activity.

- The number of workers declines because of the disappearance of a foreign affiliate but imports can be made by other firms with other activities.

- The number of workers declines because of the disappearance of a firm controlled by the residents of a country which nevertheless maintains activities abroad. Then imports may occur through trading firms but may not appear in the statistics if they are classified in another category.

    ii) *In the absence of offshoring:*

- The number of workers declines due to domestic outsourcing.

- The number of workers declines due to a strong rise in productivity or reduction in over-capacity.

- Reduction in the number of workers due to poor competitiveness.

b) **Growth of imports without a decline in the number of workers**

    i) *In the case of offshoring:*

- The number of workers in importing firms does not decline if imports of goods and services relate to second-tier subcontracting and are intended for firms which have outsourced these goods and services on the domestic market.

- The number of workers does not decline if there is job creation in secondary activities classified in the principal activity.

- The number of workers may even increase if there is new foreign investment (new foreign affiliates) in the same sectors.

- If there are new acquisitions in the domestic market by firms which relocate.

- If the people who have lost their jobs are transferred to other activities or granted leave of absence.

    ii) *In the absence of offshoring:*

- Imports increase to satisfy additional domestic demand which local producers cannot satisfy without a decline in the number of workers.

- The growth in imports may be accompanied by the creation of new jobs in the same import sectors.

On the other hand, when sectoral data are used, the presumptions of relocation are more difficult if not impossible to establish. For that it is important to consider two questions:

- Is it possible in a case of offshoring to have a reduction in the number of workers without a growth in imports?

- Can growth in imports be not accompanied by a reduction in the number of workers?

The above description shows that when offshoring occurs in a particular sector with job losses, in many cases, the available data does not necessarily allow detection of reductions in the number of jobs nor significant rises in imports. Other limitations can be added to the above cases, the most important of which might be:

3.3.1. Changes in the classification or principal activity of firms

When there are changes in classification, an enterprise might be classified at the beginning of the period under consideration in one sector and in a sector in a different category at the end of the period. A similar phenomenon can arise with aggregated sectoral data, when a firm changes its principal activity between the beginning and the end of the period under consideration.

3.3.2. Problems of confidentiality

Identifying the country of offshoring and the sector concerned, especially with regard to the activity of multinational firms, requires the use of tables which cross reference the countries of origin and destination to sectors. For reasons of confidentiality, these tables, where they exist, are likely to be much too aggregated to allow identification of all the sectors and countries concerned.

3.3.3. Successive small-scale relocations abroad

Some enterprises may progressively relocate their activities in such a way that job losses, the decline in production and exports and the growth in imports are only significant over a long period. Some national surveys not relating to relocations do not take account of job losses in a firm if they affect less than ten people.

3.3.4. Competition from exporting affiliates

Figure 8 shows that when activities with a high propensity to export are relocated, a significant part of the exports will be made by the affiliates located abroad. Thus these affiliates will be in direct competition with other domestic enterprises which export the same goods and services to the same markets. It is possible that these firms will reduce their workforce because they have difficulties in exporting.

3.3.5. Impact of offshoring on subcontractors

Often when large multinationals offshore certain activities, their subcontractors are forced to follow them abroad. When this happens, it is a classic case of offshoring. However, if that is not the case, subcontracting firms may have to reduce their workforce, without that being accompanied by imports. Even if imports do occur, they may involve sectors other than those which relocated their activities.

3.3.6. Second or third-tier subcontracting

One of the characteristics of subcontracting is "cascade subcontracting". The prime contractor contracts a first subcontractor who in turn contracts a second or even third-tier subcontractor. Thus a firm located in Country A may outsource one of its activities abroad to a firm located in Country B if it produces at a lower cost. However, the firm in Country B may regularly subcontract this activity to another firm located in Country C. The added value will then be shared between several firms. In some cases, the firm located in Country B may subcontract the activity to another firm also located in Country B. This second-tier subcontractor could be an affiliate of an enterprise located in Country A. In the latter case, Country A will be the double beneficiary. This example illustrates the objective difficulties in estimating the impact on employment of such complex transactions.

3.3.7. Competition between firms which have moved offshore and those which have not

Certain firms may reduce their workforce because they are subject to strong competition from other firms in the same sector which have moved offshore some of their activities. In general, a reduction in the number of workers due to poor competitiveness is not necessarily linked to the phenomenon of offshoring and should not be counted in job losses due to offshoring. However, when the loss of competitiveness is due to competition from firms which have moved offshore certain of their activities, it would be hard not to establish a relationship between the two phenomena. But it should be recognised that this relationship is very hard to establish even with access to individual firms' data.

3.4. Indirect measures to assess the employment impact of offshoring

3.4.1. Employment equivalent of imports

When it is possible to quantify imports resulting from offshoring and the decline in the value of exports due to offshoring, it is important to relate these changes to the corresponding employment. As regards imports in particular, the equivalent in direct jobs implied by these imports is obtained by the formula (1):

$$L_{it}^{m} = \sum_{i} M_{it} \frac{L_{it}}{Y_{it}} \quad (1)$$

where: L_{it}^{m} is the employment equivalent of imports in sector i for year t.

M_{it} : the flow of imports in sector i for year t.

Y_{it} : the output by value in sector i for year t.

In other words, this means calculating the number of jobs necessary if the imported goods and services were produced domestically.

Equation (1) only concerns direct jobs. To the extent that production of the goods and services concerned in sector i requires the use of intermediate output, jobs indirectly involved in the production should be taken into account. To do that, input-output tables must be used, assuming that a given amount of imports replaces an identical amount of domestic production.

If $A = [aij]$ i, j = 1, ...n is the technical coefficients matrix where:

Aij: the quantity of consumption of intermediate goods i required to manufacture one unit of a good j.

n = the number of sectors.

If $Y = [Y_i]_j$ $i = 1, ...n$ is the production vector of each sector and

$D = [d_i]_j$ $i = 1, ...n$ is the final demand vector for each sector

Then: AY + D = Y   (2)

This equation shows the distribution of production between intermediate consumption and final consumption. The variation in final demand on production will be given by the following equation:

$$Y = (I - A)^{-1} D \qquad (3) \qquad \text{(unit diagonal matrix)}$$

The employment equivalent of imports is then determined in relation to the production structure of the domestic economy (Li/Yi would be the mean coefficients for each sector where employment L corresponds to the total of direct or indirect jobs).

Limitations

The fact of choosing the coefficients Li/Yi based on a country's production structure and then applying them to imports (or exports) raises certain problems. First of all, it is implicitly assumed that the labour production structures are the same in the compiling country and its trading partners. This assumption, which also depends on the country involved, may not be realistic. In reality the jobs content of imports from low-wage countries is higher than that of production in the compiling country. The jobs content of the foreign production, therefore, needs to be known. If the imported goods and services had been produced in the compiling country, the price of those goods and services would have been higher and thus demand for them weaker. Moreover, this approach implies the same labour productivity in enterprises in the same sector. But experience shows that the most export-oriented firms have higher labour productivity and use higher-skilled workers than the others. Thus imports of a given value will cause more job losses than exports of the same value will create jobs.

In addition, it should not be overlooked that in the case of imports of intermediate goods, part of the goods could be processed and then re-exported. The absence of such information will further complicate evaluation of the employment equivalent of imports.

Finally, substitution between imported and domestic goods implies that the unit prices of the imported and domestic goods are the same. Again, this assumption is not realistic in the case of trade between North and South. The imported goods are generally cheaper. Consequently, an import value is substituted for a considerably higher output volume in the compiling country corresponding to the same value of domestic production.

3.4.2. *An alternative method of evaluating employment*

Another indirect measure of the impact of offshoring on employment could be achieved by means of an econometric estimation of demand for labour (L). In principle, offshoring implies job losses in the compiling country. If there were perfect mobility between sectors in the labour market, job losses in one sector could be offset by gains in another. Because of the rigidities in the labour market, the result is a net loss of jobs, at least in the short term. It was seen above that relocation can be a source of job creation by improving firms' competitiveness.

Thus demand for labour L_{it} in an industry i and year t could be estimated as follows:

$$\ln L_{it} = a_0 + a_1 \ln W_{it} + \beta \ln \omega_{it} + \delta \ln \gamma_{it} \tag{1}$$

where W = the wage rate

ω = vector for the price of other inputs

y = level of production.

The question is what input prices to use for outsourcing abroad. A multinational firm can decide what labour to be used in the compiling country and abroad. However, not all forms of outsourcing involve multinationals and it is very difficult to identify wages for inputs from abroad, especially in the case of imported services. The lower the prices of imported inputs, the greater the tendency towards outsourcing abroad.

In order to allow for this tendency to outsource abroad, an "outsourcing index" is suggested as an indicator. This indicator for a country is constructed from outsourcing abroad of an industry i and refers to both services and material goods. Thus for an industry i and for a set of categories of services j (or material goods) the outsourcing index (OI_i) is measured thus:

$$OI_i = \sum_i \left[\frac{purchases\ of\ inputs\ \ j\ excluding\ energy\ by\ industry\ i}{total\ inputs\ excluding\ energy\ used\ by\ i} \right] \bullet \left[\frac{M_j}{D_j} \right] \tag{2}$$

where M_j = imports of goods or services j

D_j = domestic demand for goods or services j

The services j (or material goods) which constitute the inputs of industry i must be defined in advance.

The first term of the outsourcing index is calculated from input-output tables. The second term, which is the rate of penetration of imports of services j (or material goods) must be calculated from data for trade in services (or material goods). Unfortunately, this ratio is more difficult to calculate for services because of the lack of detailed data collected in relation to the balance of payments.

After calculating for industry i the outsourcing index for both services (OI_i^s) and goods (OI_i^g) these can be introduced into equation (1) which determines changing demand for labour (Δ).

$$\Delta \ln L_{it} = a_o + a_1 \Delta \ln W_{it} + a_2 \Delta \ln OI_{it}^s + a_3 \Delta \ln OI_{it}^g + \beta \Delta \ln \omega_{it} + \gamma \Delta \ln Y_{it} + \delta D_t + \varepsilon_{it} \quad (3)$$

The term D_t corresponds to the fixed effects for year t which are common through all industries such as changes concerning the cost of capital.

Thus from equation (3) it could be said:

- That growth in wages W_{it} would have a negative effect on employment.

- Faster growth in the outsourcing indices $\left(OI_{it}^s \ et \ OI_{it}^g \right)$ would also have a negative impact on employment.

- Growth in the price of other inputs ω_{it} would encourage firms to replace these inputs with labour.

- Finally, growth in production Y_{it} would have a favourable effect on employment.

The greater the disaggregation of the level at which the estimate is calculated, the more outsourcing will be negatively related to employment. On the other hand, at a more aggregated level, it is the sectoral composition of employment that would change and not necessarily total employment.

3.5. Other approaches adopted to measure the impact of offshoring on employment

The approaches proposed in the preceding sections, concerning indirect measure-ments which allow a presumption of offshoring, suggest:

- Firstly, that only the suggested measurements applied to individual firms' data could provide results closer to reality.

- Secondly, that the statistical units used must be establishments and not enter-prises.

However, even when calculations are made on the basis of detailed data concerning individual firms, some evaluations cannot be made either because of the lack of certain categories of data or because of the difficulty of collecting them or because the changes are small and not detected by the surveys. If, for example, the survey sample only includes firms which abolish more than ten jobs at a time, firms which reduce less than ten jobs in many establishments and over a long period will not be included in the survey sample.

3.5.1. General equilibrium models

One of the major difficulties with the proposed approaches is to relate the factors that determine the location of a production unit abroad to the measurements used. In the majority of cases, the suggested measurements capture other phenomena as well and are not limited to the principal motive which is optimisation of factor costs.

On the other hand, the general equilibrium approach makes it possible to formalise the causes of the redistribution of capital and correct the measurement of offshoring for phenomena external to the redistribution of capital. The general equilibrium models allow the possibility of testing empirically everything that was described in Section 2.3, notably the remuneration of factors of production, skilled and unskilled labour, changes in the terms of trade, growth in exports and imports, etc. They also allow measurement of the gains achieved between partner countries.

Limitations

The principal limitation of these models is their complexity while the breakdown of the different elements that come into play is quite difficult. Moreover, the results are very sensitive to the many assumptions underlying the models.

3.5.2. *The foreign direct investment approach (FDI)*

Another approach consists of measuring the scale of offshoring through foreign direct investment. It was seen above that offshoring in the strict sense involves a capital flow to the destination country where a new affiliate is established or the capacity of an existing affiliate is expanded. More precisely, it is the financing abroad of an activity identical to that which was stopped in the compiling country.

This method is generally applied to emerging countries with low labour costs. Thus the share of direct investment in emerging countries can be calculated.

Limitations

The direct investment approach, however, has a number of disadvantages. First, it does not take account of offshoring in the broad sense, *i.e.* involving subcontracting. Then, not all direct investment in an emerging country is necessarily the result of offshoring, because it does not have to mean the cessation of the same activity in the compiling country.

Moreover, financing of an affiliate abroad may take different forms, and, especially in the case of an existing production unit, it may involve a purely financial transaction (*e.g.* exchange of shares). It may also be financed by another affiliate in the same group located in another country, unless the statistics take account of the country which is the ultimate beneficiary.

Lastly, if the information is not supplemented by other indicators, notably those suggested in Section 3.1, it will not be possible to relate them to employment.

3.5.3. *Input-output models and exchange of intermediate inputs*

This approach seeks to identify the foreign content of domestic output, by taking account of the share of intermediate inputs in the production process. These measurements are then used to evaluate how many domestic workers have been replaced by workers abroad.

These measurements seek to capture international outsourcing, namely the decision by firms to replace domestic added value (internal to the country) by production abroad. They also show the impact of fragmentation of production on domestic output.

Some studies draw a distinction between offshoring in the strict sense and the broad sense. Offshoring in the broad sense takes account of intermediate inputs imported by an industry on behalf of all industries, while offshoring in the strict sense takes account of intermediate inputs imported from the same industry.

Then, to evaluate the impact on employment, a cost function is used (*e.g.* translog type). By using this approach, it is possible to analyse the impact of offshoring on the structure of skills in demand for labour.

Limitations

This approach which is one of the most rigorous seeks to measure the impact on employment of the offshoring of activities.

The chief disadvantage is that the concept of "offshoring" if the definition in Chapter 1 were not taken into account is much broader than that of relocation abroad. Not every imported intermediate input necessarily relates to activities stopped in the compiling country and relocated abroad. From this point of view, the impact on employment is over-estimated compared with that for relocation abroad.

3.5.4. Various approaches based on individual firms' data

It was emphasised above that only the use of individual firms' data allows a close approximation of the reality concerning the impact of offshoring on employment. The use of individual firms' data also offers other possibilities for analysis.

An alternative approach to measuring the impact of offshoring on employment would be to observe what would have happened if the firms had not relocated their activities. These approaches have not yet been developed and it is no doubt too early to discuss their limitations.

3.5.5. Employment potentially affected by offshoring

Another approach consists of evaluating jobs by occupation which would potentially be affected by offshoring. This approach is based on the links between skills in information and communication technology (ICT) and employment by occupation in different industrial sectors. It involves first identifying which jobs classified by occupation are intensive users of information technology (IT) and their share of total employment. The principle of this approach is based on the idea that the more a job classified by occupation is an intensive user of information technology, the more it will potentially be affected by offshoring. This is because thanks to information technology, the output of such work can be distributed throughout the world, irrespective of the place of production.

To identify jobs by occupation in this category, four main criteria are used.

- Intensive use of information technology.

- The output of such work must be capable of being delivered with the aid of information technology (which means that it is part of a marketable service).

- The work must have a high information or "knowledge" content.

- The work does not require physical presence.

Other criteria could also be taken into account such as: *a)* major wage differentials for the same job by occupation in the destination countries; *b)* establishment of low set-up barriers; *c)* low social networking requirements.

The criteria mentioned above make it possible to take account both of skilled and unskilled jobs by occupation and efforts have been made to make the classification of data by occupation as comparable as possible between countries.

Some authors have also tried to identify jobs by occupation which present a "risk of offshoring" by classifying the jobs concerned as "high risk", "low risk" or "no risk". The results obtained give for each year the percentage of potentially offshorable jobs by occupation compared with total employment. Additional econometric studies also identify factors which influence these trend patterns.

Limitations

On the technical plane, one limitation concerns the differences in appraisal by countries in the evaluation of the information technology content of the same category of job by occupation. Other limitations relate to the approach itself and the significance of the results obtained.

One of the conclusions of these studies is that about 20% of total employment could be potentially affected by offshoring. On this point, the evaluation methods and the significance of the word "potentially" offshorable raise some questions. Certain jobs by occupation considered to be potentially non-offshorable abroad because of their need for physical presence can also be offshoring. A car mechanic cannot do repairs at a distance. However, when his company is offshored, his job will also be offshored. In fact, these cases are not taken into account in the calculations. Moreover, other jobs by occupation such as teachers are considered as non-offshorable abroad to the extent that in the vast majority of cases these jobs require physical presence.

However, distance learning is developing very rapidly in all countries and in certain categories of higher education could very soon take on considerable significance. In reality, only a small percentage of occupations classified as potentially offshorable are in fact offshored, and equally a small percentage of jobs classified as non-offshorable are in fact offshored. Given this volatility, the question arises of the relevance of distinguishing between jobs as potentially offshorable or non offshorable.

It should not be forgotten either that technology changes very rapidly and that in occupations where physical presence at a particular time was essential, that might no longer be so. At the same time, the objective of governments is that information technology should be introduced on a massive scale in all occupations. As this process advances, it might be imagined that the proportion of potentially offshorable jobs by occupation out of total employment would increase substantially.

The difficulty involved in attributing to each of the types of employment that are potentially vulnerable to offshoring a high rate of likelihood of offshoring means that the results that are obtained are difficult to use as a tool for measuring the magnitude of the offshoring phenomenon.

Chapter 4

PRELIMINARY RESULTS

This chapter presents some preliminary results on the affect of offshoring on employment for a limited number of OECD countries, with in-depth looks at the United States and France. The results are based on sector-specific industrial data, detailing the extent of offshoring within various industrial sectors, the imported share of offshoring production for each of the sectors, as well as employment changes. The impact of outsourcing abroad on employment is measured in manufacturing as well as services, and the positive effects of offshoring on domestic economies are also discussed.

The results that are shown in this chapter are provisional. As explained above, in view of the lack of systematic survey findings, we must fall back on indirect measurements which constitute the presumption of relocation abroad. In most cases, these are results that derive from databases of the OECD Secretariat collected at the sectoral level, and which are not confidential in nature.

The findings shown here do not address the indirect impact of relocation abroad on employment, and do not deal with the most recent years. From this point of view they reflect all the constraints that are described in the preceding chapter.

The approach followed in this chapter is to examine the trends in the key mechanisms which pertain to offshoring, the phenomenon of outsourcing, the imported share of offshoring production and the development of employment.

4.1. The outsourcing of manufacturing and service activities

A general indicator for detecting the degree of outsourcing or "externalization" (E) in a sector is the share of value added (VA)[*] in the turnover (TUR)[**]:

$$E = VA/TUR.$$

In principle, the more a sector outsources its activities, the more likely the value added ratio/turnover is to be low.

Conversely, this ratio cannot distinguish between domestic outsourcing inside a country and outsourcing abroad. Figure 10 shows that generally speaking, for the whole of the economy and for the countries for which data is available, the countries that outsource most are Japan, Hungary and the Czech Republic and those that outsource the least are the United States and the United Kingdom. Between 1995 and 2004 the ratio of value added/turnover has gone down in France, Austria, the Netherlands and Hungary which means that these countries have globally outsourced more. During the same period the outsourcing for the entire economy in other countries has declined.

Figure 11 measures the same ratio in 2004 for the manufacturing and services sectors. The results show that most of the countries outsource slightly more in service industries than in manufacturing industries with the sole exception of Germany. Nonetheless, for Germany it is likely that there is a higher degree of equilibrium between the outsourcing of services and of the manufacturing industry to the extent that financial and social services were not taken into account.

With regard to outsourcing, Figures 12 and 13 distinguish firms controlled by the residents of reporting countries from firms that are foreign-owned. In most countries, the subsidiaries under foreign control outsource more than firms under the control of residents. With regard to manufacturing industry, Ireland and Turkey are exceptions inasmuch as the VA/TUR ratio is higher for foreign subsidiaries than for nationally-owned firms.

---

[*]   The gross value added of an establishment, an enterprise, an industy or a sector may be defined as "the value of output less the value of intermediate consumption" (SNA 1993, §6.222).

[**]   The turnover of a reference period corresponds to sales to third parties on the market for goods or services. Turnover includes all taxes levied on goods or services except value added tax. It also includes all other expenses (transport, packaging, etc.) charged to customers.

Figure 10. The ratio of value added to turnover for the whole of the economy in certain OECD countries

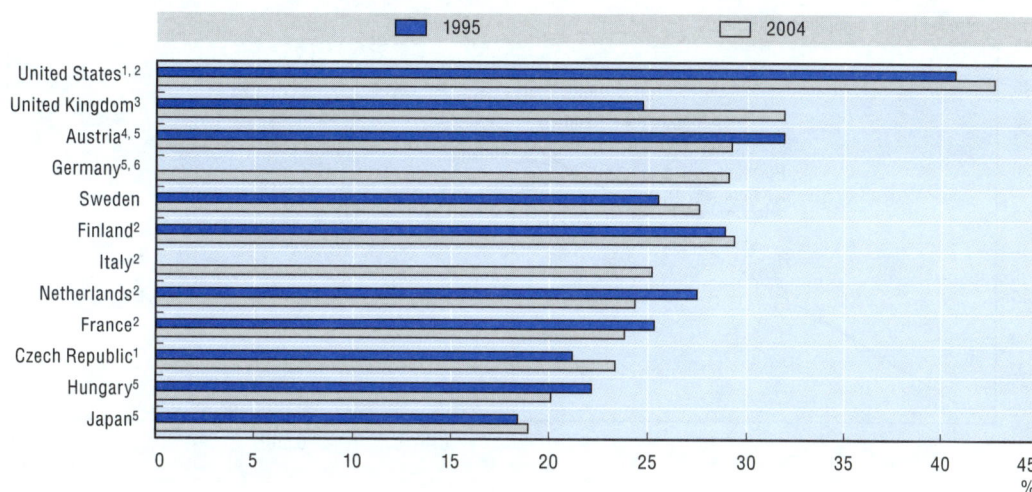

1. 1997.

2. 2002.

3. Excluding parts of mining, financial intermediation and parts of social and personal services.

4. Excluding agriculture and social and personal services.

5. 2003.

6. Excluding agriculture, financial intermediation and social and personal services.

Source: OECD, AFA and FATS databases.

StatLink: http://dx.doi.org/10.1787/447748461060

Figure 11. Ratio of value added to turnover in the manufacturing and services sectors

2004 or last year available

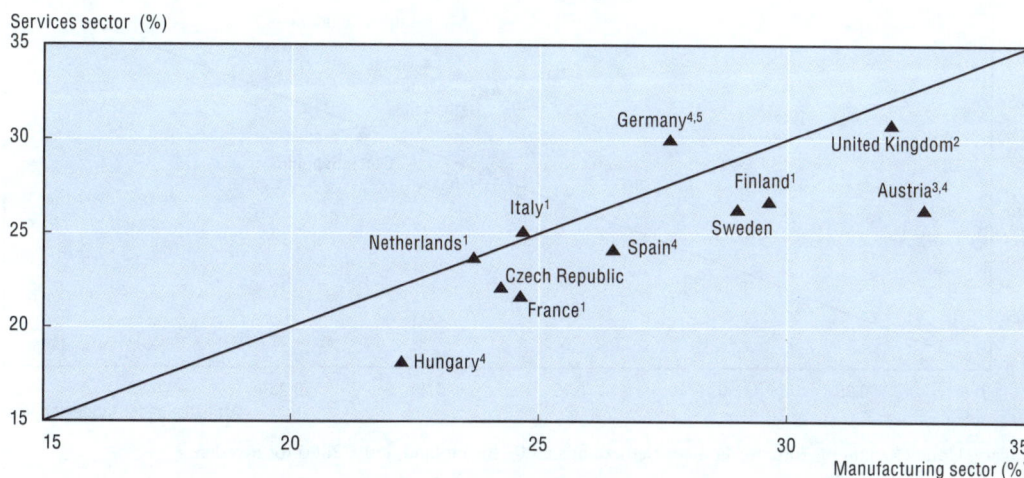

1. 1997.

2. 2002.

3. Excluding parts of mining, financial intermediation and parts of social and personal services.

4. Excluding agriculture and social and personal services.

5. 2003.

6. Excluding agriculture, financial intermediation and social and personal services.

Source: OECD, AFA and FATS databases.

StatLink: http://dx.doi.org/10.1787/148466518006

Figure 12. Ratio of value added to turnover in the manufacturing sector, 2004[*]

Firms controlled by the compiling countries

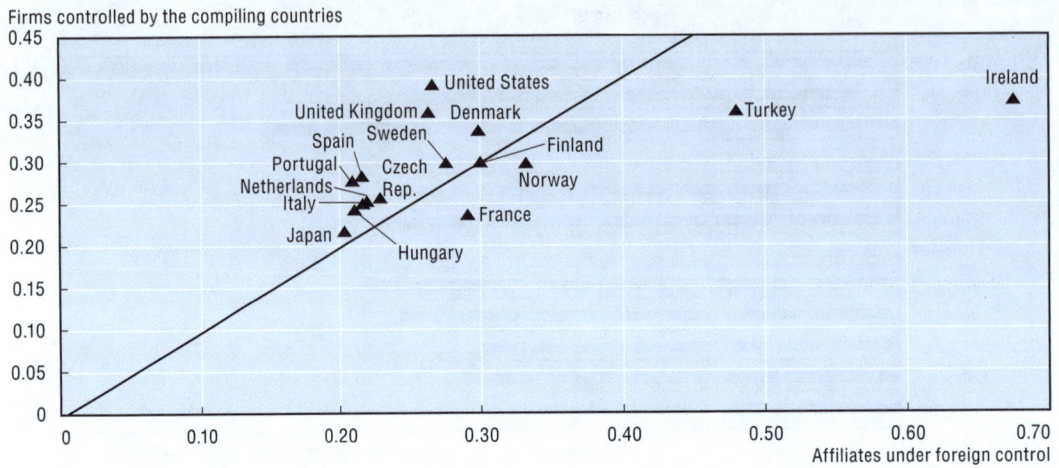

Affiliates under foreign control

* 2001 for Turkey. 2002 for Denmark, Finland, Italy, Netherlands and Portugal. 2003 for the United States, Japan, Ireland, Norway, Spain and Hungary. Ireland: production instead of turnover.

Source: OECD, AFA and FATS databases.

StatLink: http://dx.doi.org/10.1787/602746680516

Figure 13. Ratio of value added to turnover in the services sector, 2004[*]

Firms under control of residents

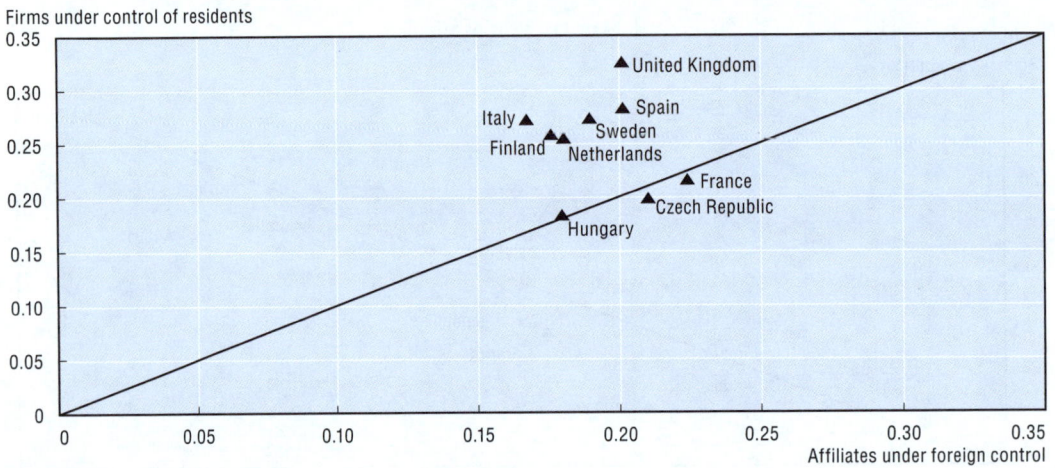

Affiliates under foreign control

* 2003 for Hungary, United Kingdom. 2002 for France, Netherlands. 2001 for Finland, Italy. 2000 for Sweden.

Source: OECD, FATS database.

StatLink: http://dx.doi.org/10.1787/541330328068

The above-described measurements cannot assess the relative shares of domestic and foreign outsourcing; for that, one must prepare a foreign outsourcing index of the type proposed in the preceding chapter. A summary of its preparation is shown in Box 8.

Box 8. Index of outsourcing abroad

The index of outsourcing abroad $\left(OI_i\right)$ is constructed as follows:

For a sector i and for a set of goods and services j the index of outsourcing $\left(OI_i\right)$ is:

$$OI_i = \sum_i \left[\frac{purchases\ of\ non\ energy\ inputs\ j\ by\ industry\ i}{total\ non-energy\ inputs\ used\ by\ i} \right] \cdot \left[\frac{M_j}{D_j} \right]$$

where M_j : imports of goods or services j

D_j : domestic demand for goods or services j

where $\left(D_j = Y_j - X_j + M_j\right)$ with: Y_j : production of goods or services j

X_j : exports of goods or services j

In other words, the more imports of goods or services j are purchased by industry i as input for its production, the more the outsourcing of industry i is important.

These indices make it possible, firstly at an aggregate level (but also at the sectoral level), for a compiling country to measure the extent of outsourcing abroad of its manufacturing industry with respect to both goods and services, as well as the extent of outsourcing abroad of services with respect to both goods and services.

This presupposes that goods and services j are well defined. These calculations can be made from input-output tables and trade data.

Figure 14. Index of outsourcing abroad in selected OECD countries

- Manufacturing intermediate import ratio of manufacturing sector
- Manufacturing intermediate import ratio of services sector
- Services intermediate import ratio of manufacturing sector
- Services intermediate import ratio of services sector

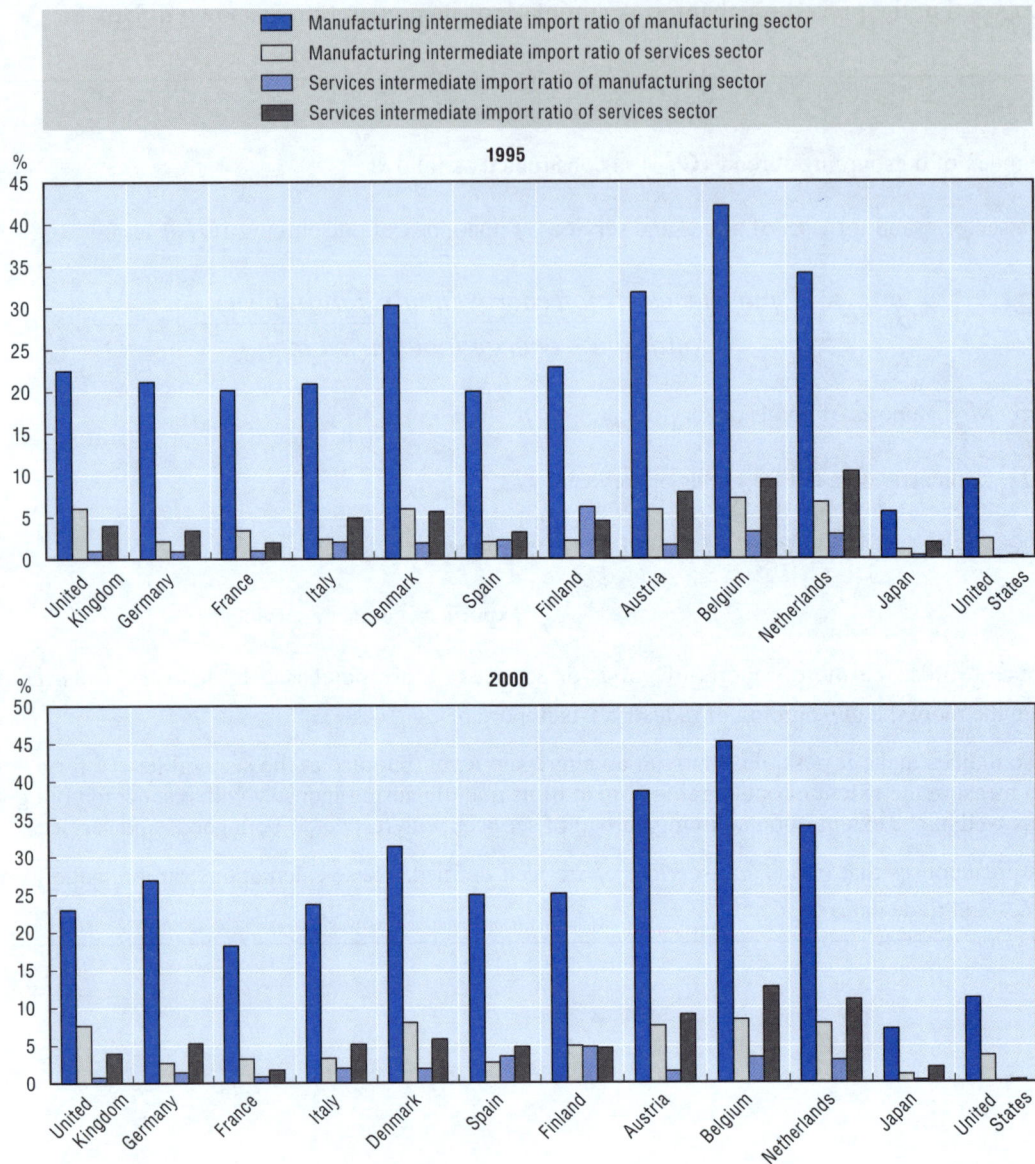

Source: OECD, Input-Output database.

StatLink: http://dx.doi.org/10.1787/715242787612

The results of the index of outsourcing abroad as shown by Figure 14 applied to the totality of both the manufacturing and services sectors show that:

- For all the available countries, the outsourcing of goods by the manufacturing sector is the largest foreign type of outsourcing. In second position comes outsourcing of goods by the services sector.

- The outsourcing of services by the services sector is in third place, and the outsourcing of services by the manufacturing sector is in last place.

- The countries whose manufacturing industries outsource most goods are Belgium, the Netherlands, Austria and Denmark. The United Kingdom, Germany, France and the United States outsource their activities abroad to a lesser degree.

- Japan is the country whose manufacturing industry outsources the least abroad. This result, contrasting with Japan's general outsourcing indicator which is among the highest, could indicate that subcontracting inside Japan is very highly developed.

- Between 1995 and 2000, the outsourcing abroad of goods by the services sector and the outsourcing abroad of services by the services sector have shown the strongest growth. Despite these trends, the relative proportions of the forms of outsourcing abroad have not significantly changed in any of these countries.

4.2. Employment trends

Figures 15 and 16 show that net job losses in OECD countries between 1995 and 2003 have exclusively occurred in the manufacturing industry. During this time, 20 countries have lost jobs in this sector while 10 other countries have recorded net job creation.

Conversely in the services sector, all countries have benefited from net creation of jobs. Figure 17 also shows that, apart from three countries (Japan, Slovakia and the Czech Republic) all the others have compensated for the losses recorded in the manufacturing sector by the jobs created in the services sector. In Japan and Slovakia, jobs created in services have not offset the losses recorded by the manufacturing sector. In the case of the Czech Republic, the overall decline of manning levels is due exclusively to agriculture, mining and quarrying, and construction.

Figure 15. Trends in total employment in the manufacturing sector, 1995-2003

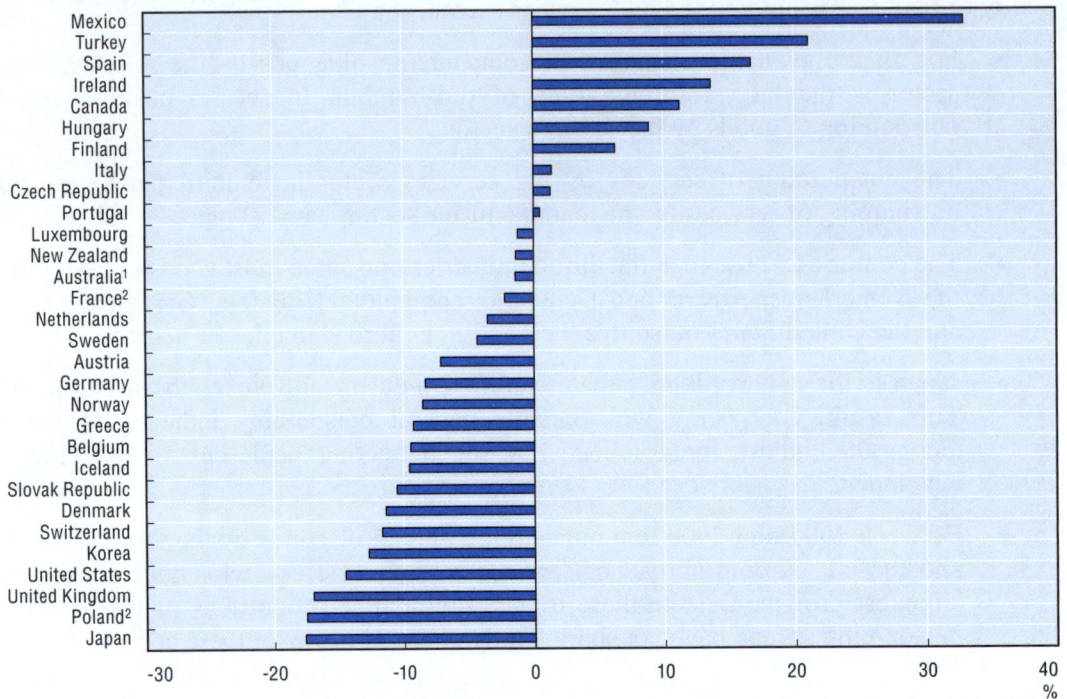

1. 1995-2001.
2. 1995-2002.

Source: OECD, STAN database and *Labour Force Statistics*.

StatLink: http://dx.doi.org/10.1787/631052168016

Figure 16. Trends in total employment in the services sector, 1995-2003

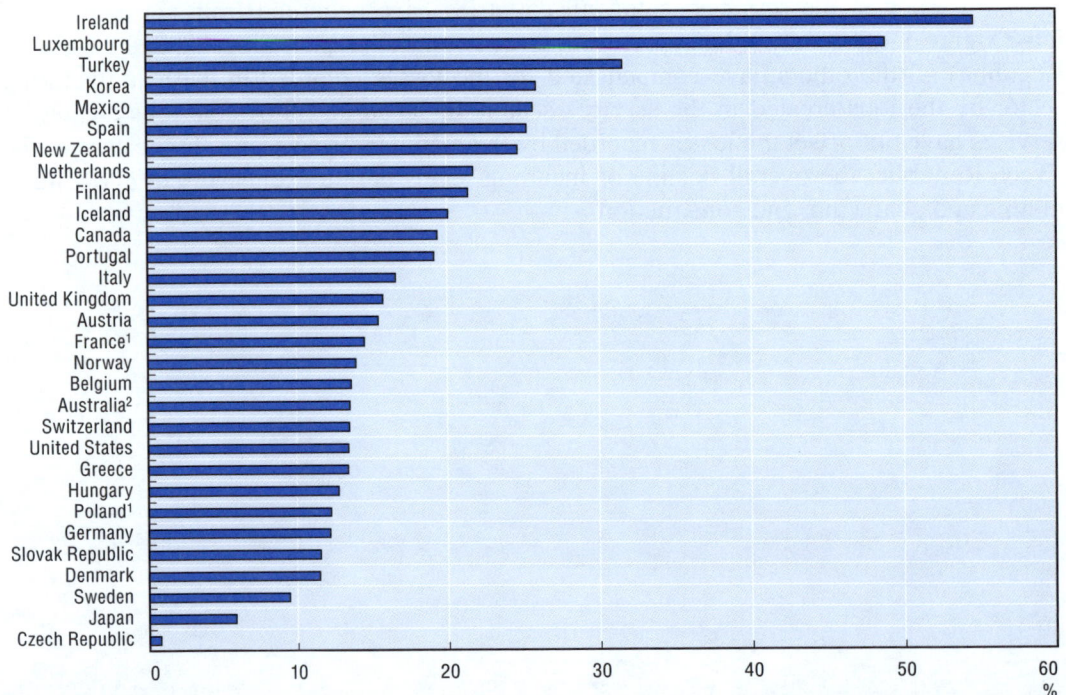

StatLink: http://dx.doi.org/10.1787/481044107808

Figure 17. Trends in total employment in the whole economy, 1995-2003

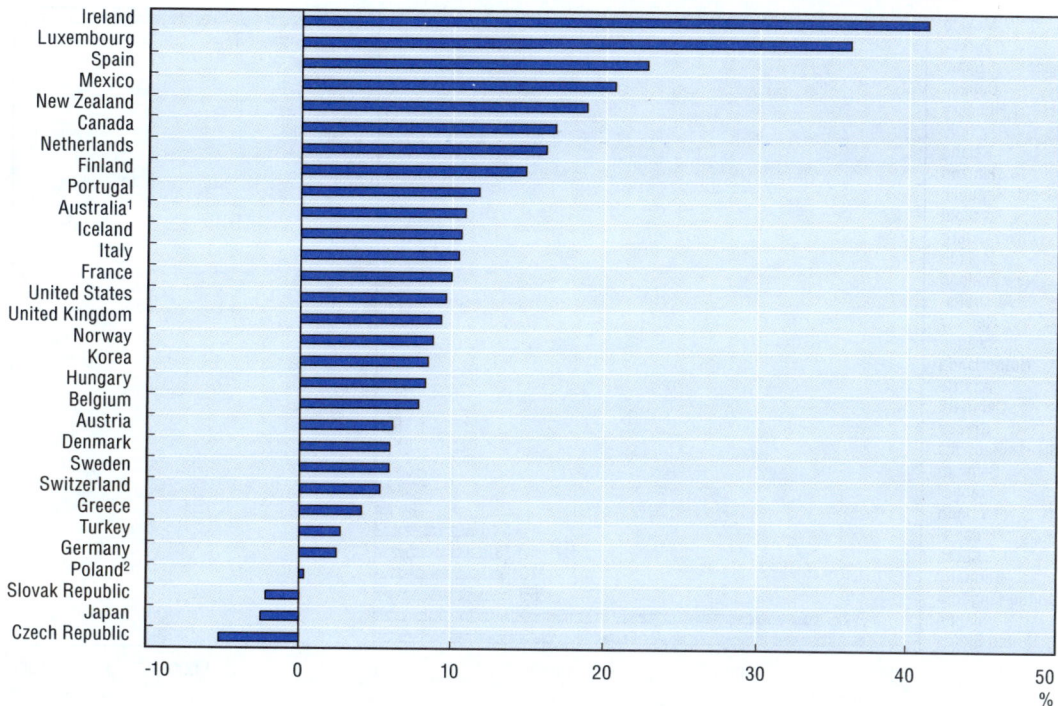

1. 1995-2001.

2. 1995-2002.

Source: OECD, STAN database and *Labour Force Statistics*.

StatLink: http://dx.doi.org/10.1787/234062465713

Figures 18 and 19 show how many jobs (in absolute figures) were concerned by net losses or gains in manufacturing industry and the service sector between 1995 and 2003. It can be seen, for example, that the United States lost 2.6 million jobs in manufacturing over the period in question, but created 14.1 million jobs in services. The trend was less favourable in Japan in that 2.4 million jobs were lost in manufacturing, while the service sector created only 2.3 million. Amongst the European countries, the biggest job losses in manufacturing industry were recorded in the United Kingdom and Germany (755 000 and 701 000, respectively), but the United Kingdom did create more jobs than Germany in services. Where the other European countries are concerned, mention should be made of the big manufacturing job losses in Poland (-544 000), half of them in the textile industry (-224 000) and a quarter in non-electrical machinery (-110 000).

The only conclusions that can be drawn from the above figures in regard to offshoring is that in services the job losses attributable to offshoring are largely offset by the creation of new jobs.

With regard to the manufacturing sector, it could be said that in general there are no direct links between import penetration trends and employment trends (Figure 20). At this level of aggregation, if these links are not established, it is going to be even more difficult to find them exclusively among imports that are attributable to offshoring.

Figure 18. Change in total employment in the manufacturing sector, 1995-2003

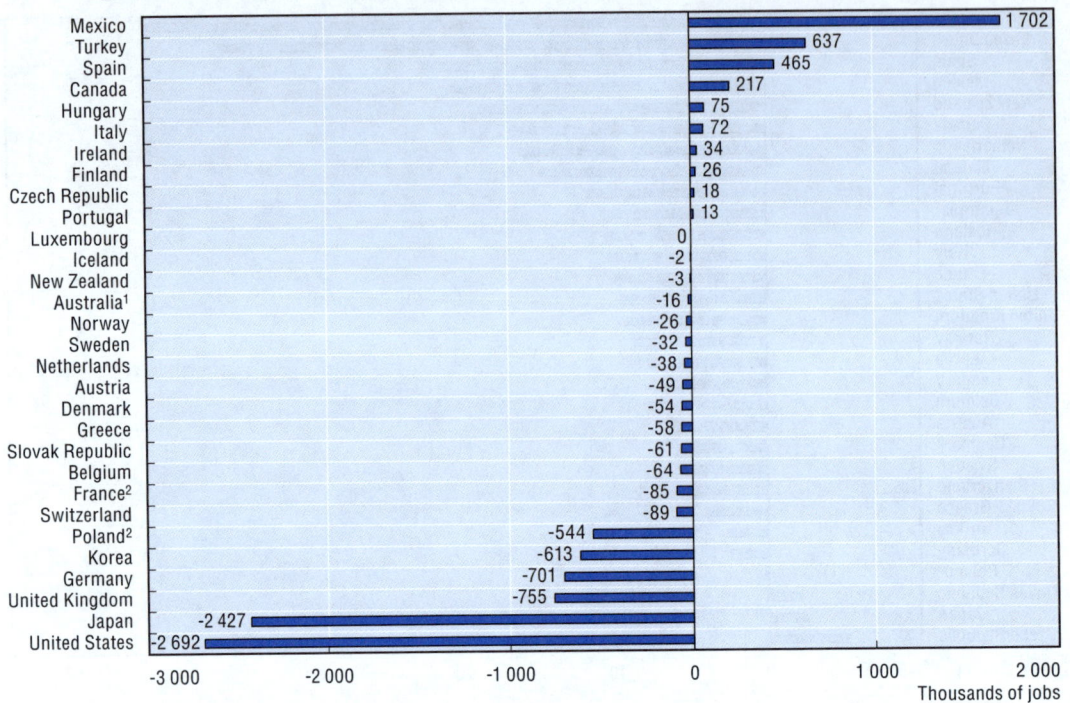

Mexico	1 702
Turkey	637
Spain	465
Canada	217
Hungary	75
Italy	72
Ireland	34
Finland	26
Czech Republic	18
Portugal	13
Luxembourg	0
Iceland	-2
New Zealand	-3
Australia[1]	-16
Norway	-26
Sweden	-32
Netherlands	-38
Austria	-49
Denmark	-54
Greece	-58
Slovak Republic	-61
Belgium	-64
France[2]	-85
Switzerland	-89
Poland[2]	-544
Korea	-613
Germany	-701
United Kingdom	-755
Japan	-2 427
United States	-2 692

Thousands of jobs

1. 1995-2001.
2. 1995-2002.

Source: OECD, STAN database and *Labour Force Statistics*.   *StatLink:* http://dx.doi.org/10.1787/447248725321

Figure 19. Change in total employment in the services sector, 1995-2003

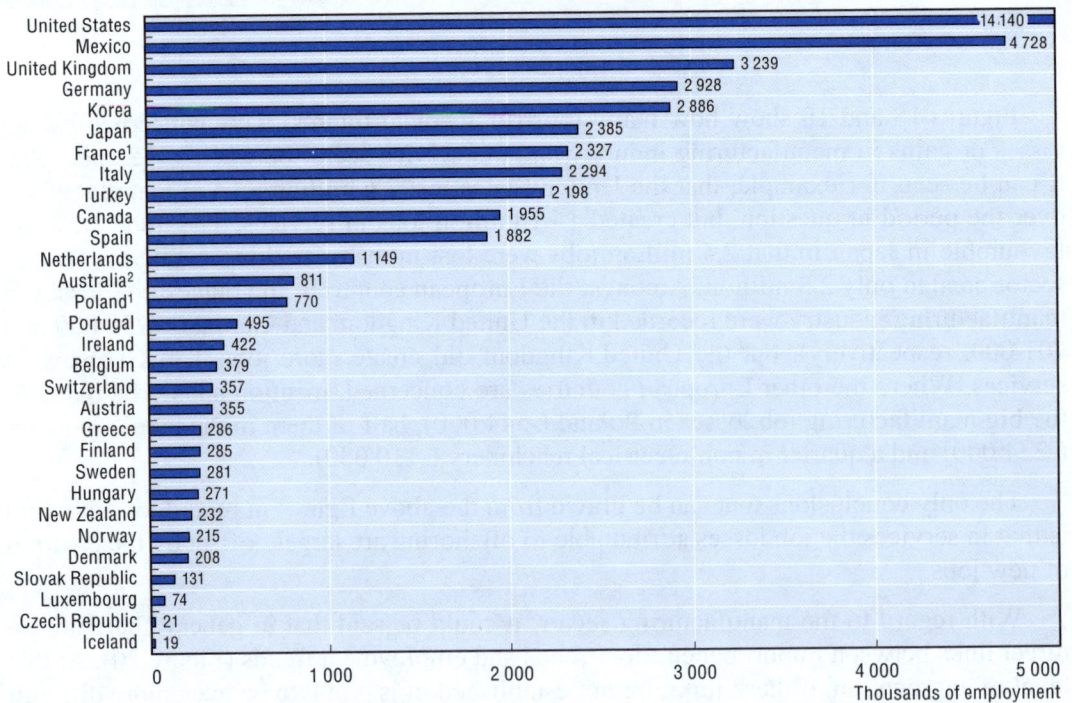

United States	14.140
Mexico	4 728
United Kingdom	3 239
Germany	2 928
Korea	2 886
Japan	2 385
France[1]	2 327
Italy	2 294
Turkey	2 198
Canada	1 955
Spain	1 882
Netherlands	1 149
Australia[2]	811
Poland[1]	770
Portugal	495
Ireland	422
Belgium	379
Switzerland	357
Austria	355
Greece	286
Finland	285
Sweden	281
Hungary	271
New Zealand	232
Norway	215
Denmark	208
Slovak Republic	131
Luxembourg	74
Czech Republic	21
Iceland	19

Thousands of employment

1. 1995-2001.
2. 1995-2002.

Source: OECD, STAN database and *Labour Force Statistics*.   *StatLink:* http://dx.doi.org/10.1787/043772378032

Figure 20. Trends in employment and import penetration rate in the manufacturing sector, 1995-2003

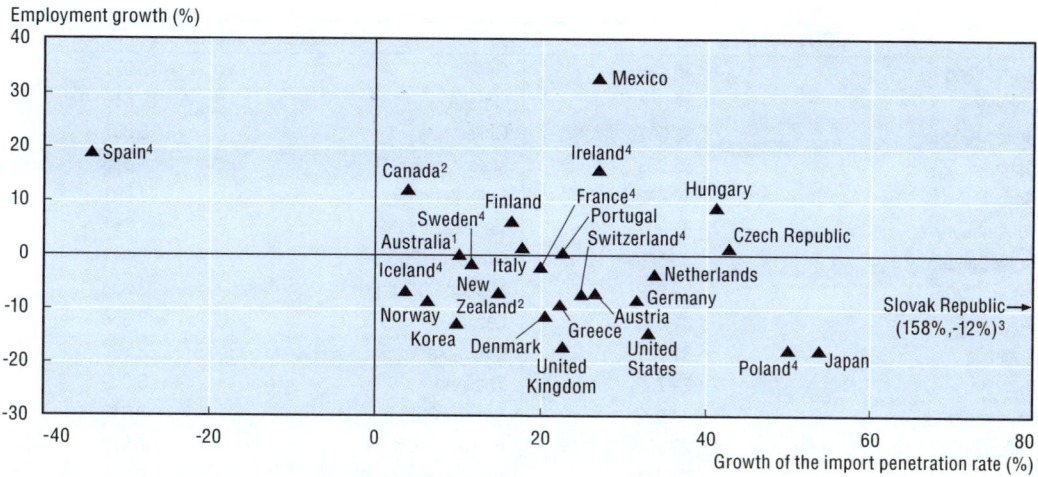

1. 1995-99.
2. 1995-2001.
3. 1997-2001.
4. 1995-2002.
Source: OECD, STAN database.

StatLink: http://dx.doi.org/10.1787/107644011635

4.3. Some explanatory factors

In the second chapter of this document, we observed how certain factors play an important role in the offshoring process.

Three factors that can play an important role will be discussed here: wage costs, labour productivity and corporate taxation.

4.3.1. Wage costs

Table 3 gives an approximate idea of wage differences between OECD countries and the less developed countries in 2004.

These data, which give only an approximate idea of the scale and do not take social charges into account, first of all show the considerable disparities in wages between workers inside the OECD area. It is therefore not surprising to find that certain countries in Central and Eastern Europe are chosen for offshoring, and that these decisions are prompted by cost considerations.

Table 3. Average annual earnings per worker (USD), 2004

OECD countries		Other countries	
Switzerland	40 496	Cyprus	17 071
Norway	37 366	Croatia	12 610
United Kingdom	36 507	Chile	5 867
Denmark (2003)	36 335	Malaysia (2001)	4 835
Germany	36 242	Estonia (2003)	4 291
Luxembourg	35 907	Venezuela (1997)	4 151
Netherlands	33 540	Lithuania (2003)	3 411
Japan (2005)	32 909	Morocco (2002)	3 386
Belgium	31 596	Latvia	3 368
Australia	31 121	Colombia	3 108
Sweden	29 752	Thailand	3 059
Ireland (2002)	28 922	Brazil (2002)	3 010
Finland	28 308	Algeria (1996)	2 632
Canada	28 241	Russian Federation (2003)	2 601
United States (2003)	27 507	Philippines (2003)	2 412
Iceland (2002)	26 641	China	1 937
Korea	26 141	Romania (2003)	1 741
France (2003)	23 453	Bulgaria	1 579
Austria (2003)	23 421	Ukraine	1 335
New Zealand (2003)	22 313	India (2003)	281
Spain	17 547		
Italy (2003)	17 475		
Greece (2003)	13 609		
Portugal	13 448		
Hungary	6 282		
Turkey (2003)	5 519		
Poland	5 513		
Slovak Republic	5 050		
Czech Republic (2003)	4 984		
Mexico	4 260		

Source: International Labour Organization (ILO), Laborsta database and Eurostat.

With regard to those countries outside the OECD zone, Ukraine and India have lower wage costs than most countries, but they also have skilled labour. By way of comparison, Table 4 shows the differences in hourly wages in some occupations between India and the USA in 2002 and 2003.

Table 4. Hourly wage (in USD) for selected occupations in the US and India, in 2002-2003

Occupation	Hourly wage (USD)	
	In the United States	In India
Telephone operator	12.57	1.00
Health record technologists / Medical transcriptionists	13.17	1.50-2.00
Payroll clerk	15.17	1.50-2.00
Accountant	23.35	6.00-15.00
Financial analyst	33.00-35.00	6.00-15.00

Source: "The New Wave of Outsourcing", A.D. Bardhan and C. Kroll, 2003.

Table 5. Labour productivity and corporate taxation, 2005

	Labour productivity GDP per hour worked, USD	Hours worked per year and per person (1)	Statutory corporate tax rates (2)
Australia	40.1	1,730	30.0
Austria	40.1	1,656	25.0
Belgium	52.9	1,534	34.0
Canada	38.5	1,736	36.1
Czech Republic	21.7	2,002	26.0
Denmark	43.3	1,551	28.0
Finland	40.1	1,714	26.0
France	49.0	1,546	35.0
Germany	44.0	1,437	38.9
Greece	30.8	2,053	32.0
Hungary	22.4	1,994	16.0
Iceland	36.6	1,794	18.0
Ireland	50.5	1,638	12.5
Italy	38.1	1,801	33.0
Japan	34.4	1,775	39.5
Korea	19.7	2,354	27.5
Luxembourg	64.7	1,557	30.4
Mexico	14.2	1,909	30.0
Netherlands	50.1	1,367	31.5
New Zealand	28.0	1,809	33.0
Norway	63.5	1,360	28.0
Poland	18.1	1,994	19.0
Portugal	24.1	1,685	27.5
Slovak Republic	22.9	1,739	19.0
Spain	36.9	1,669	35.0
Sweden	43.0	1,587	28.0
Switzerland	39.0	1,659	21.3
Turkey	13.6	1,918	30.0
United Kingdom	40.1	1,672	30.0
United States	48.3	1,713	39.3

1. The estimates of annual hours worked for Austria, Canada, Greece, Japan, United Kingdom and United States refer to hours worked per job. Data for France, Greece, Italy and Switzerland are estimates.

2. This column shows the basic combined central and sub-central (statutory) corporate income tax rate given by the adjusted central government rate plus the sub-central rate.

Source: OECD, Productivity and Tax databases.

4.3.2. Labour productivity and corporate taxation

Data concerning the level of labour productivity and corporate taxation are only available at the moment for OECD countries. They can therefore be taken into account only as a partial explanation for some of the offshoring trends that have taken place in the OECD area.

4.4. Results for each country

In principle, this section ought to present a short monograph for each country for which data is available. The main issue addressed in this paper is how to measure the magnitude of offshoring and the number of jobs involved. The other consequences of offshoring are undoubtedly more significant than the mere number of jobs at stake. In any case, it will not be possible to carry out such analyses until an evaluation of the magnitude of the offshoring phenomenon has been made.

Without losing sight of the ultimate objective, in this version of the paper, only two countries—the USA and France—will be addressed, while for a number of other countries, the results for outsourcing abroad will be shown in Appendix 1. The USA has been chosen because of the wealth of data available in different areas, notably the activity of multinational companies.

Most work carried out in the USA, as well as a considerable number of public debates about offshoring, has focused on services. However, policymakers continue to ponder the future of the manufacturing industry and the consequences of offshoring for this sector.

France has also been chosen because it is the only OECD country in which policy makers have sought to evaluate assumptions concerning the direct impact of offshoring on employment in the following methodological approach recommended for one year now by the Secretariat. The results thus obtained deserve our special attention.

The method of calculating the indices for outsourcing abroad which have been calculated for the goods and services of some 20 countries is shown in Box 8. Figures 21, 22 and 23 show that in general smaller countries outsource their activities abroad more than larger countries. Moreover, the level of outsourcing is a lot higher for goods than for services. It is also interesting to observe that, unlike Japan, the United States has an index for outsourcing abroad which is higher for manufacturing industry than for services. One possible explanation could be that, in the United States, services outsourced abroad are insignificant compared to demand for services on the domestic market, while the former is no doubt more substantial in Japan.

In view of the fact that the input-output tables that serve as a basis for calculating the indices for outsourcing abroad are updated only every 5 years, the last year available in the harmonised tables is only 2000. This is undoubtedly a considerable limitation, given that relocating abroad accelerated after 2003.

Figure 21. Index of outsourcing abroad of goods and services

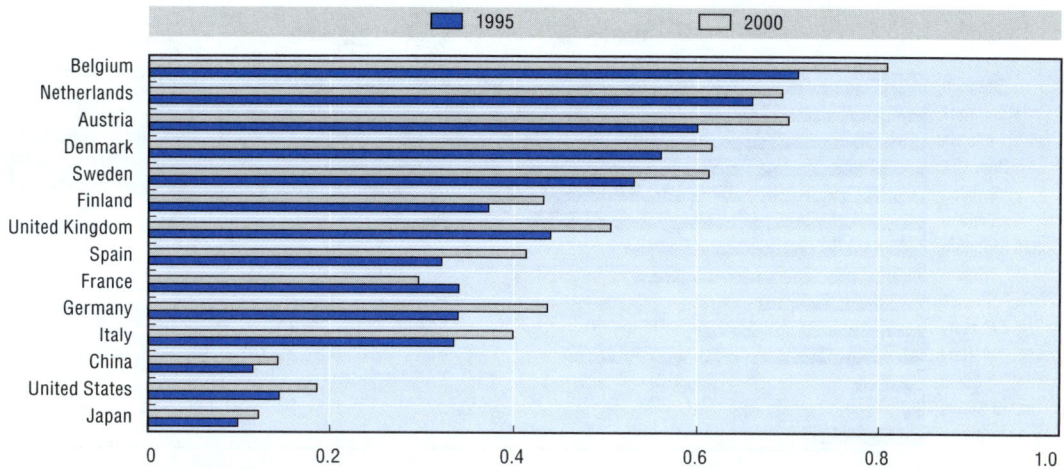

Source: OECD, Input-Output database.

StatLink: http://dx.doi.org/10.1787/172106241038

Figure 22. Index of outsourcing abroad of goods

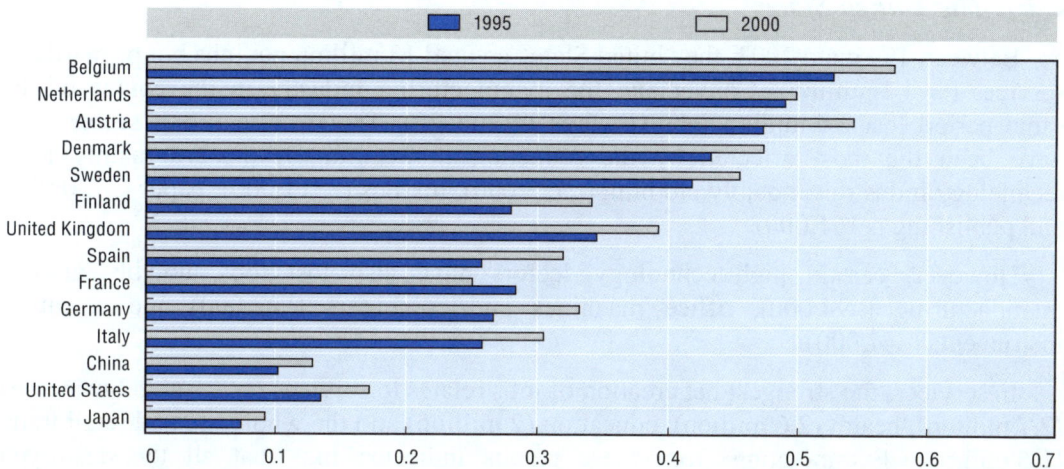

Source: OECD, Input-Output database.

StatLink: http://dx.doi.org/10.1787/286350867824

Figure 23. Index of outsourcing abroad of services

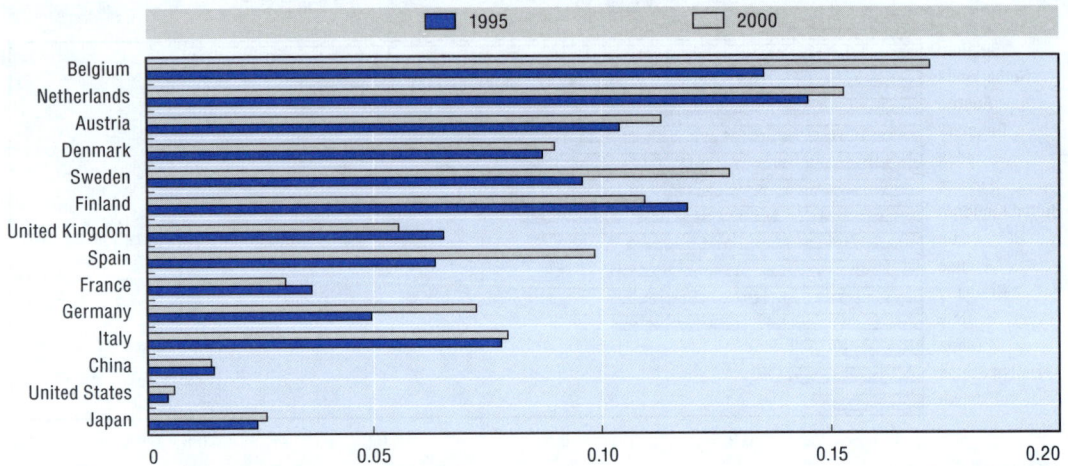

Source: OECD, Input-Output database.

StatLink: http://dx.doi.org/10.1787/731357412480

4.4.1. The United States

Between 1995 and 2003, the United States created 13 million net jobs but primarily in services (+14.1 million). Conversely, the manufacturing industry in the course of the same period lost 2.6 million jobs (Figures 24 and 25). The manufacturing sectors that have been the most affected by the reduction in manning levels are mainly low-technology industries, notably clothing (–425,000), textiles (–311,000), paper (–120,000) and publishing (–161,000).

However, certain high-technology sectors have also lost jobs, notably aircraft manufacturing (–94 000), office machines and computers (–82,000) and scientific instruments (–47,000).

In services, the strongest net creation of jobs relates to services rendered to businesses (2.7 million), health (2.6 million), education (2 million) and the wholesale and retail trade (1.5 million). Extrapolating from these results indicates first that all the destroyed manufacturing jobs have not been destroyed due to offshoring. Conversely, the fact that in services there is practically no sector (at least at the level of data aggregation available) which has lost jobs does not mean that services have lost no jobs, simply that in those sectors which have recorded declines there has been a net creation of jobs.

Consequently, the key question is how to identify the sectors which have lost jobs as the result of relocation abroad as well as the magnitude of those losses.

It has been emphasized above that such an analysis can only be conducted in a rigorous manner if it is based on data relating to individual firms. Nonetheless, in this paper, which uses only non-confidential sectoral data, our aim is to identify the most conspicuous cases which provide evidence concerning the presumptive impact of offshoring.

Figure 24. Trends relating to the number of employees in the manufacturing sector between 1995 and 2003

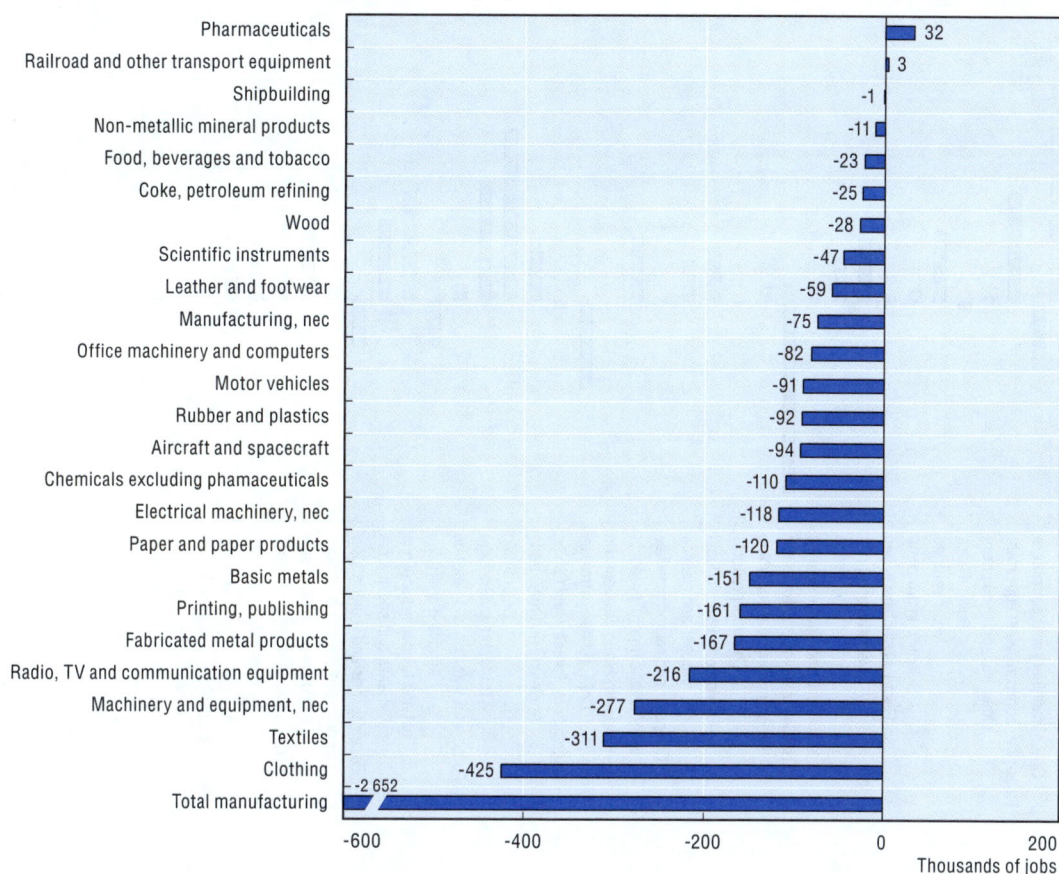

Pharmaceuticals	32
Railroad and other transport equipment	3
Shipbuilding	-1
Non-metallic mineral products	-11
Food, beverages and tobacco	-23
Coke, petroleum refining	-25
Wood	-28
Scientific instruments	-47
Leather and footwear	-59
Manufacturing, nec	-75
Office machinery and computers	-82
Motor vehicles	-91
Rubber and plastics	-92
Aircraft and spacecraft	-94
Chemicals excluding phamaceuticals	-110
Electrical machinery, nec	-118
Paper and paper products	-120
Basic metals	-151
Printing, publishing	-161
Fabricated metal products	-167
Radio, TV and communication equipment	-216
Machinery and equipment, nec	-277
Textiles	-311
Clothing	-425
Total manufacturing	-2 652

Thousands of jobs

Source: OECD, STAN database.

StatLink: http://dx.doi.org/10.1787/237586467276

Figure 25. Trends in the numbers of employees in services between 1995 and 2003

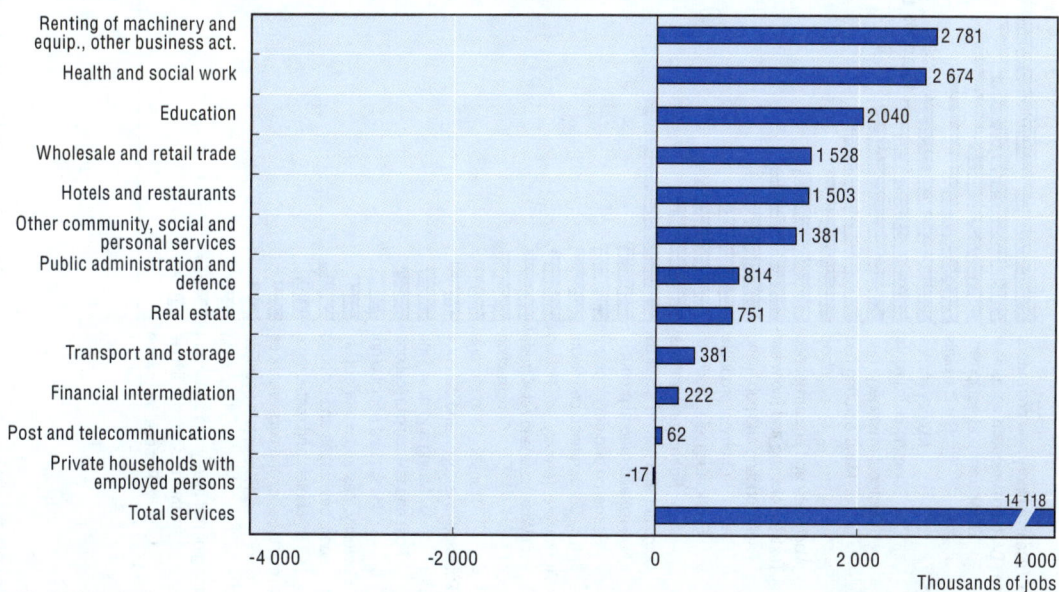

Renting of machinery and equip., other business act.	2 781
Health and social work	2 674
Education	2 040
Wholesale and retail trade	1 528
Hotels and restaurants	1 503
Other community, social and personal services	1 381
Public administration and defence	814
Real estate	751
Transport and storage	381
Financial intermediation	222
Post and telecommunications	62
Private households with employed persons	-17
Total services	14 118

Thousands of jobs

Source: OECD, STAN database.

StatLink: http://dx.doi.org/10.1787/417334674670

Figure 26. USA - Index of outsourcing of goods abroad by the goods and service industries

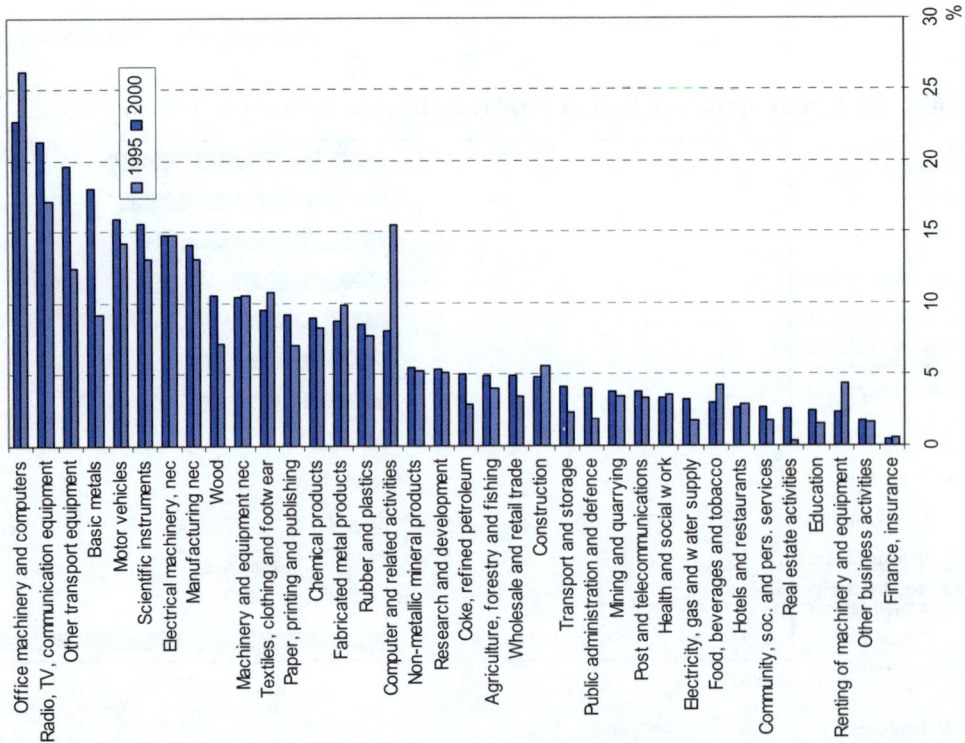

Source: OECD, Input-Output database. *StatLink:* http://dx.doi.org/10.1787/614564155840

Figure 27. USA - Growth of employment 1995-2000

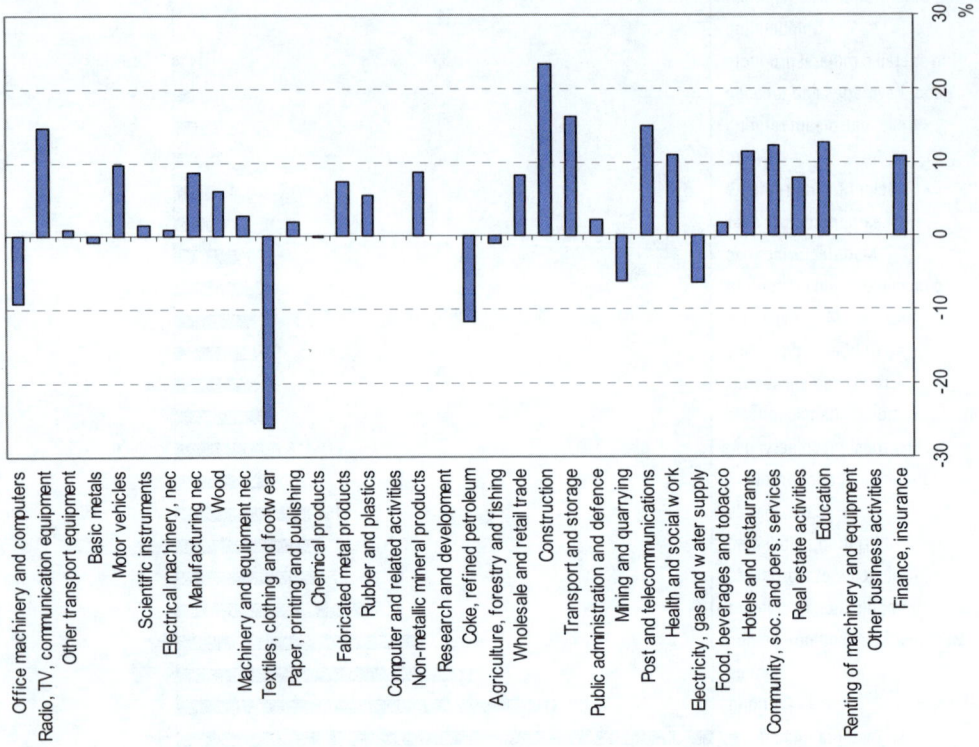

Source: OECD, STAN database. *StatLink:* http://dx.doi.org/10.1787/805230365571

Figure 28. USA - Index of outsourcing of goods abroad by the goods and service industries

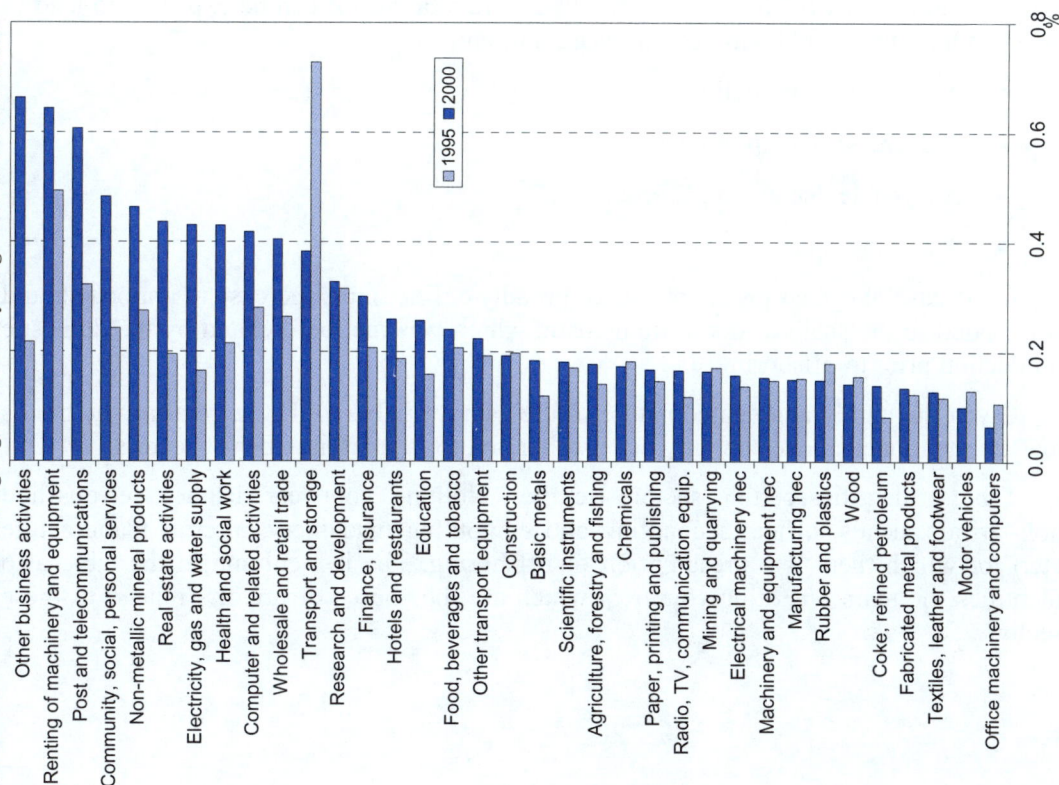

Source: OECD, Input-Output database. *StatLink:* http://dx.doi.org/10.1787/266653682616

Figure 29. USA - Growth of employment 1995-2000

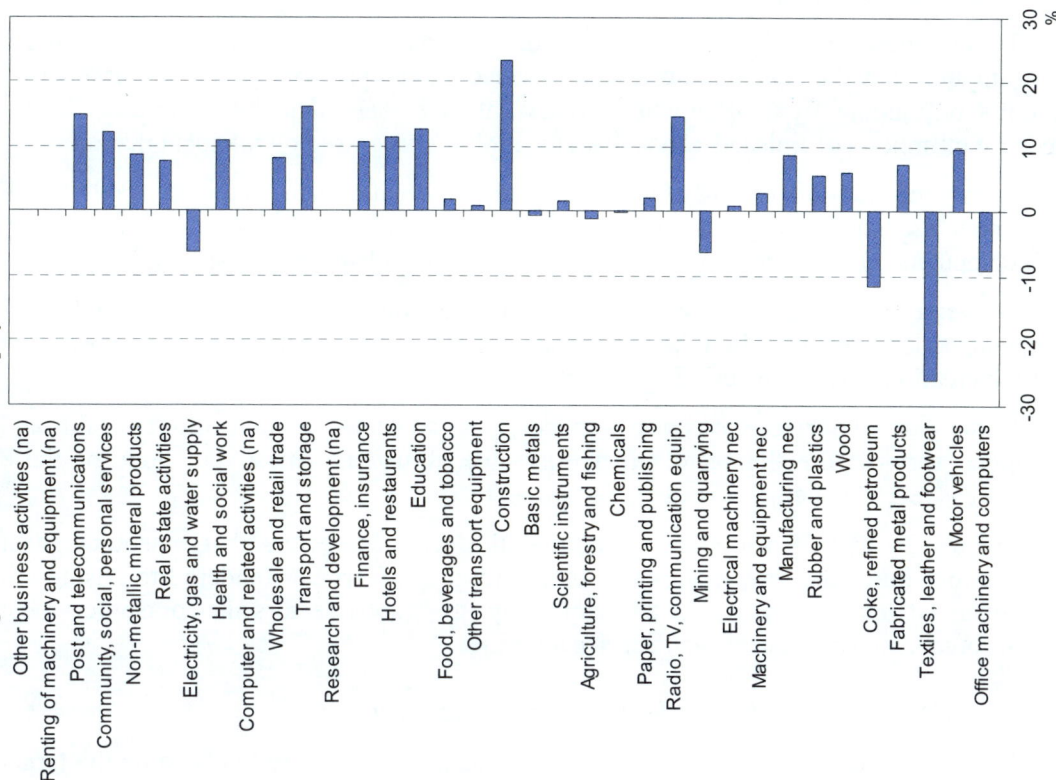

Source: OECD, STAN database. *StatLink:* http://dx.doi.org/10.1787/801857247817

The establishment of foreign outsourcing indices for the manufacturing and service industries (Figures 26 and 28) marks a first step.

These indices reveal the importance of imports that serve as the intermediary consumption for the manufacturing and service industries. Given the importance of imports originating from offshored activities, it is evident that these indices take no account of imports of finished goods that are resold unprocessed on the local market.

The indices for outsourcing of goods abroad show that certain sectors of goods which are among the most heavily outsourced, such as textiles, clothing, shoes, office machinery and computers, construction and oil refining have also cut back their manning levels.

Conversely, other sectors, such as automobile manufacture or radio, TV and other communications devices which have a relatively high index of outsourcing have recorded net job creation during the period under consideration.

In the case of services, business services, post and telecommunications, health and computer services are the sectors that outsource abroad the most, but none of these sectors has recorded net job losses.

Figures 26 and 28 show moreover that the services sectors that outsource most services outsource the fewest activities linked to goods (services rendered to businesses and financial intermediation). In the same way, the goods sectors that outsource most goods, outsource very few of their service activities.

Presumptions of offshoring in the manufacturing industry

Table 6 facilitates the task of identifying those sectors that are likely to be the target of offshoring. In accordance with the definitions shown in the first part of this paper (Boxes 1 and 3), the offshoring that affects a particular sector can be expected to lead in the short term to the following results as a minimum:

- A decline in production.
- A decrease in employment.
- A possible decline in exports.
- A rise in imports.

In the case of offshoring (narrowly or broadly defined), the increase in imports should correspond to the share of domestic demand which was met beforehand by the domestic production prior to offshoring.

Given the highly aggregated nature of the data available to the Secretariat, the trends that are mentioned above can only be corroborated for a small number of sectors.

Table 6 identifies certain sectors (textiles, clothing, footwear, leather, ferrous and non-ferrous metals, office, accounting and computing machinery, aircraft manufacture etc.) for which there is a presumption of offshoring. The last column in the table also identifies the main emerging countries which are the source of imports related to these sectors.

Table 6. Simultaneous decline in production, employment and exports and growth in imports, by sector, in the manufacturing sector

ISIC3	Sector	Growth of imports (%) 1995/2004			Decline in employment	Decline in production	Decline in exports		Main countries of origin of imports (low-wage)[1]
		total	from OECD	from non-OECD			1995/04	1999/04	
15 to 16	Food products, beverages and tobacco	102	113	83	X		X		Mexico (3), China (5)
17 to 19	Textiles, clothing, leather and footwear	76	51	85	X	X			China (1), Mexico (3), India (4)
20	Wood and products of wood and cork	130	111	191	X		X	X	China (2), Brazil (3), Chile (4)
21 to 22	Paper, printing and publishing	31	20	133	X		X		China (2), Mexico (3)
23	Coke, refined petroleum products and nuclear fuel	251	290	216	X				Russia (4), Mexico (7)
24	Chemicals and chemical products	164	156	210	X				China (6)
2423	Pharmaceuticals	398	386	567					Singapore (9)
25	Rubber and plastics products	112	96	143	X				China (2), Mexico (4)
26	Non-metallic mineral products	102	66	209	X				China (1), Mexico (2), Brazil (5)
27	Basic metals	70	40	143	X	X			Russia (3), Mexico (4), Brazil (5)
271	Ferrous metals	83	42	192	X	X			Mexico (2), Brazil (3), Russia (5)
272	Non-ferrous metals	59	37	106	X	X			Russia (3), South Africa (4)
28	Fabricated metal products	116	81	182	X				China (1), Chinese Taipei (3), Mexico (4)
29	Machinery and equipment, nec	76	56	216	X				China (2), Mexico (5)
30	Office, accounting and computing machinery	50	-16	128	X	X		X	China (1), Malaysia (2), Mexico (4)
31	Electrical machinery and apparatus, nec	87	66	143	X				Mexico (1), China (2)
32	Radio, television and communication equipment	51	26	89	X			X	China (1), Mexico (2), Malaysia (5)
33	Medical, precision and opt. instruments, watches and clocks	126	125	132	X				Mexico (2), China (4)
34	Motor vehicles	82	79	268	X				Mexico (3)
35	Other transport equipment	119	101	256	X			X	Brazil (5), China (6)
353	Aircraft and spacecraft	124	105	405	X			X	Brazil (4)
36 to 37	Manufacturing nec	128	64	171	X				China (1), Mexico (4), India (5)

1. Figures in brackets refer to the countries' ranks among all countries of origin of imports for the selected industry.

Source: OECD, Bilateral Trade and STAN databases.

The second and third columns of Table 6 specify whether most of the growth in imports comes from the OECD zone or from countries that do not belong to the OECD. The presumption of offshoring of sectors as indicated in Table 6 may be confirmed by Figure 26 which presents the index of outsourcing of goods abroad.

In theory a significant share of the imports attributable to offshoring in the strict sense involve intra-firm imports. Nonetheless, if one examines the trends in intra-firm imports (Figure 30), the results do not bear out this assertion for a number of reasons.

First, the available published data do not make it possible to cross-check the sectors and the countries of origin. When one identifies, for example, that for certain categories of goods there has been relocated to China, then intra-firm imports from U.S. parent companies originating from their subsidiaries in China apply to the totality of goods and are not broken down by sector.

Figure 30. Intra-firm imports of the United States in goods in the total trade of the United States and by partner country

Share of intra-firm imports of goods by the United States in total imports of goods by partner country, 2003

Share of intra-firm imports of goods by the United States in total imports of goods by industry

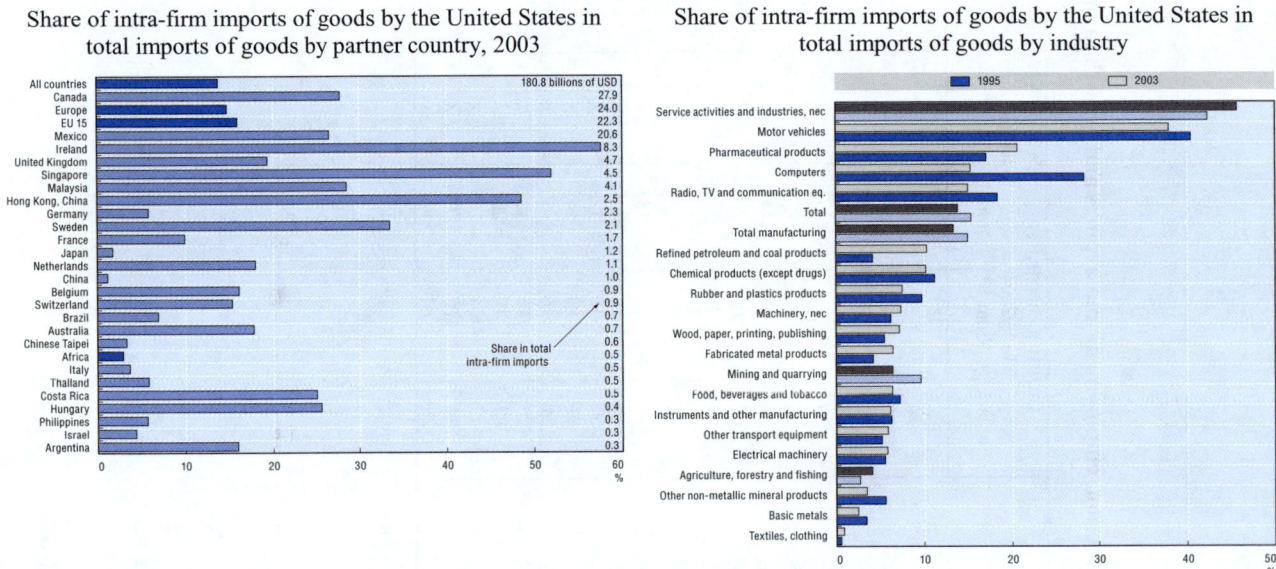

Source: OECD, AFA and STAN databases, and International Trade by Commodity Statistics.
StatLink: http://dx.doi.org/10.1787/370158680712   *StatLink:* http://dx.doi.org/10.1787/263636708474

Another key reason is that for a sector the intra-firm imports do not necessarily reflect the nature of goods imported but rather reflect the main activity of the firms that make up the sector. Thus, the textile imports originating from U.S. subsidiaries abroad will not necessarily be made by firms in the same group whose main activity is textiles but rather by businesses whose main activities are wholesaling and distribution.

Figure 31 presents intra-firm imports of the American parent companies originating from their foreign subsidiaries. The countries in question are the emerging countries, which are identified in Table 6 as delocalization countries. We observe the strong growth in intra-firm imports originating from Mexico (from 9 million dollars to 40 million dollars between 1990 and 2002) and the rise of imports originating from China, especially beginning from 1998, at a time when imports from Malaysia, Brazil and the Philippines were going down. However, if one compares these findings with the results in Table 8 we note that the intra-firm imports originating from American subsidiaries in Mexico are at present significantly more substantial than those originating from China. Consequently, this means that the manufacturing activities are more relocated in Mexico than in China.

Figure 31. Imports of goods of by US parent companies originating from subsidiaries abroad

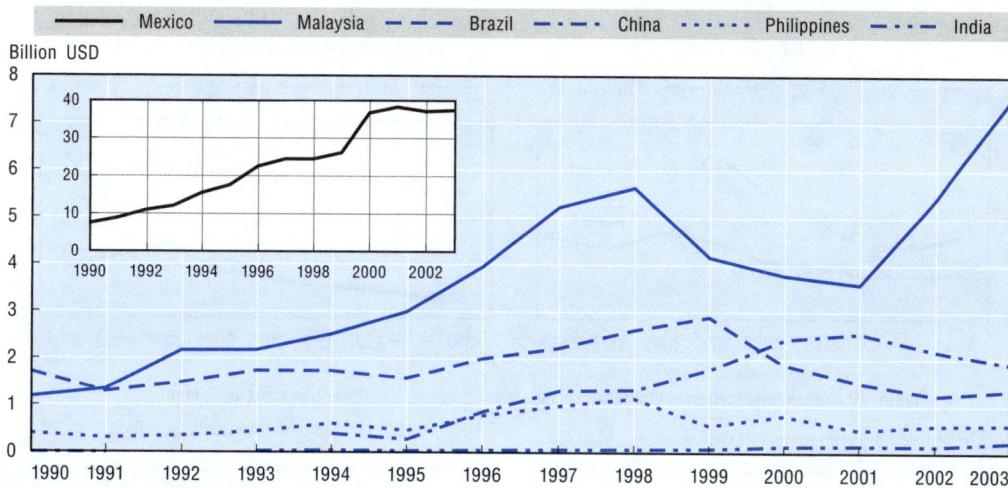

Source: OECD, AFA database.

StatLink: http://dx.doi.org/10.1787/211133161548

The decline in jobs identified in Table 6 cannot be attributed solely to offshoring, and the same applies in sectors where there is strong prima facie evidence of offshoring.

In order to measure job losses linked to offshoring in the manufacturing industry, it will be necessary to evaluate the rise in imports with regard to those sectors for which there is a presumption of offshoring, as well as the changes in exports over the same period.

Figure 32. Import penetration rate

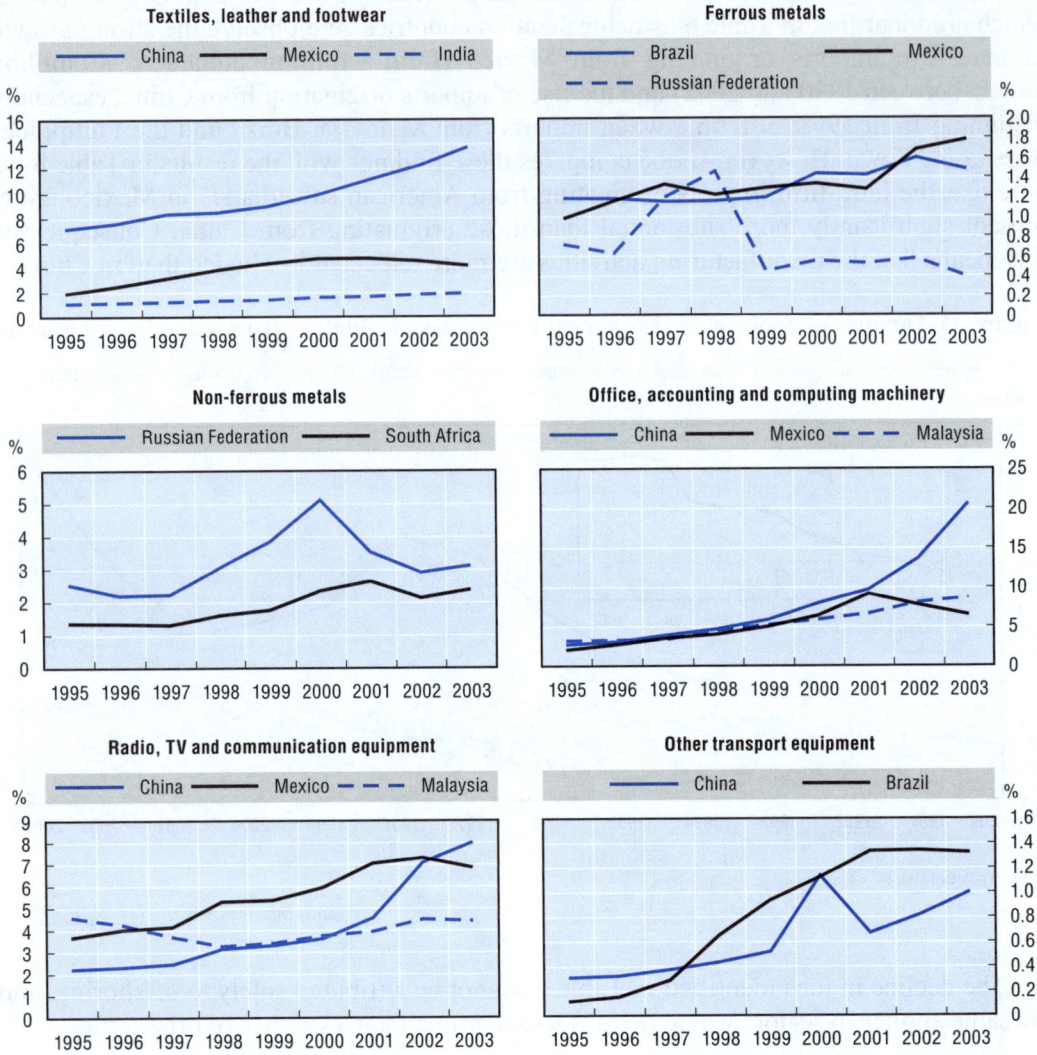

Textiles, leather and footwear

China — Mexico — — India

Ferrous metals

Brazil — Mexico
— — Russian Federation

Non-ferrous metals

Russian Federation — South Africa

Office, accounting and computing machinery

China — Mexico — — Malaysia

Radio, TV and communication equipment

China — Mexico — — Malaysia

Other transport equipment

China — Brazil

Source: OECD, Bilateral Trade database.

StatLink: http://dx.doi.org/10.1787/283085557567

Table 7. United States trade balance, 2004

Millions of USD

	Imports	Exports	Balance
Textile, clothing, leather			
China	35 980	892	-35 088
Mexico	8 893	5 521	-3 372
India	4 728	42	-4 686
Ferrous metals			
Mexico	2 598	1 535	-1 063
Brazil	2 591	61	-2 530
Russian Federation	1 760	14	-1 746
Non-ferrous metals			
Russian Federation	2 878	4	-2 873
South Africa	2 124	27	-2 097
Office machinery, computers			
China	36 575	1 397	-35 179
Malaysia	11 371	655	-10 717
Mexico	7 749	8 228	479
Radio, TV, communication equipment			
China	26 847	4 230	-22 617
Malaysia	10 501	6 002	-4 500
Mexico	19 346	12 470	-6 877
Other transport equipment			
Brazil	2 635	102	-2 533
China	1 922	2 193	271

Source: OECD, Bilateral Trade database.

The next step is to calculate the jobs which are incorporated into net imports (imports-exports) using this equation:

$$\text{US jobs embodied} = \begin{pmatrix} \text{Change in US output} \\ \text{necessary to replace} \\ \text{US net imports} \end{pmatrix} \times \begin{pmatrix} \dfrac{\text{Employment US}}{\text{Output US}} \end{pmatrix}$$

To calculate the first term, one must again use the input-output tables. It is as well to point out the limitations of these trends as discussed in the preceding chapter. For total trade, these calculations show (Figure 33) that approximately 2.6 million jobs were necessary in order to produce the equivalent of net American imports in 2003. Among these jobs, 2.5 million would be necessary to produce the equivalent of net imports of durable goods, and 1.3 million for non-durable goods. Conversely, given that services generate surpluses, the USA is exporting an output equivalent to 1.2 million jobs (these figures appear in Figure 33 as minuses).

Figure 33. US jobs embodied in net imports

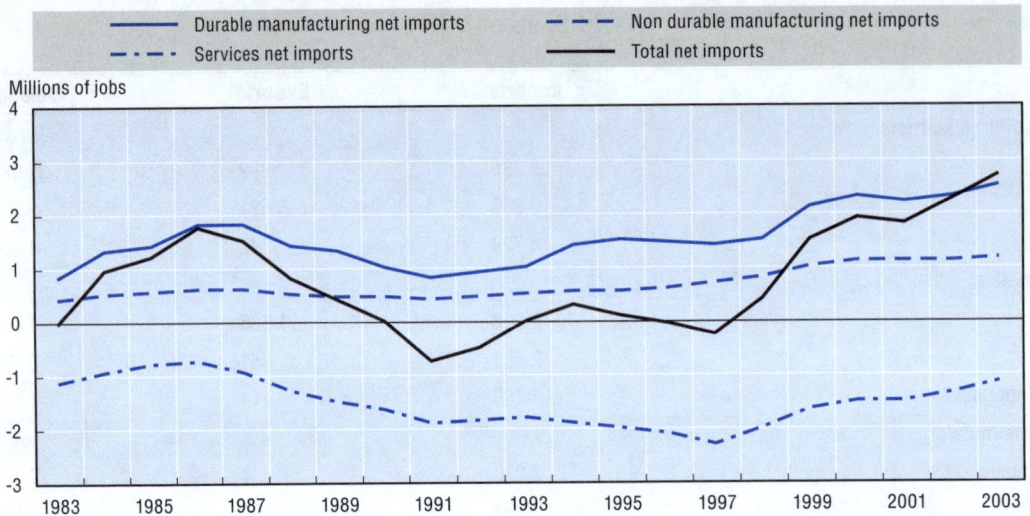

Source: US Department of Labor, Bureau of Labor Statistics, US Department of Commerce, Bureau of Economic Analysis.

StatLink: http://dx.doi.org/10.1787/241206168730

Presumptions of relocation abroad in services

Figure 25 shows that between 1995 and 2003, virtually all the services sectors were net job creators. Unfortunately, the employment data come from industrial surveys and are classified according to ISIC Classification Rev. 3 while the data on trade are collected in the context of balances of payments and their disaggregation is not compatible with the breakdown for employment.

Moreover, Figures 28 and 29 show that there is no link between a strong outsourcing of services abroad and a decline in jobs.

However, the fact that in the USA all services sectors (at least at the level of data aggregation available) are net job creators, does not mean to say that there is no destruction of jobs or no relocation abroad.

Figure 34 shows that imports intended for businesses (finance, computing, communications, insurance etc.) some of which have a high foreign outsourcing rate, such as financial intermediation, account for relatively modest sums. At the same time, all the sectors except insurance generate trade surpluses (Figure 35) and are net job creators.

The computation of jobs, incorporated in the total of American imports in the sector of services to businesses is not expected to yield very high figures. To the extent that one party to these imports is directly or indirectly linked to offshoring, this means that the impact on employment of the offshoring of the services is expected to be fairly moderate.

As opposed to the situation with the manufacturing industry, the largest share of the offshoring of services has occurred with developed countries.

Figure 34. Imports of services from the United States

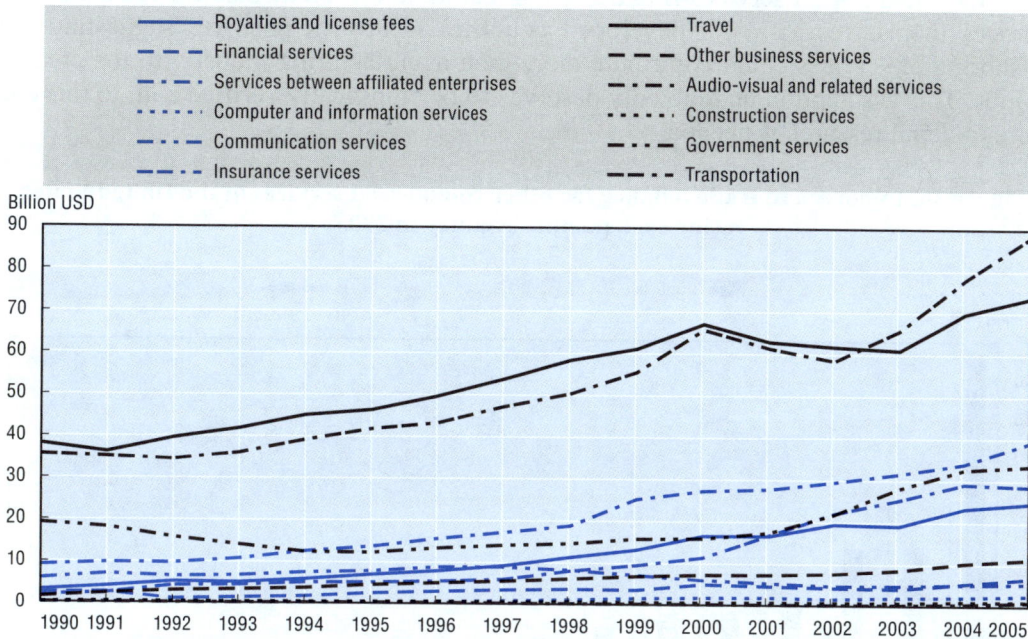

Legend:
- Royalties and license fees
- Financial services
- Services between affiliated enterprises
- Computer and information services
- Communication services
- Insurance services
- Travel
- Other business services
- Audio-visual and related services
- Construction services
- Government services
- Transportation

Source: IMF, Balance of Payments Statistics.

StatLink: http://dx.doi.org/10.1787/647445123515

Figure 35. Trade balance in services, United States

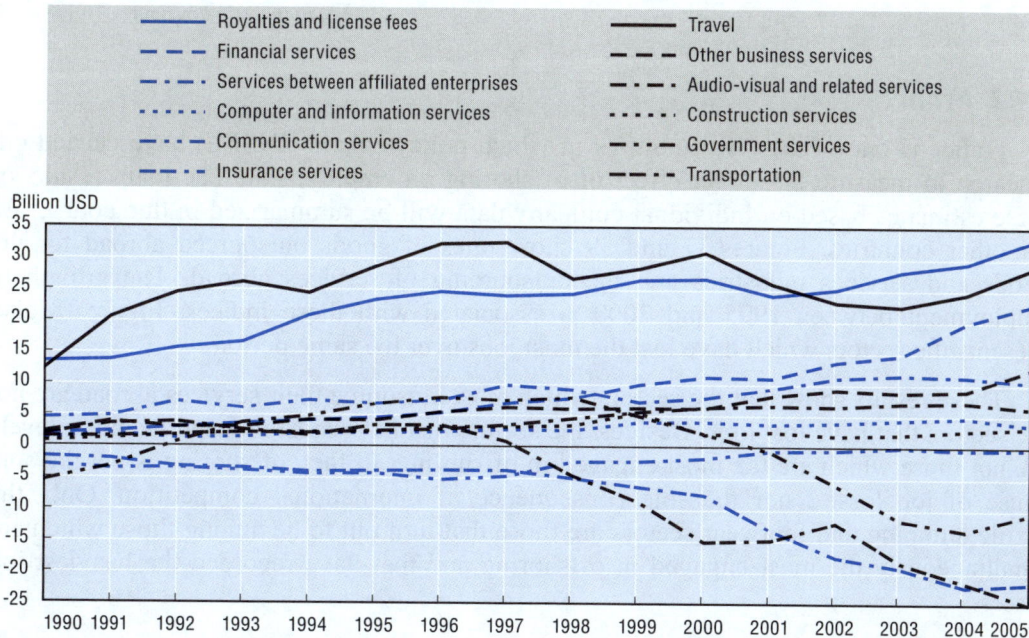

Legend:
- Royalties and license fees
- Financial services
- Services between affiliated enterprises
- Computer and information services
- Communication services
- Insurance services
- Travel
- Other business services
- Audio-visual and related services
- Construction services
- Government services
- Transportation

Source: IMF, Balance of Payments Statistics.

StatLink: http://dx.doi.org/10.1787/620306521634

The emerging countries with their low manpower costs account for a more modest share of global import services (Figure 36). In addition, the Trade balance of commercial services themselves vis-à-vis developed countries is always positive, suggesting that offshoring of services could contribute more than manufacturing industry to the creation of jobs. This assumption undoubtedly deserves to be empirically verified and, to this end, more in-depth research is needed.

Figure 36. Imports and trade balance for other commercial services of the United States, for each partner country in 2003

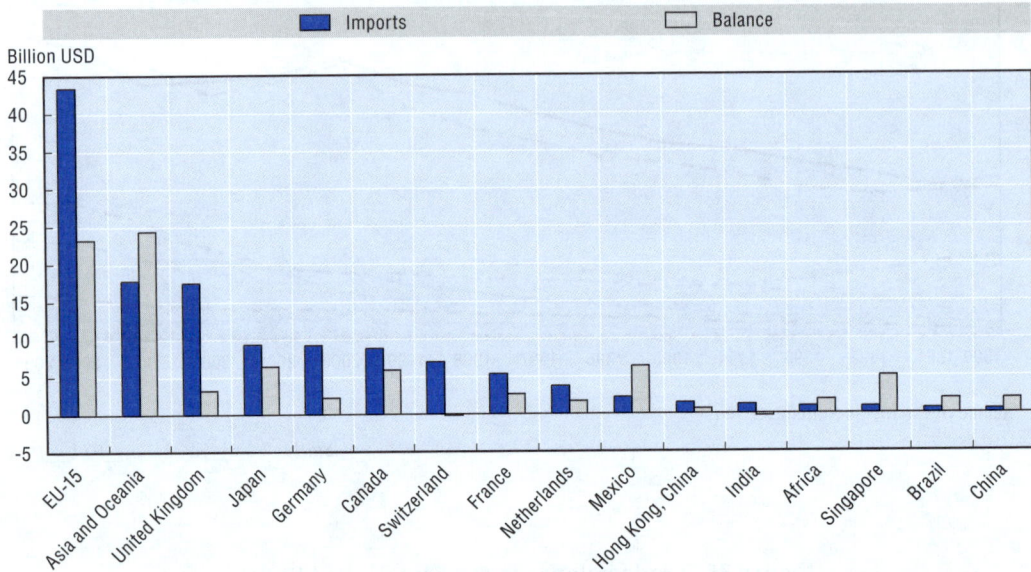

Source: OECD (2005), *OECD Statistics on International Trade in Services, Detailed tables by Partner Country, 2000-2003.*

StatLink: http://dx.doi.org/10.1787/711162631355

4.4.2. France

France is one of the rare countries in which policymakers (INSEE) have carried out research to measure the direct effect of offshoring on employment. The main results of these estimates based on individual company data will be summarized in due course. As for other countries, Figures 37 and 39 show rates of goods outsourced abroad for the goods and services industries and the outsourcing of services abroad. The growth in employment between 1995 and 2000 is associated with these indices. Figure 38 also presents the sectors which have lost the most jobs over the same period.

These results show that the sectors which most outsource their services abroad are not the sectors that have lost jobs. Besides, the sectors that have most reduced manning levels are not those which are the most engaged in offshoring. In fact, offshoring is not the sole cause of job losses, nor the sole consequence of international competition. Only the textile, clothing and footwear sectors are those that turn out to be among those which are simultaneously the most engaged in offshoring and that have recorded the heaviest job losses.

INSEE's estimates (Auber-Sillard, 2005) concerning jobs offshored were calculated using the method recommended by the OECD Secretariat. The virtue of the results which, in the absence of direct measurements, constitute presumptions of offshoring is that they have been calculated based on data relating to individual firms.

According to this study, approximately 95 000 manufacturing jobs were eliminated in France between 1995 and 2001 as the result of offshoring, corresponding to 2.4% of the total manning levels of the manufacturing industry.

Offshoring in France may thus have come about as much because of downsizing as through the outright closure of businesses.

Among offshoring jobs, a little less than half are destined for countries with so-called "low wages" while the developed countries account for 53% of jobs. Offshoring toward the developed countries largely corresponds to restructurings and the refocusing of business groups in the heart of developed countries rather than an effort to cut production costs. Offshoring is most often made in capital-intensive sectors such as the civil aviation, automobile and pharmaceutical sectors.

Among emerging countries, China is the top destination of offshoring with a third of offshored jobs during the period 1995-2001. The three large groups, employing more than 5 000 employees in France, account for more than half of the relocated abroad jobs. This proportion is slightly lower among offshoring in countries with low wages (47%).

Over the same period, ten large groups between them accounted for almost a quarter of labour shedding. Excluding these ten groups, offshoring would account for 10,500 jobs a year on average.

The foreign groups would offshoring a bit more than the French groups, especially when the offshoring is made toward a developed country. However, regarding offshoring toward countries with low wages, there is minimal difference between French and foreign groups. The European groups that are not French would offshore least toward these countries.

Figure 37. France – Index of outsourcing of goods abroad by the goods and services industries

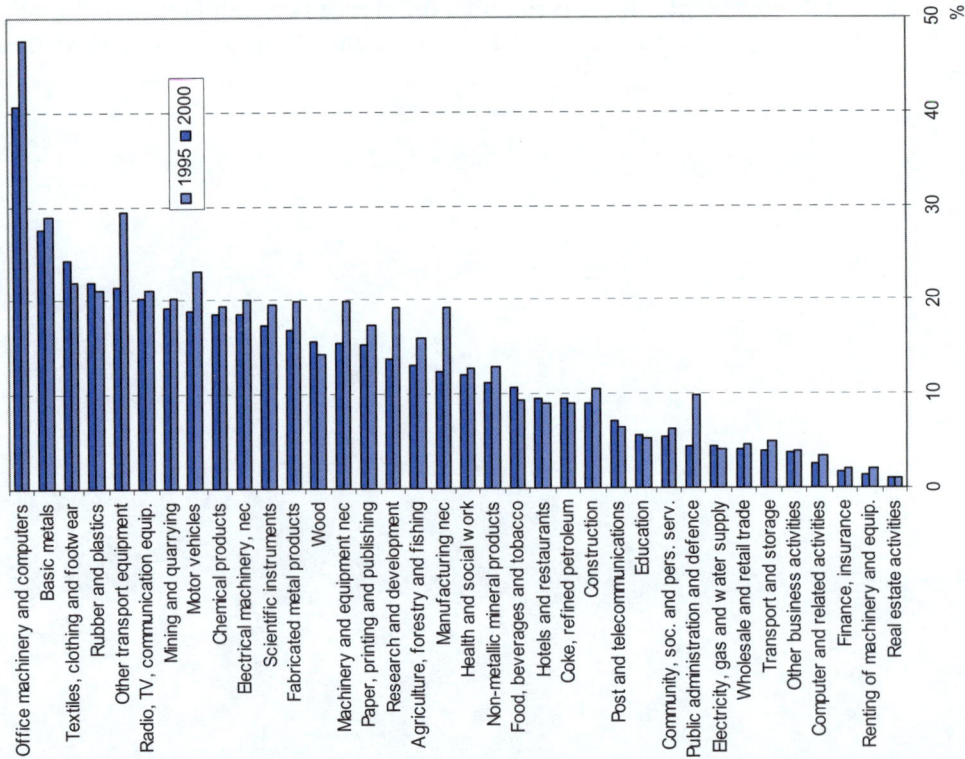

Source: OECD, Input-Output database. *StatLink:* http://dx.doi.org/10.1787/835081586266

Figure 38. France – Growth of employment 1995-2000

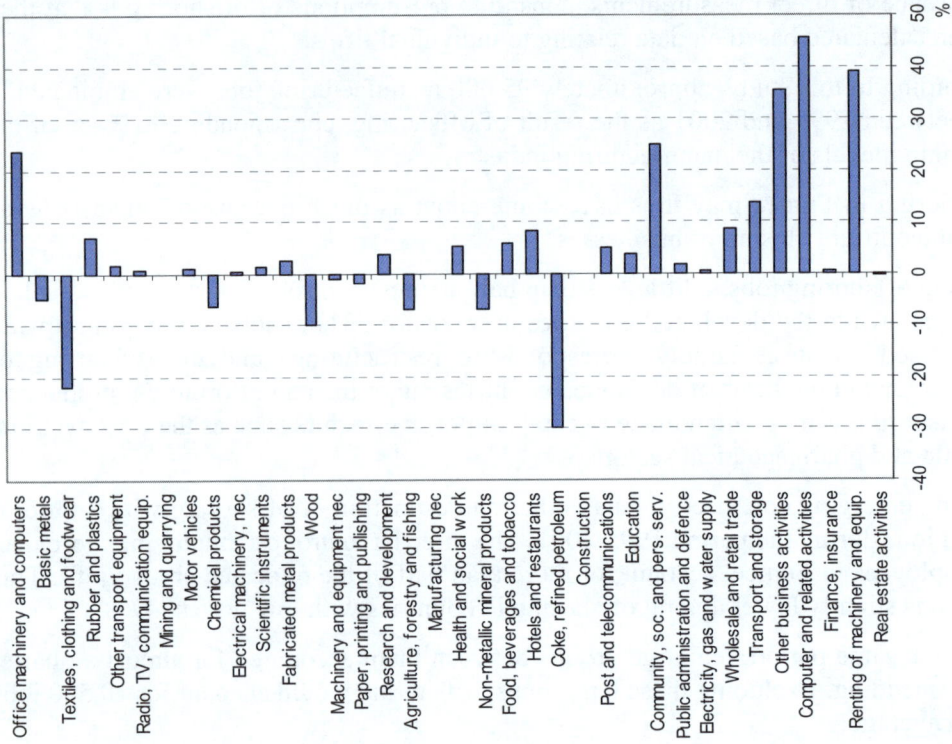

Source: OECD, STAN database. *StatLink:* http://dx.doi.org/10.1787/225023201485

Figure 40. France – Growth of employment 1995-2000

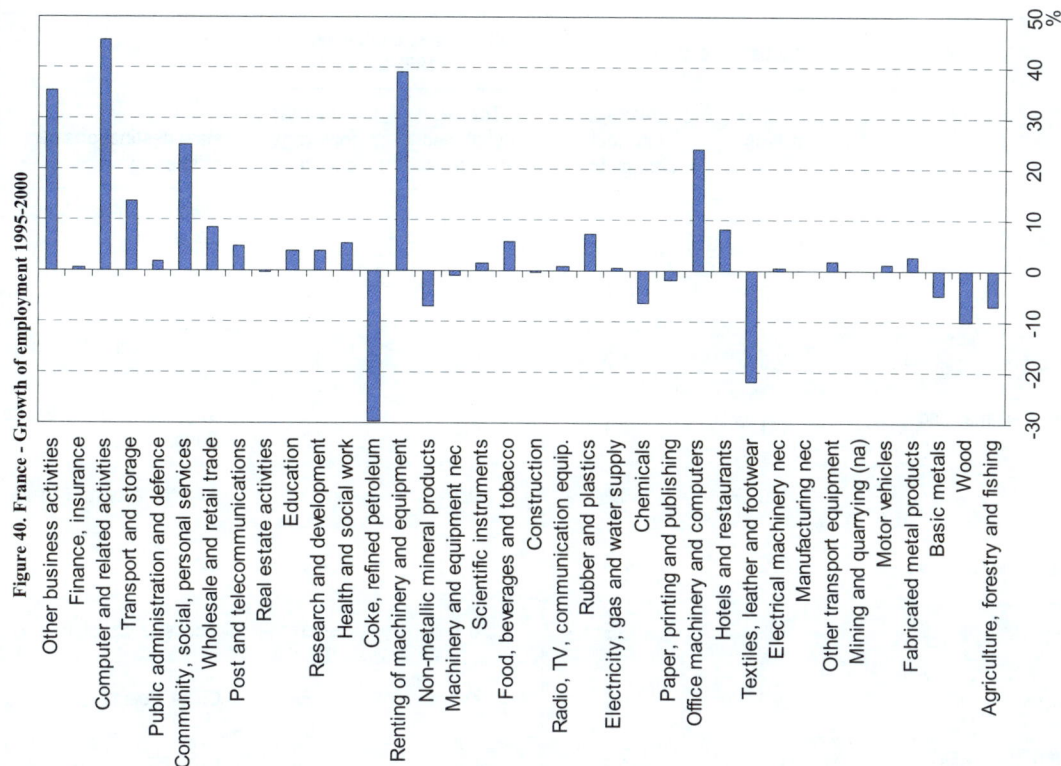

Source: OECD, STAN database. *StatLink:* http://dx.doi.org/10.1787/262563043861

Figure 39. France – Index of outsourcing of goods abroad by the goods and services industries

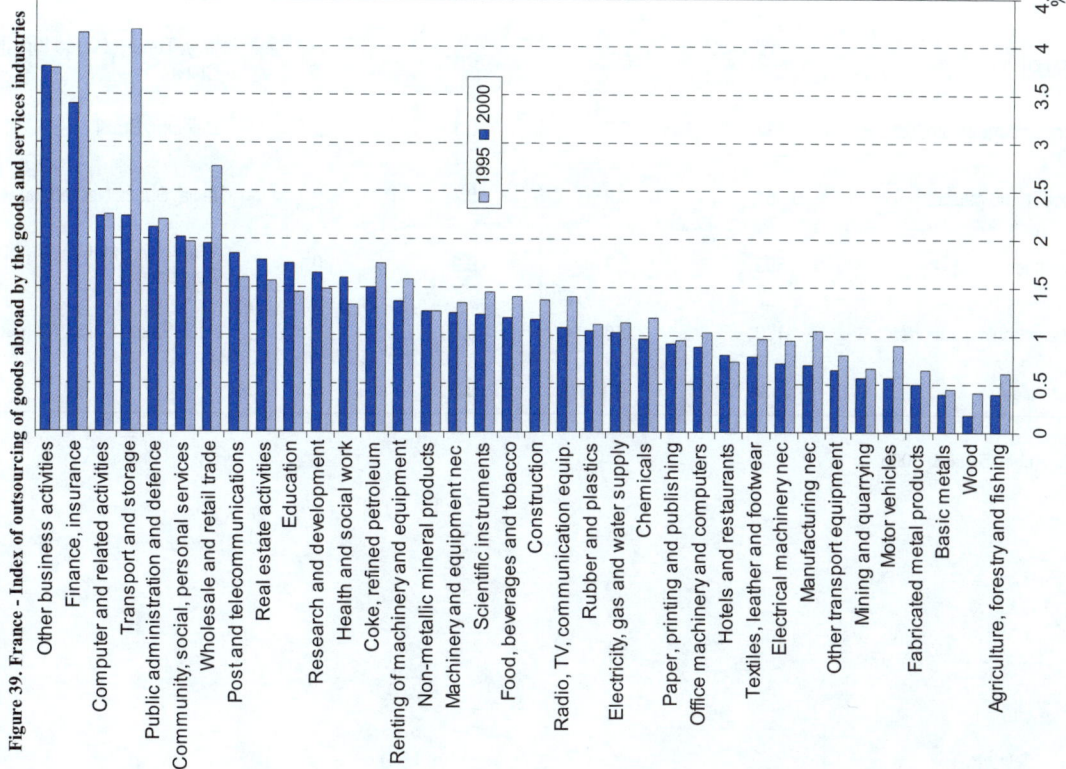

Source: OECD, Input-Output database. *StatLink:* http://dx.doi.org/10.1787/261107787430

Table 8. France: Jobs losses linked to offshoring, by sector

Sector	Industrial employment		Jobs losses, annual average, 1995-2001		Main destinations of offshoring
	In 1994	Average annual change in %	Toward developed countries	Toward low-wage countries	
Clothing, leather	197	-5.8	0.1	0.7	Morocco, Tunisia, Vietnam, China
Textile	140	-3.2	0.1	0.3	Romania, China, Italy, Mexico
Electrical and electronic equipment	265	-1.0	0.3	0.3	China, Czech Republic, United States
Pharmaceuticals, perfumes and cleaning	151	-0.9	0.6	0.0	Switzerland, United States, Germany, Ireland
Mineral products	186	-0.9	0.2	0.1	Italy, Venezuela, Belgium
Printing, publishing, reproduction	222	-0.9	0.1	0.0	Italy
Wood and paper	183	-0.5	0.1	0.1	Indonesia, Brazil, Finland
Household equipment	223	-0.4	-0.1	0.5	China, Poland
Shipbuilding, aerospace, railroad equipment	134	-0.3	0.4	0.0	United States, Germany
Motor vehicles	286	0.2	0.2	0.0	Spain
Mechanical equipment	422	0.7	0.1	0.1	Italy, Turkey, United Kingdom, China
Basic and fabricated metal products	432	0.7	0.1	0.1	Belgium, Brazil
Chemicals, rubber and plastics	354	0.9	0.2	0.1	India, Spain, Netherlands
Food and beverages	569	0.9	0.2	0.1	Germany, Netherlands, Spain, Belgium
Electrical and electronic components	170	2.6	0.4	0.3	Italy, Spain, China, Morocco
Total	3934	-0.1	0.2	0.2	

Source: INSEE, Auber-Sillard, 2005.

Offshoring toward developed countries is most often achieved by subsidiaries of companies. Conversely, when low-wage countries are involved, subcontracting is the method most heavily favoured.

Offshoring toward low-wage countries is more frequent in low technology sectors that tend to employ manpower that is not very skilled (clothing, leather, textiles etc). However, it is also found in high-tech sectors (*e.g.* electronics), but such offshoring accounts for activities with low value added, whereas those operations involving substantial value added stay in France.

The individualized data on businesses which has been used reveals that practically all sectors have been affected by offshoring, notably toward developed countries. Offshoring has occurred in the context of the restructurings of groups. Table 8 presents the sectors which are affected by offshoring and also identifies the main destinations of offshoring.

The main limitation of this work is that it does not take into account the role of exports in offshoring due to the fact that that there is no flow of imports which corresponds to these exports. Other constraints that also apply to this paper have been outlined in Section 3.2 of this report.

4.5. Main research estimating the number of jobs affected by offshoring

Other recent research has sought to estimate the number of jobs affected by offshoring. Most of this work has been carried out in the United States and has tended to focus on services.

This research could be divided into three categories:

- Estimates of the number of jobs "potentially at risk of being offshored".

- Forecasts of the number of jobs likely to be offshored.

- Estimates of the number of jobs already offshored.

Most of this research also seeks to identify the particular categories of service jobs that are vulnerable to offshoring.

Table 9 summarises the research that seeks to identify service jobs at risk of being moved offshore. While the jobs share some common features across the literature, they also show differences, and the subjectivity of the evaluations make verification and comparison difficult. These findings, the main limitations of which were presented in Section 3.5.5, give a rough idea of the number of types of jobs that could move offshore. It is likely, however, that even the most pessimistic studies underestimate the number of jobs that could potentially be sent offshore. This is due primarily to the fact that many service jobs that are considered immune from relocation abroad (see Section 3.5.5) may in fact be sent offshore if performed by a firm that itself can be relocated abroad. As a rule, the vast majority of companies can potentially be moved offshore. In contrast, there are a number of reasons to believe that, whatever the circumstances, offshoring will not exceed certain thresholds:

- While a large number of managerial jobs in companies are technically offshorable, the firms in question could never be run remotely.

- Many occupations classified as potentially offshorable involve small and medium-sized enterprises that lack the resources to move some of their activities offshore. Such SMEs might be compelled to outsource only some of their activities, but to do so domestically.

- Some of these occupations are exercised by self-employed persons who presumably would have no particular reason to move abroad. Other reasons are presented in Section 2.5 as well.

Table 9. Estimates of service jobs that could potentially be moved offshore

Authors	Number of jobs concerned	Countries concerned	Percentage of total employment	Year
Jensen and Kletzer	9.4 million	United States	9.4%	2000
Garner	14 million	United States	10%	2000
Van Welsum	23 million	United States	18.1%	2002
Beedham and Kroll	15 million	United States	11.7%	2003
McKinsey Global Institute	160 million	World-wide	11%	2003
Blinder	28-42 million	United States	20-25%	2004

Source: National Academy of Public Administration (2006).

Table 10 presents forecasts of the number of jobs that could be moved offshore.

Most of this research is based on interviews conducted with experts in order to make projections into the future.

Table 10. Forecasts of jobs likely to be moved offshore

Researcher	Forecast job losses	Time frame	Sector	Annual average	Estimated offshoring losses relative to aggregate annual job loss (%)
Goldmann Sachs	Up to 6 million	2003-2013	Services and manufacturing	600 000	2 %
McKinsey Global Institute	4.1 million	2005-2008	Services world-wide	1.36 million	–
Forrester Research	3.4 million	2005-2015	Services	340 000	1 %
Deloitte Research	850 000	2003-2008	Financial services	170 000	9 %

Source: National Academy of Public Administration (2006).

The Goldmann Sachs study suggests that the extent of offshoring by US businesses will depend on the magnitude of potential savings, logistical constraints and labour-supply constraints in the offshore destinations.

The McKinsey analysis, which is more comprehensive and does not focus on the United States alone, stipulates that the gap between the potential for jobs to be offshored and the jobs likely to be offshored depends on a number of factors including cost pressures, competition for resources, size of the company and the legal, regulatory, social and political environment in the receiving country. The Forrester research is based essentially on interviews and surveys of companies and information technology professionals in the United States and India. The Deloitte study, which assumes that the United States and Germany each has the same percentage of its workforce employed in financial services (3.7%), estimates the overall cost savings from the offshoring of financial services at 15%. This leads to 850 000 job losses in order to remain competitive. Table 11 summarises the findings of research estimating the number of jobs already sent offshore.

Table 11. Estimates of actual jobs affected by offshoring

Researcher	Job losses	Time frame	Sector	Annual average	Estimated offshoring losses relative to aggregate annual job loss (%)
Bronfenbrenner and Luce	48 000	1/1-31/3/2004	Manufacturing	192 000	8 %
Brown	16 073	1-9/2004	Services and manufacturing (private)	16 073	< 1 %
Garner	218 000	2000-2002	All services	109 000	< 1 %
McKinsey Global Institute	565 000	2005	Service sector world-wide	–	N.D.
Schulze	155 000-215 000	2000-2003	Services, construction and public works	52 000-72 000	1 %

Source: National Academy of Public Administration (2006).

Bronfenbrenner and Luce, through interviews with corporate executives and using data on actual or announced production shifts out of the United States, estimated that 48 000 jobs had been offshored to low-wage countries, including China, India and Latin American countries, during the first quarter of 2004. They concluded that the US government would need to set up a reporting system to track production shifts out of the United States.

Sharon Brown's study, by means of questionnaires formulated by the Bureau of Labor Statistics, identified 10 722 jobs that were shifted out of the country between January and September 2004, either within the same company or to another one.

The Garner study estimated that of the 14 million service jobs at risk of being offshored in 2000, some 218 000 were in fact moved offshore between 2000 and 2002.

The McKinsey Global Institute study found that 565 000 service jobs world-wide had been offshored in 2005 – figures based on case studies in eight sectors. MGI expects job losses in those same eight sectors to double by 2008.

Charles Schulze, in a policy brief for the Brookings Institution, estimated that increased service imports between 2000 and 2003 would suggest between 155 000 and 215 000 lost jobs in the construction and public works sector alone. He cautioned, however, that it was unclear whether those job losses were due to offshoring or to other factors.

All these estimates would prompt different comments. First, there is a certain consensus that several characteristics of service jobs make them more vulnerable to offshoring. Even certain highly skilled jobs can be at risk. Second, these estimated job losses are relatively modest when compared with aggregate annual job losses in the United States. Even so, it is possible that the job losses are far more substantial in certain particular categories. Last, the differentials between the estimates from one study to another remind us of the extent to which the results depend on the methodologies used.

4.5.1. Estimating the jobs affected by offshoring in Europe

Evaluations of jobs lost in Europe because of offshoring were conducted recently by the European Restructuring Monitor (ERM) and published by the European Foundation for the Improvement of Living and Working Conditions. The evaluations covered firms that were being restructured. The type of restructuring and the reasons behind it were identified. National correspondents analysing the data were asked to take part in the exercise. It is not certain, however, that all cases were identified properly or that offshoring's indirect employment effects were taken into account.

Table 12 presents the number of jobs lost in 2005 because of offshoring. The figures indicate job losses that were announced, but the losses may not actually happen until after 2005. The greatest (absolute) number of job losses because of offshoring was observed in Germany, followed by the United Kingdom, Portugal and France.

It is interesting to note in Table 12 that certain countries, such as Slovenia, Slovakia and Ireland, which are considered destination countries for offshoring, have also lost jobs because of activities that have been moved to other countries (see also Box 13 – Offshoring Within the European Union). In terms of sectors and in absolute numbers, the sectors that lose the most jobs in absolute numbers are in metals, followed by the motor sector, the electric sector and financial services. As a percentage of total job losses, however, the hardest hit sectors are computer services, textiles and chemicals (see Figure 41).

Table 12. Total job losses due to offshoring announced in the ERM, by country, in 2005

Total job losses		Job losses due to offshoring		Offshoring as a % of the total	
United Kingdom	200 706	Germany	7 765	Portugal	54.7
Germany	108 233	United Kingdom	6 764	Austria	29.6
France	45 405	Portugal	2 448	Denmark	28.8
Poland	27 117	France	2 080	Slovak Republic	25.2
Netherlands	22 111	Slovenia	1 516	Slovenia	24
Sweden	16 691	Denmark	1 505	Ireland	23.6
Czech Republic	14 949	Ireland	1 345	Finland	15.9
Spain	13 963	Italy	1 171	Italy	15.7
Hungary	10 960	Finland	1 153	Belgium	10.9
Italia	7 467	Sweden	904	Germany	7.2
Finland	7 240	Hungary	620	Hungary	5.7
Slovenia	6 327	Poland	610	Sweden	5.4
Ireland	5 697	Slovak Republic	600	France	4.6
Belgium	5 266	Belgium	576	United Kingdom	3.4
Denmark	5 234	Austria	505	Spain	2.3
Portugal	4 478	Spain	320	Poland	2.2
Lithuania	3 398	Netherlands	160	Czech Republic	0.9
Slovak Republic	2 383	Czech Republic	130	Netherlands	0.7
Austria	1 708	Cyprus	0	Cyprus	0
Estonia	1 068	Estonia	0	Estonia	0
Malta	850	Latvia	0	Latvia	0
Latvia	600	Lithuania	0	Lithuania	0
Cyprus	60	Malta	0	Malta	0

Source: ERM, 2005.

Figure 41. Job losses due to offshoring by sector in 2005 in the European Union

Percentages of total losses

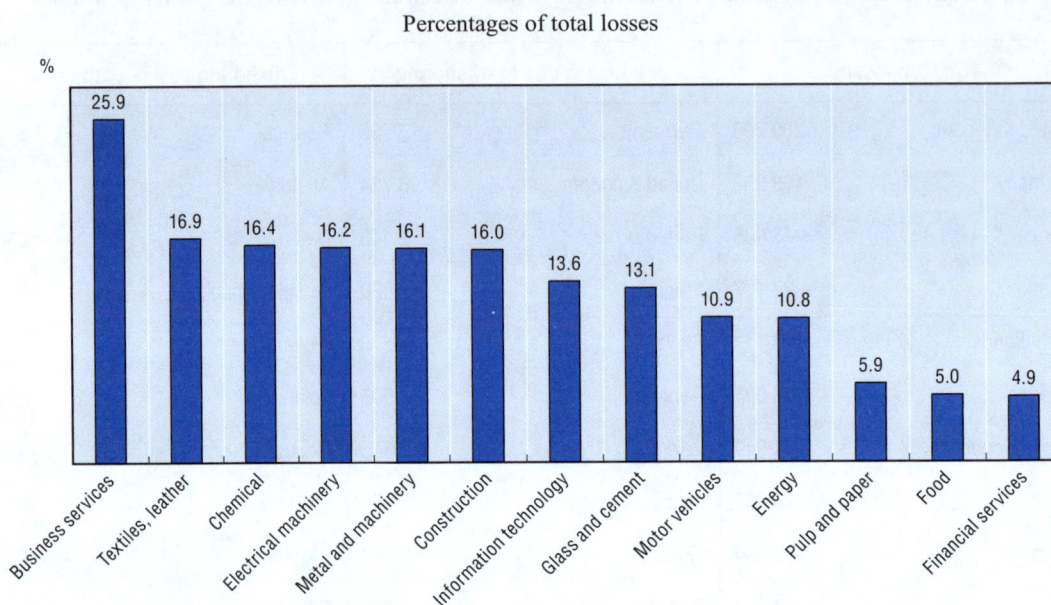

Source: ERM, 2005.

StatLink: http://dx.doi.org/10.1787/465788655438

4.6. Measuring the impact on the demand for labour of outsourcing production abroad

The most relevant recent analysis of the impact on domestic employment of the offshoring of services is the one carried out by Mary Amiti and Shang-Jin Wei (2004).

To measure offshoring trends, the authors computed the respective shares of five categories of imported services in manufacturing-sector output in 2000: management services (12%), financial services (2.4%), telecommunications (1.3%), insurance (0.5%) and information technology (0.4%).

In their analysis of 450 economic sectors, Amiti and Wei observed that the offshoring of services had brought about a roughly 0.4% loss of employment in the manufacturing industry. However, when the calculations were made at a higher level of aggregation – using 96 sectors – it would seem that the offshoring of services had no notable effect on employment. In other words, growth in demand for other economic sectors was enough to offset the negative repercussions.

The offshoring of services can affect the demand for labour in three ways. First is through a substitution effect via the price of products or services entering into production. In other words, the drop in prices for imported services triggers a reduction in the demand for labour to the extent that labour and imported services are interchangeable.

Second, if offshoring enhances productivity, that means that businesses can produce just as much but spend less. In other words, for a given level of output, offshoring can theoretically trigger a reduction in the demand for labour.

Third, offshoring can affect this demand through demand for the product. Because of more extensive offshoring, a business or an industry can bolster its efficiency and competitiveness, feeding through to greater demand for products and thus for labour.

In any given sector, offshoring can therefore have either a positive or a negative effect on employment, depending on whether or not the beneficial impact on demand outweighs the detrimental substitution or productivity effects. For the US economy as a while, Amiti and Wei concluded that the offshoring of services had had only a very slight impact on aggregate employment.

4.6.1. *Estimates by the OECD Secretariat*

The OECD Secretariat undertook a series of estimations based on the same model as that of Amiti and Wei, but differing in certain respects. Amiti and Wei worked with highly detailed sectoral data covering a single country (alternately the United States and the United Kingdom) and available over a long period.

In contrast, the OECD Secretariat worked on sectoral data for 12 OECD countries covering the years 1995 and 2000, using harmonised input-output tables for those countries.

To estimate the effect of offshoring on domestic sector employment three types of models, were used adding each time some more flexibility. Always the starting point was production function where gross output is obtained using a combination of labour, capital stock and intermediate inputs. First, we assume that all inputs other than labour are quasi-fixed and that output is exogenous. Second, we assume that the inputs are variable but that output is fixed, and finally we also allow output to vary.

In the first model, labour demand would simply be the inverted production function solved for labour as a function of gross output, intermediate inputs and capital stock, if labour would compensate for the sluggishness in the adjustment of the other inputs. However, it may well be that the desired production level is not met because labour itself is subject to hiring and firing costs. The industry employment equation is:

$$\Delta \ln L_{it} = \beta_0 + \beta_1 \Delta \ln Y_{it} + \beta_2 \Delta \ln K_{it} + \beta_3 \Delta \ln M_{it} + \beta_4 \Delta \ln OI_{it} + \beta_I D_I + \beta_C D_C + \eta_{it} \qquad (1)$$

Where:

L_{it}: is the demand for labour in industry i in year t.

Y_{it}: is the production (gross output) in industry i in year t.

K_{it}: is the capital stock used in industry i in year t.

M_{it}: is the level of intermediate inputs used in industry i in year t.

OI_{it}: is the overall outsourcing index for industry i in year t.

D_I: denotes industry dummies.

D_C: denotes country dummies.

Δ: is the first difference operator.

η_{it}: is a random error term i.i.d. distributed accounting for left-out variables.

The model is estimated in first differences to eliminate time-invariant industry effects in labour demand.

In the second model it is assumed that all inputs are variable and that the observed levels result from a cost minimization subject to a constrained level of output and exogenous factor prices. The technology can be represented by a dual representation, such as a cost function. The demand for labour is obtained by applying Shephard's lemma to the cost function. This approach corresponds to Amiti and Wei's model specification. The estimating equation is as follows:

$$\Delta \ln L_{it} = \alpha_0 + \alpha_1 \Delta \ln W_{it} + \alpha_2' \Delta \ln \omega_{it} + \alpha_3 \Delta \ln Y_{it} + \alpha_4 \Delta \ln OI_{it} + \alpha_I D_I + \alpha_C D_C + \varepsilon_{it} \qquad (2)$$

Where W_{it} is the wage rate in industry i in year t.

ω_{it} is the price vector of capital and intermediate inputs in industry i in year t.

ε_{it} is a random error term i.i.d. distributed accounting for left-out variables

Factor demands are homogeneous of degree zero in factor prices. Therefore was imposed the parametric restriction that $\alpha_1 + \alpha_2' = 0$. Again first differences were taken to eliminate time-invariant individual industry effects. A double log functional form is specified for the labour demand, which is consistent with a Cobb-Douglas production function.

The third model differs from the second model in that output is also considered to be endogenous. The decision maker is seen as a profit maximiser that determines simultaneously on the inputs and the output level on the basis of exogenously given input and output prices. The estimating equation is given by:

$$\Delta \ln L_{it} = \gamma_0 + \gamma_1 \Delta \ln W_{it} + \gamma_2' \Delta \ln \omega_{it} + \gamma_3 \Delta \ln p_{it} + \gamma_4 \Delta \ln OI_{it} + \delta_I D_I + \delta_C D_C + \nu_{it} \quad (3)$$

Where p_{it} is the output price in industry i in year t.

ν_{it} is a random error term i.i.d. distributed accounting for left-out variables.

This time was imposed the parametric restriction that $\gamma_1 + \gamma_2' + \gamma_3 = 0$ to account for homogeneity of degree zero of factor demand in factor and output prices. Again we take first differences to eliminate time-invariant industry effects and we use a double log functional form, which is consistent with a Cobb-Douglas production function.

In all three models we experiment with industry and country dummies to account for industry and country specificities not only in the levels but also in the changes of employment.

Complete data were available for 12 countries (Austria, Belgium, Denmark, Finland, France, Germany, Greece, Italy, Korea, Norway, Sweden, United States) and 26 industries for two years, *i.e.* 1995 and 2000, except for Greece (where data were available for 1995 and 1999) and Norway (where data are for 1997 and 2001). As explained in Annex 2 industries were defined on the basis of two digit ISIC codes, with some regrouping to have the same comparable industrial definitions across all countries. The base year for converting current to constant value is the year 2000.

The variables used in the analysis are: outsourcing index for manufacturing (OIM) and services (OIS), Wage rates (WAGES), Investment price deflator (INVP), Intermediate input (INPUT), Intermediate input price deflator (IIP), Output (OUTPUT), Output price deflator (POUT), and Capital Stock (CAP). These variables are defined as follows.

The outsourcing index measures the proportion of intermediate inputs that are imported. It is computed in the following way:

$$OI_i = \sum_j \left[\frac{purchase\ of\ inputs\ j\ excluding\ energy\ by\ industry\ i}{total\ inputs,\ excluding\ energy,\ used\ by\ i} \right] \bullet \left[\frac{M_j}{D_j} \right]$$

Where M_j denotes import of intermediate input j, and

D_j is the domestic demand for input j.

In other words, was applied the percentage of imported final demand of commodity/service j to the intermediate input use of commodity/service j by industry i to compute the indirect import of commodity/service j by industry i. They then sum the imported commodities/services used as intermediate inputs in sector i and express them in percentage of total intermediate inputs of commodity/services in sector i.

The percentage of imported intermediate inputs was measured directly from the tables in the STAN input-output tables. The following formula has been used:

$$OI_i = \frac{total\ imported\ input\ used\ by\ industry\ i}{total\ input\ used\ by\ industry\ i}$$

Different coefficients for the outsourcing index were used for manufacturing and services (OIM and OIS) by interacting the outsourcing index with manufacturing and services dummies.

Wages has been computed as the ratio of labour compensation of employees (worksheet LABR) to the full time equivalent employees (worksheet EMPE_FTE) wherever we got data for EMPE_FTE. In other cases, such as Belgium, Denmark, Finland, and Germany, the number of employees (worksheet EME) has been used rather than full time equivalent employees, as worksheet EMPE_FTE was not available for these countries. In case of Sweden total employment (number engaged; worksheet EMPN) has been used as a proxy of full time employees due to lack of other data.

INVP has been computed as the ratio of gross fixed capital formation at current prices to the gross fixed capital formation at constant prices.

INPUT is the value of intermediate inputs at constant prices while IIP has been derived as the ratio of the value of intermediate inputs at current prices to the value of intermediate inputs at constant prices. Similarly OUTPUT is the value of output at constant prices whereas POUT is the ratio of the value of output at current prices to the value of output at constant prices.

Variable CAP has been measured as the value of gross fixed capital formation at constant prices. Data were not available on physical capital stock and no annual data to construct a capital stock from investment data. Hence we assumed that the capital stock is proportional to gross fixed capital formation.

Table 13 presents the estimation results obtained from the inverted Cobb-Douglas production function. A likelihood ratio test clearly rejects the absence of industry and country-specific influences on sector labour demand. Industry dummies control for sector-specific technical change and country dummies control for country-specific labour market regulations and rigidities. Results will be commented from the last column of Table 1. If all inputs could be adjusted instantaneously then the elasticity of labour with respect to output should be the inverse of labour share in the value of output. In the short term we expect rigidities in labour adjustment: it takes time to hire the desired type of worker, and laws and regulations make it difficult in many countries, especially in European countries, to lay off workers without costs. This is why labour reacts slowly to increases in the level of production. The elasticity is of 0.11. Labour follows the movement of the other inputs: the elasticity of labour with respect to intermediate inputs is 0.11 and its elasticity with respect to capital is close to zero. *These results clearly indicate that foreign outsourcing decreases labour demand in manufacturing.* If the index increases by 10%, labour demand decreases by 1.2% in manufacturing. Whereas the coefficient of foreign outsourcing, while remaining significant and negative, decreases in absolute magnitude when we control for industry effects and country effects, the effect of foreign outsourcing in services becomes negative and significant only after we control for industry-specific effects.

4. PRELIMINARY RESULTS – **99**

Table 13. Employment and foreign outsourcing in OECD countries, 1995-2000*

(Conditional labour demand equation with quasi-fixed inputs, in growth rates)

Variables	Dependent variable: Δ ln (Employment)				
	No dummies	Country dummies	Industry dummies	Country & industry dummies	Remarks
Δ ln(OIM)	-0.1805**	-0.1716**	-0.1292**	-0.1242**	Outsourcing index in manufacturing
	(-2.5433)	(-2.3117)	(-2.4425)	(-2.3511)	
Δ ln(OIS)	0.0258	0.0135	-0.0737***	-0.0967***	Outsourcing index in services
	(0.7198)	(0.3518)	(-2.6439)	(-3.3914)	
Δ ln(INPUT)	0.1160***	0.1438***	0.0872***	0.1096***	Intermediate input
	(4.3702)	(4.4982)	(3.7371)	(4.3382)	
Δ ln(CAP)	0.0472**	0.0377	0.0240	0.0042	Capital formation
	(2.1606)	(1.6068)	(1.4734)	(0.2478)	
Δ ln(OUTPUT)	0.1473***	0.1176***	0.1464***	0.1084***	Output
	(5.1095)	(2.8598)	(5.9360)	(3.0381)	
Log likelihood	190.8472	198.3123	293.0747	313.8220	
N	264	264	264	264	
R^2	0.1987	0.2428	0.6306	0.6844	

Note: * $p < 0.1$; ** $p < 0.05$; *** $p < 0.01$; + Figures in parentheses are t-values.

The results do not change a lot when we let the other inputs adjust to their optimal level, *i.e.* when the levels of capital and intermediate inputs were replaced by the prices of labour and intermediate inputs relative to investment (Table 14). The likelihood ratio test again concludes that the most preferred specification is the one corresponding to the last column, *i.e.* with industry and country dummies. It is thus not sufficient to correct for industry and country-specific fixed effects in the levels, but there are also specific industry and country effects in explaining the growth rates. According to the cross-price elasticities, labour is a substitute for intermediate inputs and slightly complementary to the capital stock. *The outsourcing index has a negative coefficient in both manufacturing and services industries. The detrimental effect on labour from foreign outsourcing is slightly stronger in manufacturing than in services. A 1% increase in the proportion of imported intermediate inputs for the manufacturing leads to a 0.13% reduction in sectoral employment in the home country while in the case of imported intermediate input for services , the reduction in sectoral employment in the home country is 0.10%.(Table 14).*

Table 14. Employment and foreign outsourcing in OECD countries, 1995-2000*

(Conditional labour demand equation with variable inputs, in growth rates)

Variables	Dependent variable: Δ ln (Employment)				Remarks
	No dummies	Country dummies	Industry dummies	Country & industry dummies	
Δ ln(OIM)	-0.2679***	-0.2304***	-0.1621***	-0.1334**	Outsourcing index in manufacturing
	(-3.6582)	(-3.0069)	(-3.0367)	(-2.5126)	
Δ ln(OIS)	0.0202	0.0246	-0.0847***	-0.1003***	Outsourcing index in services
	(0.5322)	(0.6110)	(-2.9930)	(-3.4934)	
Δ ln(WAGES)- Δ ln(INVP)	-0.0728	-0.1945**	-0.1688***	-0.2557***	Wages/investment deflator
	(-1.340)	(-2.5866)	(-3.7020)	(-4.4651)	
Δ ln(IIP)- Δ ln(INVP)	0.0618	0.0996*	0.1954***	0.2292***	Intermediate input/ investment price
	(1.1495)	(1.7534)	(3.5876)	(4.1174)	
Δ ln(OUTPUT)	0.1134***	0.1981***	0.0694***	0.1206**	Gross output
	(3.9290)	(4.5216)	(2.9698)	(3.2965)	
Log likelihood	177.5445	187.2284	290.1022	313.6965	
N	266	266	266	266	
R^2	0.1271	0.1884	0.6255	0.6864	

Note: * $p < 0.1$; **$p < 0.05$; *** $p < 0.01$; + Figures in parentheses are t-values.

When output to varies and the labour demand equation is unconditional on output (as suggested by Amiti and Ekholm, 2006), the likelihood ratio test again gives the preference to the inclusion of industry and country dummies. There is little sign of any substitutability or complementarity between labour and other two factors of production. What is interesting is to notice is that a 1% increase in the price of output increases by 0.3% to demand for labour. As output increases following the increase in the price of output, the demand for labour by almost as much as following a 1% reduction in the wage rate. The output expansion effect is not negligible. *Regarding the two outsourcing indexes, this still cannot exclude a labour destroying effect due to foreign outsourcing, by about twice as much in manufacturing as in services. A 1% increase in the proportion of imported intermediate inputs for manufacturing leads to 0.15% reduction in sectoral employment in the home country and around 0.08% in the case of imported intermediate inputs for services. (Table 15).*

Table 15. Employment and foreign outsourcing in OECD countries, 1995-2000*

(Unconditional labour demand equation, in growth rates)

Variables	Dependent variable: Δ ln (Employment)				Remarks
	No dummies	Country dummies	Industry dummies	Country & industry dummies	
Δ ln(OIM)	-0.2615***	-0.2769***	-0.1613***	-0.1546***	Outsourcing index in manufacturing
	(-3.5617)	(-3.6522)	(-2.9828)	(-2.9734)	
Δ ln(OIS)	0.1182***	0.1089**	-0.0421	-0.0865**	Outsourcing index in services
	(2.7019)	(2.2986)	(-1.2310)	(-2.4554)	
Δ ln(WAGES)- Δ ln(INVP)	-0.1327**	-0.0759	-0.2649***	-0.2832***	Wages/investment deflator
	(-2.1633)	(-1.0124)	(-4.9402)	(-4.6440)	
Δ ln(IIP)- Δ ln(INVP)	-0.0441	-0.1768*	0.1408**	-0.0046	Intermediate input/ investment price
	(-0.5148)	(-1.7687)	(1.9944)	(-0.0577)	
Δ ln(POUT)- Δ ln(INVP)	0.1251	0.2454**	0.1208*	0.3032***	Relative price output/investment
	(1.5088)	(2.5624)	(1.7073)	(3.7848)	
Log likelihood	175.8774	185.1119	285.2146	313.3326	
N	264	264	264	264	
R²	0.0978	0.1588	0.6059	0.6815	

Note: * $p < 0.1$; **$p < 0.05$; ***$p < 0.01$; + Figures in parentheses are *t*-values.

It should be noticed that when we used industry definitions which are more disaggregated in some countries and non-existent in others, the results did not differ substantially from those presented above. The solution with more aggregated data is preferable because then industries have the same definitions in all countries. The qualitative results (signs and significance of the coefficients) for outsourcing were also the same when a value-added specification of output (in which case there is no intermediate input) is used. But the gross output specification precisely is preferable because it examined the outsourcing of intermediate inputs.

Using a cross-section of growth rates in labour employment in 26 industries of 12 OECD countries, using a measure of foreign outsourcing directly obtained from input-output data, the conclusion is that foreign outsourcing is detrimental to sectoral domestic employment, especially in manufacturing but also in services. The results do not depend on the assumed flexibility in factor demand and output supply. Even though there could be a boomerang effect from lower production costs due to foreign outsourcing that translate into higher demand and ultimately more employment, the direct domestic job-destroying effect predominates, at least over the five-year period which was taken into consideration.

While this method of estimation may be the best one possible if special survey data and access to individual firm data are unavailable, it nonetheless has certain limitations. Its main limitation, which arises from the particular form that it was necessary to use, is the lack of long series on outsourcing indices generated from input-output tables. This compelled us to work on variations between two periods without being able to refer to specific countries or industries (cross-section analysis). This difficulty may be overcome in the near future, however, which would pave the way for dynamic analysis by country and by industry.

In contrast, it will be more difficult to find short-term solutions for three other limitations.

Inclusion of imported intermediate inputs excludes all imports of finished goods that are resold without transformation on the domestic market. The offshoring of production involves intermediate and finished goods alike.

Another limitation is that offshored production involving only exported goods and services is not included insofar as it generates no import flows to the country of origin.

Lastly, no study to date has been capable of overcoming the major difficulty of ascertaining offshoring's indirect effects on employment. We shall come back to this difficulty later in the report.

Annex 2 presents a number of particularities and difficulties regarding the data used.

4.7. Quantifying the positive effects of offshoring

While to measure the employment impact of offshoring raises methodological difficulties that are sometimes insurmountable, assessing the benefits derived from offshoring is just as ambitious and difficult a challenge.

Even when data on individual firms (microdata) are accessible, it is very difficult to quantify the benefits of offshoring and even more difficult to establish a causal relationship.

The problem here is not, in fact, to quantify the gains from foreign trade, direct investment or outsourcing abroad, *i.e.* in more general terms the benefits of globalisation; rather, it is an attempt to identify the benefits stemming exclusively from offshoring, and not from other factors.

In Section 2.4, the main benefits mentioned were:

- Growth in consumers' incomes.
- Improved competitiveness and productivity in enterprises.
- Export growth.
- Control of inflation.
- Better returns on capital.

This list is certainly not exhaustive, yet even with access to each firm's cost accounting it would be very difficult to determine the benefits stemming from offshoring alone, and probably even more difficult to identify the share accruing to each beneficiary (shareholders, managers, employees, consumers, subcontractors), as well as to a country in its entirety.

4.7.1. Growth in consumers' incomes

L Offshored goods and services are theoretically imported for less than the cost of producing them domestically. Box 9 gives a brief description of a method for assessing the potential gains to consumers stemming from these differences in price. Nevertheless, these gains are overestimated and probably not actually realised, insofar as demand for these goods would be significantly less if they were sold on the domestic market at higher prices.

Figure 42 provides only a rough illustration of the potential gain per capita could derive thanks to price differentials.

Figure 42. Potential per capita income gains due to imports of offshored goods in USD

Average 2003-2005

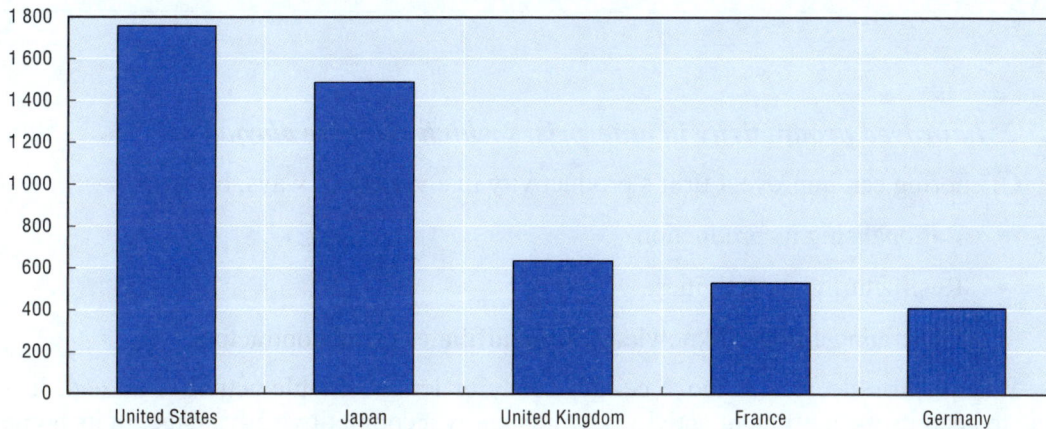

Source: CEPII.

StatLink: http://dx.doi.org/10.1787/532020630216

> **Box 9. Measuring consumers' gains due to domestic market sales of imports resulting from offshoring**
>
> Offshoring enables firms to sell goods on the domestic market for lower prices than if the same goods had been manufactured and sold in the country of origin. Quality being equal, the price differential between imports from offshoring and the same goods sold prior to offshoring constitutes the main gain for consumers' income.
>
> A very approximate method, proposed by Professor Fontagne of the CEPII, for estimating the effects on consumers' incomes stemming from imports of goods whose production has been moved offshore would be to identify the firms, industries and countries concerned. If one is working with individual firms' data, it is necessary to evaluate the domestic consumption that is no longer satisfied by national production but by imports of activities that have been moved offshore. If these data are not available, another, rougher approach would be to identify imports from offshore countries and to compute their unit value $\left(= \dfrac{Value\ of\ imports}{Quantities} \right)$. These calculations can be limited to consumer goods as defined in UN statistics. The next step is to compute the unit values of exports of these same goods. The ratio between the two categories of unit values is weighted by the structure of imports of these goods from the countries concerned. Lastly, the difference is multiplied by the number of imports actually observed, which corresponds to the overall gain for the year in question. This gain can then be divided by the number of households in each country to measure the savings or the gain for each household.

4.7.2. Improved productivity in enterprises which relocate abroad

Offshoring can improve a firm's productivity in a variety of ways, by:

- Rationalising its production.

- Restructuring its activities.

- Generating a flow of knowledge from affiliates or subcontractors.

When a firm decides to move certain costly or less profitable activities abroad, it is able to keep its most efficient activities, which enjoy a competitive advantage, in its home country. This rationalisation of production enables the firm to bolster its productivity and strengthen the activities in which it is most efficient. The work force that remains in the firm after offshoring is theoretically more productive.

After moving some of its activity offshore, a firm can restructure so as to divest itself entirely of unprofitable activities, reap greater benefits from economies of scale, invest in activities having a higher technological content and upgrade the products and services it sells both at home and abroad. In addition, the firms can acquire and exploit patents developed by their affiliates or adopt technological innovations proposed in some cases by their associates and subcontractors abroad, and this can enhance productivity.

According to estimates by Amiti and Wei, in the United States, between 1992 and 2000, the foreign outsourcing of services accounted for between 11% and 13% of productivity growth, and that of goods for between 3% and 6%.

For European countries, the evidence would seem less clear. However, for British firms, Girma and Görg (2004) and Criscuolo and Leaver (2005) found a positive correlation between offshoring and productivity growth (both labour productivity and total factor productivity) at the establishment level. This correlation, involving foreign outsourcing of services, is positive and significant only for firms classified as belonging to the service sector, and not for manufacturing firms. Another study, commissioned by Logical CMG, concluded that pursuit of the offshoring trend in the United Kingdom would shrink the productivity gap of British firms by 10% as compared to their main competitors.

Similar results have been found in respect of the Netherlands and Denmark (Griffith, 2005 and Jensey, 2006). More recently, empirical research by F. Davari, M. Iommi and C. Jona-Lasimio has shown that in Italy's case it is the offshoring of intermediate goods alone that shows a positive correlation with productivity growth, while other forms of offshoring show no tangible links with productivity growth.

Figure 43. Outsourcing abroad index for goods (2000) and productivity growth (1997-2002) in the United States

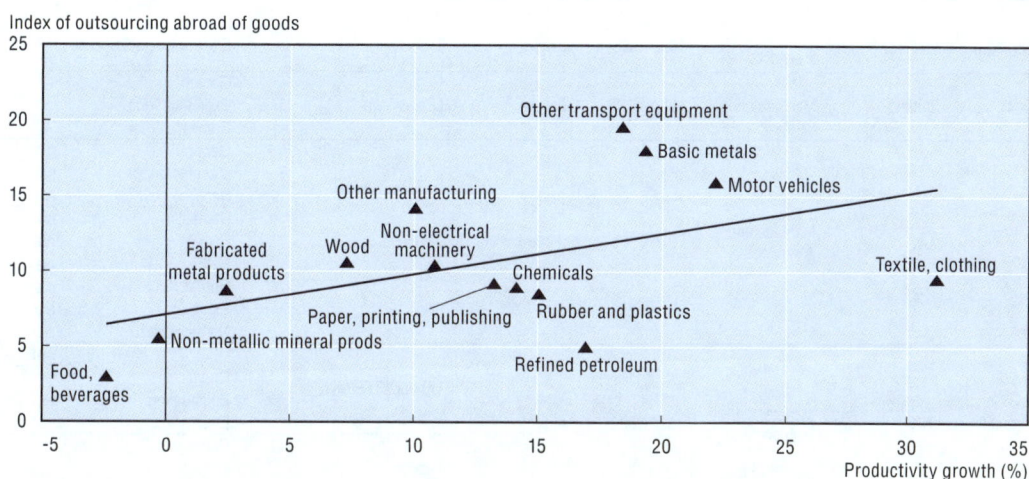

Source: OECD Input-Output and STAN databases.

StatLink: http://dx.doi.org/10.1787/175400811626

Figure 43 shows, in respect of the United States, that most of the industries that do the most offshoring record relatively high productivity growth, but the linkages do not seem fairly strong in all industries. Given industry particularities and the fact that productivity is affected by many other factors besides offshoring, it would be difficult to draw such correlations from these figures. However, the level of aggregation of the data used precludes identification of the firms that send some of their activities offshore, which makes it more difficult to draw conclusions. It would probably be better when using these data to introduce offshoring into the equation as an explicatory variable of productivity trends, but it would be preferable to use microdata to work with data per establishment.

Table 16, proposed by Karsten Olsen (2006), summarises the main research carried out recently to explore the linkages between foreign outsourcing and productivity. While until now these linkages have not been explored sufficiently in empirical studies, some general conclusions do seem to be emerging from the existing literature.

Table 16. Empirical evidence on outsourcing and productivity

Source	Country	Industy	Period	Type of outsourcing	Productivity measure	Remarks	Productivity effects from outsourcing		
Aggregate level							M	S	SC
Egger & Egger (2001b)	EU-12	Manufacturing	1992-1997	Offshore	Low-skill labour level	Short-run effect	-	n/a	n/a
						Long-run effect	+	n/a	n/a
Amity & Wei (2006)	US	Manufacturing	1992-2000	Offshore	Labour growth	General	+	++	n/a
					TFP growth	General	+	++	n/a
Amity & Wei (2004b)	US	Manufacturing	1992-2001	Offshore	Labour growth	General	0	+	n/a
Egger et al. (2001)	Austria	Manufacturing	1990-1998	Offshore	TFP growth	General	+	n/a	n/a
Plant level							M	S	SC
Görzig & Stephan (2002)	Germany	Manufacturing & services	1992-2000	Any	Return per employee	Short-run effect	++	-	+
						Long-run effect	++	+	+
Görg & Hanley (2003b)	Ireland	Manufacturing & services	1990-1995	Offshore	Labour growth	Electronics sector	0	0	n/a
					Labour level	Electronics sector	0	0	n/a
					Labour level & growth	Upstream firms	0	0	n/a
						Downstream firms	0	+	n/a
							M	S	MS
Görg & Hanley (2005)	Ireland	Manufacturing & services	1990-1995	Offshore	TFP level	Electronics sector	n/a	n/a	+
							+	0	n/a
Görg et al. (2004)	Ireland	Manufacturing	1990-1998	Offshore	Labour level	General	+	0	n/a
						Exporting firms	+	0	n/a
						Domestic firms	0	0	n/a
Criscuolo & Leaver (2005)	UK	Manufacturing & services	2000-2003	Offshore	TFP level	General	n/a	+	n/a
						Manufacturing	n/a	0	n/a
						Services	n/a	+	n/a
						Domestic	n/a	+	n/a
						Foreign	n/a	0	n/a
						MNEs	n/a	0	n/a
						Non-MNEs	n/a	+	n/a
						Exporter	n/a	0	n/a
						Non-exporterr	n/a	+	n/a
							MS	MS * FO	
Girma & Görg (2004)	UK	Manufacturing (sub-sectors)	1980-1992	Any	Labour / TFP level	Chemicals	+/+	+/+	
						Engineering	++/++	++/++	
						Electronics	0/0	0/0	
					Labour / TFP growth	Chemicals	0/0	0/0	
						Engineering	0/+	+/+	
						Electronics	0/0	0/0	
							(see type of out.)		
Lui & Tung (2004)	Chinese Taipei	Manufacturing	2000/2001	FDI offshore	Labour level	General	-		
						Export outsourcing	+		
					Labour growth	General	-		
						Export outsourcing	+		

Note: TFP = total factor productivity, M = material outsourcing, S = services outsourcing, SC = outsourcing work/labour cost, MS = material + services outsourcing, FO = foreign ownership. A +(-) indicates a positive (negative) significant effect, whereas 0 indicates insignificant effects. Double signs indicate that effects are larger relative to single signs for the same study. Not all effects depicted here are necessarily robust over all model variations in the different studies.

First, it would seem that the productivity effects of the outsourcing of goods by manufacturing firms are either slight or insignificant. In contrast, the productivity effects of outsourcing services are significant only when the services are outsourced by service companies and not by firms belonging to the manufacturing sector.

In addition, the positive productivity effect of outsourcing goods is far greater if the firm in question is already highly active internationally. Nevertheless, the productivity effects of outsourcing goods abroad are often tied in with strategic elements that are firm-specific.

4.7.3. Control of inflation

Consumer price inflation has moderated considerably in all OECD countries over the past 25 years. In the OECD area, the level of inflation, which was roughly 10% in the early 1980s, declined to about 2% over the decade from 1995 to 2005. These developments have coincided with a marked increase in the extent of globalisation, with the production of many goods and services becoming increasingly internationalised and growth in the volume of trade in goods and services between the OECD countries and non-member economies, in particular because of low labour costs.

Recent work by the OECD Secretariat (2006), extending work undertaken by the IMF, the BIS and the US Federal Reserve Board, has set out to quantify the possible effects of globalisation on price levels in the OECD countries. This research does not focus in particular on offshoring-related imports, but its conclusions are relevant in that area as well.

This research finds that the impact of import prices on domestic prices in all countries over the past decade has been significantly larger than the weight of imported goods and services in domestic demand, suggesting that competition from lower-priced imports has placed pressure on domestic producers in import-competing industries to lower the mark-ups of prices over domestic costs.

The low import price inflation in OECD countries can in part be attributed to the rising trade integration of low-cost countries from Asia and Latin America. The share of non-OECD members in total world trade has increased from about a quarter in 1990 to roughly a third in 2005. The rise in the trade share of non-OECD countries reflects both an increased openness of these countries as well as higher GDP growth rates compared with OECD countries.

During the period from 1996 to 2000, imports from China mechanically deducted 0.1 percentage points per annum from inflation in the United States. In contrast, there was little discernible effect in the euro area. Since 2000, imports from China have contributed to lower inflation in the euro area, deducting an average 0.2 percentage points per annum from inflation. For the United States, the contribution of imports from China to lower inflation since 2000 was similar to that in the previous five-year period (Table 17).

It is clear that trade with lower-cost economies can have different effects in particular importing economies, not just in terms of the magnitude of the effects, but also in the channels through which they arrive. The results for the euro area also suggest that the downward pressure from lower-cost economies may have accelerated since the year 2000, in at least some economies.

Table 17. Computing the mechanical globalisation impact on inflation

	A. Imports from China	B. Imports from other dynamic Asian economies	Total A + B
United States	-0.02	-0.01	-0.03
1991-1995	-0.09	-0.04	-0.12
1996-2000	-0.11	0.00	-0.11
2001-2005			
Euro area			
1991-1995	-0.02	-0.01	-0.03
1996-2000	0.00	0.05	0.05
2001-2005	-0.19	-0.09	-0.28

Source: OECD (2006), Economics Department

The impact on inflation of imports from activities sent offshore will probably be far less. Such an assessment will demand additional research. Moreover, it would be interesting in future work to try to factor in the role of imports from emerging countries in the wage moderation of the OECD countries.

4.7.4. Possible growth in exports of firms that move activities offshore

One of the positive effects of offshoring may be growth in the exports of firms that move activities offshore. The factors fostering the export growth of such firms are many; among the most important are:

- Complementary effects between exports and foreign direct investment.

- Expanded export capacity due to improved competitiveness.

- Better specialisation of businesses that move offshore with goods and services for which there is strong demand abroad.

- The fact that income growth in the offshore countries also bolsters their demand for imports.

Much empirical research has shown that during periods when flows of foreign investment do not diminish, the relationship between exports and foreign direct investment is more one of complementarity than of substitution. Export flows to offshore countries may be in the same industry as in the home country or in other industries. This complementary relationship relates only to offshoring via affiliates abroad rather than through subcontracting abroad.

If offshoring enhances corporate competitiveness, firms can also win new foreign markets without altering the structure or nature of their production. Moreover, if a firm that moves offshore improves its profitability and generates additional resources, it can specialise to a greater extent in products and services that are higher-range and in greater demand. This can also enable it to win new markets through exports.

In most cases, the offshore destination countries increase their income and consumption thanks to foreign investment and subcontracting orders. Most often, the additional consumption is satisfied by new imports. In such a case, the question that arises is whether the country that moves offshore is in a position to satisfy this new demand through exports. It should be stressed, however, that if the country of origin is able to increase exports to the offshore destination countries, the firms that have moved some of their activities to those countries will not necessarily be the only ones to benefit from the exports.

If the relocating countries have an appropriate investment and specialisation policy, they will be able to offset the import flows from the offshore destination countries with new export flows and to restore their trade balances with those countries. In this case, the restored trade balance could trigger the creation of new jobs destined for additional exports. Unfortunately, this is frequently not the case, which heightens trade imbalances between certain countries, especially when offshoring-related trade accounts for only a small share of bilateral trade.

Figure 44. Outsourcing abroad index for goods in 2000 and growth in the export rate between 1997 and 2003 in the United States

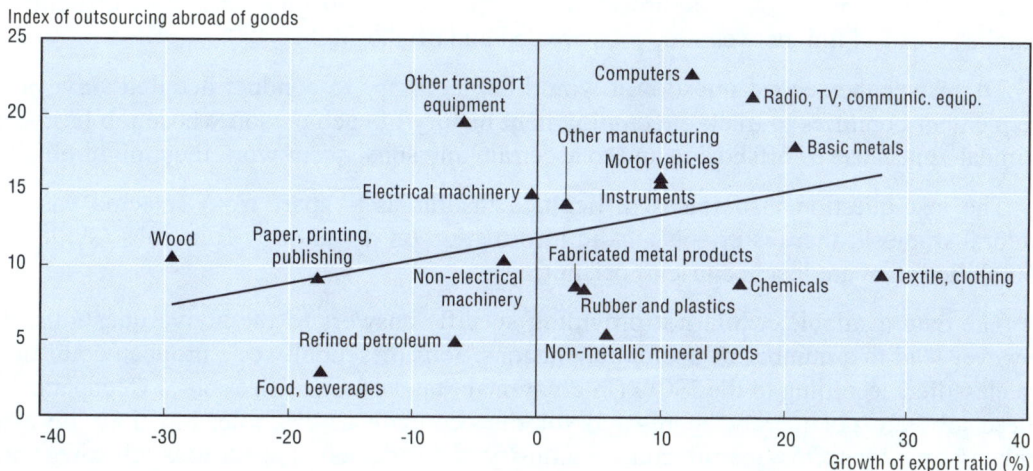

Source: Input-Output and STAN databases.

StatLink: http://dx.doi.org/10.1787/208440663381

Figure 44, using the United States as an example, looks for a correlation between the outsourcing abroad of various manufacturing industries and growth in those same industries' propensity to export (exports / production).

The propensity to export of sectors that outsource the most abroad, *i.e.* computers, electronics (radio, TV and communications), basic metals, motor vehicles and instruments, experienced the greatest growth. The only sector that outsources heavily and whose propensity to export declined was "other transport equipment", consisting essentially of the aeronautical industry. This trend may reflect industry-specific cyclical factors. The high propensity to export of certain sectors, such as textiles and wearing apparel, is due essentially to a sharp drop in production, which explains the job losses and more moderate growth in exports.

4.7.5. Creation of skilled jobs

The enhanced competitiveness of firms that move some of their activities offshore enables them to expand their market shares and their profits, and to increase capital investment. Theoretically, in most cases the improved activity of firms also feeds through to the creation of new jobs. This raises a number of questions, the most important of which could be summarised as follows:

- Does the creation of new jobs offset the destruction of the jobs moved offshore?

- Are the new jobs that are created filled by the people whose jobs were destroyed because of offshoring, or by other people?

- Are the newly created jobs as skilled, more skilled or less skilled than the jobs moved offshore?

These questions cannot be answered precisely from the data currently available without carrying out more highly specialised surveys.

To answer the first question would entail clear knowledge of the number of jobs lost because of offshoring. Yet we have seen that the best estimations yield fairly approximate results and do not factor in indirect effects. Regarding job creations, it is difficult to establish a causal link between the jobs created and offshoring.

To answer the second question it would be necessary to conduct detailed surveys in the member countries to track the employment history of each person whose job has been eliminated because of offshoring and to ascertain any subsequent work they might obtain.

The last question also raises difficulties insofar as – apart from selected case or sectoral studies – there is no systematic information on the nature of the jobs (skilled or non-skilled) that are lost because of offshoring.

The data available, while not providing specific answers to the above questions, do however lead to a number of useful conclusions. Jobs (essentially of European countries) are classified according to the ISCO (International Standard Classification of Occupations). These jobs are not merely aggregated for the economy as a whole, but they are also broken down by sector (manufacturing industry and services). The various job categories can also be combined according to their level of skills (see Box 10). No groupings by skills have been adopted internationally, but the one proposed in this document can illustrate the major trends.

Only data on European countries are expressed using the ISCO classification, and they are harmonised and mutually comparable, whereas data on the United States and Japan are based on national classification systems. Japanese data do not provide sufficient detail, whereas the United States revised its national classification system in the middle of the reference period, which makes comparisons more difficult.

The results in Figure 45 involve growth in skilled and unskilled jobs in manufacturing and in services for most of the European Union countries (see Annex 4 as well). In manufacturing, which in most countries has lost jobs overall, skilled jobs are on the rise. In services, in which all countries are net job creators, skilled jobs are growing significantly faster than unskilled ones in the vast majority of countries.

These results have nothing at all to do with offshoring. They simply show that, in spite of offshoring, manufacturing in particular, which overall is losing jobs in a majority of countries, is a net creator of skilled jobs.

Box 10. Job classifications by level of skills (ISCO* classification)

Highly skilled jobs

ISCO1:   Legislators, senior officials and managers.

ISCO2:   Professionals.

ISCO3:   Technicians and associates.

Low-skilled or unskilled jobs

ISCO8:   Plant & machine operators & assemblers.

ISCO9:   Elementary occupations.

Other categories

ISCO4:   Clerks.

ISCO5:   Services workers & shops & market sales workers.

ISCO6:   Skilled agricultural and fishery workers.

ISCO7:   Craft & related workers.

*   ISCO = International Standard Classification by Occupation.

Figure 45. Growth of skilled and low-skilled jobs in the European Union

Growth 1997-2004 as a percentage

Manufacturing

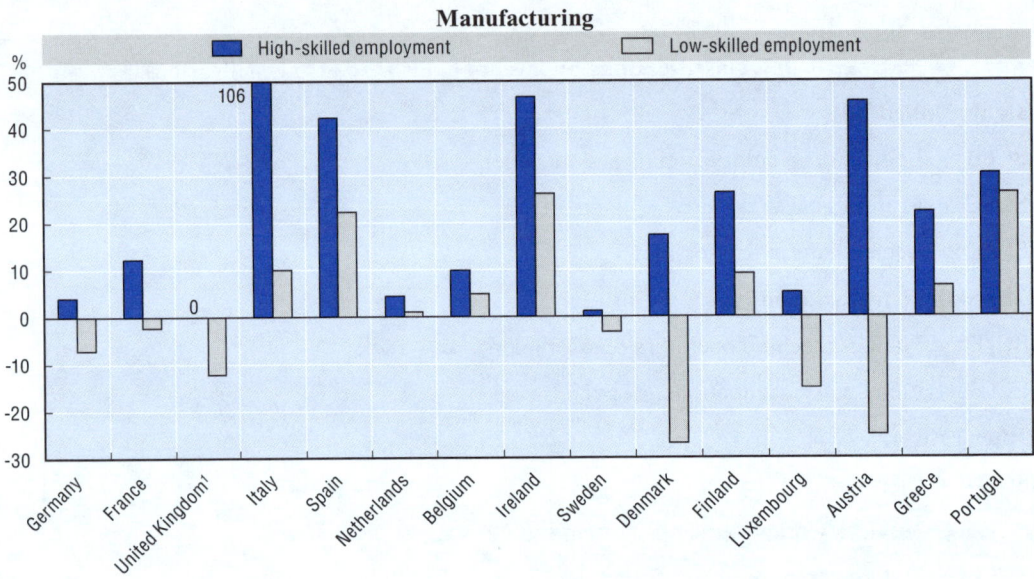

StatLink: http://dx.doi.org/10.1787/823841178484

Services

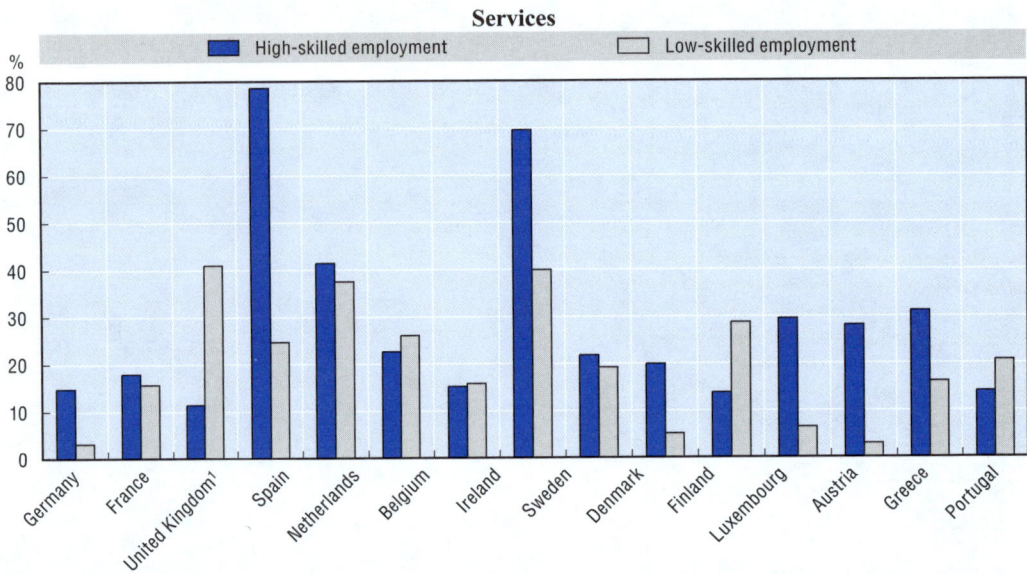

StatLink: http://dx.doi.org/10.1787/526771082752

Source: OECD calculations using Eurostat data.

To draw correlations with offshoring, comparisons are made in Figure 45 between trends in skilled and unskilled jobs in the sectors that resort the most to offshoring (see Annex 4, Table 1). For the three largest European Union countries, it can be seen that skilled jobs were on the rise in Germany and France, while other job categories receded. With regard to the United Kingdom, where aggregate employment in the leading offshoring sectors was in decline, skilled jobs remained stable.

The main conclusion from these trends is that skilled jobs stand up much better, and may in fact increase, in the face of globalisation-induced adjustment costs, and especially offshoring. Box 11 summarises the main limitations of approaching job trends by occupation and by skills level.

Figure 46. Employment trends in the sectors that resort most to offshoring

Growth 1997-2004 as a percentage

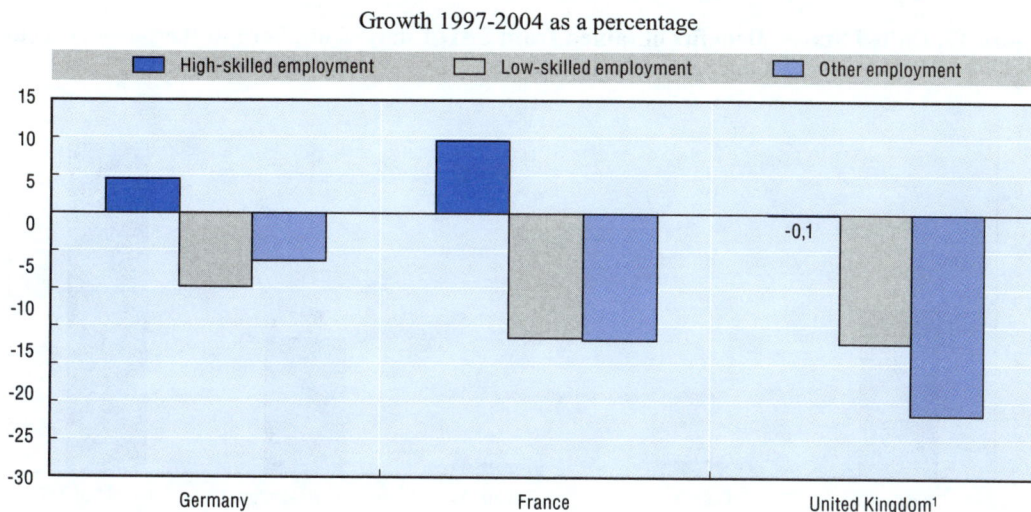

StatLink: http://dx.doi.org/10.1787/276626423811

Box 11. Main limitations on the use of job data by occupation

- Except for data on European Union countries, which are broken down according to the ISCO (International Standard Classification by Occupation), data on other countries are compiled using national classification schemes. International comparisons become more difficult insofar as the level of aggregation and the details available differ from one country to another.

- The ranking of occupations by skills level is somewhat subjective. For example, the same occupation as listed in the classification schemes may require very different skills, depending on whether the occupation is exercised in a small business or a very large multinational firm.

- The available data make no distinction between jobs created and jobs lost, giving only the net change.

- No information is available about the quality of the jobs in question. For example, are the jobs stable or insecure, part-time, chosen or imposed, with or without social benefits, well-paid or low-paid?

4.7.6. Other work on the benefits of offshoring

The presentation will be limited to the work done in 2005 by the McKinsey Global Institute (MGI). The Institute quantified the economic benefits that individual firms have been able to derive from shifting services abroad. Those benefits were measured for the United States, France and Germany. Figure 47 shows the results for the United States. According to these calculations, for every USD 1 that is moved offshore in the services sector, the United States repatriates:

- USD 0.58 because of reduced labour costs.

- USD 0.05 because of induced additional exports.

- USD 0.05 in repatriated profits.

- USD 0.47 in gains due to the re-employment of persons affected by offshoring.

Figure 47. United States: Benefits obtained from USD 1 moved offshore in the services sector

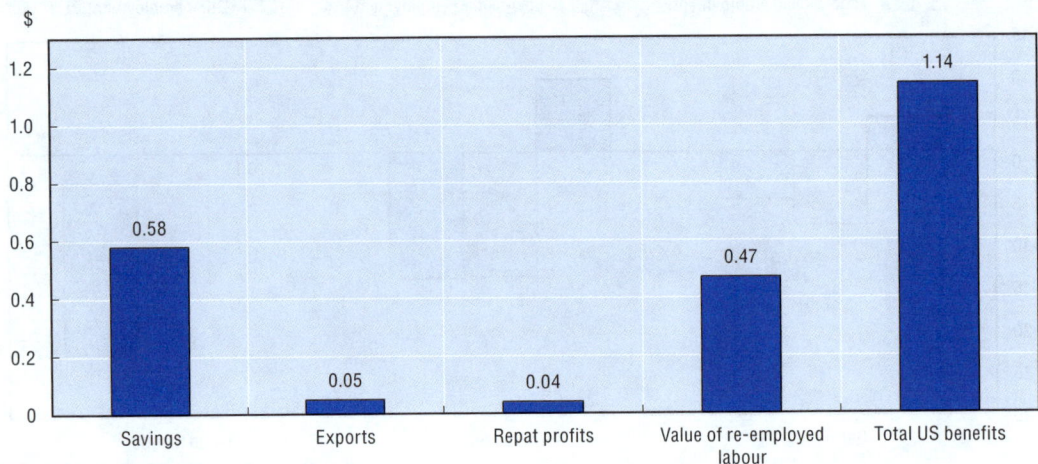

Source: McKinsey and Company.

The same evaluations for France and Germany yield less satisfactory results insofar as, according to Kinsey, for EUR 1 moved offshore, France repatriates EUR 0.86 and Germany EUR 0.74.

Three main reasons explain the differences with the United States. First, the labour cost savings are less in France and Germany because wages in their destination countries are higher than in those of the United States. Essentially, the countries involved are India for the United States and Eastern European and North African countries for France and Germany. Second, the United States takes greater advantage of the wealth created in the destination countries, and their additional demand, exporting more to those countries. And third, persons who lose their jobs to offshoring in the United States tend to find other work more quickly than is the case in France, for example. Thus, about 60% of French workers find new jobs within one year – a lower rate than in the United States (69%). The re-employment rate is a key driver of the net economic impact of offshoring in services: increasing it by 9 points for France (equivalent to the US) could generate EUR 0.13 extra benefit and practically offset the current economic loss for the country. Given current unemployment levels in France and the difficulty of creating new jobs, improving the re-employment rate for workers at risk will be a key challenge for French policymakers and businesses.

From these findings, it should not be concluded that it is not in the interests of France or Germany to offshore. In point of fact, without offshoring the costs for those countries would be significantly higher. Without commenting on the technical details of the evaluations in McKinsey's work, some of which are still relatively opaque, two main limitations warrant mention. First, in respect of the United States, the firms included in the case of offshoring are those that have a long and successful history of shifting services to India. There is no guarantee that any other American firm would reap the same benefits if it wanted to move its activities offshore. A second limitation stems from the fact that it is difficult to extrapolate for a country's economy as a whole the benefits drawn from a panel of firms. Certain macroeconomic effects (impact on the terms of trade, *i.e.* the cost of financing additional imports) should be factored in as well.

4.7.7. *Main benefits for destination countries*

The benefits reaped by destination countries are many, and they correspond to the benefits derived from direct investment and subcontracting orders. Without being exhaustive, it could be said that direct investment contributes to host countries' growth, job creation, technology transfers and enhanced productivity of the firms involved. In the case of research laboratories, a further benefit is all the spillover effects to firms that co-operate with these foreign laboratories.

Nevertheless, the benefits depend on the nature of the investment. If the choice of destination countries has been motivated solely by low labour costs, the resultant benefits might be only temporary, because as growth and living standards progress in those countries, labour costs will increase as well. Under the circumstances, foreign investors may be tempted to shift their activities to other countries where labour costs would be cheaper.

The benefits can be longer-lasting if the firms that move activities offshore choose the countries involved not only for their low labour costs, but also for the skills and quality of the work force. The more foreign investment involves highly technology-intensive activities (such as computer services, software, telecommunications, pharmaceuticals, etc.), the greater – and especially longer-lasting – the benefits will be for the host countries. Foreign investment will be more stable if another selection criterion for the host country is a large and fast-growing domestic market (as in China, India, etc.).

Geographical proximity can also play an important role that can benefit the countries to which activities are relocated, especially at a time when transport costs are rising significantly. Section 2.5 presents certain factors that are unfavourable for offshoring. Destination countries ought to take these factors into account to ensure that foreign investment will remain there over the medium term.

Chapter 5

POLICY RESPONSES

This chapter outlines how OECD countries are addressing the phenomenon of offshoring, be it via existing or new regulations and policy measures. Some measures to be taken into consideration in order to facilitate adjustments to offshoring are presented at the end of the chapter.

5.1. Causes for concern

Studies carried out thus far show that job losses due to offshoring account for only a very low percentage of the total number of jobs destroyed. According to the European Monitoring Centre on Change (EMCC) in Dublin, relocate abroad is responsible for less than 5% of total labour shedding in Europe, far behind bankruptcies, closures and restructurings. Under these conditions, it might seem puzzling that relocation abroad has triggered so many debates and heightened such concern in so many countries.

Figure 48. Jobs losses in Europe

Industry and services, from 1 January 2002 to 15 July 2004, in %

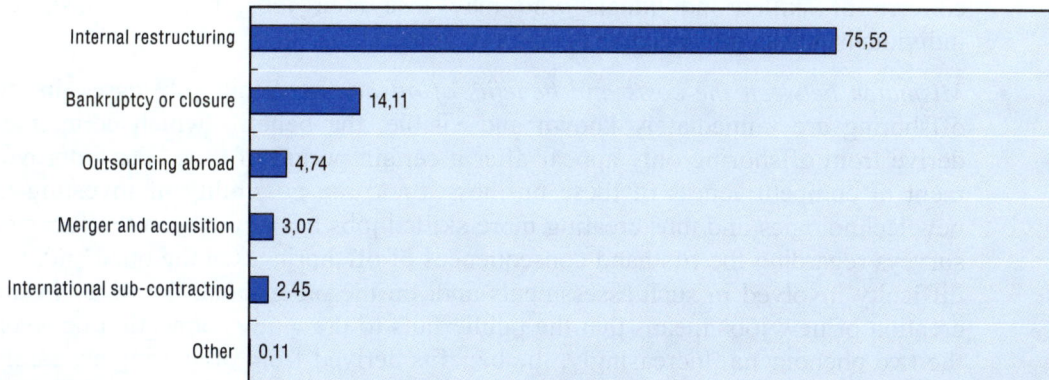

Source: EMMC/Dublin.

A number of factors could explain these concerns:

- *Underestimation of the impact.* Firstly, in the absence of official surveys and due to the complexity of the offshoring phenomenon, it is highly likely that the results of studies underestimate the true impact of offshoring. In chapter 3, as well as in Box 12, we saw how the many indirect effects were never measured, while for the direct effects only partial and indirect measurements are taken into account. . Therefore, a part of the restructuring of multinationals has relocating implications as many activities are scaled back or eliminated in a country while being strengthened in others. At the same time, the bankruptcies or closure of factories could well be indirectly linked to offshoring, if the businesses in question have failed to move offshore certain activities when they ought to have done so and were unable to stay competitive as a result.

- *Chronic high unemployment.* The reactions of those who lose their jobs as the result of offshoring might differ if in their own countries unemployment were at tolerable levels and if the average time-scale for finding a new job were lower. In such cases offshoring is not a major problem because those who lose their jobs can easily find another in a relatively short space of time.

- *Regional and sectoral impact.* Offshoring can have a more important impact on certain regions, notably when the activities that have been wiped out were at the heart of the economic life of the regions. Even so, some sectors are more affected than others, and it is this aspect that makes the effects of offshoring so conspicuous.

- *The attractiveness of new emerging countries.* The emergence of new countries that are large in size, that have manpower that is not very costly and which is becoming increasingly skilled (for example, China, India, Brazil, Russia etc,) in the context of a new division of labour and world competition, creates a sense of insecurity. If sectors that are relatively protected, such as the computer sector, are insufficiently sheltered from international competition, this will heighten the concern of skilled individuals who may lose their jobs, but also unskilled individuals whose jobs become even more vulnerable.

- *Mismatch between the costs and benefits of offshoring.* While job losses due to offshoring are immediately known and visible, the benefits which companies derive from offshoring only appear after a certain period of time. The improvement of competitiveness of these businesses and the possibility of investing in new technologies and thus creating more skilled jobs has never been the focus of surveys regarding the firsthand consequences of offshoring. On the one hand, the difficulty involved in such assessments and, on the other hand, the delay in the creation of new jobs means that the public fails to draw any connection between the two phenomena. Increasingly, the benefits derived from offshoring are rarely announced in the media and most of the time the new jobs demand new skills and are not necessarily intended for those individuals who lost their jobs due to offshoring.

Box 12. Offshoring that has an indirect impact difficult to assess

- A business trims its workforce by outsourcing certain operations to other domestic firms. Those other firms in turn subcontract operations to other companies abroad.

- When a firm offshores operations that generated exports and its exports are then carried out by offshore affiliates, other domestic firms that do not move operations abroad and that export to the same markets may trim their workforce because they are no longer competitive enough to export to those markets.

- A business will be prompted to cut its staff when its main competitors have moved operations offshore and sell goods and services in the domestic market at more-competitive prices.

- A business may replace a domestic subcontractor with a subcontractor abroad. The job losses relate to the subcontractor alone, who is not responsible for the decision.

- Businesses that receive government subsidies or contracts use many domestic sub-contractors, some of whom make use of second- or third-degree subcontractors abroad.

5.2. The reaction of public authorities: what must be avoided

To gauge political reactions when faced by offshoring, the Secretariat has distributed a brief questionnaire to member countries for which the results will be presented in Annex 5.

Faced with the concerns which have sometimes appeared to be exaggerated and which are often divorced from reality, some politicians and local officials are tempted to propose measures intended to hamper or penalise firms that move operations offshore. But these proposed measures could be counterproductive in the long term (see Section 5.3) and often in contradiction with countries' international engagement. This could probably explain why, to date, no country has taken coercive measures vis-à-vis offshoring.

The most frequently proposed measures are:

Cancelling or requiring repayment of government aid to firms that shift operations offshore

At the present time, some countries make certain types of government assistance subject to certain conditions, including a pledge to maintain employment, especially on a regional level. In such cases it is only right that companies that accept this conditional aid should comply with its rules of attribution. In contrast, if the aid were granted unconditionally, it would be illegal to ask firms that shift operations abroad to refund it.

Excluding firms that shift operations offshore from government contracts

And a policy of making firms that shift operations offshore ineligible for government contracts would conflict with the aim of limiting budget deficits by reining in on public spending. As more and more companies shifted operations offshore, the central govern-ment would have fewer suppliers from which to choose. Moreover, such a provision would run counter to the laws of competition and the country's international commit-ments.

Preventing trademarks from being moved offshore

The issue of a ban on the offshoring of trademarks warrants certain explanations. First, a trademark is a sign that a company uses to distinguish its products and services from those of other firms. It gives its owner the right to prevent third parties from using the brand. Like patents, trademarks are registered with national or regional registry offices. Within the European Union, for example, it is the Office for Harmonization in the Internal Market (OHIM), located in Spain, that is the public authority in charge of procedures for registering trademarks.

The owner of a trademark is free to choose the country or countries that can produce the products that will bear that trademark. No national legislation can prohibit the owner from making that choice. The owner's only obligation is to indicate the country of manufacture if such notification is compulsory. Procedures for indicating the country of manufacture are already well regulated at the international level.

Taxing the offshoring-related imports of companies that fail to comply with environmental rules

The proposal to tax offshoring-related imports of firms that fail to comply with environmental rules raises a number of questions. It is true that in some countries multi-national firms finding themselves subject to stiff environmental legislation decide to shift some of their activities to countries whose environmental legislation is lax or in some cases non-existent. The aim of taxing these firms' imports from countries that are non-compliant with environmental rules would be to force the firms to tailor their production systems to the country of origin rather than to move their activities offshore. But such taxes would be in violation of WTO rules.

Box 13. Offshoring within the European Union

In principle, offshoring within a unified market should not raise particular problems. In the case of the European market the main objection involves the fact that some countries use low corporate tax rates to convince a great many companies to move their operations there (see Table 5).

At the beginning of this report, it was seen that the two main reasons why businesses shift operations abroad were to cut costs and be closer to customers (Figure 3). On the other hand, tax considerations were paramount for parent companies, corporate headquarters or centres of decision-making (Figure 5).

Many examples confirm the low importance attached to corporate taxation with regard to offshoring of production. Some companies which had set up their activities in Ireland in the 90s prefer later to relocate to Eastern Europe, even though the corporate tax rate was higher than in Ireland which remained unchanged at 12.5% – the lowest in Europe. In contrast, in Eastern Europe wages are still several times lower than those of Ireland.

5.3. The cost of not moving offshore

Here the main question is to ascertain the cost to firms, consumers and national economies if businesses, for a variety of reasons, were unable to relocate or were prevented from relocating their operations abroad.

If governments were to take some of the above measures so as to limit or hamper offshoring, it could have a significant administrative cost. The State should thus be in a position to assess the state of competition regarding each product and service of firms that move operations offshore, and should take a position on the extent of immediate or future risk run by the firms so as to ascertain whether offshoring is justified or not. Such costly assessments, which to date no country has attempted, might be more difficult to carry out, given the complexity involved in detecting the multiple indirect effects of offshoring.

While to quantify them would be an extremely difficult undertaking, the main costs of not shifting operations offshore could be summarised briefly as follows:

- In the most unfavourable instances, plants could be shut down entirely. This would entail far more job losses than initially expected.

- If offshoring can preserve other jobs at home, then not offshoring cannot save them.

- Not offshoring prevents firms from consolidating their financial positions and restoring competitiveness. In such cases, firms will lack the resources they need to invest, upgrade products and services, innovate, adopt new technologies or create new, and in many cases more highly skilled, jobs.

- Consumers are denied the benefit of more-competitive prices and suffer a decline in their income.

- The fall-off in business due to impaired corporate competitiveness may trigger more lob losses than layoffs as a result of offshoring.

- The central government cannot use the resulting lost tax revenue to assist workers who lose their jobs.

- More generally, the country cannot reap the benefits of offshoring mentioned in Sections 2.4 and 4.7.

The truth of the matter is that in an economy open to international competition, there is no effective way to prevent offshoring from taking place over the long term if a business considers it vital. Apart from the costs mentioned above, to raise obstacles can have other detrimental consequences in the medium term:

- In order to avoid labour unrest or penalties, some businesses may move even faster to relocate many of its operations abroad once and for all.

- From this standpoint, many companies prefer to do all of their job creation abroad.

- Domestic businesses are weakened by a loss of competitiveness and become more vulnerable to hostile take-overs by foreign firms.

It should also be stressed that to be concerned only with the number of jobs moved offshore, without looking at the types of jobs involved, is to take a highly short-term perspective. To want to save certain jobs at all costs, via government subsidies or coercive measures, when in the context of international competition those jobs will never be competitive, could constitute improper use of public funds. In contrast, it is important to help the people involved to train for other, more highly skilled jobs and to enhance the country's attractiveness in order to promote innovation and high value added, higher-range activities, especially in services and high-tech industries.

5.4. Facilitate adjustments

Before exploring certain ways to facilitate adjustment, it would be necessary to recognise that: for many businesses, offshoring could be a vital step to take. Businesses operate in an extremely competitive economic environment which is changing fast. To remain competitive, they are compelled to adjust continuously to market conditions. For many firms, moving operations abroad is just one of many ways to adjust. For some, it could be vital to their survival, whereas for others it may be another means of preserving their competitive position. The costs of failure to offshore could be substantially greater than the costs of offshoring. It would be useful not to lose sight of the fact that offshoring is a fact of business life, and that it would be counterproductive to erect obstacles that would stand in the way of such efforts. Protectionism is wholly inappropriate, even as a short-term response to the problem of offshoring.

In this respect, offshoring adjustment is not necessarily different from the other types of structural adjustment. The main policy challenges appear, however, to be the same – regardless of the ultimate source of structural change: *i)* to create the general conditions in order to facilitate a smooth transfer of resources from declining to expanding activities; while *ii)* providing adequate assistance to those who experience adjustment costs as a result of structural change.

The policy challenge is therefore to facilitate reallocation so as to take advantage of new possibilities, while at the same time limiting adjustment costs for individuals, communities and society as a whole. By this standard, successful countries would not necessarily be characterised by stable sector patterns of production and employment or by the presence of particular industries. Instead, they would be characterised by their capacity to manage structural changes without experiencing long-lasting increase in unemployment and/or inactivity rates among working-age persons, while at the same time improving living standards as resources move into new and expanding areas. Successful countries would also ensure that the resulting gains in overall living standards are not achieved at an unacceptably high cost to adversely affected workers and community.

A number of policies may impact on the capacity of countries to adjust in the face of structural shocks. Reintegrating displaced workers is particularly challenging and involves policies to ensure sufficient work and hiring incentives, as well as employability. In addition, regulations and related policies should favour a mobile labour force and a business environment supportive of growth and job creation. In some cases, targeted policies are useful for assisting displaced workers to re-integrate into employment. However, the overriding advice to countries is to aim for good general policies to handle structural adjustments.

Measures that could facilitate structural adjustment include:

Organise continuous lifelong staffing training at the national and local levels

Various studies show that the most highly educated and best-trained people tend to keep their jobs, or that if they lose their jobs they will be able to find other ones readily. This is more evident when microdata (at the firm level) are used. *OECD Employment Outlook*[2] provides direct evidence that workers receiving training are both less likely to be laid-off and recover more rapidly in the event that they do lose their jobs. The OECD publication *"Promoting Adult Learning"* provides a wealth of material about how governments encourage the provision of cost-effective training to the adult force. The educational system must also factor in the new needs of a knowledge economy. It cannot restrict itself to conveying knowledge but must develop the abilities students need to acquire new knowledge and assimilate it rapidly throughout their entire careers. What is needed is to cultivate a desire to learn, to be creative and at the same time to have independent critical faculties and to want to take risks. If teachers are to take on such a role, their profession will have to be upgraded. The organisation of lifelong training for business personnel is one of the key issues in the quest to reduce unemployment and restore public confidence. This requires close co-operation between governments, including local authorities, social partners and businesses.

Use social policy to help those individuals who lose their employment due to offshoring

The use of social policy could be justified for those individual who have lost their employment due to offshoring and who have difficulty in finding other employment.[3] It is necessary to have a good overall employment policy framework in place which reinforces the structural adjustment capacity of labour markets and fosters high employment. Two other elements could play an important role in the co-ordinated policies: propose an adequate income support and a direct re-employment assistance to workers (*e.g.* job search assistance and selective training). The adjustment costs can be higher for workers who are elderly, have limited skills and are working in the manufacturing rather than the service sector.

Except measures mentioned above, an economic framework that favours business creation, other measures could also be taken into consideration in order to increase the adjustment capacity of the economies affected by offshoring.

---

2.   *OECD Employment Outlook 2004*, Chapter 4.

3.   An excellent analysis of these problems can be found in Chapter 1 of the *OECD Employment Outlook 2005,* entitled "Trade Adjustment Costs in OECD Labour Markets".

Invite multinational firms to comply with labour standards and discuss their offshoring plans with employees

Good management by multinational enterprises of employment and industrial relations can make an important contribution to addressing concerns about relocation abroad. Public policies to promote responsible business conduct are identified in the *OECD Policy Framework for Investment* and include effective enforcement of labour and other relevant laws, clear communication on expected business conduct to enterprises, supporting private sector initiatives for corporate responsibility, and active participation in international instruments such as the *ILO Tripartite Declaration of Principles concerning Multinational Enterprises and Social Policies and the OECD Guidelines for Multinational Enterprises*.

The OECD Guidelines are detailed recommendations to multinational enterprises by 39 adhering governments in all major areas of business ethics. In the area of employment and industrial relation, they cover all internationally recognised core labour standards. They also provide that in particular in the case of the closure of an entity involving collective lay-offs or dismissals, enterprises should provide reasonable notice to representatives of their employees and co-operate with the employee representatives and appropriate governmental authorities so as to mitigate to the maximum extent practicable adverse effects, and that in the context of bona fide negotiations, enterprises should not threaten to transfer the whole or part of an operating unit from the country concerned in other countries in order to influence unfairly those negotiations. Adhering governments have established a unique mechanism to implement the Guidelines – the National Contact Points and the "specific instances" facility by which they offer their good offices to help the parties to resolve disputes and build trust.

Expand research and development efforts and innovation

In a context of a globalised economy and keen international competition, ongoing innovation alone can limit the need for offshoring. More particularly, technological innovation can lead to the development of new products and services and new manufacturing processes, but it entails a sustained research effort. It must enable the creation of centres of excellence and close co-operation between the public and private sectors and between industry and academia. Research is vital not just for developing new technologies, innovating and thus contributing to growth and new job creation, but also for making it possible to absorb and assimilate advanced technologies that are developed abroad.

To remain competitive, businesses need to master new technologies and focus on the production of goods and services that are high-end or high-value added. Activities with a strong technological content do not merely encompass the traditional high-tech sectors but also others, for high-tech niches are to be found in all sectors. The non-stop breakthroughs in these niche categories can create or maintain many jobs. But by the same token this calls for a major effort in terms of R&D and the ongoing training of personnel. This effort to promote top-of-the-line specialisation and a knowledge-based economy ought not to exclude the small and medium-sized companies that are less well-equipped to innovate or train their staffs.

Make science and technology appealing once again

In many OECD countries, one can observe a lack of interest on the part of young people for the engineering and scientific professions and, more generally, for the culture of technology. Look no further than India, which has more than 700 000 engineers, and where approximately 80 000 engineers are trained every year. The dearth of scientists and engineers can create serious problems for R&D and the technological innovation of companies. Such a situation can promote certain types of relocation toward countries where manpower is better trained and cheaper. In other cases, businesses will have no option but to rely on foreign scientists and engineers.

Abolish barriers to trade and investment

Job losses due to offshoring could be offset by the growth of exports intended for the countries where offshoring has occurred. A vertical specialisation between parent companies and subsidiaries can favour complementarities in their interactions. More particularly, in the case of emerging countries the steady increase in revenue creates a supplementary demand for imports which could be met by the countries that are the source of offshoring.

Improve quantitative cost/benefit assessments of offshoring

At the present time knowledge of the scale of the phenomenon of offshoring, and of its anticipated social costs and benefits, is still patchy and inadequate. A better grasp of the subject will not in itself restore confidence, but it will provide better guidance with regard to the policies to be followed and will ensure policy consistency both in the short and long terms.

CONCLUSIONS

The foregoing analysis has demonstrated the complexity of the phenomenon of offshoring while illustrating the difficulties involved in measuring its impact on employment. In this regard, to evaluate offshoring's positive and negative effects on employment, three difficulties can be distinguished. The first of these involves the lack of regular, official surveys in most of the OECD countries. The data needed for these evaluations cannot be taken from other existing data, either because those data are confidential and thus not accessible, or because the data are not collected by a large number of countries (*e.g.* intra-firm trade). Even when confidential data by firm or by establishment can be accessed, it is very difficult to gauge the indirect employment effects that offshoring firms may have on their competitors that do not engage in offshoring, as well as on their own subcontractors.

The second difficulty concerns the measurement of positive effects. It is fairly difficult to quantify the various benefits accruing to a firm from the enhanced competitiveness it derives from outsourcing, and it is especially difficult to apportion them among the various parties involved: consumers, shareholders and employees of the firm.

Lastly, the third difficulty stems from the need to attribute the positive and negative effects of offshoring over a country's economy as a whole, and then to translate them in terms of jobs. Finding suitable solutions to all these evaluation difficulties will no doubt be an extremely ambitious undertaking. Nevertheless, whatever the outcome of these quantitative measures, the most important consideration lies in the realm of policy.

There is every reason to believe that offshoring will continue. It may gather pace, especially if growth in the emerging countries remains far greater than in the OECD countries, if their labour force becomes increasingly skilled and if the bulk of future demand lies in those emerging countries. Moreover, the rapid computerisation of services, their industrialisation and automation, along with their greater opening to global trade, may further foster the offshoring of services. Such a development could, however, raise a number of limitations (see Sections 2.4 and 2.5.3), especially because of the sharp rise in the wages of the more highly skilled workers in the emerging countries, a certain scarcity in that labour force which is already apparent.

It would therefore be counterproductive to throw up obstacles, which could be only temporary, to the offshoring of activities that are not crucial to a country's future. Rather, conditions should be created that are conducive to keeping the most innovative high-tech or high-value added activities at home. Sight should not be lost of the fact that if, in the medium term, market growth, demand for goods and services, and know-how shift to the emerging countries, the cause for concern would no longer be offshoring, but rather the trend for businesses to create the bulk of new jobs in those emerging countries and not within the OECD area. Conversely, the growth of the emerging countries holds out enormous opportunities for the exports of the OECD countries, which must therefore redouble their efforts to ensure a satisfactory outcome for the multilateral negotiations now underway at the WTO.

Annex 1

Simultaneous decline in production, employment and exports and growth in imports, by sector, in the manufacturing sector

- **France**
- **Germany**
- **Japan**
- **United Kingdom**

Table 1. FRANCE: Simultaneous decline in production, employment and exports and growth in imports, by sector, in the manufacturing sector

ISIC3	Industry	Growth of imports (%) 1995/2004			Decline in employment 1995/02	Decline in production 1995/02	Decline in exports		Main low-wage economies source of imports[1]
		Total	From OECD	From non-OECD			1995/03	1998/03	
15 to 16	Food products, beverages and tobacco	25	24	29					Brazil (8)
17 to 19	Textiles, clothing, leather and footwear	45	24	77	X	X			China (3), Turkey (7), India (9)
20	Wood and products of wood and cork	57	51	76	X				China (8), Brazil (9)
21 to 22	Paper, printing and publishing	15	14	34	X				
23	Coke, refined petroleum products and nuclear fuel	138	88	268	X				Russia (1), OPEP (5), Eastern Europe
24	Chemicals and chemical products	63	60	119					-
2423	Pharmaceuticals	160	160	156					
25	Rubber and plastics products	58	52	136					China (7), Eastern Europe
26	Other non-metallic mineral products	41	35	177	X				China (6), Eastern Europe
27	Basic metals	30	30	32	X				Chile (6)
271	Iron and steel	50	48	79	n.a.	n.a.			South Africa (9)
272	Non-ferrous metals	8	5	20	n.a.	n.a.	X	X	Chile (2), Russia (10)
28	Fabricated metal products	67	58	190					China (5), Eastern Europe
29	Machinery and equipment, n.e.c.	48	40	322	X				China (8), Eastern Europe
30	Office, accounting and computing machinery	35	5	191	X	X	X	X	China (1), Chinese Taipei (8), Singapore (10), Eastern Europe
31	Electrical machinery and apparatus, n.e.c.	70	51	216					China (3), Eastern Europe
32	Radio, television and communication equipment	71	48	139					China (1), Singapore (8), Malaysia (10), Eastern Europe
33	Medical, precision and opt. instruments, watches and clocks	79	77	92					China (6)
34	Motor vehicles	78	78	82					Turkey (7), Eastern Europe
35	Other transport equipment	100	106	21					
353	Aircraft and spacecraft	112	114	51					-
36 to 37	Manufacturing n.e.c.	71	52	129					China (1), Poland (8)

1. Figures in brackets refer to the economies' ranks among all countries of origin of imports for the selected industry.

Source: OECD, Bilateral Trade and STAN databases.

Table 2. GERMANY: Simultaneous decline in production, employment and exports and growth in imports, by sector, in the manufacturing sector

ISIC3	Industry	Growth of imports (%) 1995/2004			Decline in employment 1995/02	Decline in production 1995/02	Decline in exports 1995/03	1998/03	Main low-wage economies source of imports[1]
		Total	From OECD	From non-OECD					
15 to 16	Food products, beverages and tobacco	16	13	39	X				Poland (8), Brazil (10)
17 to 19	Textiles, clothing, leather and footwear	-4	-21	28	X	X			China (2), Turkey (3), India (5), Poland (6), Czech Rep. (10)
20	Wood and products of wood and cork	-19	-32	32	X	X			Poland (2), China (5), Czech Rep. (7), Russia (8)
21 to 22	Paper, printing and publishing	17	16	48	X				-
23	Coke, refined petroleum products and nuclear fuel	88	78	170	X				Russia (3), China (5), Poland (6)
24	Chemicals and chemical products	83	83	102	X				-
2423	Pharmaceuticals	250	254	179	n.a.	n.a.			-
25	Rubber and plastics products	37	31	105	X				Czech Rep. (5), China (8)
26	Other non-metallic mineral products	-11	-16	68	X	X			China (4), Czech Rep. (6), Poland (9)
27	Basic metals	19	19	21	X				Russia (6)
271	Iron and steel	17	16	35	n.a.	n.a.			Poland (9)
272	Non-ferrous metals	21	22	16	n.a.	n.a.			Russia (1)
28	Fabricated metal products	31	24	81	X				China (2), Czech Rep. (3), Poland (8)
29	Machinery and equipment, n.e.c.	48	41	159	X				Czech Rep. (5), China (8)
30	Office, accounting and computing machinery	56	18	179	X				China (1), Chinese Taipei (8), Singapore (9), Malaysia (10)
31	Electrical machinery and apparatus, n.e.c.	62	43	192	X				China (1), Czech Rep. (3), Hungary (8)
32	Radio, television and communication equipment	100	56	265	X				China (1), Singapore (5), Hungary (6), Malaysia (8), Chinese Taipei (9)
33	Medical, precision and opt. instruments, watches and clocks	67	64	87	X				China (5), Hungary (9), Eastern Europe
34	Motor vehicles	85	82	233					Hungary (7), Slovak Rep. (8)
35	Other transport equipment	125	122	168	X				Poland (8)
353	Aircraft and spacecraft	143	143	142	n.a.	n.a.			-
36 to 37	Manufacturing n.e.c.	27	9	75	X				China (1), Poland (2), Czech Rep. (4)

1. Figures in brackets refer to the economies' ranks among all countries of origin of imports for the selected industry.

Source: OECD, Bilateral Trade and STAN databases.

Table 3. JAPAN: Simultaneous decline in production, employment and exports and growth in imports, by sector, in the manufacturing sector

ISIC3	Industry	Growth of imports (%) 1995/2004			Decline in employment 1995/03	Decline in production 1995/03	Decline in exports		Main low-wage economies source of imports[1]
		Total	From OECD	From non-OECD			1995/03	1998/03	
15 to 16	Food products, beverages and tobacco	-4	-3	-5	X	X		X	China (2), Thailand (4)
17 to 19	Textiles, clothing, leather and footwear	10	-44	39	X	X		X	China (1), Indonesia (7), Thailand (8)
20	Wood and products of wood and cork	-13	-34	10	X	X	X		China (1), Indonesia (2), Malaysia (4)
21 to 22	Paper, printing and publishing	-15	-32	82	X	X			China (3), Indonesia (4)
23	Coke, refined petroleum products and nuclear fuel	71	83	66	X		X		OPEC (1), China (4), Indonesia (5)
24	Chemicals and chemical products	44	27	111	X	X			China (3), Chinese Taipei (10)
2423	Pharmaceuticals	37	30	124					China (10)
25	Rubber and plastics products	82	18	170	X	X			China (1), Thailand (4), Chinese Taipei (5)
26	Other non-metallic mineral products	36	-1	92	X	X			China (1), Thailand (3)
27	Basic metals	-1	-19	16	X	X			China (1), South Africa (2), Russia (3)
271	Iron and steel	-4	-19	10	X	X			China (2), South Africa (4), Chinese Taipei (5)
272	Non-ferrous metals	0	-19	19	X	X			South Africa (1), Russia (2), China (4), Indonesia (5)
28	Fabricated metal products	64	7	160	X	X		X	China (1), Thailand (4), Chinese Taipei (5)
29	Machinery and equipment, n.e.c.	66	24	229	X	X			China (1), Thailand (5), Chinese Taipei (6)
30	Office, accounting and computing machinery	67	-15	141	X	X	X		China (1), Chinese Taipei (3), Philippines (5)
31	Electrical machinery and apparatus, n.e.c.	83	11	160	X	X		X	China (1), Philippines (3), Thailand (5)
32	Radio, television and communication equipment	80	-6	222	X	X			China (1), Taipei (2), Malaysia (5), Philippines (6)
33	Medical, precision and opt. instruments, watches and clocks	87	64	173	X	X			China (2), Thailand (6), Chinese Taipei (7)
34	Motor vehicles	8	-10	602	X				South Africa (4), China (5)
35	Other transport equipment	81	76	116				X	China (2), Chinese Taipei (3)
353	Aircraft and spacecraft	89	87	461				X	Singapore (6), Malaysia (8)
36 to 37	Manufacturing n.e.c.	4	-20	22	X	X		X	China (1), Thailand (3), India (5), Chinese Taipei (6)

1. Figures in brackets refer to the economies' ranks among all countries of origin of imports for the selected industry.

Source: OECD, Bilateral Trade and STAN databases.

Table 4. UNITED KINGDOM: Simultaneous decline in production, employment and exports and growth in imports, by sector, in the manufacturing sector

ISIC3	Industry	Growth of imports (%) 1995/2004			Decline in employment 1995/03	Decline in production 1995/03	Decline in exports 1995/03	Decline in exports 1998/03	Main low-wage economies source of imports[1]
		Total	From OECD	From non-OECD					
15 to 16	Food products, beverages and tobacco	65	68	49	X	X	X	X	-
17 to 19	Textiles, clothing, leather and footwear	89	59	126	X				China (2), Turkey (4), India (6), Hong Kong, China (10)
20	Wood and products of wood and cork	63	57	81	X				Latvia (3), China (4), Brazil (8)
21 to 22	Paper, printing and publishing	18	14	77	X	21 only	21 only	21 only	China (10)
23	Coke, refined petroleum products and nuclear fuel	266	146	536					OPEC (1), Russia (2), Latvia (7)
24	Chemicals and chemical products	76	70	260	X				Singapore (7)
2423	Pharmaceuticals	244	221	1226	X^2				-
25	Rubber and plastics products	70	60	132	X		X		China (3)
26	Other non-metallic mineral products	89	71	264	X		X	X	China (5), Turkey (7)
27	Basic metals	4	10	-13		X	X	X	Russia (6), South Africa (10)
271	Iron and steel	41	31	151	X^2	X^2	X	X	Russia (8), South Africa (9), Turkey (10)
272	Non-ferrous metals	-17	-5	-39	X^2	X^2	X	X	Russia (4), South Africa (8)
28	Fabricated metal products	90	72	182	X	X			China (2), Chinese Taipei (7), India (10)
29	Machinery and equipment, n.e.c.	50	41	239	X	X			China (5)
30	Office, accounting and computing machinery	43	28	118	X	X	X	X	China (5), Taipei (7), Chinese Malaysia (8), Singapore (10)
31	Electrical machinery and apparatus, n.e.c.	40	31	108	X	X			China (2), Eastern Europe
32	Radio, television and communication equipment	71	82	73	X	X		X	China (4), Hungary (8), Eastern Europe
33	Medical, precision and opt. instruments, watches and clocks	89	100	55	X				China (8)
34	Motor vehicles	102	98	534	X				-
35	Other transport equipment	122	295	86	X				China (10)
353	Aircraft and spacecraft	135	402	63	X^2				OPEC (8)
36 to 37	Manufacturing n.e.c.	147	149	191					China (1), India (10)

1. Figures in brackets refer to the economies' ranks among all countries of origin of imports for the selected industry.

2. 1995-2002.

Source: OECD, Bilateral Trade and STAN databases.

Annex 2

Problems encountered while analysing data in Section 4.6.

Industry definition

We noticed that data for the following industries were merged with the upper-level related industries in many countries:

9 → Chemical

13 → Iron & steel

22 → Building & repairing of ships & boats

26 → Production, collection and distribution of electricity

Country-specific status is shown below:

1. Austria

- 9 includes Pharmaceuticals (10)
- 13 includes Non-ferrous metals (14)
- 22 includes Aircraft & spacecraft (23) and Railroad equipment & transport equipment n.e.c. (24)
- 26 includes Manufacture of gas (27) and Steam and hot water supply (28)

2. Belgium

- 9 includes Pharmaceuticals (10)
- 13 includes Non-ferrous metals (14)
- 22 includes Aircraft & spacecraft (23) and Railroad equipment & transport equipment n.e.c. (24)
- 26 includes Manufacture of gas and Steam and hot water supply (28)

3. Denmark

- 23 Aircraft & spacecraft includes Railroad equipment & transport equipment n.e.c. (24)

4. Finland

- 9 includes Pharmaceuticals (10)
- 13 includes Non-ferrous metals (14)
- 22 includes Aircraft & spacecraft (23) and Railroad equipment & transport equipment n.e.c. (24)
- 26 includes Manufacture of gas (27) and Steam and hot water supply (28)

5. France

- 9 includes Pharmaceuticals (10)
- 13 includes Non-ferrous metals (14)
- 22 includes Aircraft & spacecraft (23) and Railroad equipment & transport equipment n.e.c. (24)
- 26 includes Manufacture of gas (27) and Steam and hot water supply (28)

6. Germany

- 9 includes Pharmaceuticals (10)
- 13 includes Non-ferrous metals (14)
- 22 includes Aircraft & spacecraft (23) and Railroad equipment & transport equipment n.e.c. (24)
- 26 includes Manufacture of gas (27) and Steam and hot water supply (28)

7. Greece

- 9 includes Pharmaceuticals (10)
- 13 includes Non-ferrous metals (14)
- 22 includes Aircraft & spacecraft (23) and Railroad equipment & transport equipment n.e.c. (24)
- 26 includes Manufacture of gas (27) and Steam and hot water supply (28)

8. Italy

- 9 includes Pharmaceuticals (10)
- 13 includes Non-ferrous metals (14)
- 22 includes Aircraft & spacecraft (23) and Railroad equipment & transport equipment n.e.c. (24)
- 26 includes Manufacture of gas (27) and Steam and hot water supply (28)

9. Japan and 10. Korea

No merging.

11. Norvège

In 1997

Mining and quarrying (energy) (2) includes Mining and quarrying (non-energy) (3)

Manufacture of gas; distribution of gaseous fuels through mains (27), Steam and hot water supply (28) and Collection, purification and distribution of water (29) are missing. Might be merged with (26).

Land transport; transport via pipelines (33) might include Water transport (34), Air transport (35) and Supporting and auxiliary transport activities; activities of travel agencies (36)

In 2001

- 9 includes Pharmaceuticals (10)
- 13 includes Non-ferrous metals (14)
- 22 includes Aircraft & spacecraft (23) and Railroad equipment & transport equipment n.e.c. (24)
- 26 includes Manufacture of gas (27) and Steam and hot water supply (28)

12. Spain

- 9 includes Pharmaceuticals (10)
- 13 includes Non-ferrous metals (14)
- 22 includes Aircraft & spacecraft (23) and Railroad equipment & transport equipment n.e.c. (24)
- 27 includes Steam and hot water supply (28)
- Total of 27 is zero which might mean that 27 and 28 are included in 26

13. Sweden

- 9 includes Pharmaceuticals (10)
- 13 includes Non-ferrous metals (14)
- 22 includes Aircraft & spacecraft (23) and Railroad equipment & transport equipment n.e.c. (24)
- 26 includes Manufacture of gas (27) and Steam and hot water supply (28)

14. United States

In 1995

- 28 includes Sewage and refuse disposal, sanitation and similar activities (9000)

- 31 includes Manufacture of rubber tyres and tubes; retreading and rebuilding of rubber tyres (2511), part of other human health activities (8519)

- 40 includes part of Building completion (4540), part of Sewage and refuse disposal, sanitation and similar activities (9000).

- 42 includes Technical testing and analysis (7422) and Market research and public opinion polling (7413).

- 43 includes part of Non-scheduled air transport (6220), Publishing of books, brochures and other publications (2211), part of Printing (2221), News agency activity (9220), part of Dramatic arts, music and other arts activities (9214).

- 47 includes Car washes (5020), Other business activities n.e.c. (7499), Non-scheduled air transport (6220).

The import of water transport is defined as the foreign port price, international freight, insurance and customs duty in the US table. In order to keep the consistency with other country's positive imports, the imports of water transport sector are moved to exports.

In 2000

- Collection, purification and distribution of water (29) includes Steam and hot water supply (28)

In order to make comparable data for all the countries we have used aggregated data for certain industries. Aggregation of industries has been based on industry data as well data available in input-output tables. Aggregation has been done it the following manner:

Czech Republic and Poland: GFCF deflator (GFCFK) for 1995 has missing values. Aggregate data for "Mining and Quarrying" have been used in the analysis rather than taking "Mining and Quarrying (energy)" and "Mining and Quarrying (non-energy)" (industry codes 2 & 3 respectively) separately.

Aggregate data for "Chemicals" (9) and "Pharmaceuticals" (10) have been used in the analysis rather than taking Chemicals and Pharmaceuticals separately.

Aggregate data for "Iron & steel" (13), "Non-ferrous metals" (14), and "Fabricated metal products, except machinery & equipment" (15) have been used in the analysis.

Aggregate data for "Office, accounting & computing machinery" (17), "Electrical machinery & apparatus, nec" (18), "Radio, television & communication equipment" (19) and "Medical, precision & optical instruments" (20) have been used in the analysis.

Aggregate data for "Motor vehicles, trailers & semi-trailers" (21), "Building & repairing of ships & boats" (22), "Aircraft & spacecraft" (23), and "Railroad equipment & transport equipment n.e.c." (24) have been used in the analysis.

Aggregate data have been used in the analysis in respect of the following sectors:

- Production, collection and distribution of electricity (26), Manufacture of gas; distribution of gaseous fuels through mains (27), Steam and hot water supply (28), and Collection, purification and distribution of water (29);

- Land transport; transport via pipelines (33), Water transport (34), Air transport (35), Supporting and auxiliary transport activities; activities of travel agencies (36), and Post & telecommunications (37) have been used in the analysis.

- Real estate activities (39), Renting of machinery & equipment (40), Computer & related activities (41), Research & development (42), and Other business activities (43).

Annex 3

Index of outsourcing abroad and growth of employment

- **Australia**
- **Austria**
- **Belgium**
- **Canada**
- **Czech Republic**
- **Denmark**
- **Finland**
- **Germany**
- **Greece**
- **Hungary**
- **Italy**
- **Japan**
- **Korea**
- **Netherlands**
- **Norway**
- **Poland**
- **Portugal**
- **Slovak Republic**
- **Spain**
- **Sweden**
- **United Kingdom**

Australia - Index of outsourcing of goods abroad by the goods and service industries

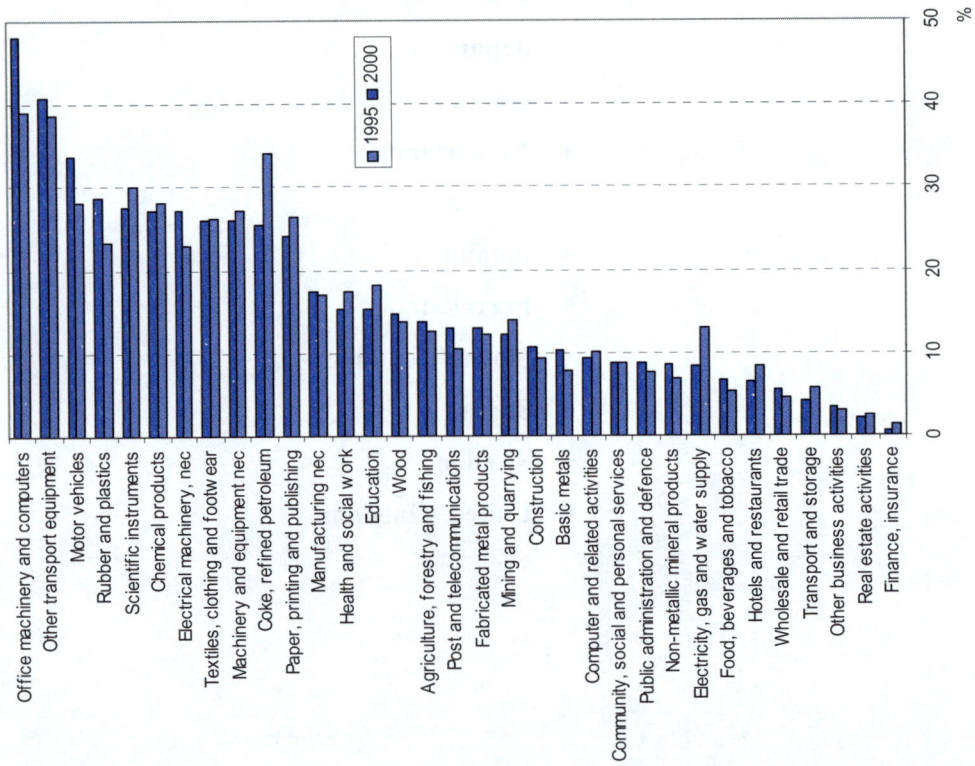

Source: OECD, Input-Output database. StatLink: http://dx.doi.org/10.1787/311545378712

Australia - Growth of employment 1995-2000

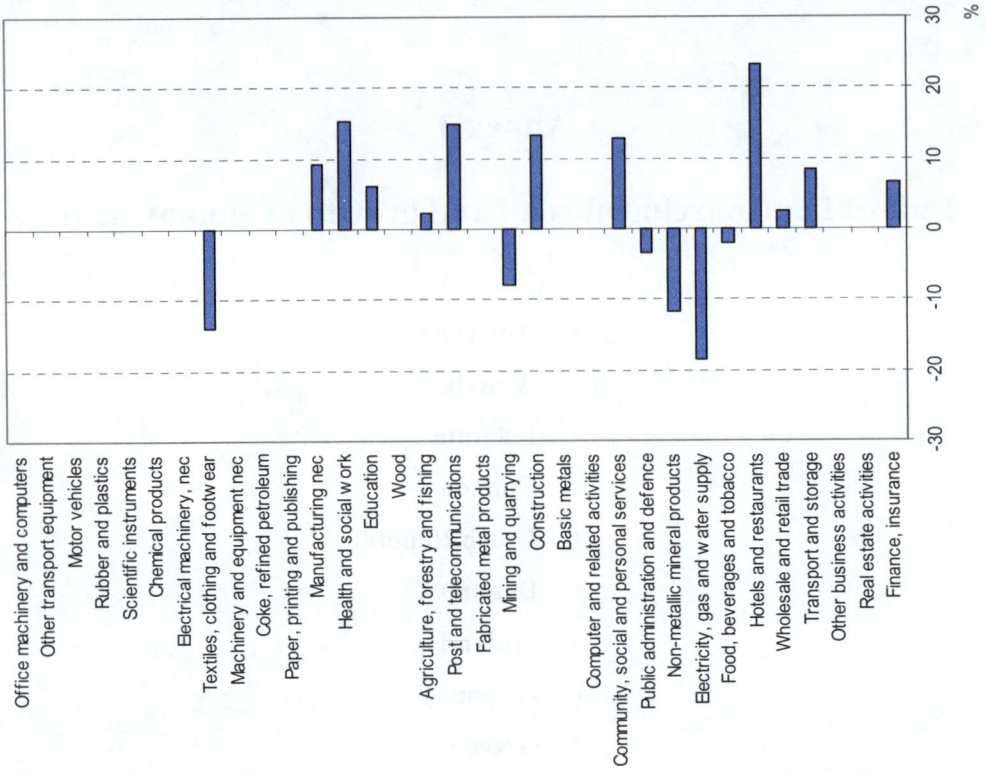

Source: OECD, STAN database. StatLink: http://dx.doi.org/10.1787/441624743357

Australia – Index of outsourcing of services abroad by the goods and service industries

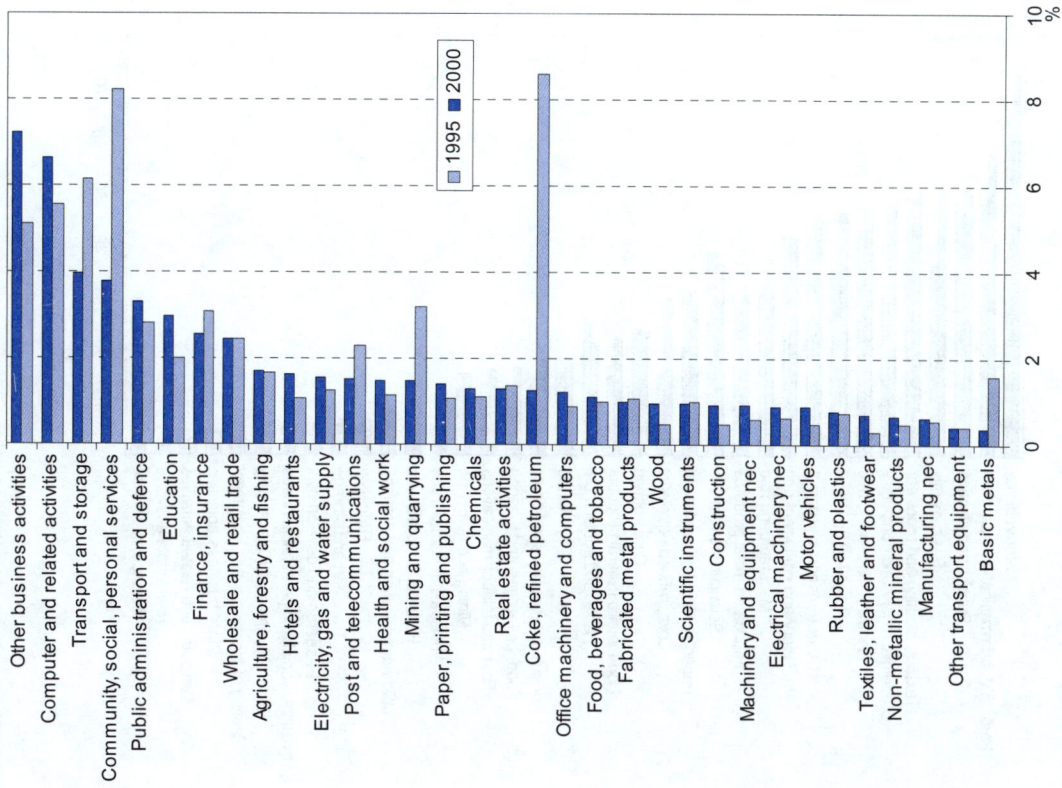

Australia – Growth of employment 1995-2000

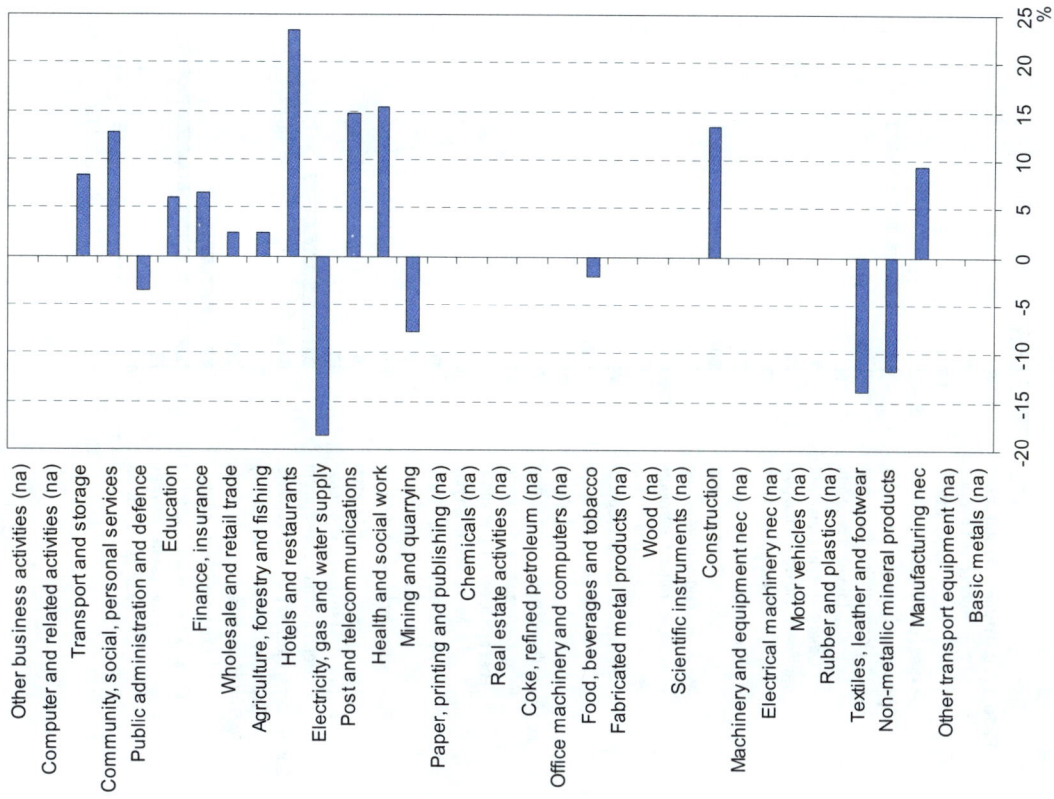

Source: OECD, Input-Output database. *StatLink:* http://dx.doi.org/10.1787/655105844768

Source: OECD, STAN database. *StatLink:* http://dx.doi.org/10.1787/653657612262

Austria - Index of outsourcing of goods abroad by the goods and service industries

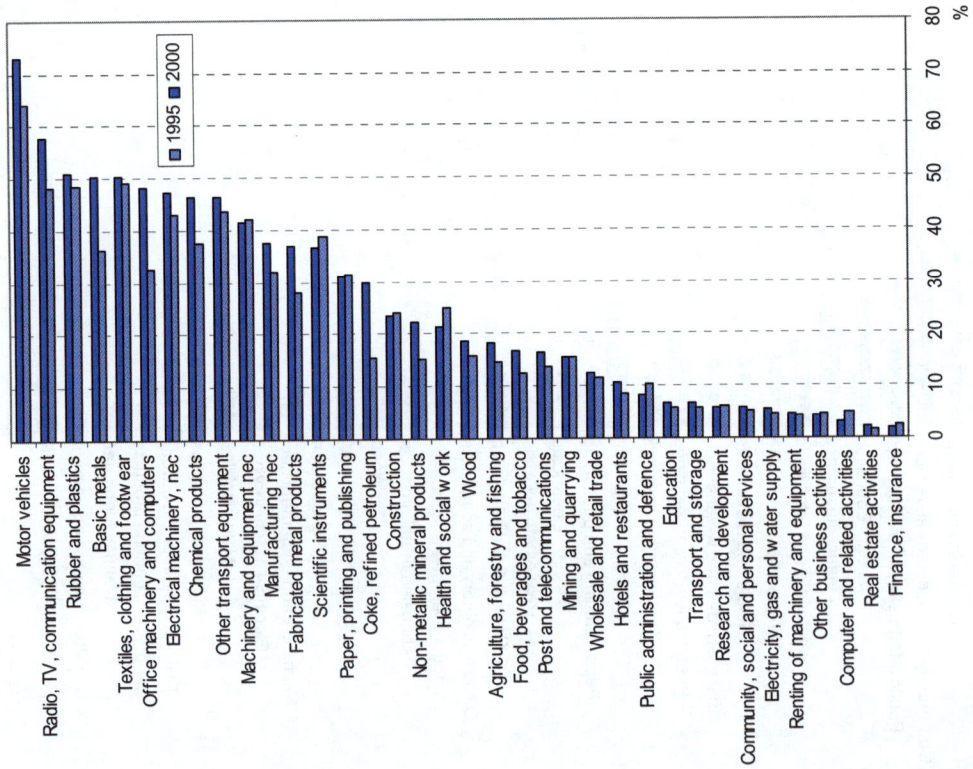

Source: OECD, Input-Output database. *StatLink:* http://dx.doi.org/10.1787/554123867613

Austria - Growth of employment 1995-2000

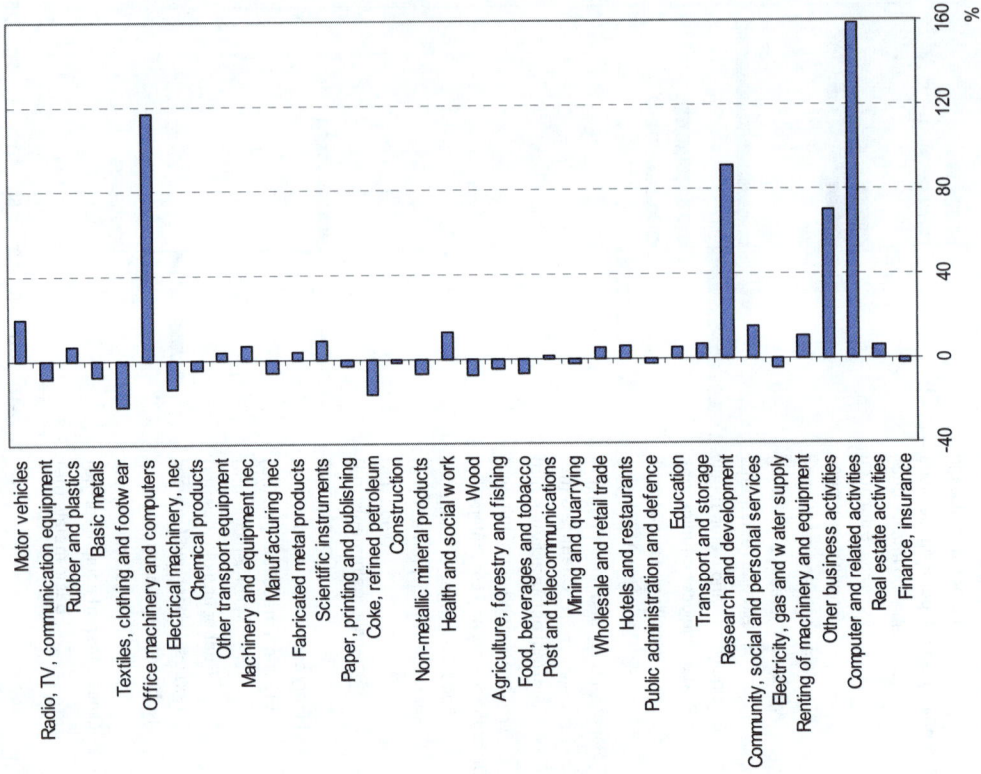

Source: OECD, STAN database. *StatLink:* http://dx.doi.org/10.1787/716807312030

Austria - Index of outsourcing of services abroad by the goods and service industries

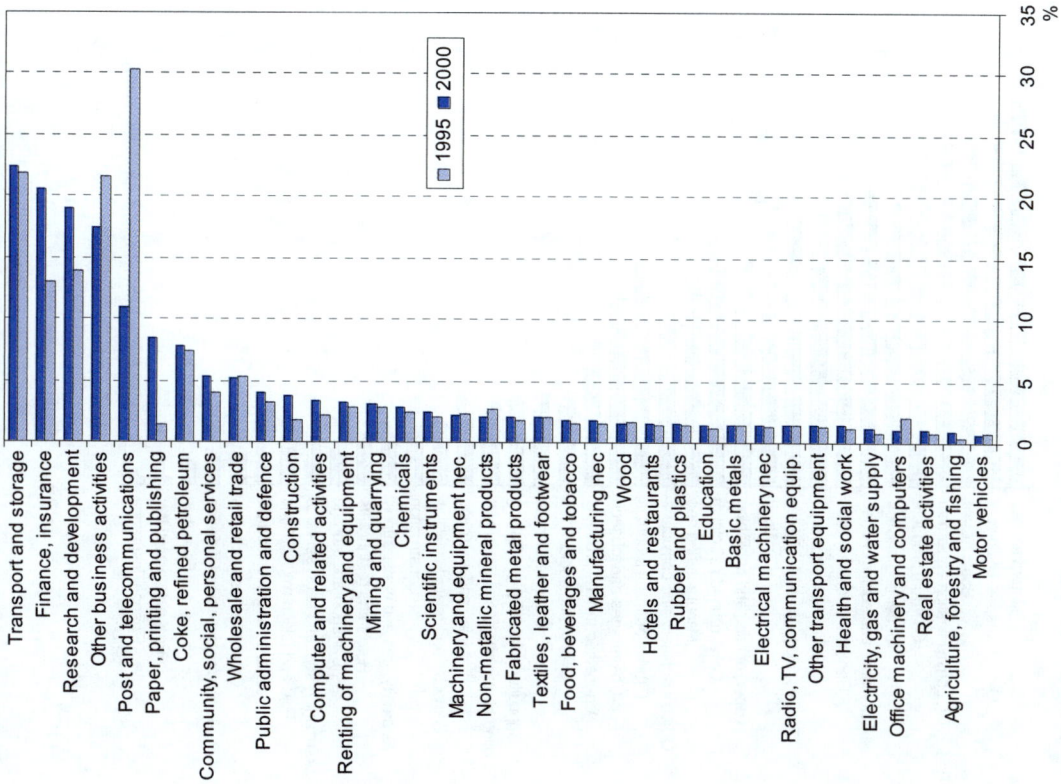

Source: OECD, Input-Output database. *StatLink:* http://dx.doi.org/10.1787/715755832346

Austria - Growth of employment 1995-2000

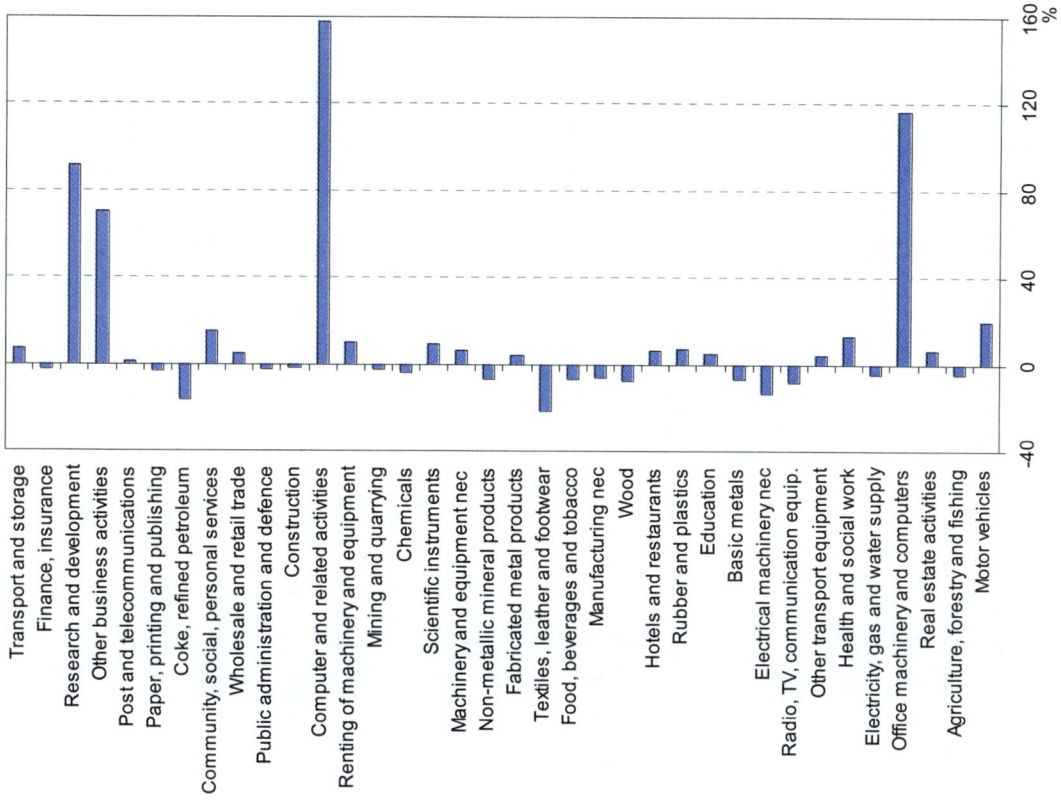

Source: OECD, STAN database. *StatLink:* http://dx.doi.org/10.1787/780115054588

Belgium - Index of outsourcing of goods abroad by the goods and service industries

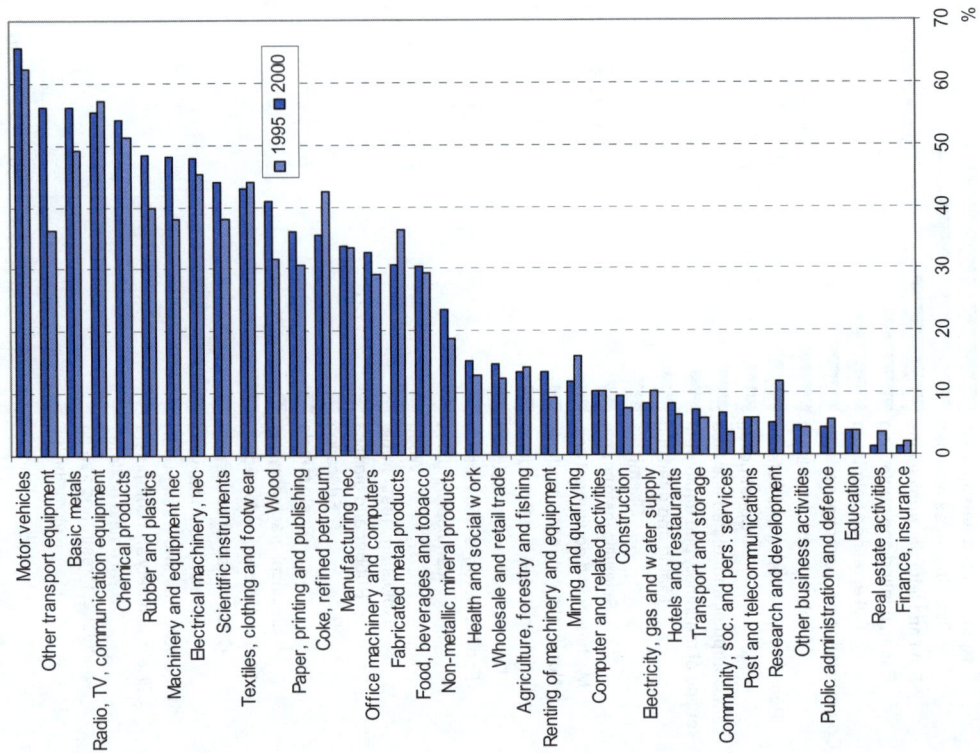

Source: OECD, Input-Output database. StatLink: http://dx.doi.org/10.1787/100842525538

Belgium - Growth of employment 1995-2000

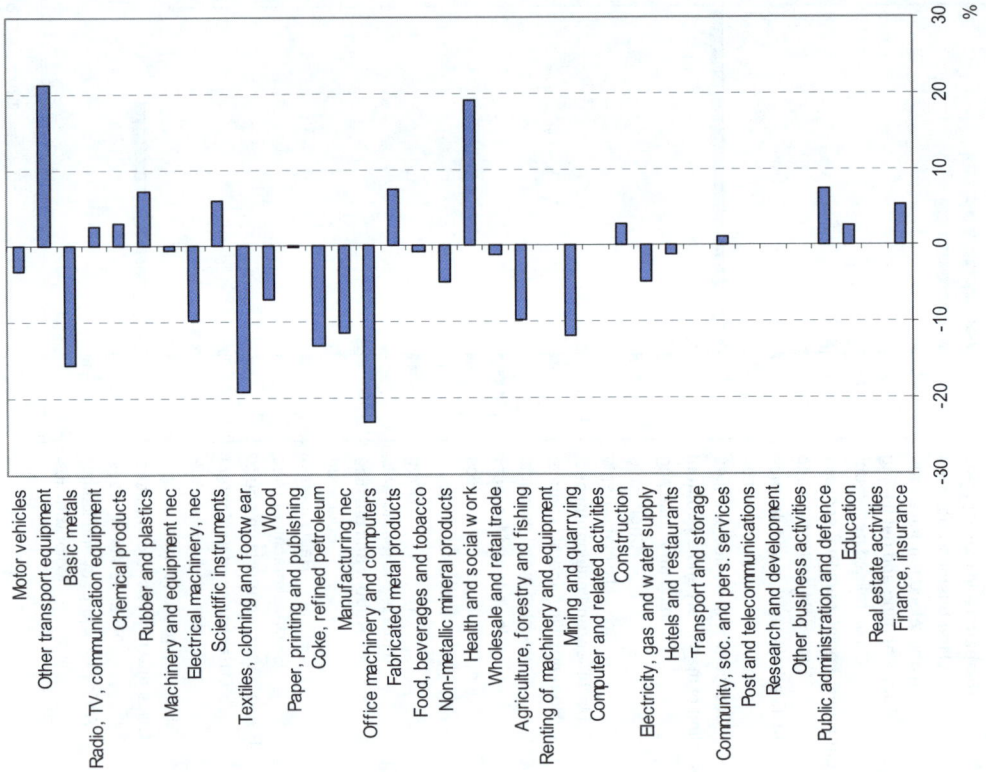

Source: OECD, STAN database. StatLink: http://dx.doi.org/10.1787/258348877603

Belgium - Index of outsourcing of services abroad by the goods and service industries

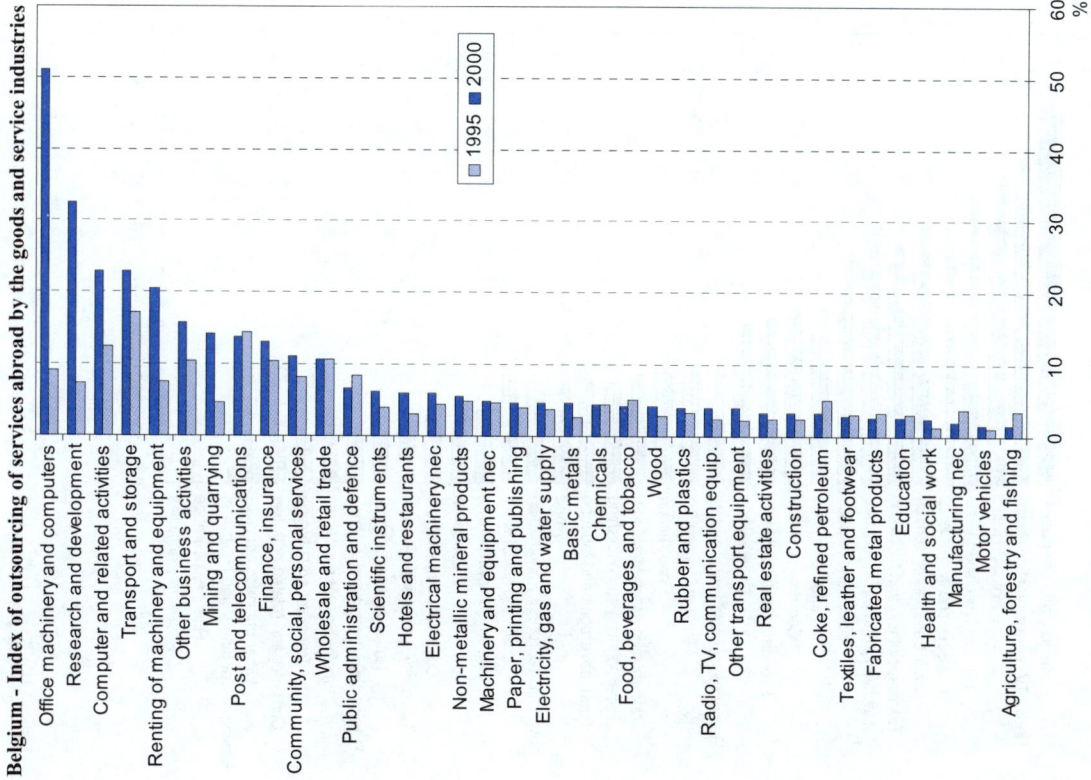

Source: OECD, Input-Output database. *StatLink:* http://dx.doi.org/10.1787/123618000756

Belgium - Growth of employment 1995-2000

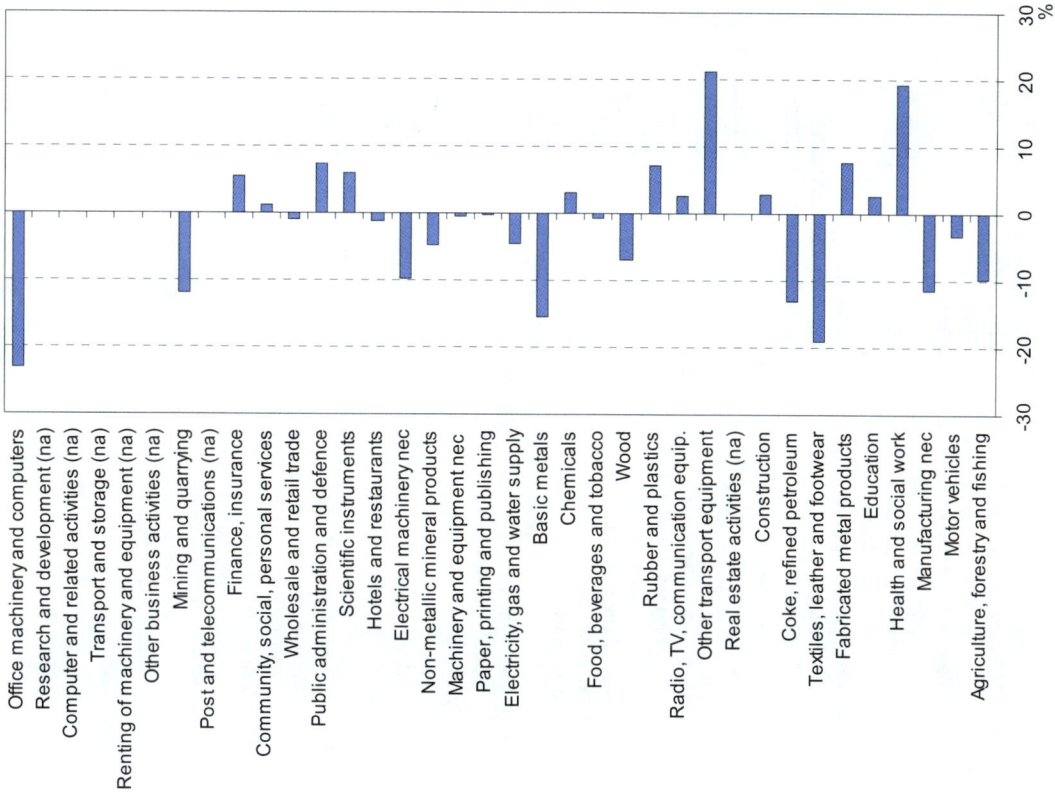

Source: OECD, STAN database. *StatLink:* http://dx.doi.org/10.1787/735453152121

Canada - Index of outsourcing of goods abroad by the goods and service industries

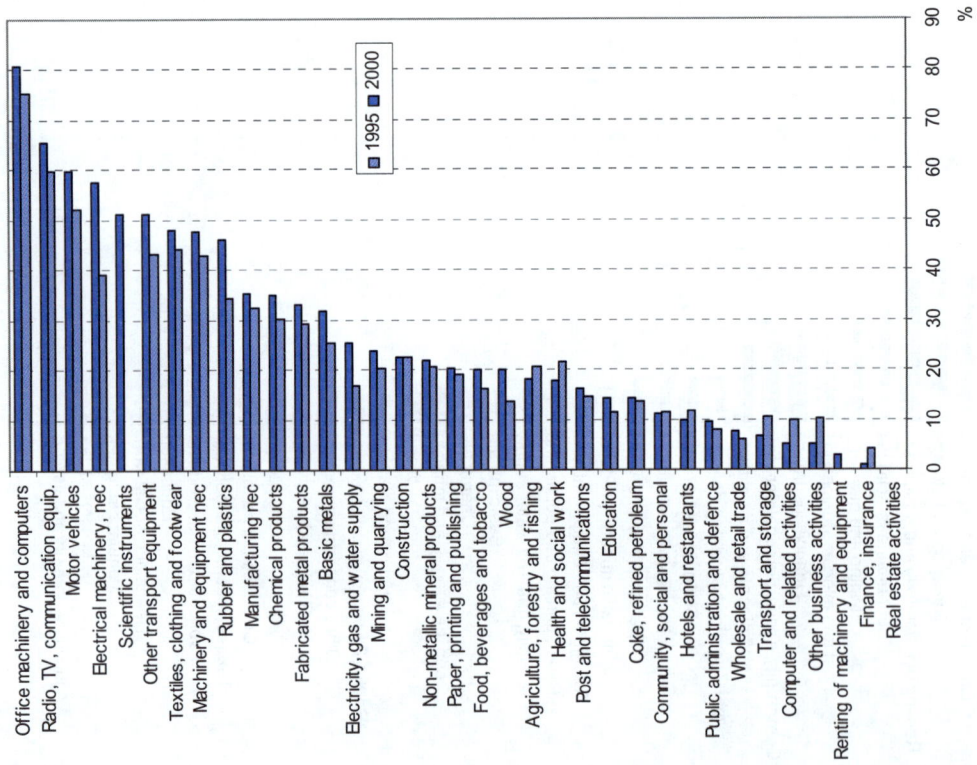

Source: OECD, Input-Output database. StatLink: http://dx.doi.org/10.1787/651263433516

Canada - Growth of employment 1995-2000

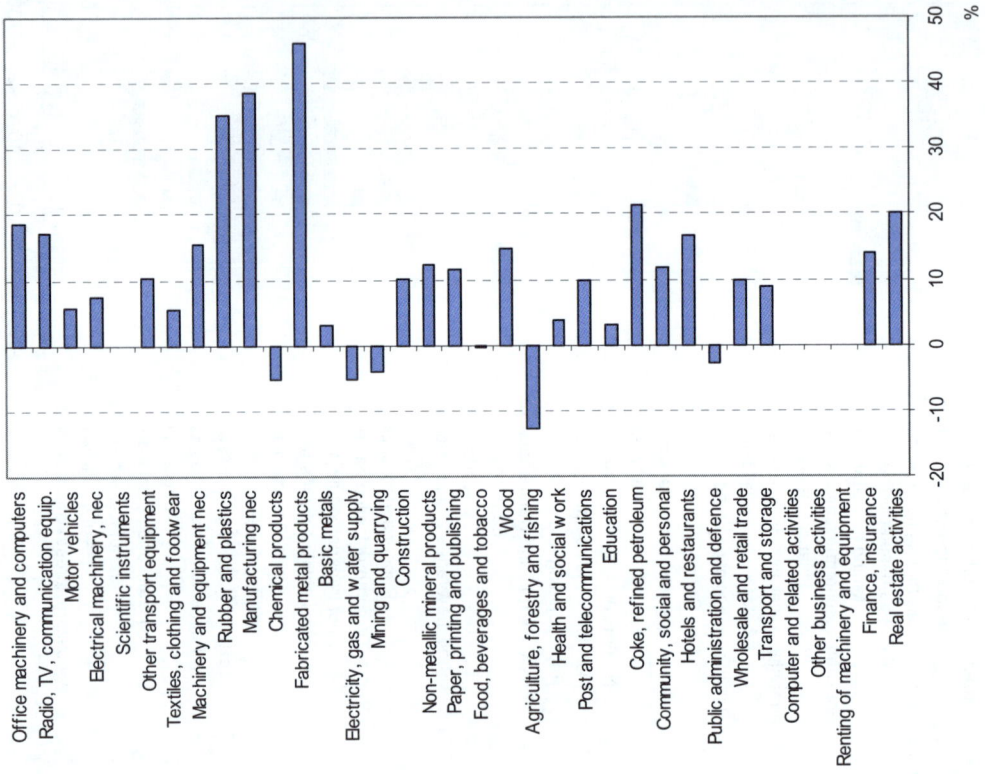

Source: OECD, STAN database. StatLink: http://dx.doi.org/10.1787/781352707152

Czech Rep. - Index of outsourcing of goods abroad by the goods and service industries

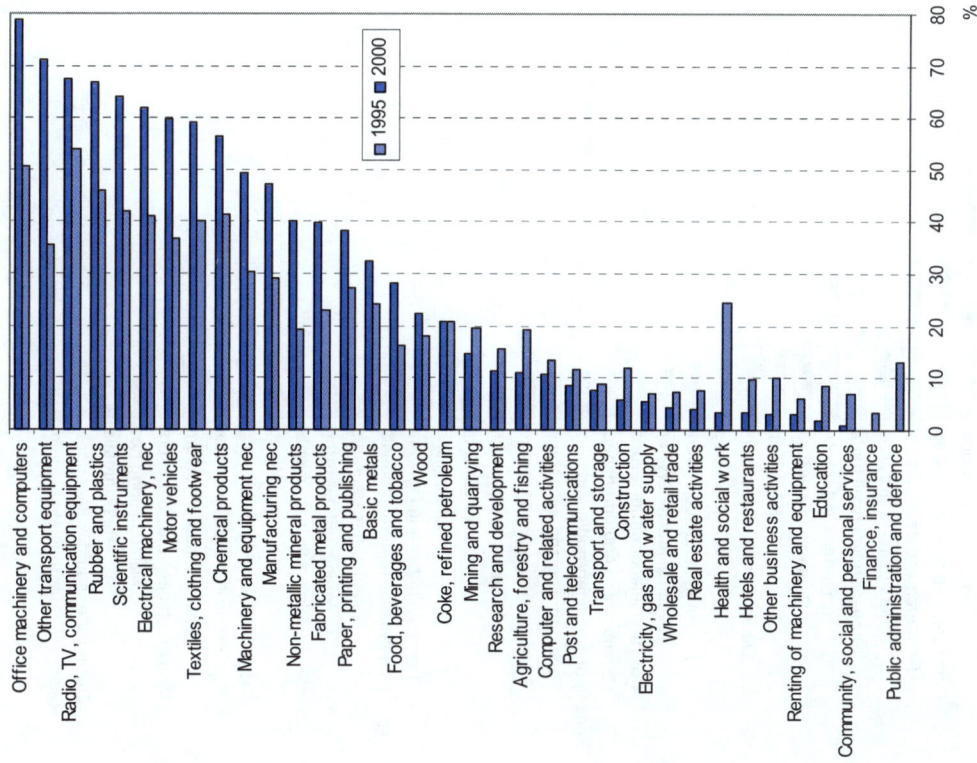

Czech Rep. - Growth of employment 1995-2000

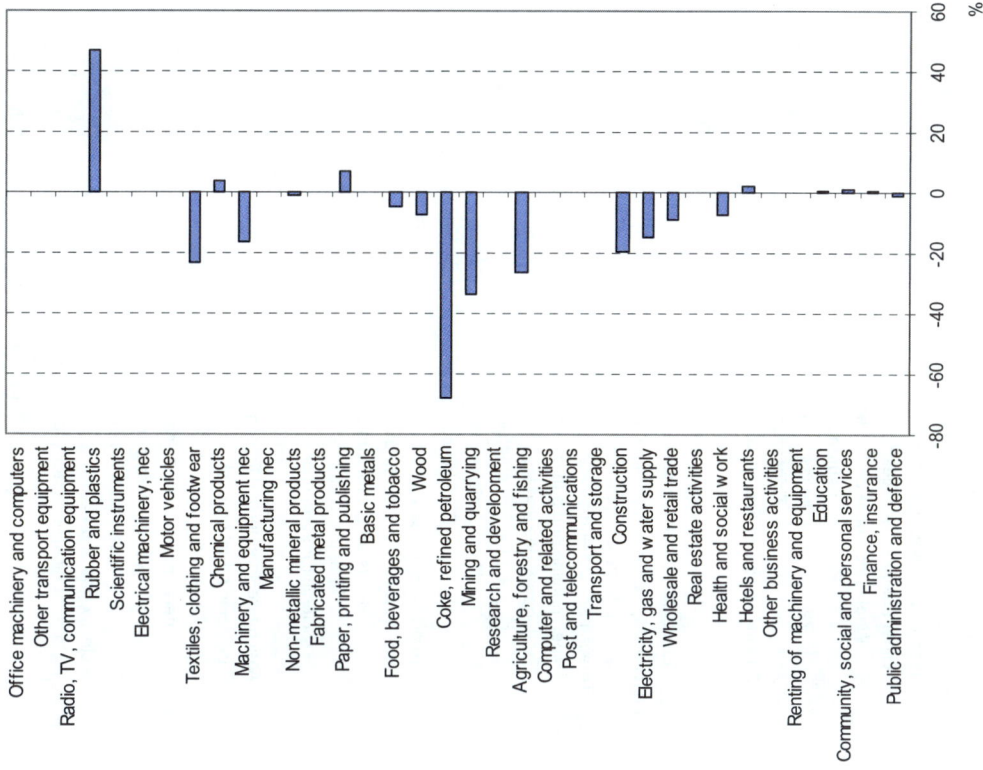

Legend: 1995 2000

Categories (both charts):

- Office machinery and computers
- Other transport equipment
- Radio, TV, communication equipment
- Rubber and plastics
- Scientific instruments
- Electrical machinery, nec
- Motor vehicles
- Textiles, clothing and footwear
- Chemical products
- Machinery and equipment nec
- Manufacturing nec
- Non-metallic mineral products
- Fabricated metal products
- Paper, printing and publishing
- Basic metals
- Food, beverages and tobacco
- Wood
- Coke, refined petroleum
- Mining and quarrying
- Research and development
- Agriculture, forestry and fishing
- Computer and related activities
- Post and telecommunications
- Transport and storage
- Construction
- Electricity, gas and water supply
- Wholesale and retail trade
- Real estate activities
- Health and social work
- Hotels and restaurants
- Other business activities
- Renting of machinery and equipment
- Education
- Community, social and personal services
- Finance, insurance
- Public administration and defence

Source: OECD, Input-Output database. *StatLink:* http://dx.doi.org/10.1787/808123141172

Source: OECD, STAN database. *StatLink:* http://dx.doi.org/10.1787/121013630676

OFFSHORING AND EMPLOYMENT: TRENDS AND IMPACTS – ISBN-978-92-64-03092-3 – © OECD 2007

Czech Rep. - Index of outsourcing of services abroad by the goods and service industries

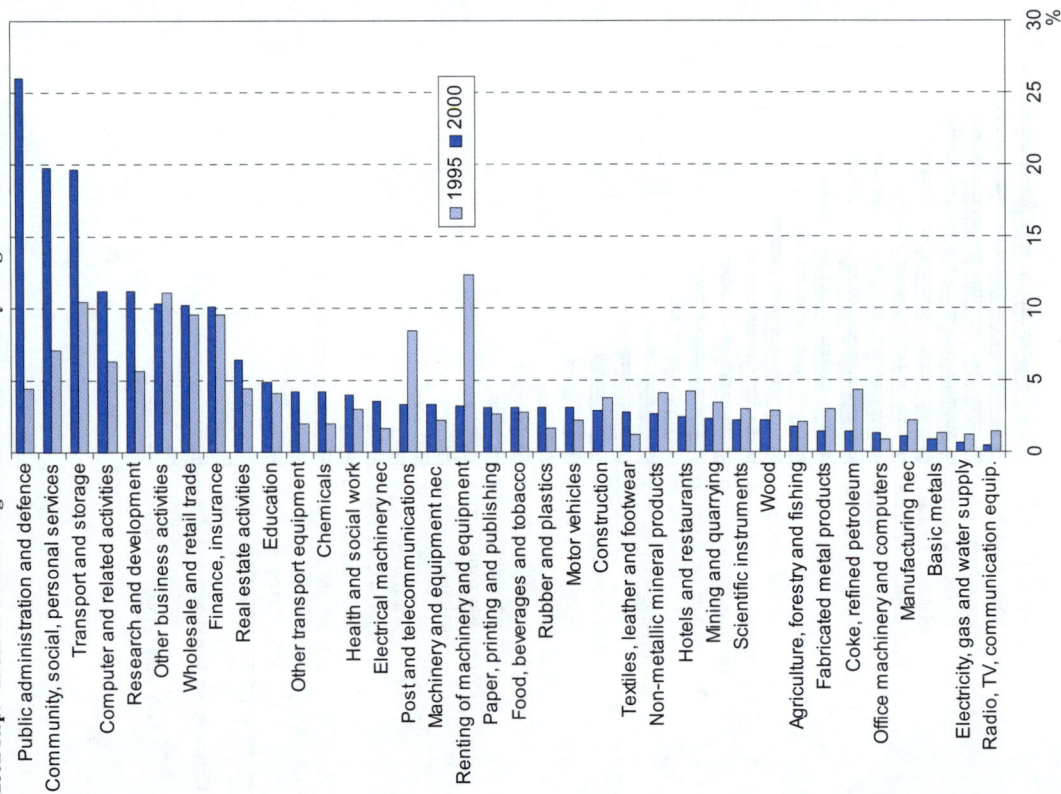

Source: OECD, Input-Output database. *StatLink:* http://dx.doi.org/10.1787/863846156687

Czech Rep. - Growth of employment 1995-2000

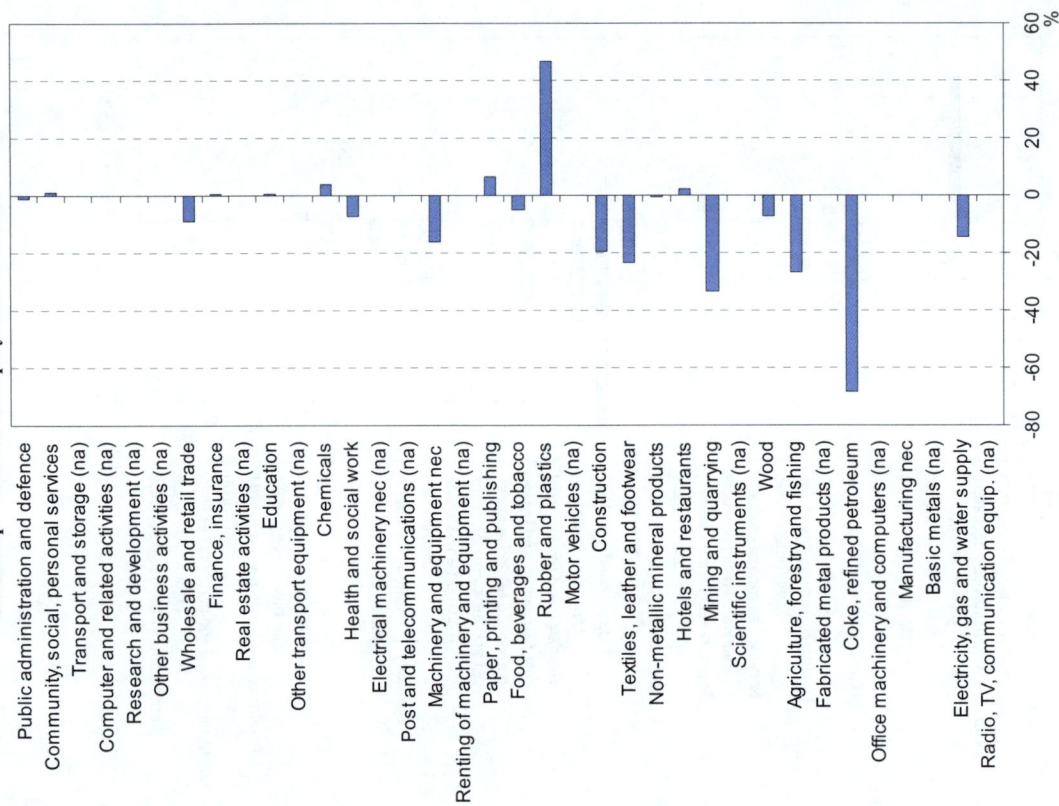

Source: OECD, STAN database. *StatLink:* http://dx.doi.org/10.1787/607261285404

Denmark - Index of outsourcing of goods abroad by the goods and service industries

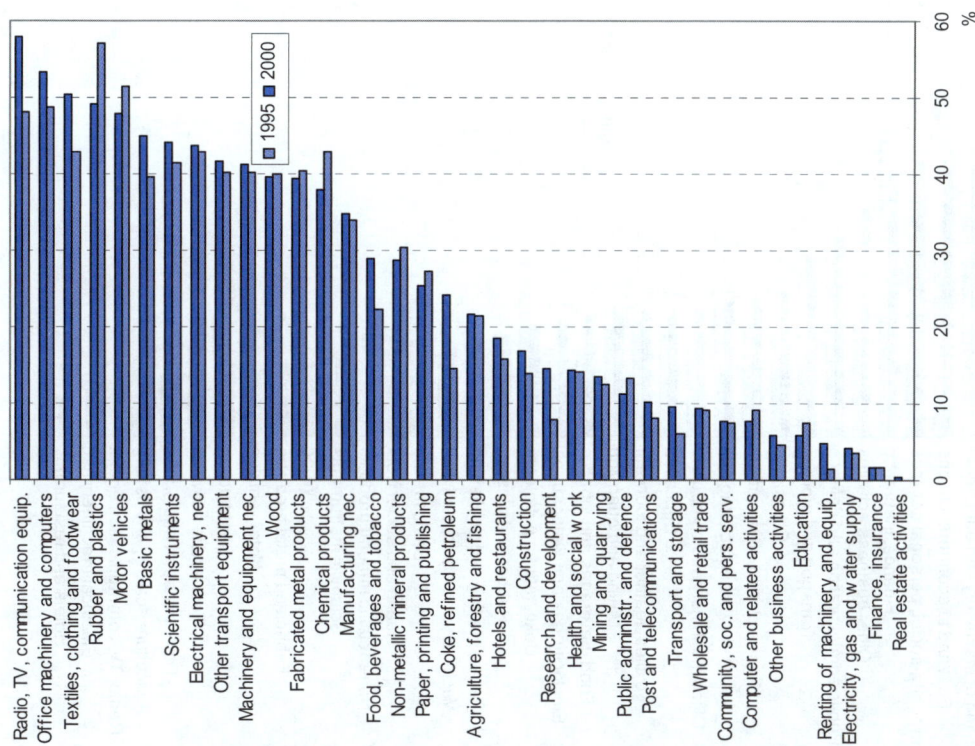

Radio, TV, communication equip.
Office machinery and computers
Textiles, clothing and footwear
Rubber and plastics
Motor vehicles
Basic metals
Scientific instruments
Electrical machinery, nec
Other transport equipment
Machinery and equipment nec
Wood
Fabricated metal products
Chemical products
Manufacturing nec
Food, beverages and tobacco
Non-metallic mineral products
Paper, printing and publishing
Coke, refined petroleum
Agriculture, forestry and fishing
Hotels and restaurants
Construction
Research and development
Health and social work
Mining and quarrying
Public administr. and defence
Post and telecommunications
Transport and storage
Wholesale and retail trade
Community, soc. and pers. serv.
Computer and related activities
Other business activities
Education
Renting of machinery and equip.
Electricity, gas and water supply
Finance, insurance
Real estate activities

1995 ■ 2000

%

Source: OECD, Input-Output database. *StatLink:* http://dx.doi.org/10.1787/176351737308

Denmark - Growth of employment 1995-2000

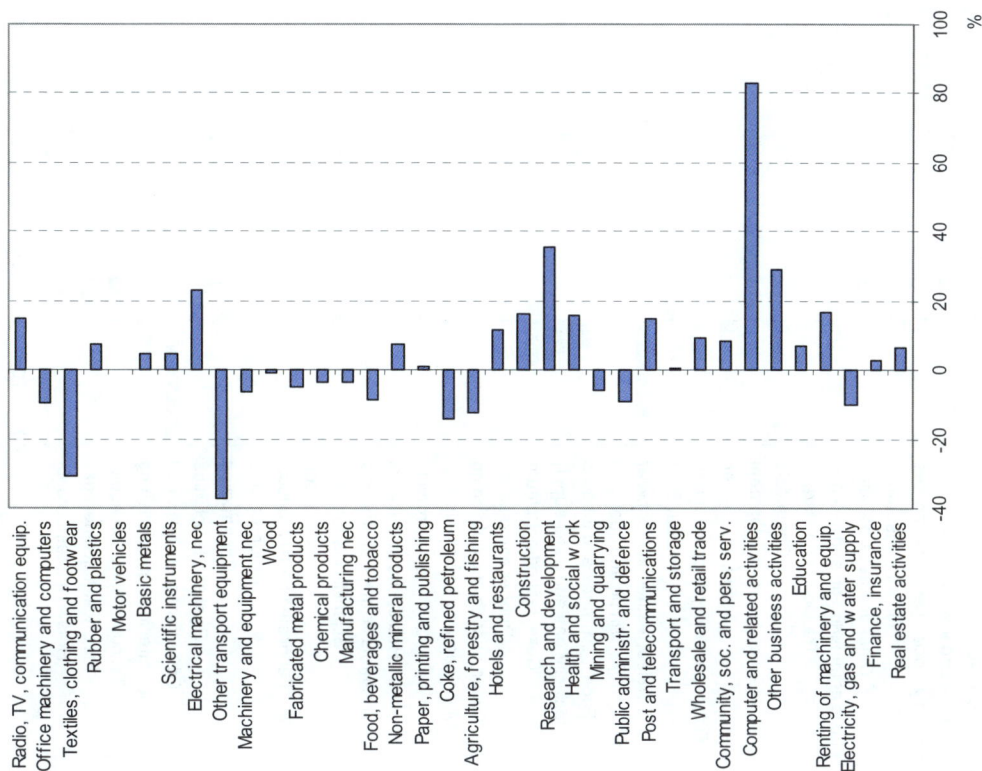

Radio, TV, communication equip.
Office machinery and computers
Textiles, clothing and footwear
Rubber and plastics
Motor vehicles
Basic metals
Scientific instruments
Electrical machinery, nec
Other transport equipment
Machinery and equipment nec
Wood
Fabricated metal products
Chemical products
Manufacturing nec
Food, beverages and tobacco
Non-metallic mineral products
Paper, printing and publishing
Coke, refined petroleum
Agriculture, forestry and fishing
Hotels and restaurants
Construction
Research and development
Health and social work
Mining and quarrying
Public administr. and defence
Post and telecommunications
Transport and storage
Wholesale and retail trade
Community, soc. and pers. serv.
Computer and related activities
Other business activities
Education
Renting of machinery and equip.
Electricity, gas and water supply
Finance, insurance
Real estate activities

%

Source: OECD, STAN database. *StatLink:* http://dx.doi.org/10.1787/563600702185

Denmark - Index of outsourcing of services abroad by the goods and service industries

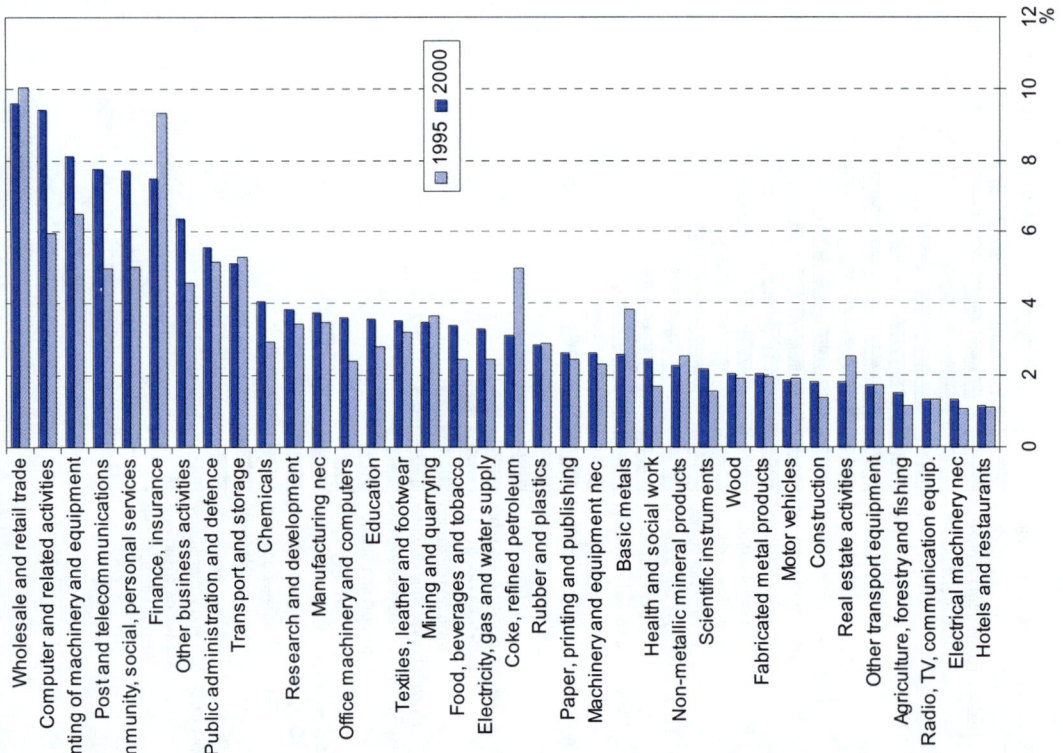

Source: OECD, Input-Output database. StatLink: http://dx.doi.org/10.1787/735485147511

Denmark - Growth of employment 1995-2000

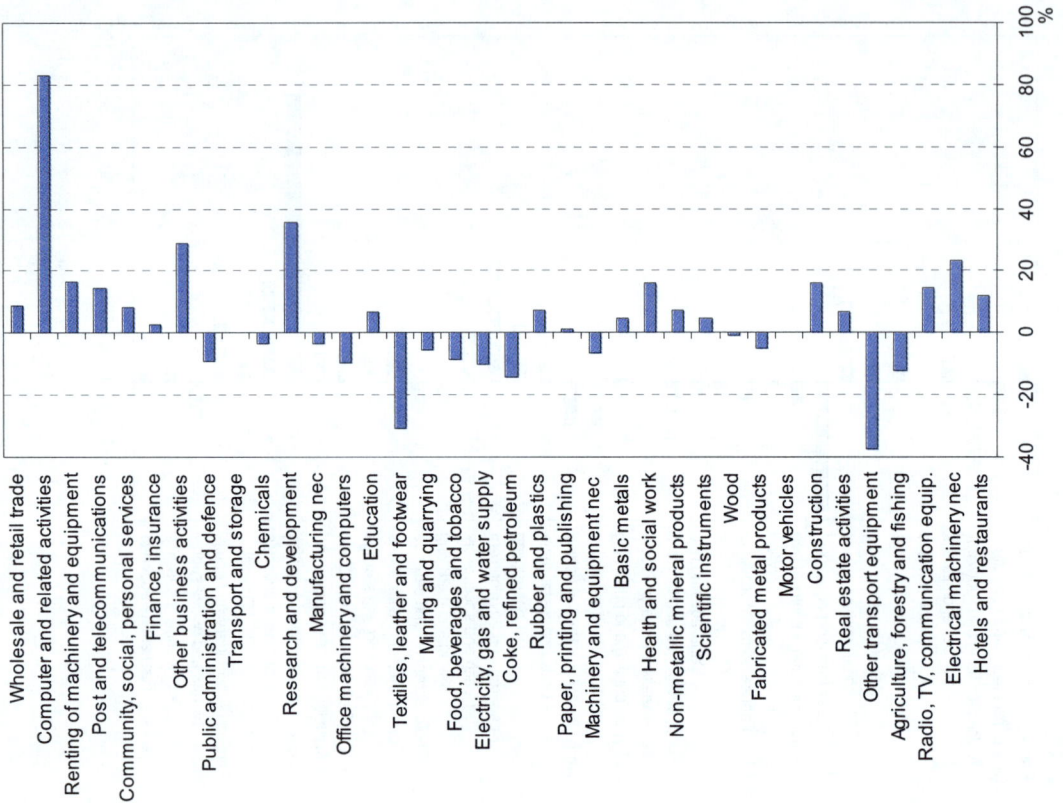

Source: OECD, STAN database. StatLink: http://dx.doi.org/10.1787/783606657672

Finland - Index of outsourcing of goods abroad by the goods and service industries

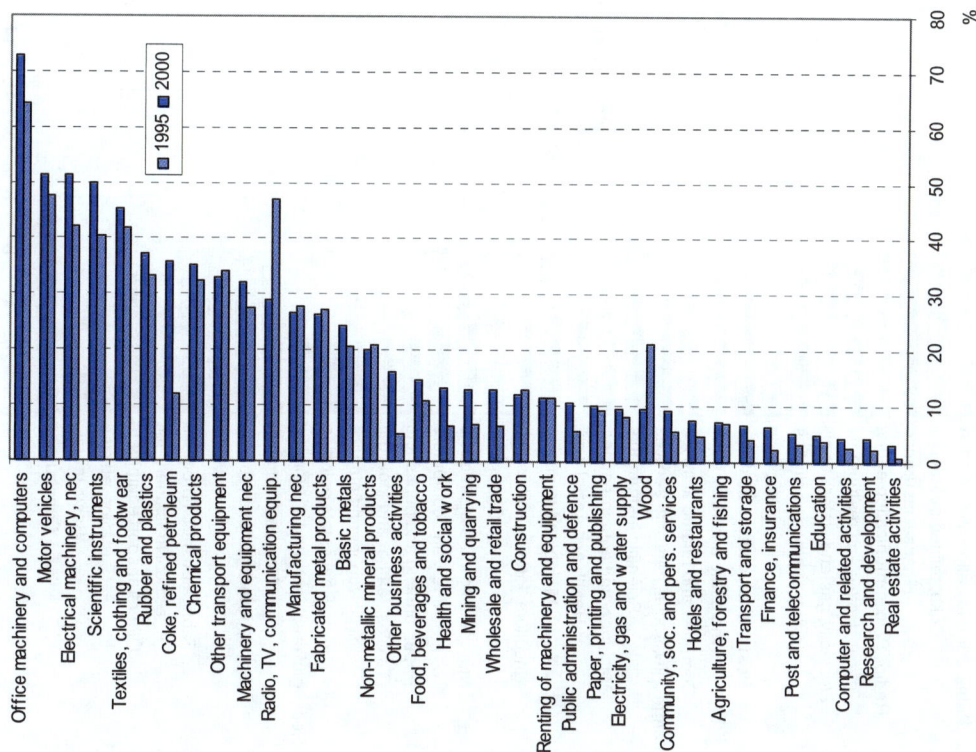

Finland - Growth of employment 1995-2000

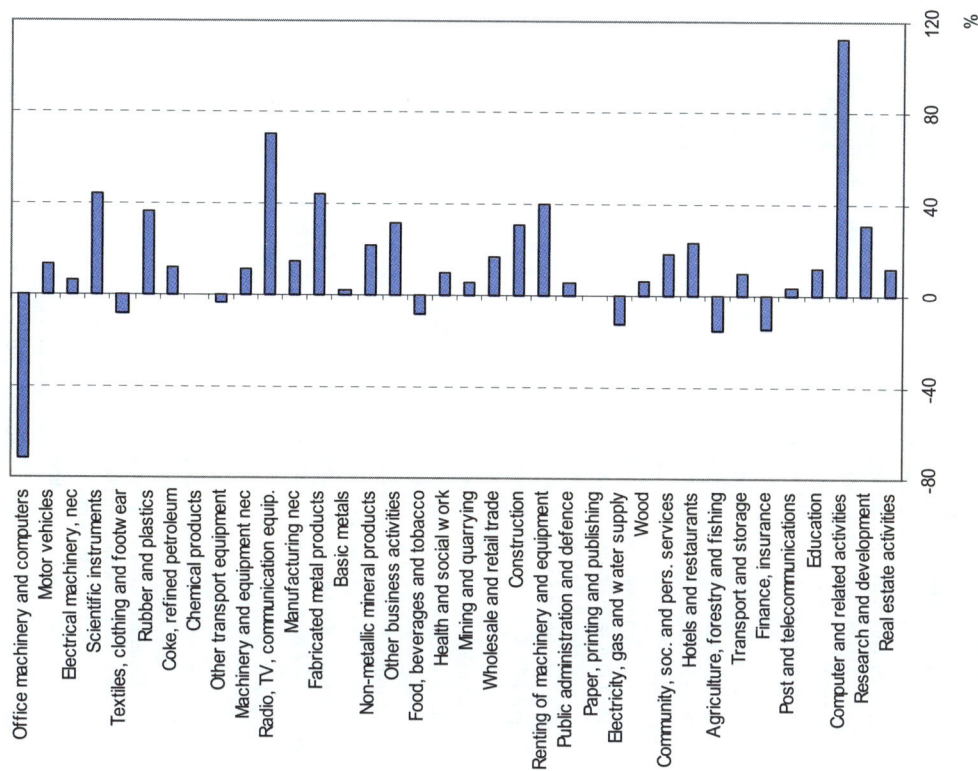

Source: OECD, Input-Output database. *StatLink:* http://dx.doi.org/10.1787/138281120806

Source: OECD, STAN database. *StatLink:* http://dx.doi.org/10.1787/848585483613

Finland - Index of outsourcing of services abroad by the goods and service industries

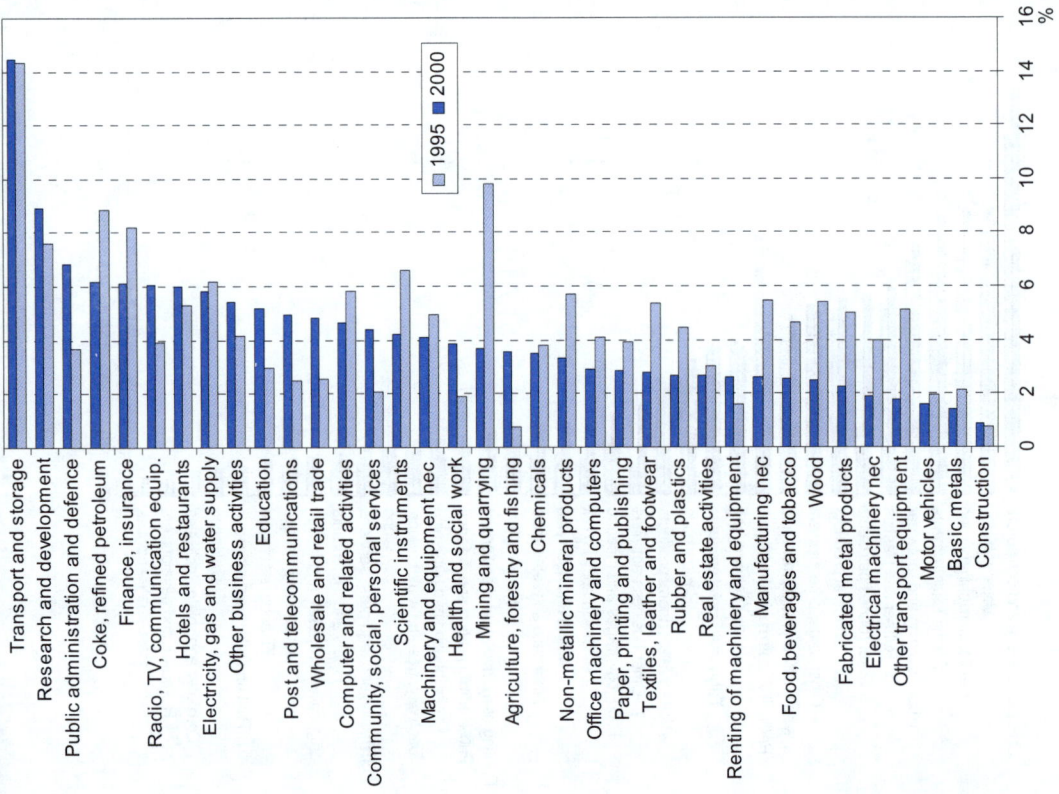

Legend: 1995, 2000

Source: OECD, Input-Output database. *StatLink:* http://dx.doi.org/10.1787/147008475144

Finland - Growth of employment 1995-2000

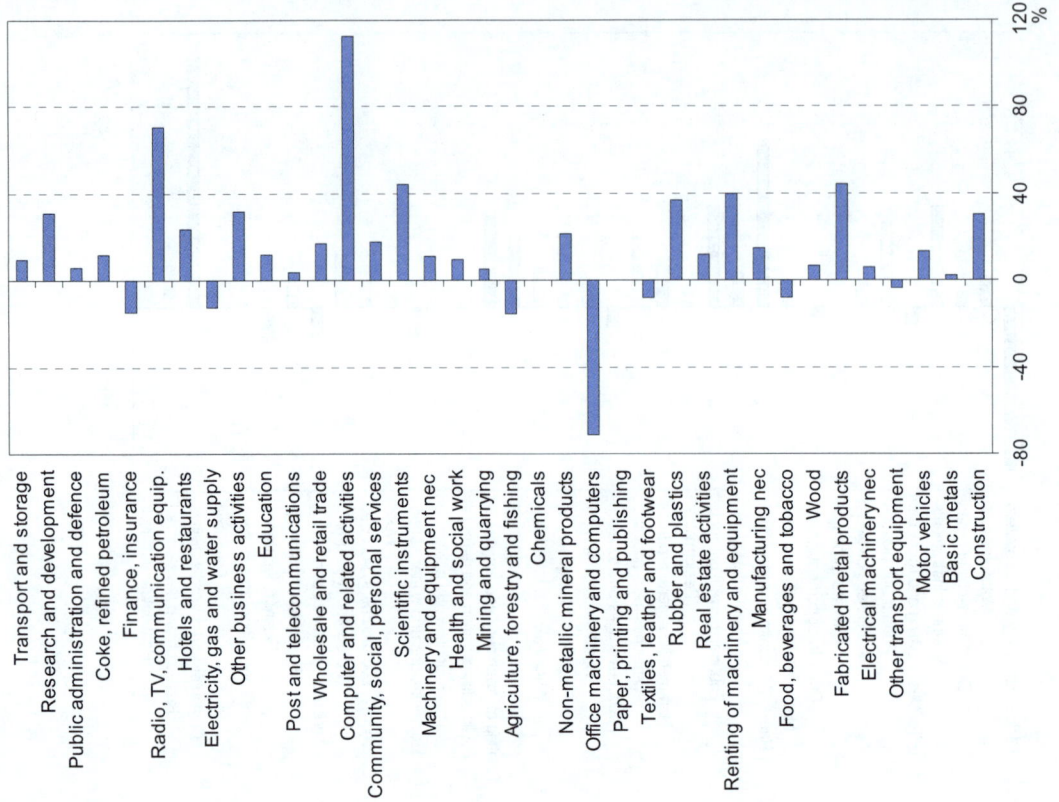

Source: OECD, STAN database. *StatLink:* http://dx.doi.org/10.1787/152762743211

Germany - Index of outsourcing of goods abroad by the goods and service industries

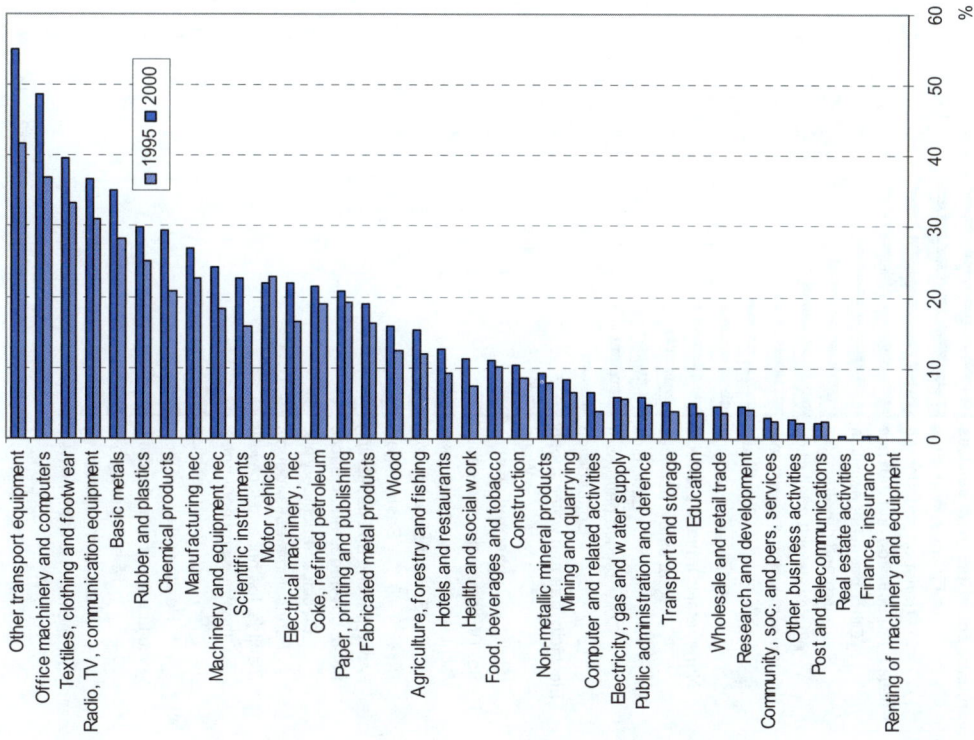

Germany - Growth of employment 1995-2000

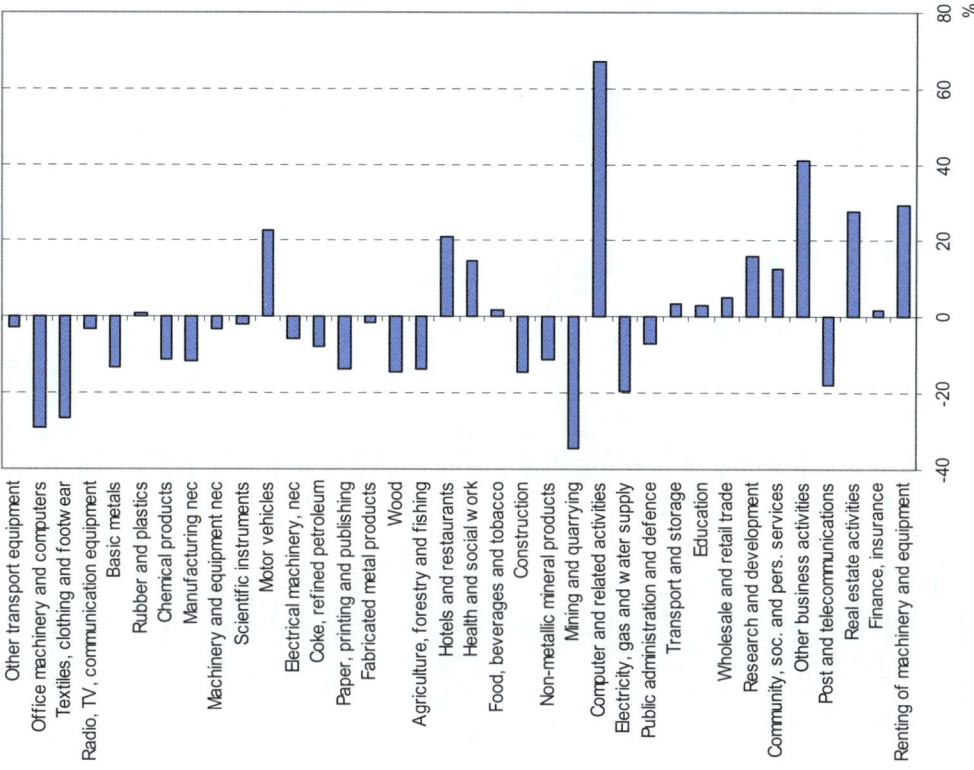

Source: OECD, Input-Output database. *StatLink:* http://dx.doi.org/10.1787/582744802005

Source: OECD, STAN database. *StatLink:* http://dx.doi.org/10.1787/638828308038

Germany – Index of outsourcing of services abroad by the goods and service industries

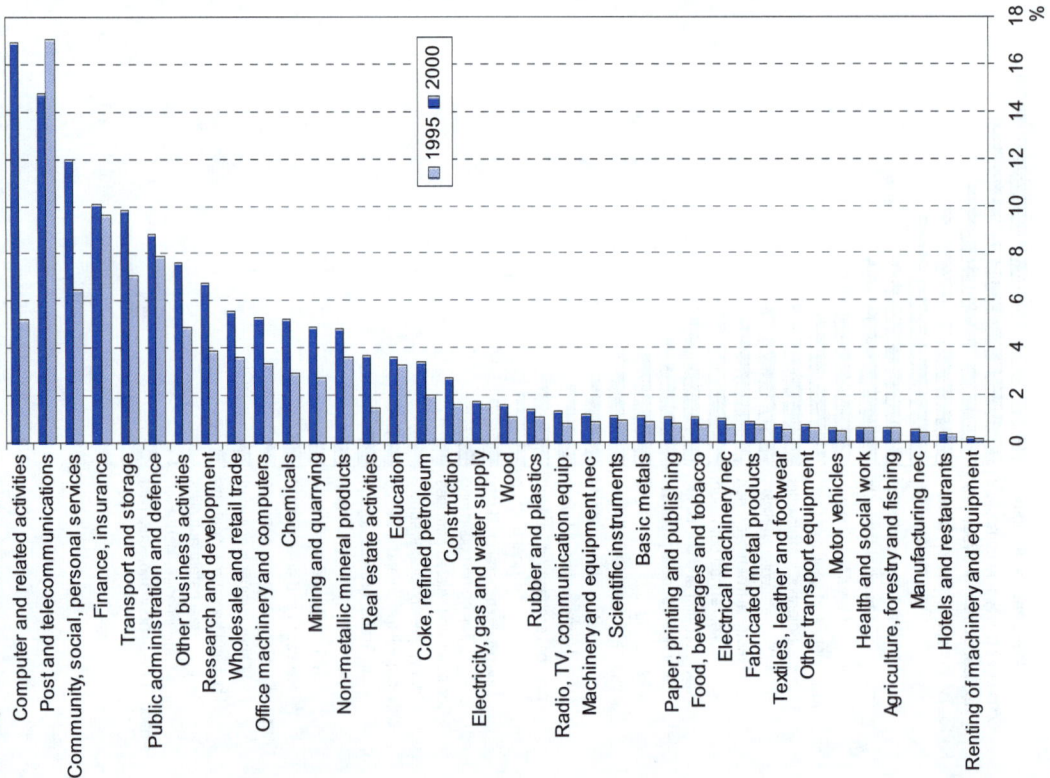

Source: OECD, Input-Output database. *StatLink:* http://dx.doi.org/10.1787/628578142205

Germany – Growth of employment 1995-2000

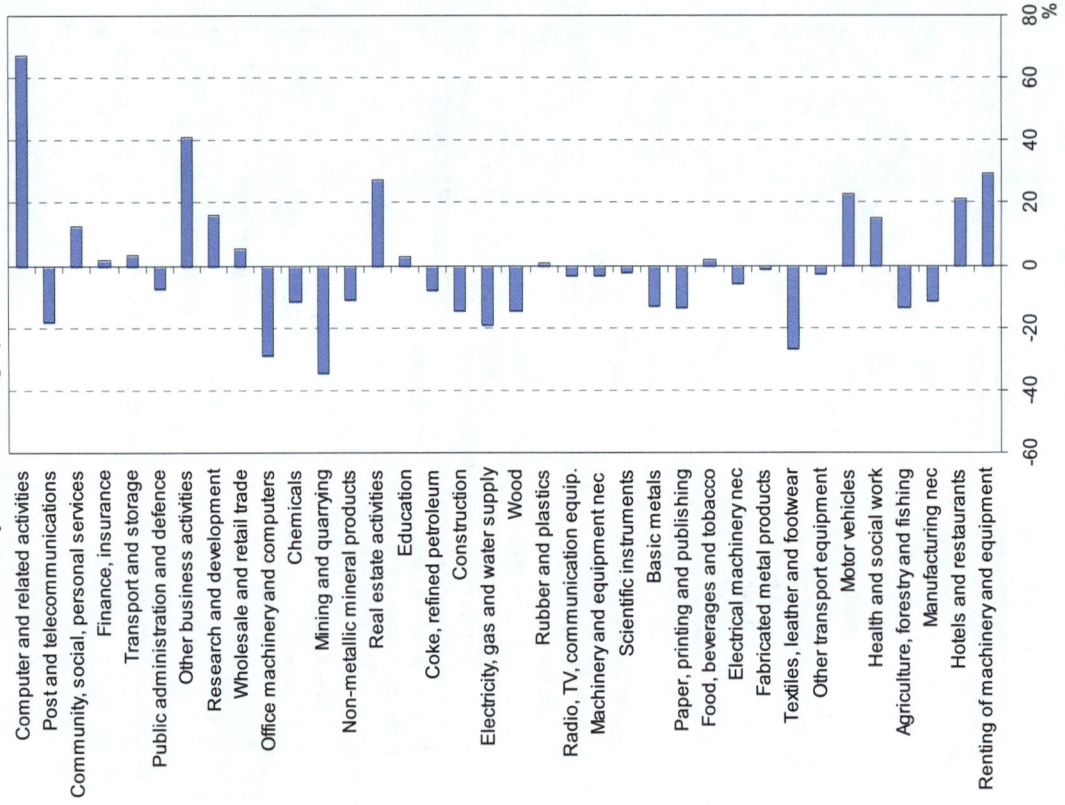

Source: OECD, STAN database. *StatLink:* http://dx.doi.org/10.1787/353784706506

Greece – Index of outsourcing of goods abroad by the goods and service industries

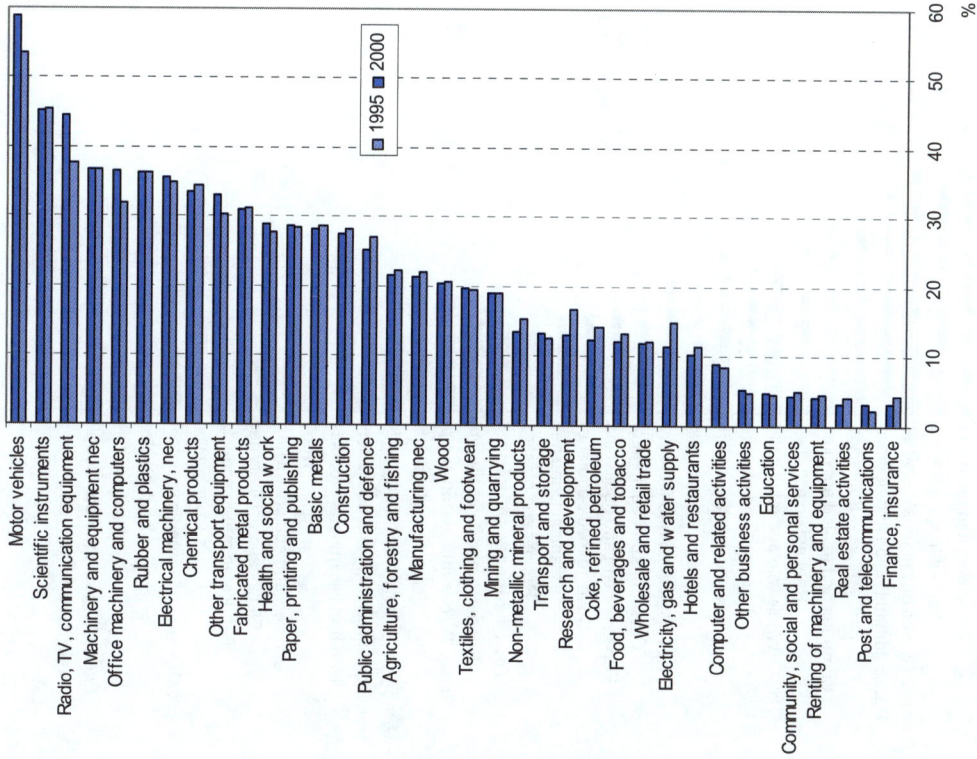

Source: OECD, Input-Output database. *StatLink:* http://dx.doi.org/10.1787/650123752382

Greece – Growth of employment 1995-2000

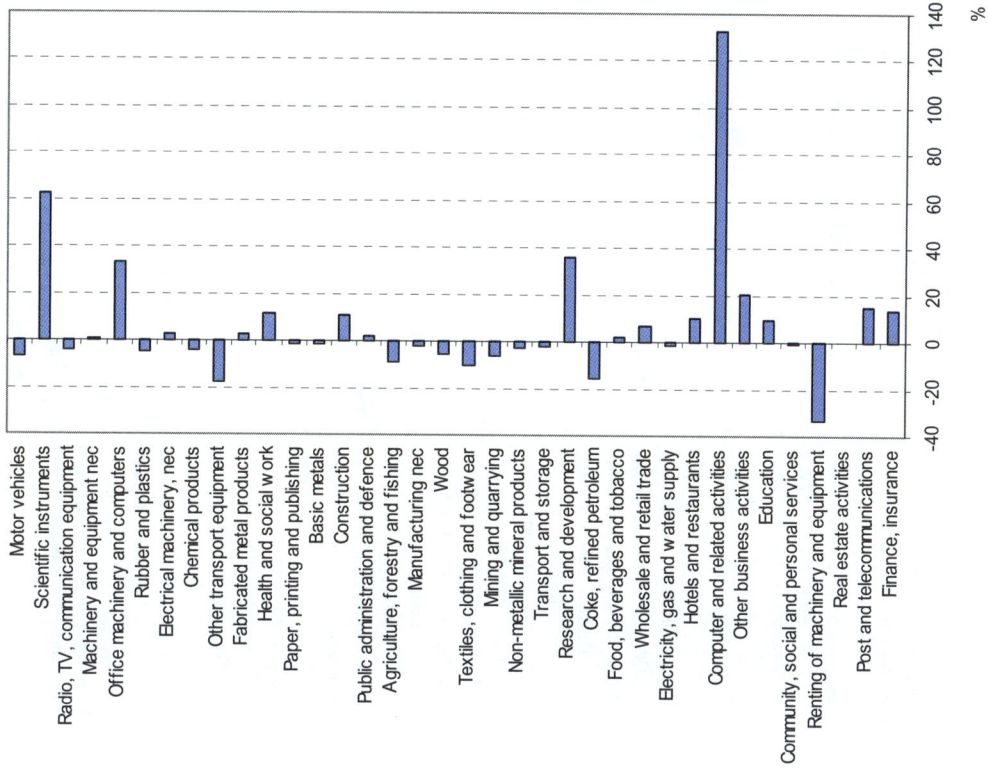

Source: OECD, STAN database. *StatLink:* http://dx.doi.org/10.1787/568478762148

Greece – Index of outsourcing of services abroad by the goods and service industries

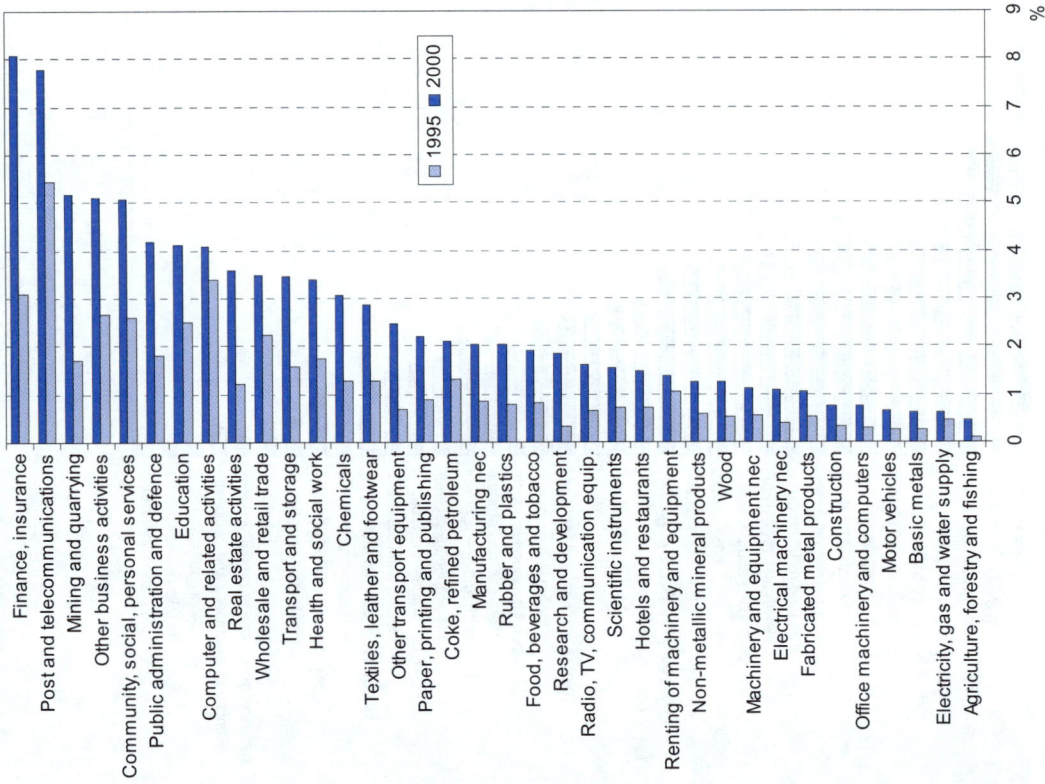

Source: OECD, Input-Output database. *StatLink:* http://dx.doi.org/10.1787/121546178427

Greece – Growth of employment 1995-2000

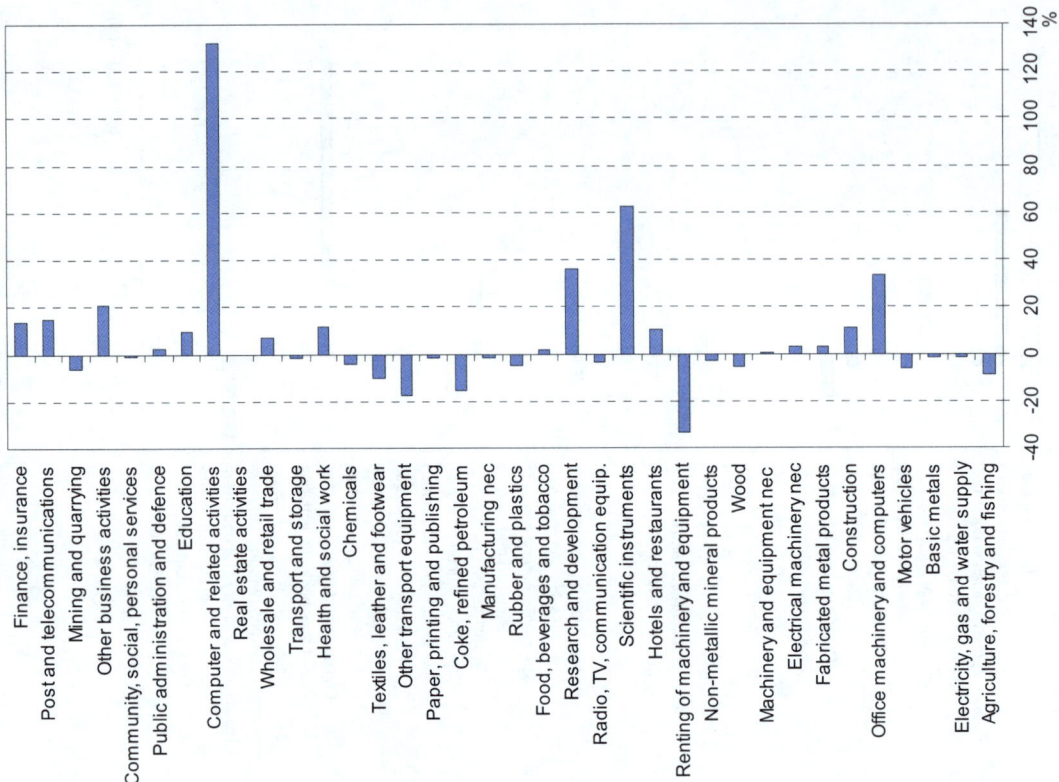

Source: OECD, STAN database. *StatLink:* http://dx.doi.org/10.1787/441363540467

Hungary - Index of outsourcing of goods abroad by the goods and service industries

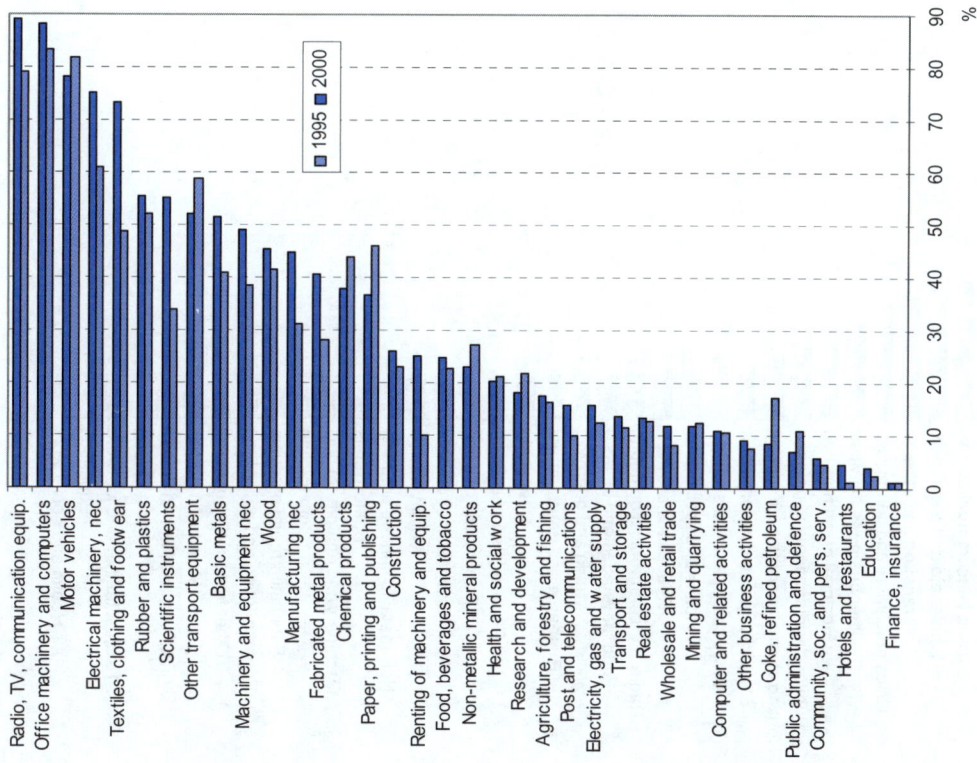

Source: OECD, Input-Output database. StatLink: http://dx.doi.org/10.1787/837612605253

Hungary - Growth of employment 1995-2000

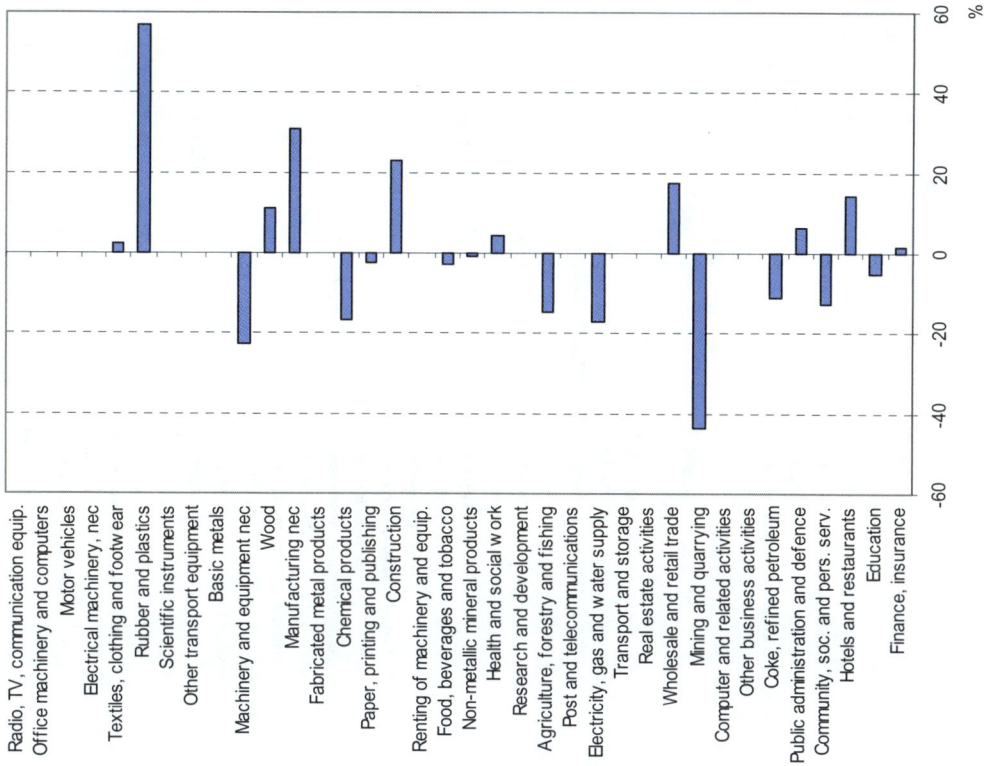

Source: OECD, STAN database. StatLink: http://dx.doi.org/10.1787/588760011532

Hungary - Index of outsourcing of services abroad by the goods and service industries

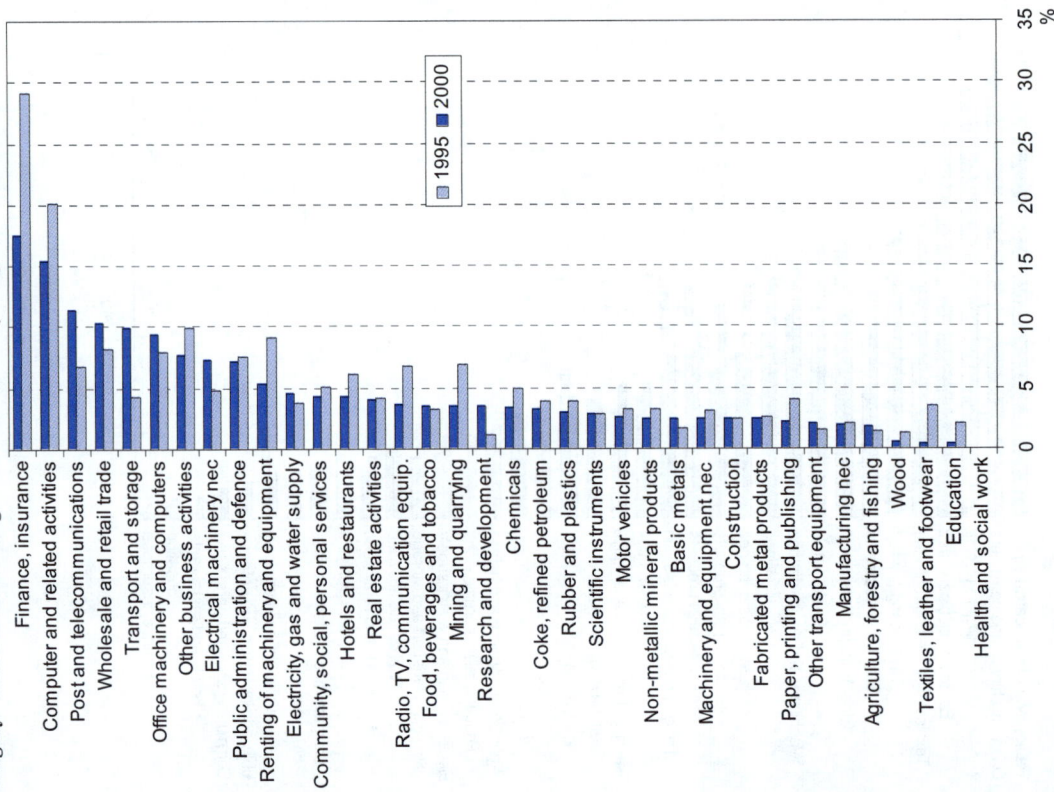

Source: OECD, Input-Output database. *StatLink:* http://dx.doi.org/10.1787/003601341284

Hungary - Growth of employment 1995-2000

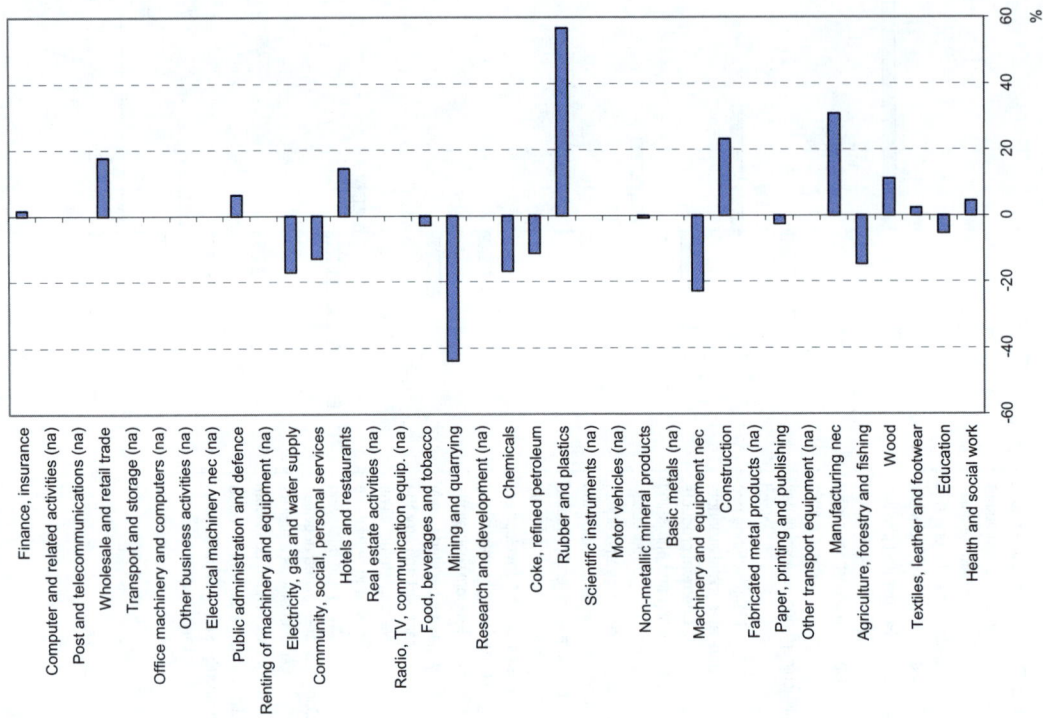

Source: OECD, STAN database. *StatLink:* http://dx.doi.org/10.1787/753877221188

OFFSHORING AND EMPLOYMENT: TRENDS AND IMPACTS – ISBN-978-92-64-03092-3 – © OECD 2007

Italy - Index of outsourcing of goods abroad by the goods and service industries

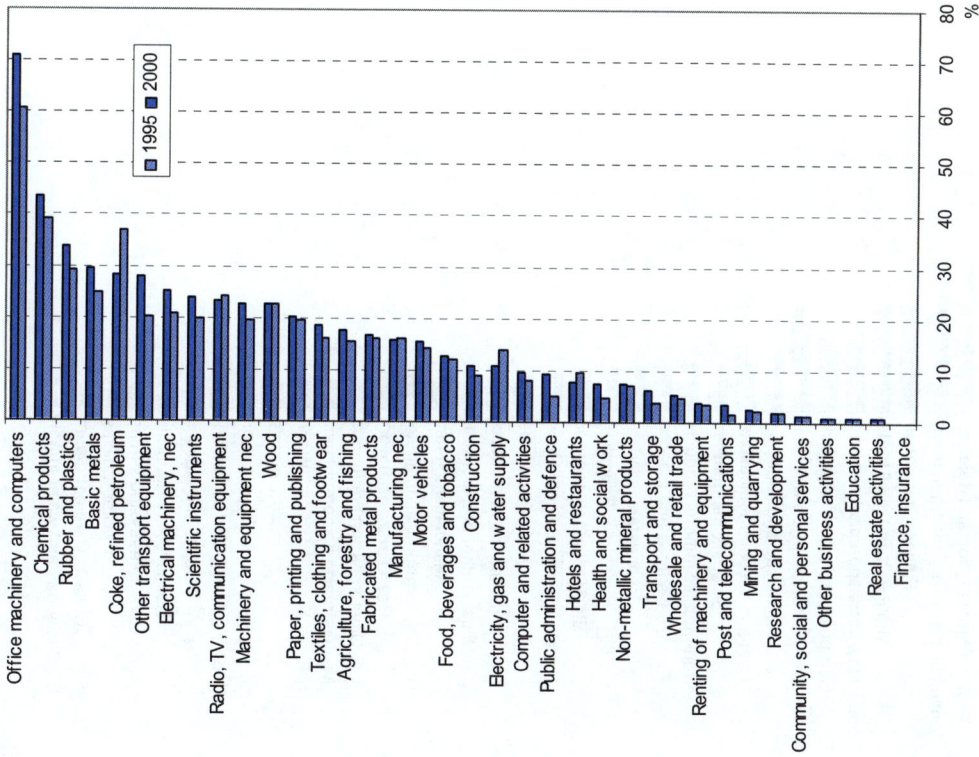

Legend: 1995 | 2000

Source: OECD, Input-Output database. *StatLink:* http://dx.doi.org/10.1787/624220118821

Italy - Growth of employment 1995-2000

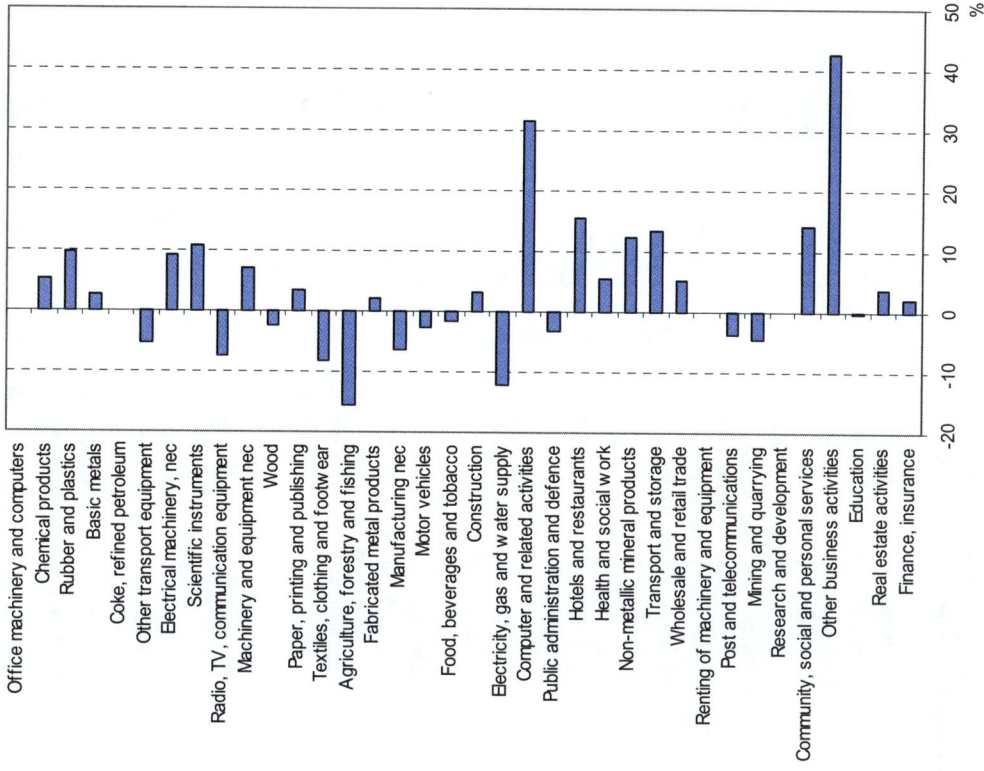

Source: OECD, STAN database. *StatLink:* http://dx.doi.org/10.1787/144146670861

Italy - Index of outsourcing of services abroad by the goods and service industries

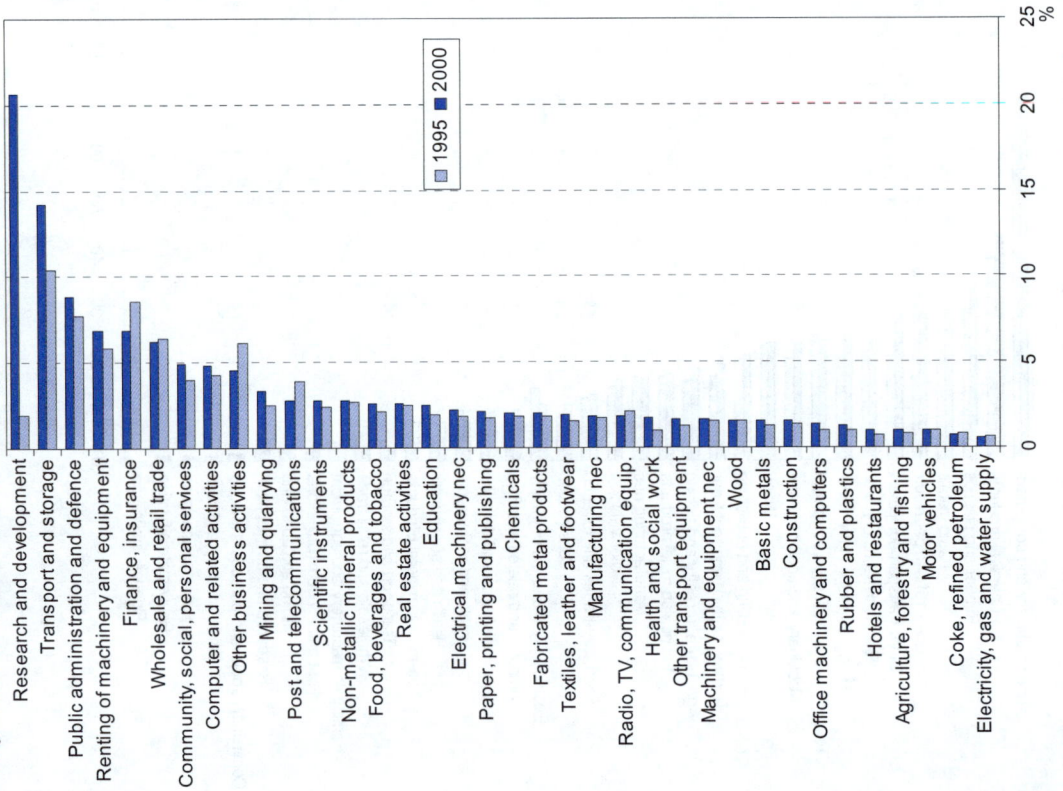

1995 ▪ 2000

Source: OECD, Input-Output database. *StatLink:* http://dx.doi.org/10.1787/182553031135

Italy - Growth of employment 1995-2000

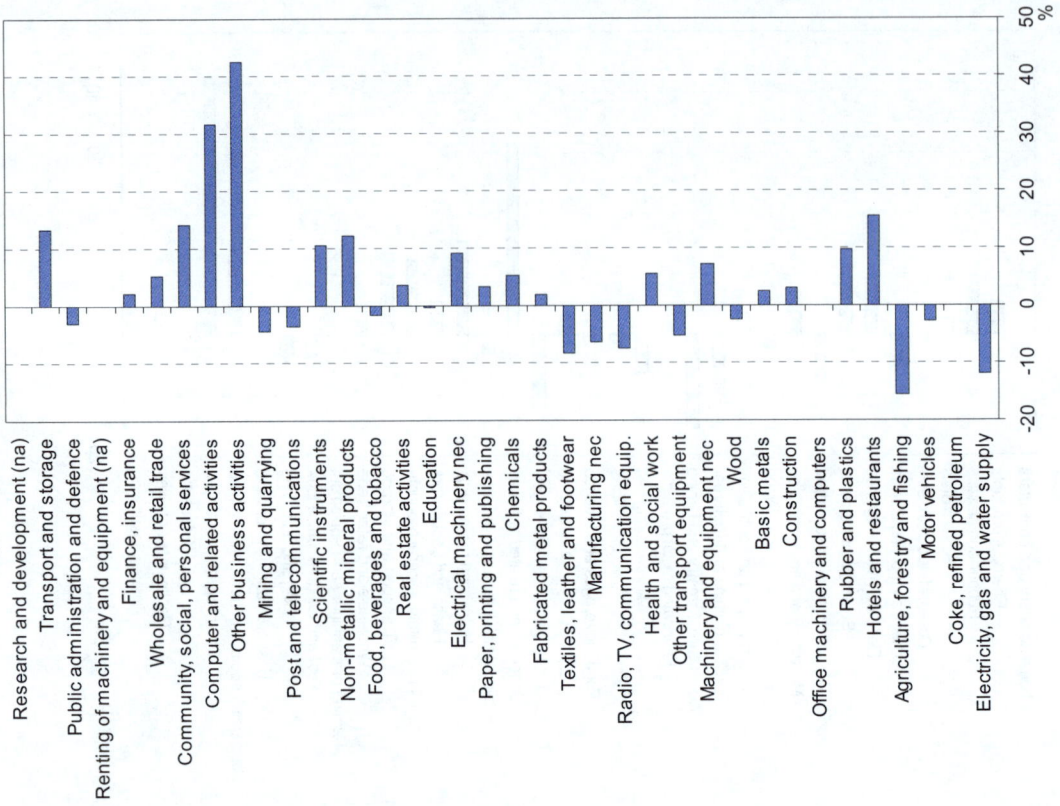

Source: OECD, STAN database. *StatLink:* http://dx.doi.org/10.1787/315630381544

Japan - Index of outsourcing of goods abroad by the goods and service industries

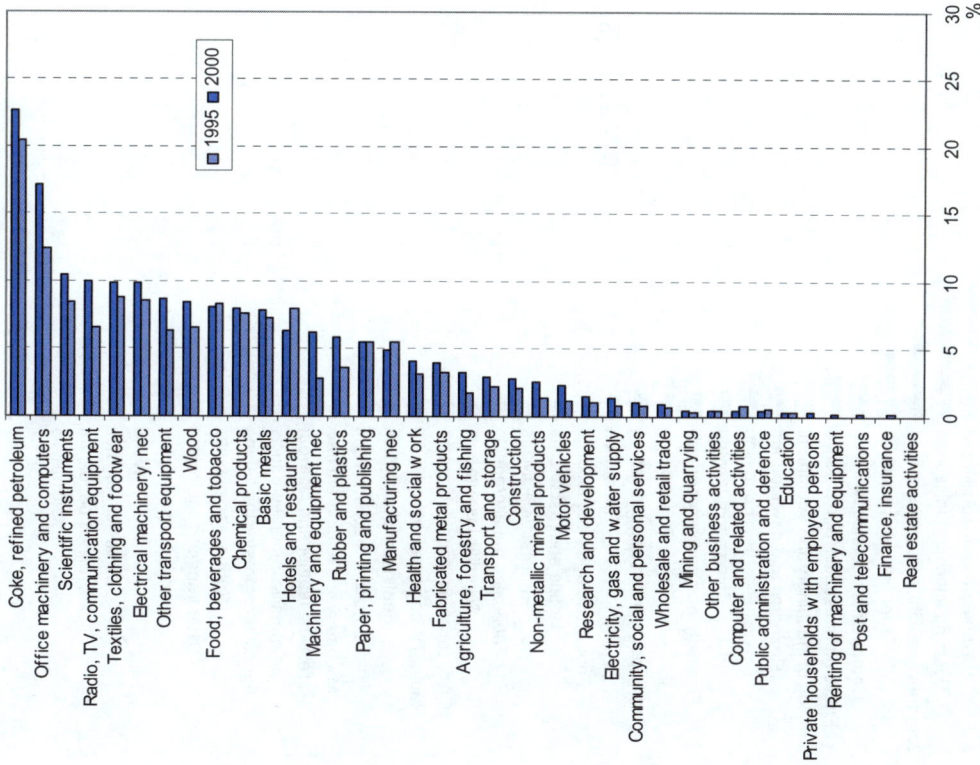

Source: OECD, Input-Output database. *StatLink:* http://dx.doi.org/10.1787/215514024278

Japan - Growth of employment 1995-2000

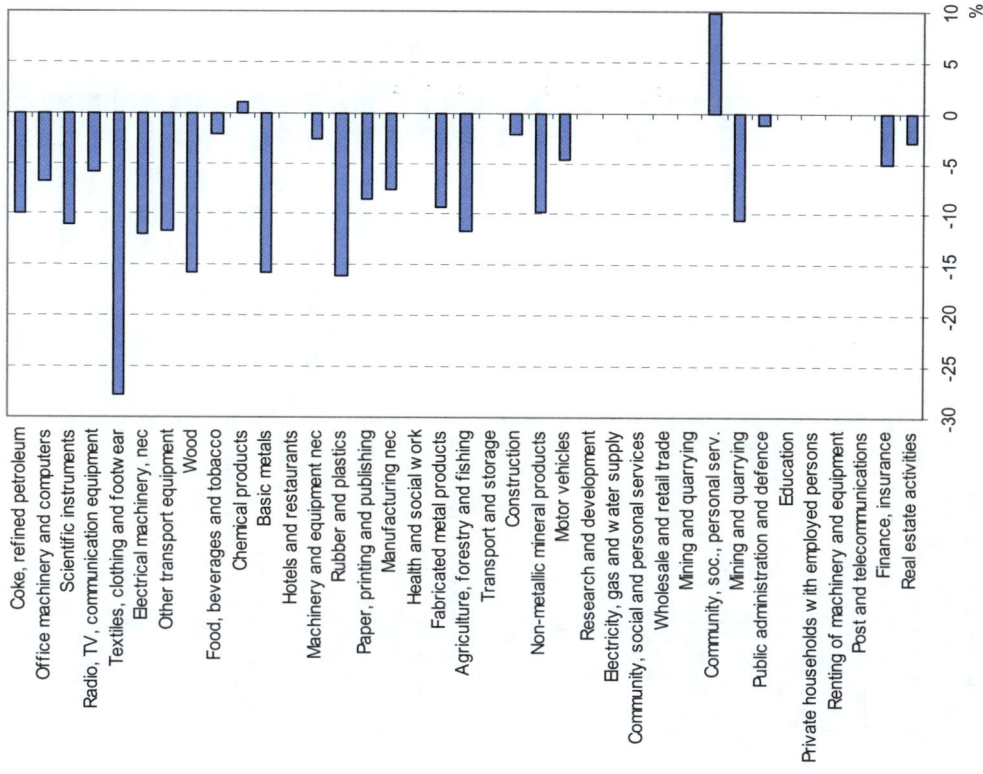

Source: OECD, STAN database. *StatLink:* http://dx.doi.org/10.1787/768004105688

Japan - Index of outsourcing of services abroad by the goods and service industries

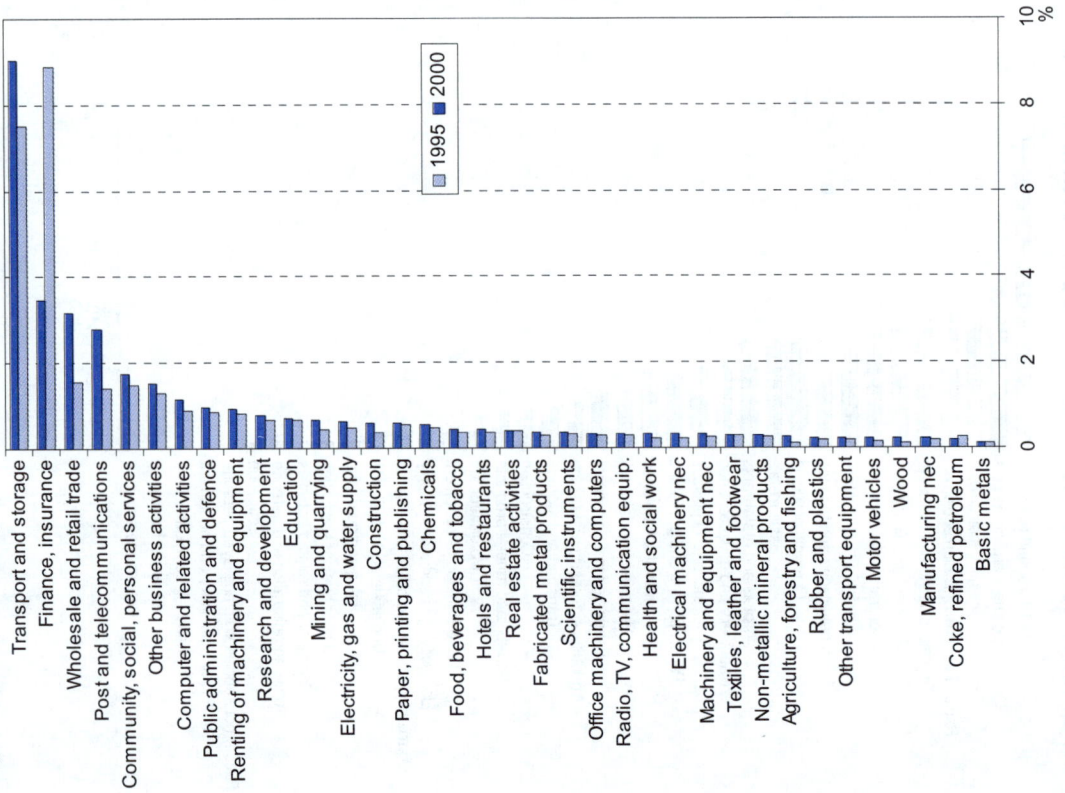

Source: OECD, Input-Output database. *StatLink:* http://dx.doi.org/10.1787/735166443701

Japan - Growth of employment 1995-2000

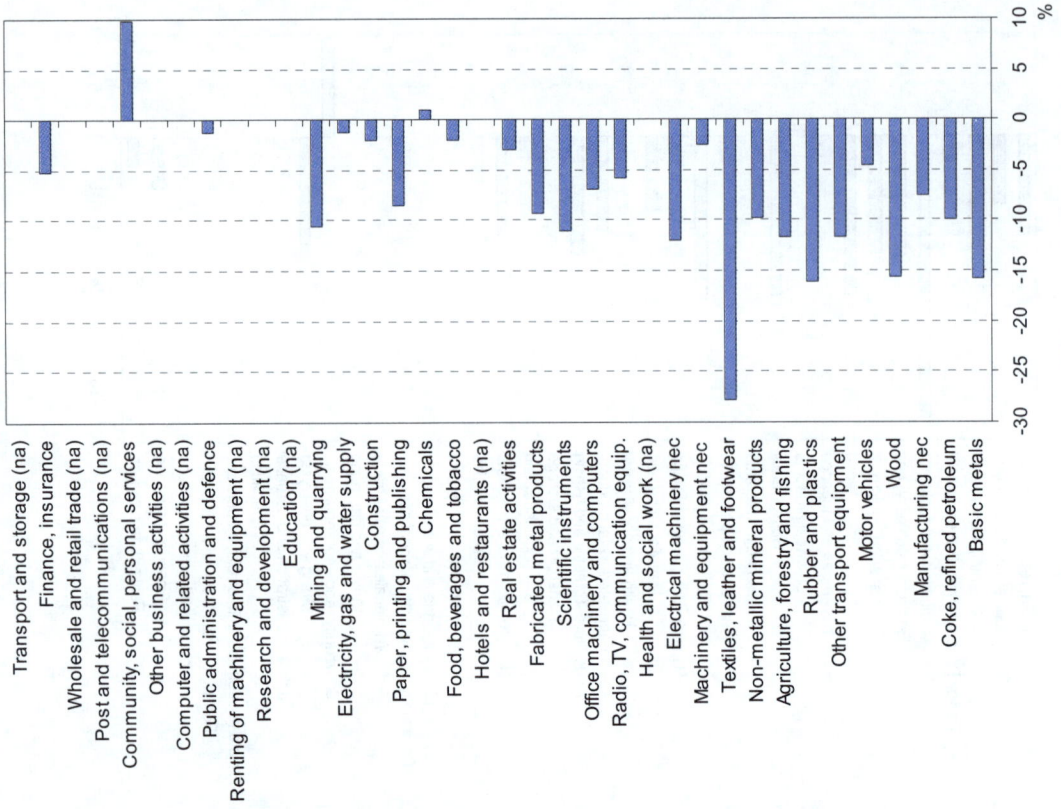

Source: OECD, STAN database. *StatLink:* http://dx.doi.org/10.1787/255083814741

Korea - Index of outsourcing of goods abroad by the goods and service industries

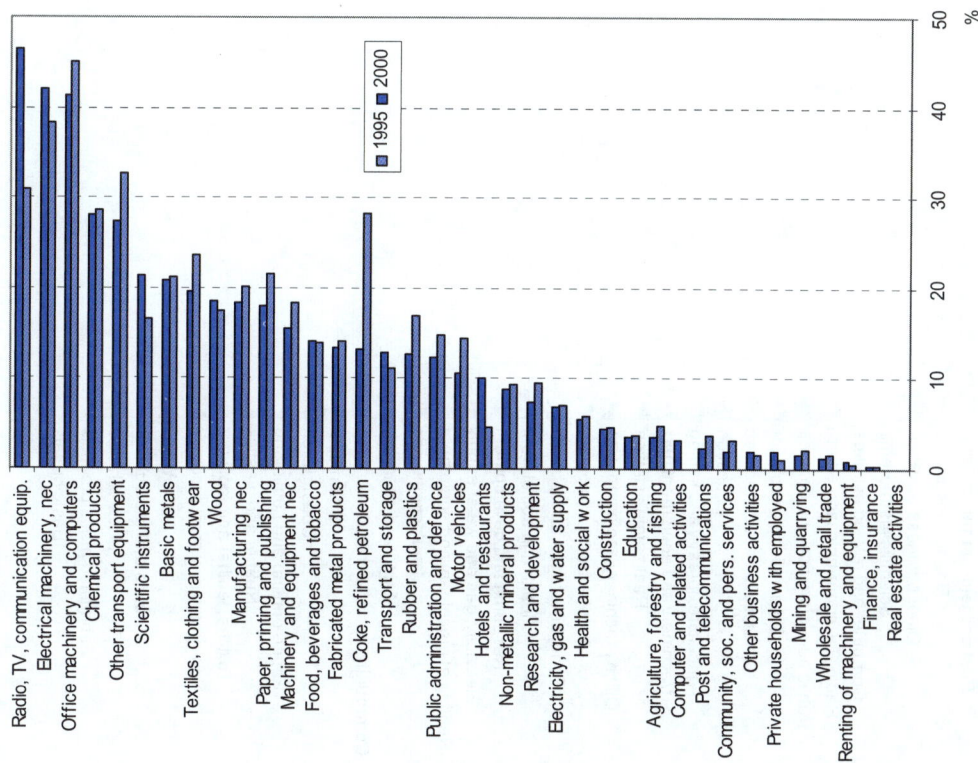

Legend: 1995 ■ 2000

Korea - Growth of employment 1995-2000

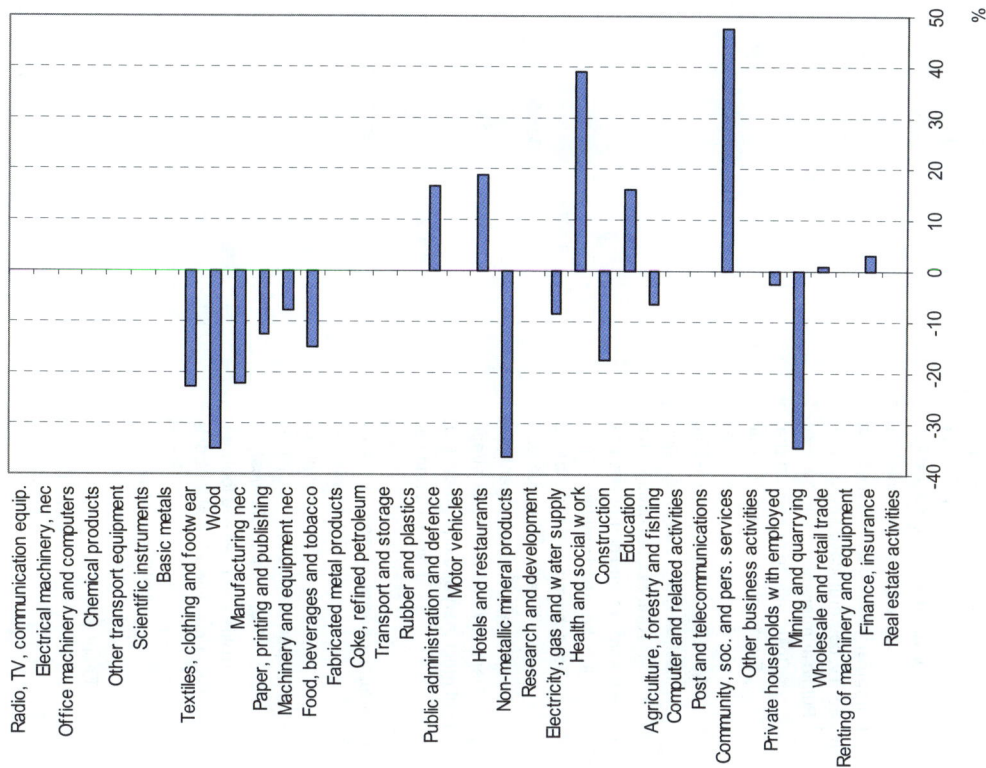

Source: OECD, Input-Output database. *StatLink:* http://dx.doi.org/10.1787/171703285235

Source: OECD, STAN database. *StatLink:* http://dx.doi.org/10.1787/774643208403

OFFSHORING AND EMPLOYMENT: TRENDS AND IMPACTS – ISBN-978-92-64-03092-3 – © OECD 2007

Korea - Index of outsourcing of services abroad by the goods and service industries

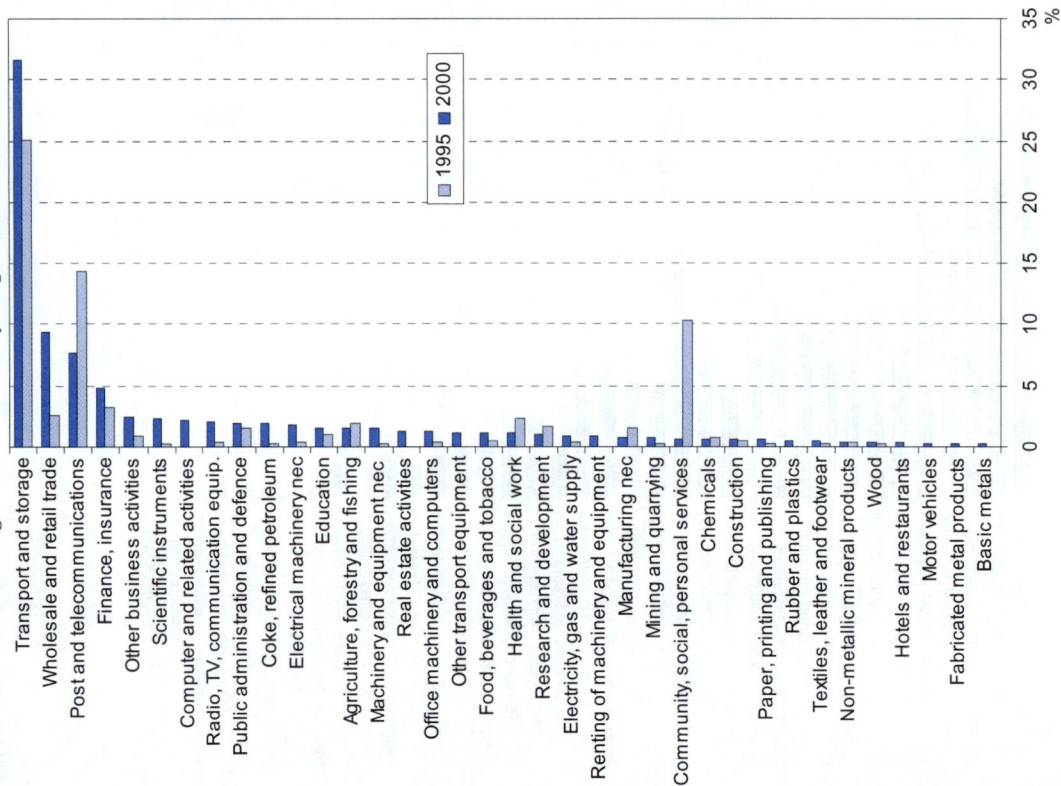

Legend: □ 1995 ■ 2000

Source: OECD, Input-Output database. *StatLink:* http://dx.doi.org/10.1787/600648330681

Korea - Growth of employment 1995-2000

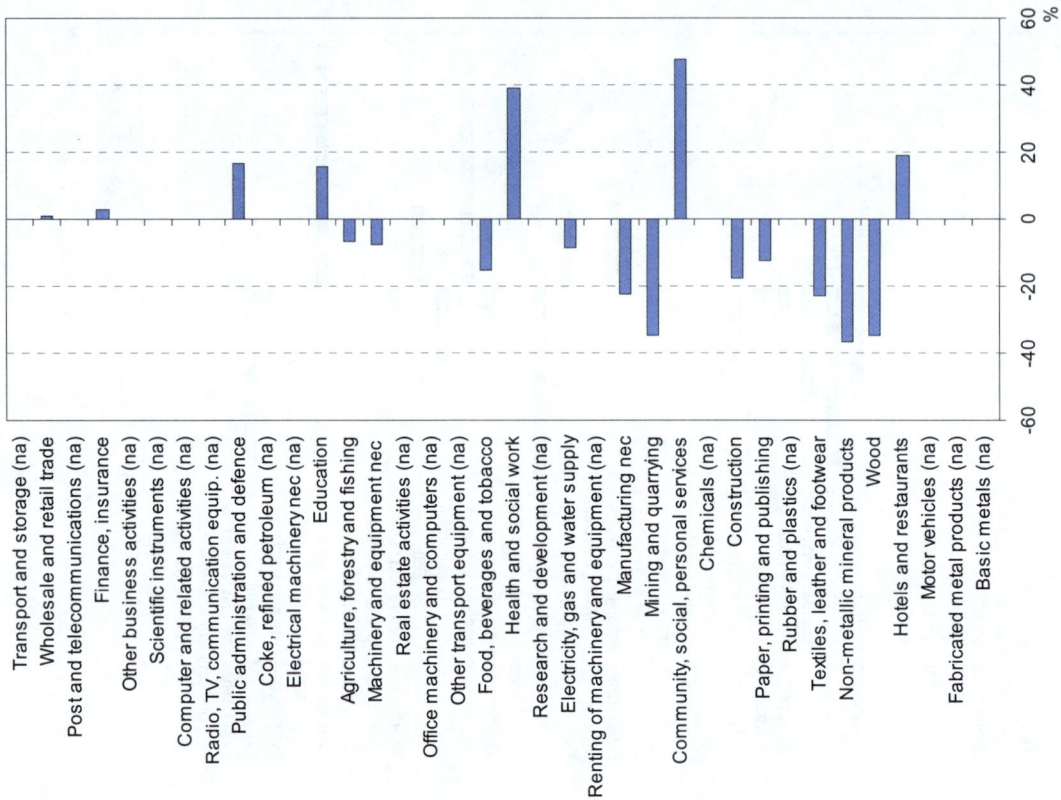

Source: OECD, STAN database. *StatLink:* http://dx.doi.org/10.1787/730632834434

Netherlands – Index of outsourcing of goods abroad by the goods and service industries

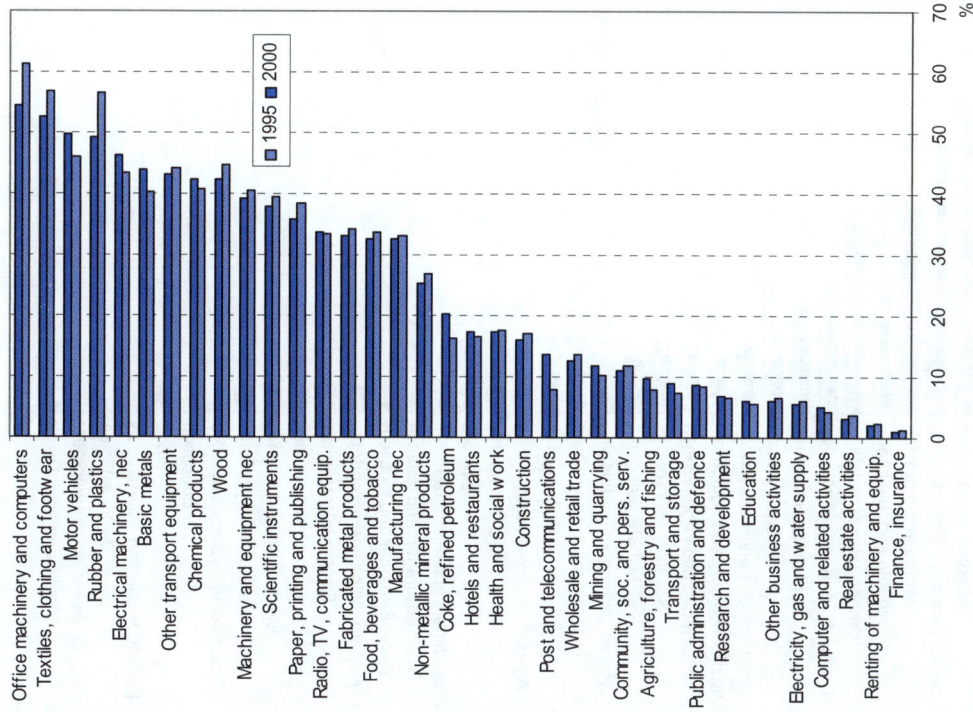

Netherlands – Growth of employment 1995-2000

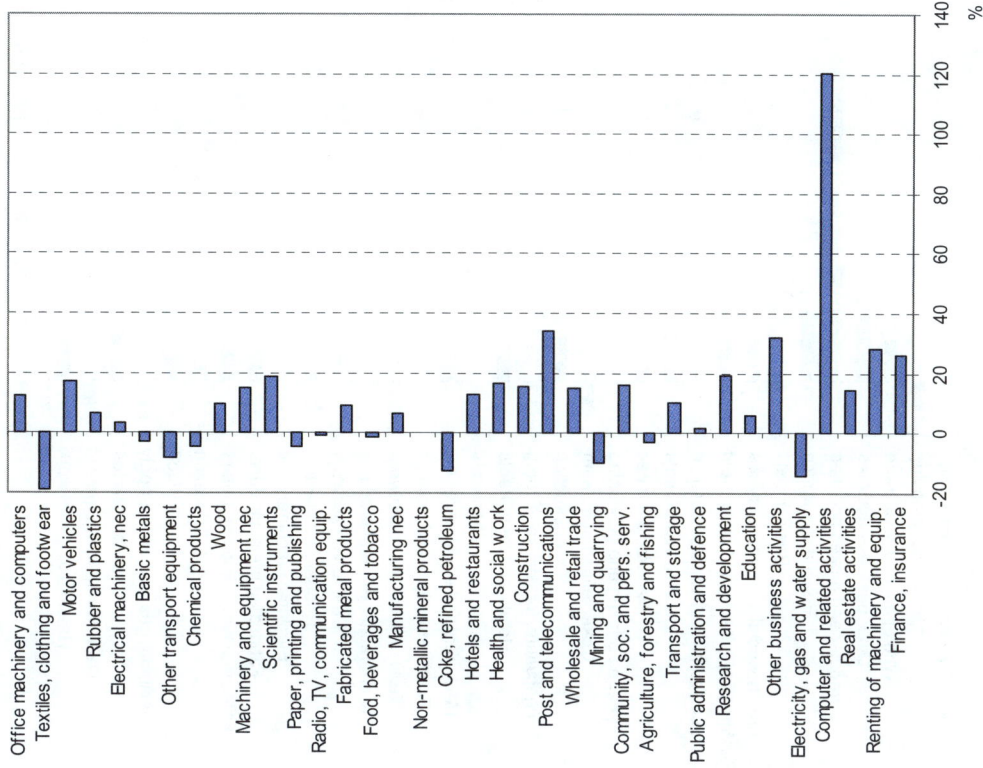

Source: OECD, Input-Output database. *StatLink:* http://dx.doi.org/10.1787/448157348728

Source: OECD, STAN database. *StatLink:* http://dx.doi.org/10.1787/614155558375

Netherlands – Index of outsourcing of services abroad by the goods and service industries

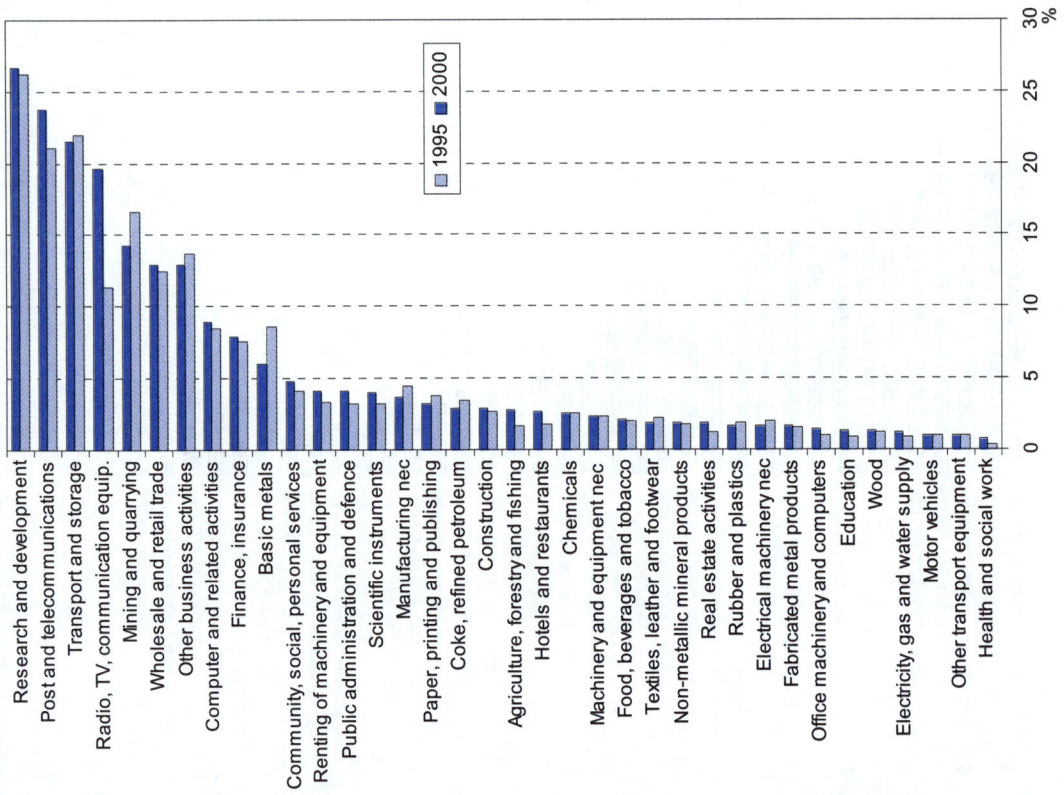

Source: OECD, Input-Output database. *StatLink:* http://dx.doi.org/10.1787/553453345823

Netherlands – Growth of employment 1995-2000

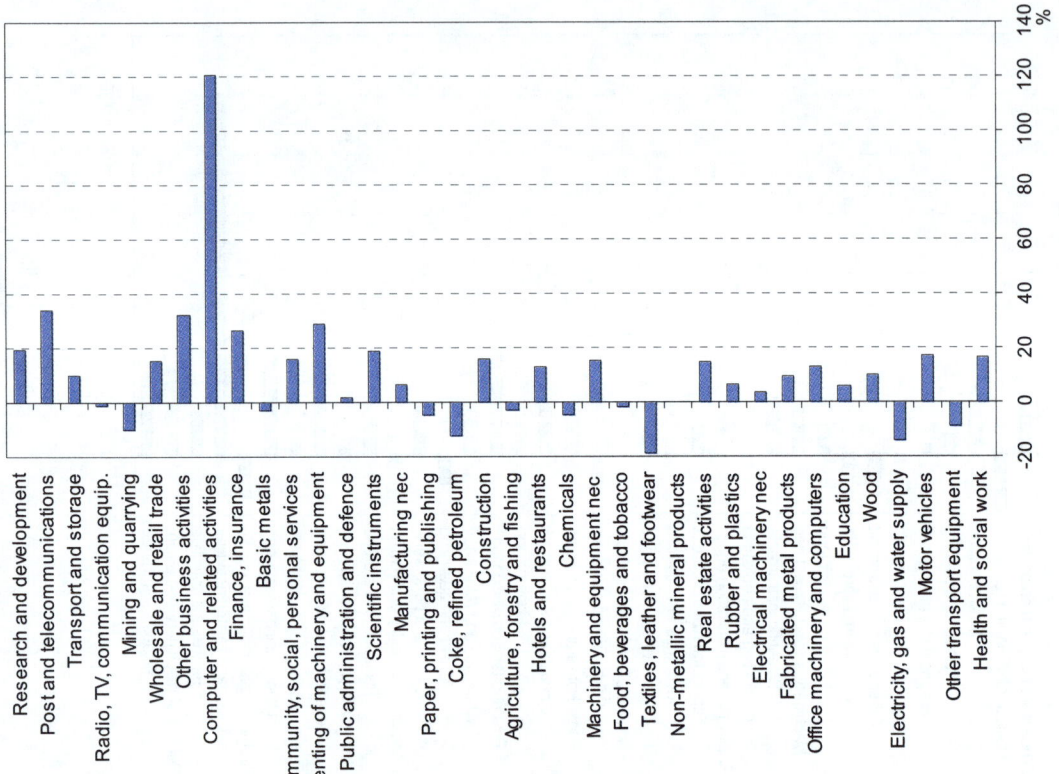

Source: OECD, STAN database. *StatLink:* http://dx.doi.org/10.1787/833866663850

Norway - Index of outsourcing of goods abroad by the goods and service industries

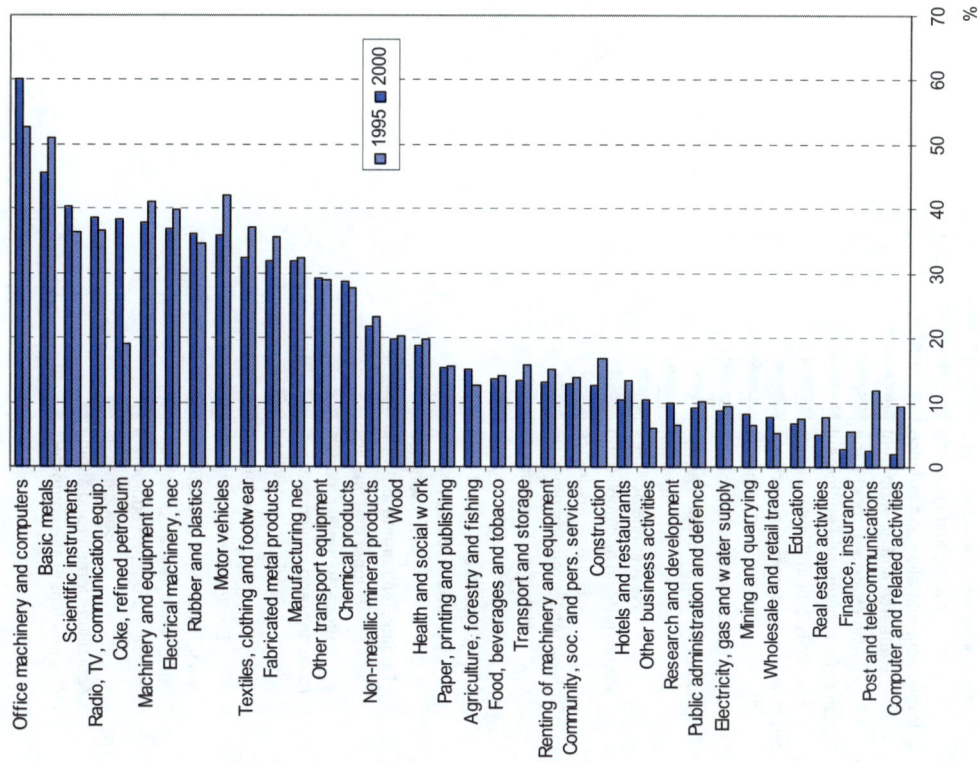

Norway - Growth of employment 1995-2000

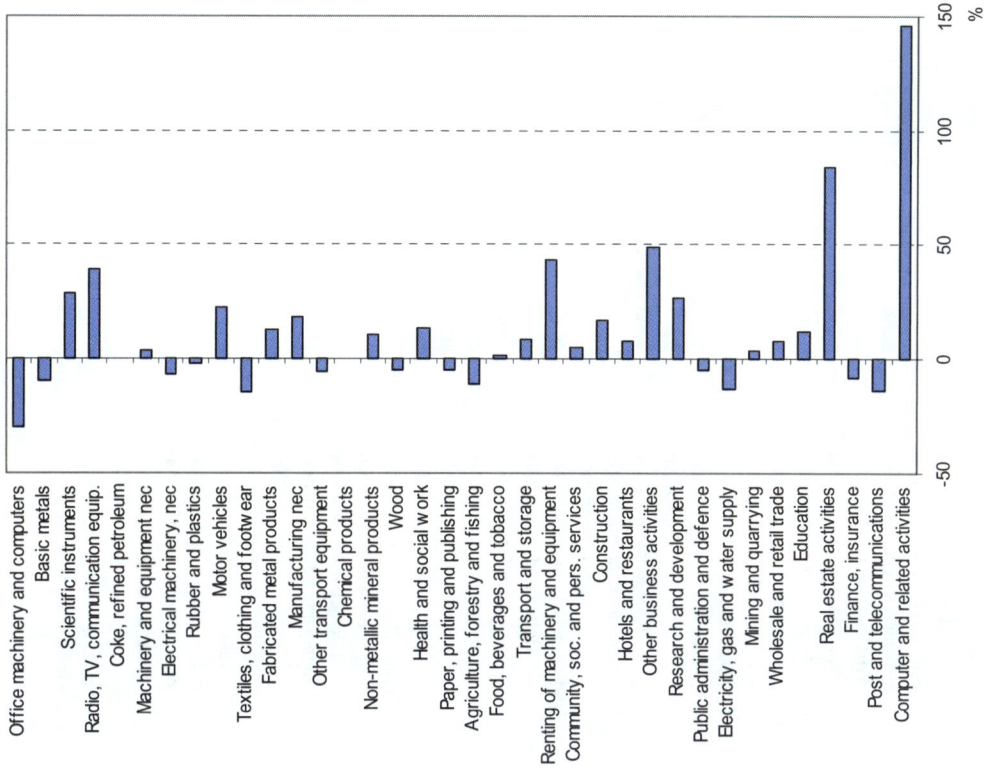

Source: OECD, Input-Output database. *StatLink:* http://dx.doi.org/10.1787/070151258883

Source: OECD, STAN database. *StatLink:* http://dx.doi.org/10.1787/318348107055

Norway – Index of outsourcing of services abroad by the goods and service industries

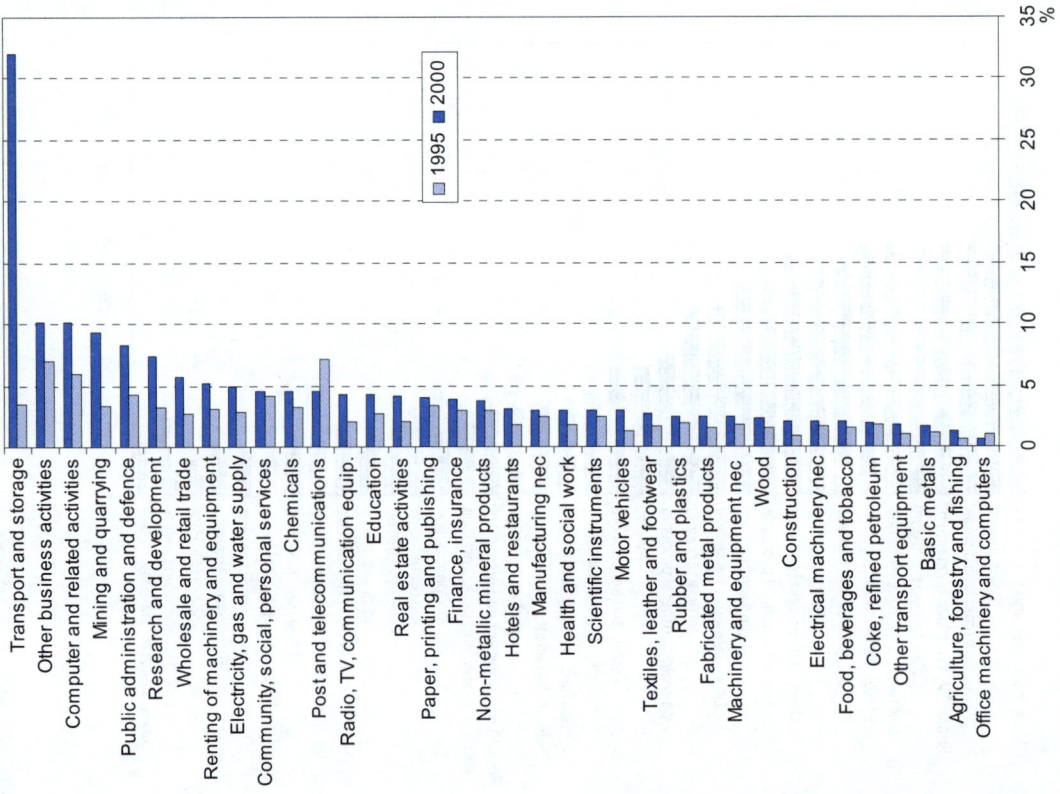

Source: OECD, Input-Output database. *StatLink:* http://dx.doi.org/10.1787/078183530103

Norway – Growth of employment 1995-2000

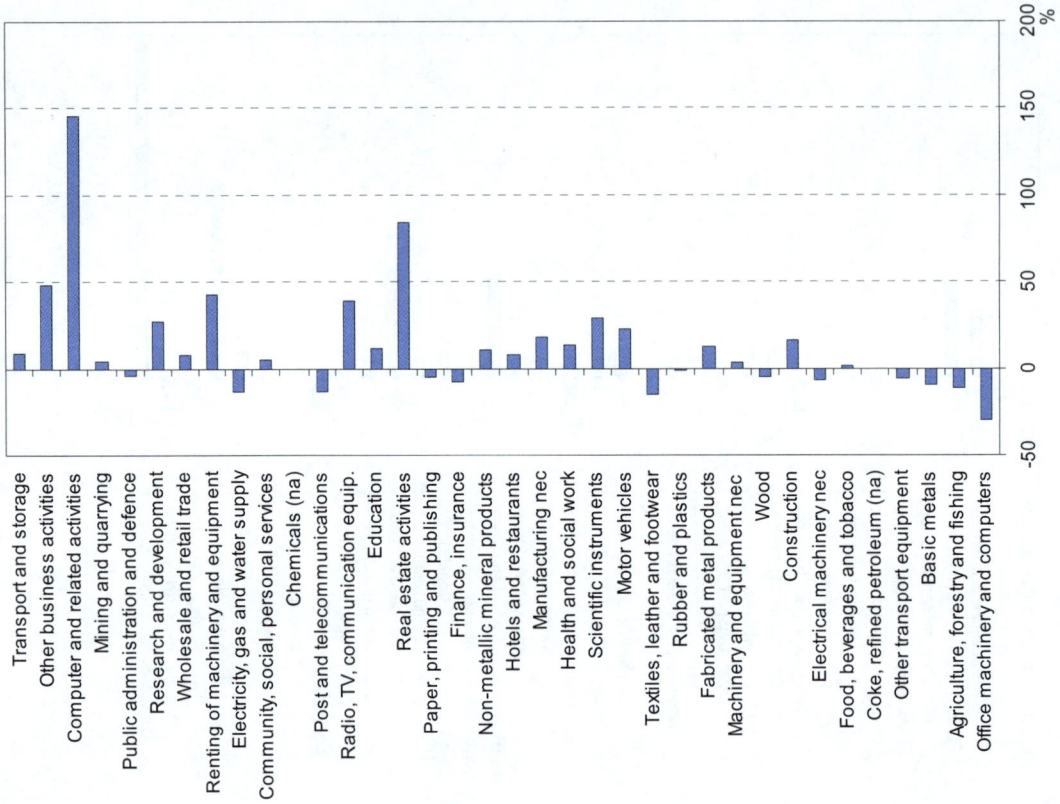

Source: OECD, STAN database. *StatLink:* http://dx.doi.org/10.1787/318481477265

Poland - Index of outsourcing of goods abroad by the goods and service industries

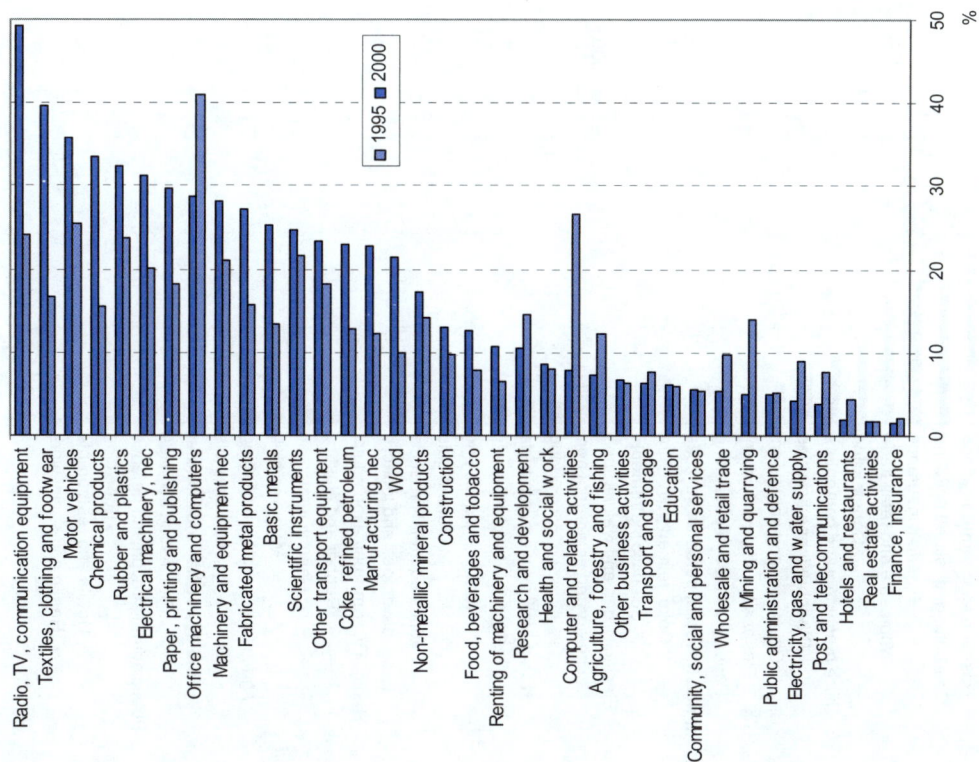

Poland - Growth of employment 1995-2000

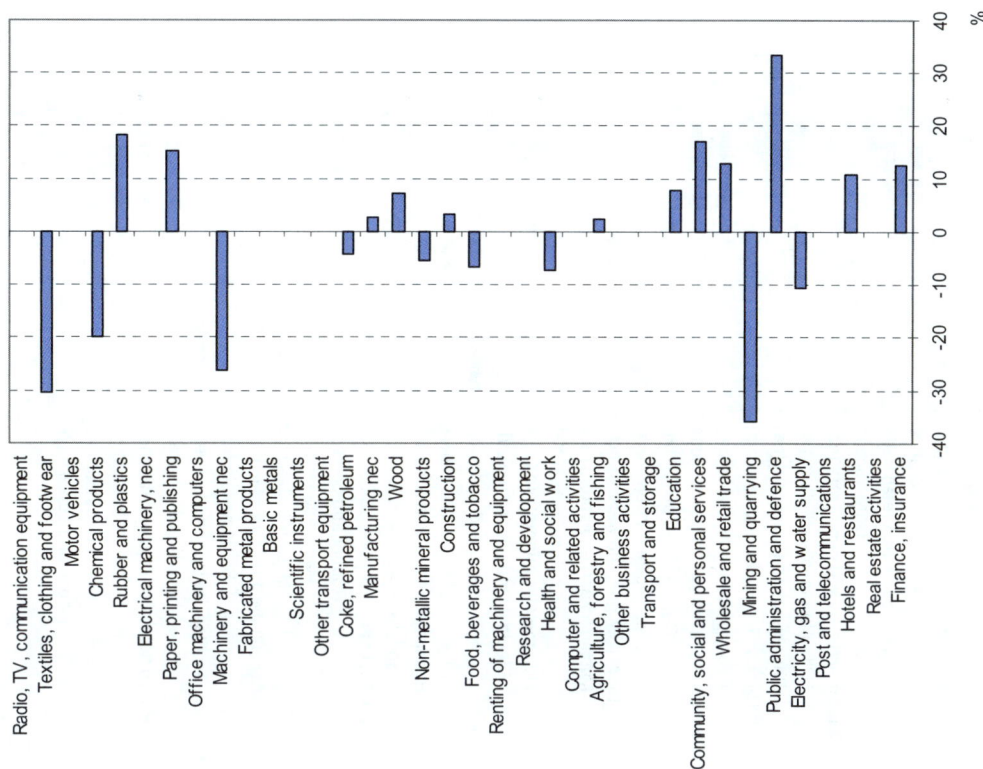

Source: OECD, Input-Output database. *StatLink:* http://dx.doi.org/10.1787/835828807607

Source: OECD, STAN database. *StatLink:* http://dx.doi.org/10.1787/080771538400

Poland - Index of outsourcing of services abroad by the goods and service industries

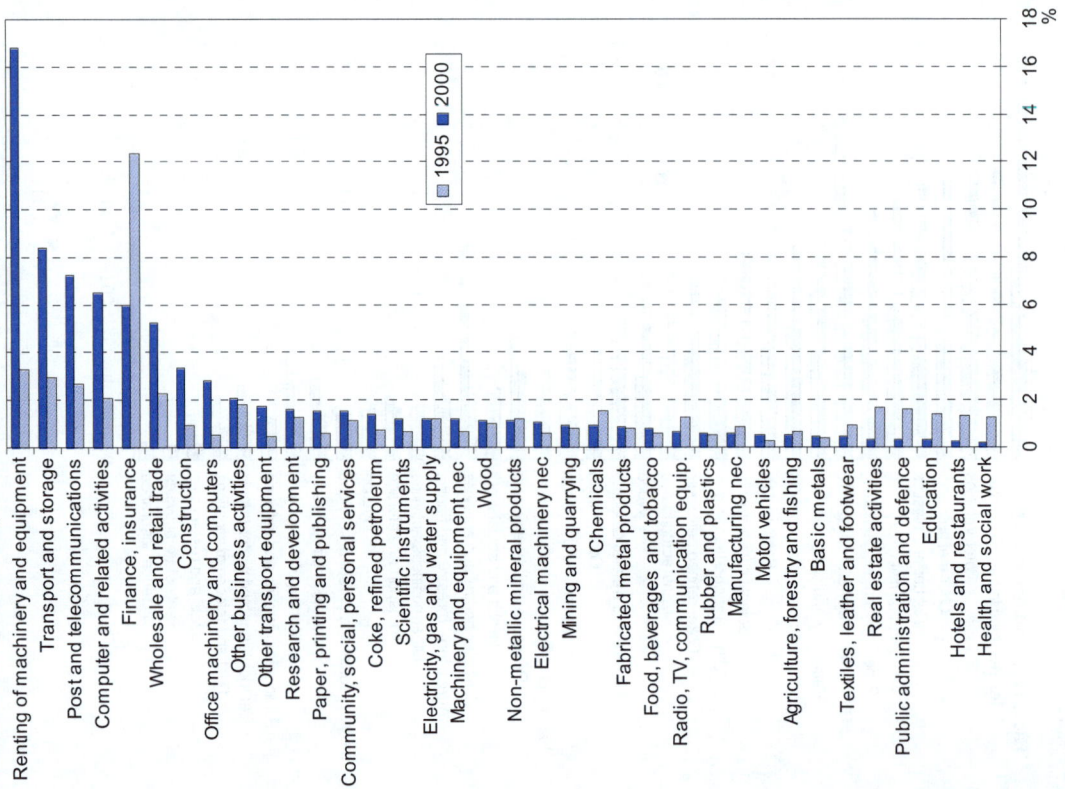

Source: OECD, Input-Output database. StatLink: http://dx.doi.org/10.1787/544483565141

Poland - Growth of employment 1995-2000

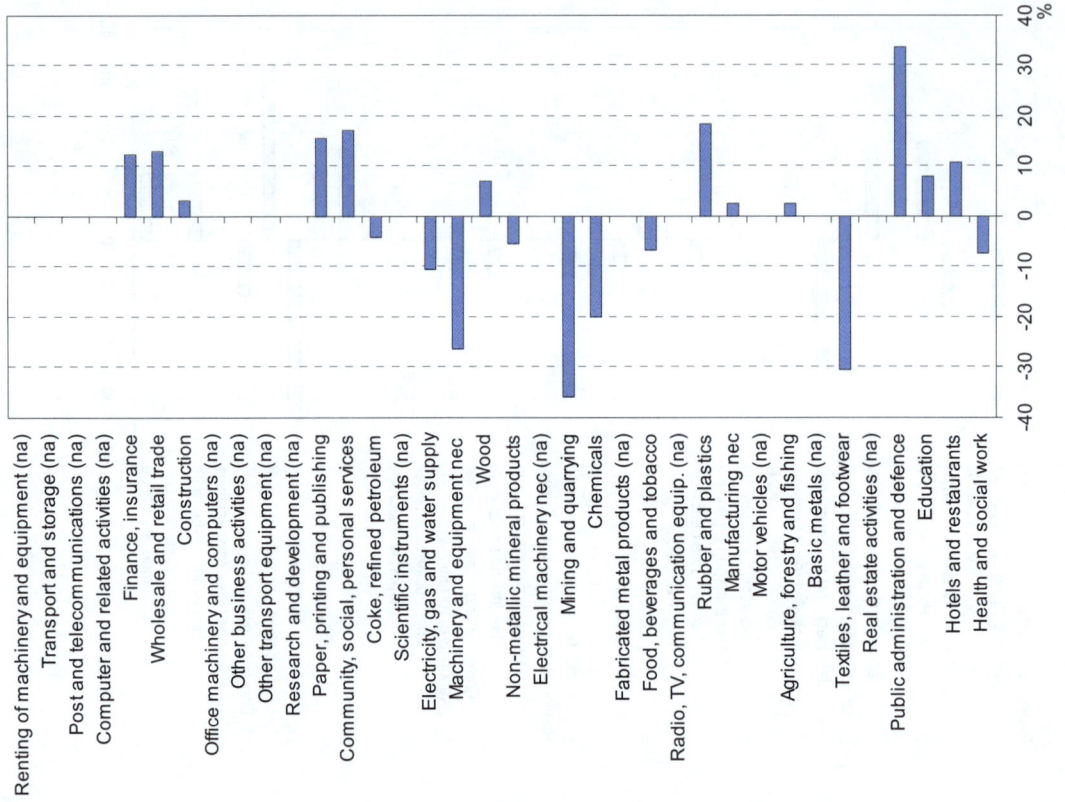

Source: OECD, STAN database. StatLink: http://dx.doi.org/10.1787/14728788O565

Portugal - Index of outsourcing of goods abroad by the goods and service industries

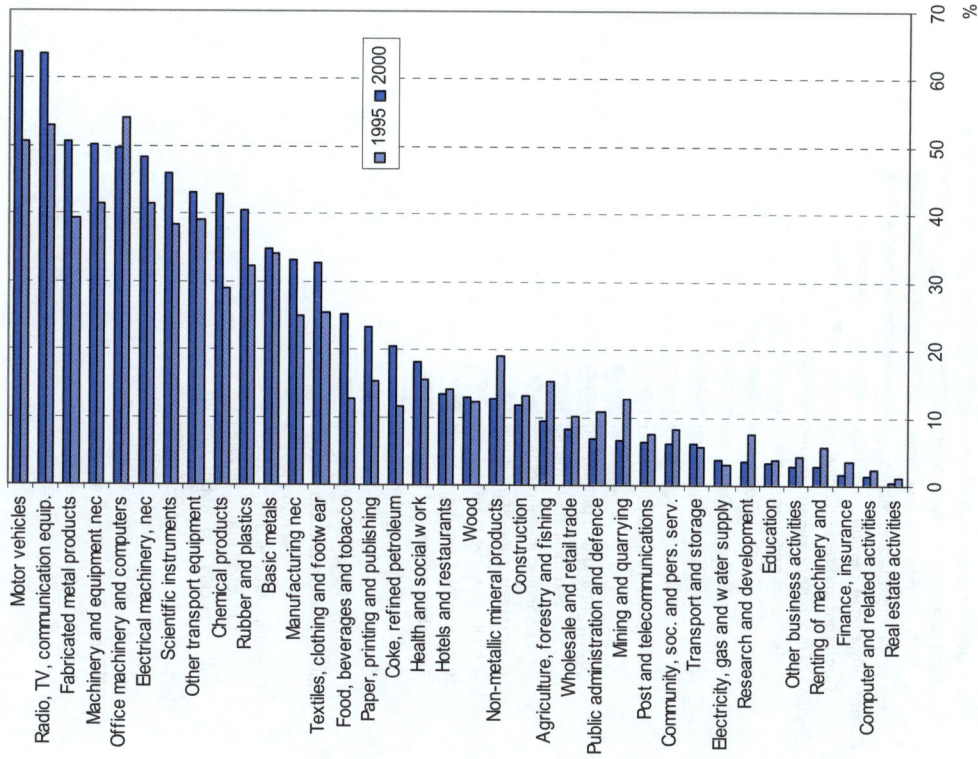

Source: OECD, Input-Output database. *StatLink:* http://dx.doi.org/10.1787/086621365067

Portugal - Growth of employment 1995-2000

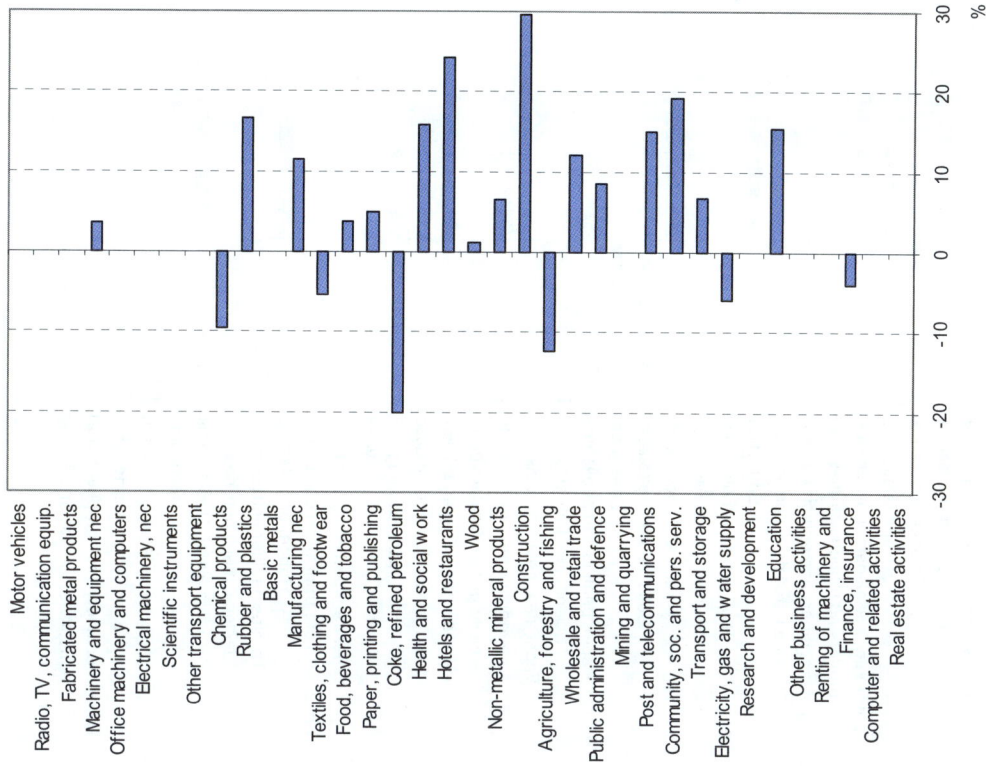

Source: OECD, STAN database. *StatLink:* http://dx.doi.org/10.1787/415421723670

Portugal - Index of outsourcing of services abroad by the goods and service industries

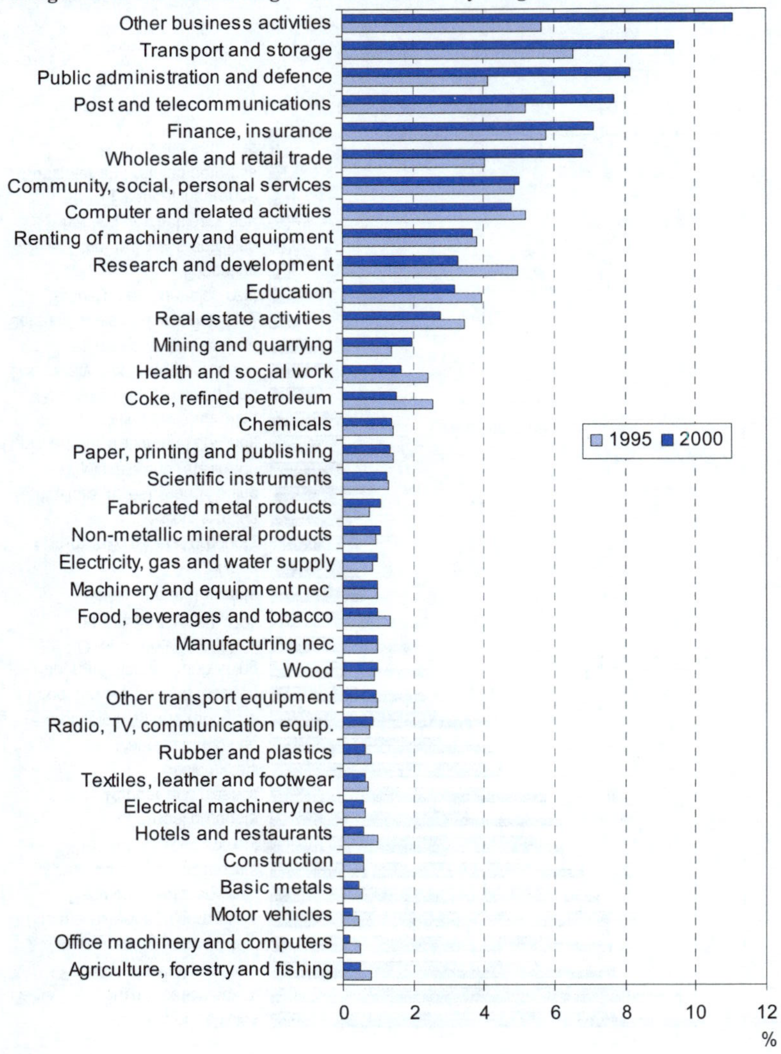
Other business activities
Transport and storage
Public administration and defence
Post and telecommunications
Finance, insurance
Wholesale and retail trade
Community, social, personal services
Computer and related activities
Renting of machinery and equipment
Research and development
Education
Real estate activities
Mining and quarrying
Health and social work
Coke, refined petroleum
Chemicals
Paper, printing and publishing
Scientific instruments
Fabricated metal products
Non-metallic mineral products
Electricity, gas and water supply
Machinery and equipment nec
Food, beverages and tobacco
Manufacturing nec
Wood
Other transport equipment
Radio, TV, communication equip.
Rubber and plastics
Textiles, leather and footwear
Electrical machinery nec
Hotels and restaurants
Construction
Basic metals
Motor vehicles
Office machinery and computers
Agriculture, forestry and fishing
1995
2000
0
2
4
6
8
10
12
%

Source: OECD, Input-Output database. *StatLink:* http://dx.doi.org/10.1787/183535088207

Portugal - Growth of employment 1995-2000

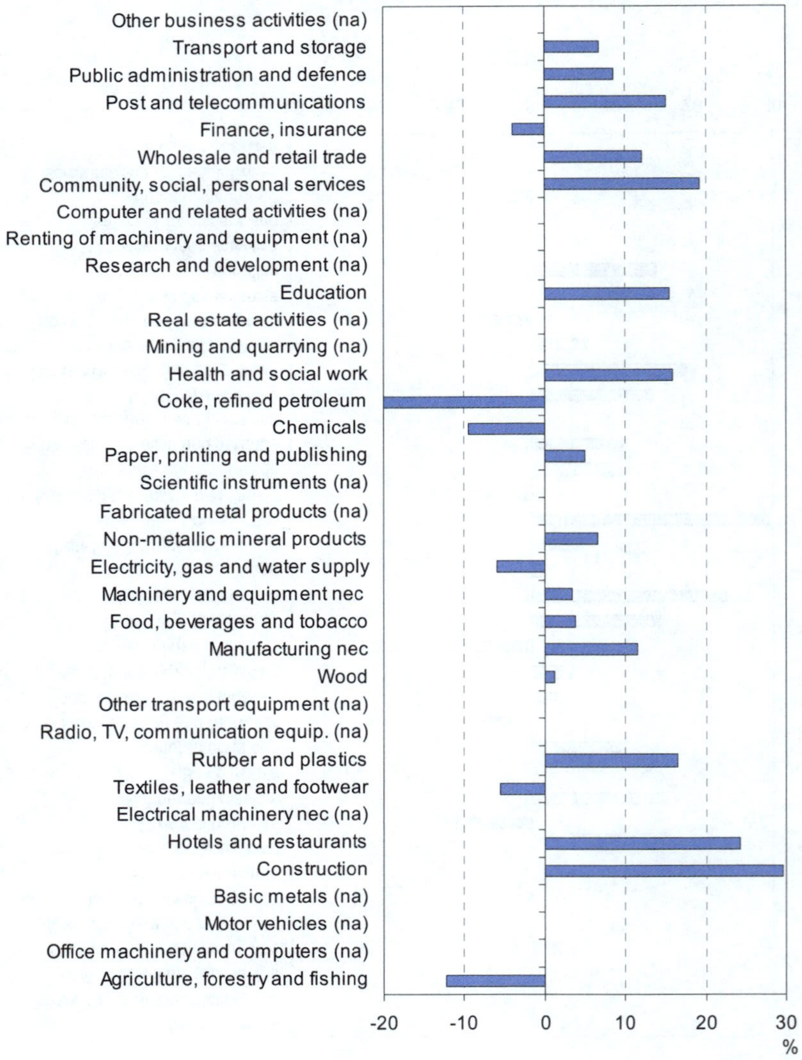
Other business activities (na)
Transport and storage
Public administration and defence
Post and telecommunications
Finance, insurance
Wholesale and retail trade
Community, social, personal services
Computer and related activities (na)
Renting of machinery and equipment (na)
Research and development (na)
Education
Real estate activities (na)
Mining and quarrying (na)
Health and social work
Coke, refined petroleum
Chemicals
Paper, printing and publishing
Scientific instruments (na)
Fabricated metal products (na)
Non-metallic mineral products
Electricity, gas and water supply
Machinery and equipment nec
Food, beverages and tobacco
Manufacturing nec
Wood
Other transport equipment (na)
Radio, TV, communication equip. (na)
Rubber and plastics
Textiles, leather and footwear
Electrical machinery nec (na)
Hotels and restaurants
Construction
Basic metals (na)
Motor vehicles (na)
Office machinery and computers (na)
Agriculture, forestry and fishing
-20
-10
0
10
20
30
%

Source: OECD, STAN database. *StatLink:* http://dx.doi.org/10.1787/413352550246

Slovak Rep. - Index of outsourcing of goods abroad by the goods and service industries

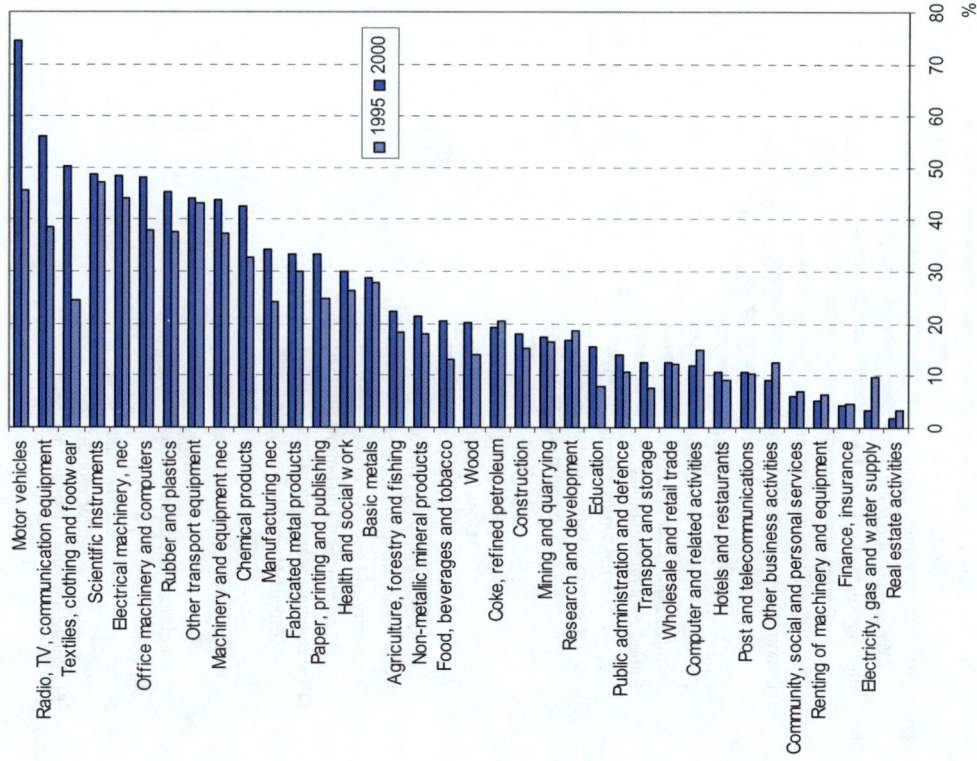

Slovak Rep. - Growth of employment 1995-2000

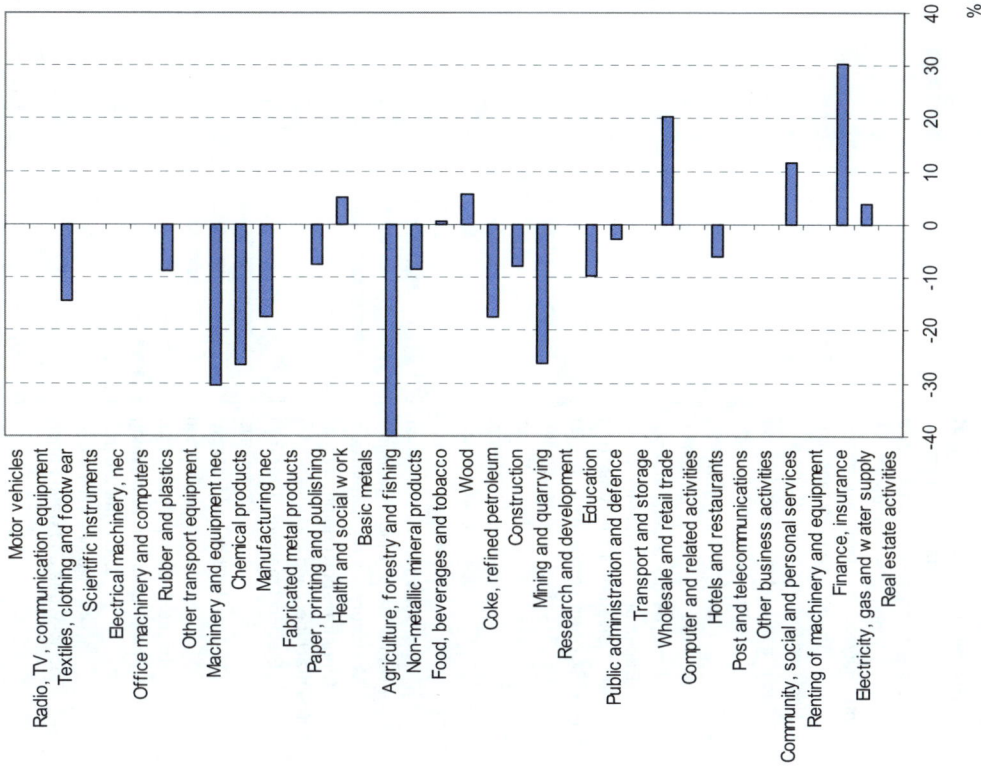

Source: OECD, Input-Output database. *StatLink:* http://dx.doi.org/10.1787/724411885427

Source: OECD, STAN database. *StatLink:* http://dx.doi.org/10.1787/221740850203

Slovak Rep. - Index of outsourcing of services abroad by the goods and service industries

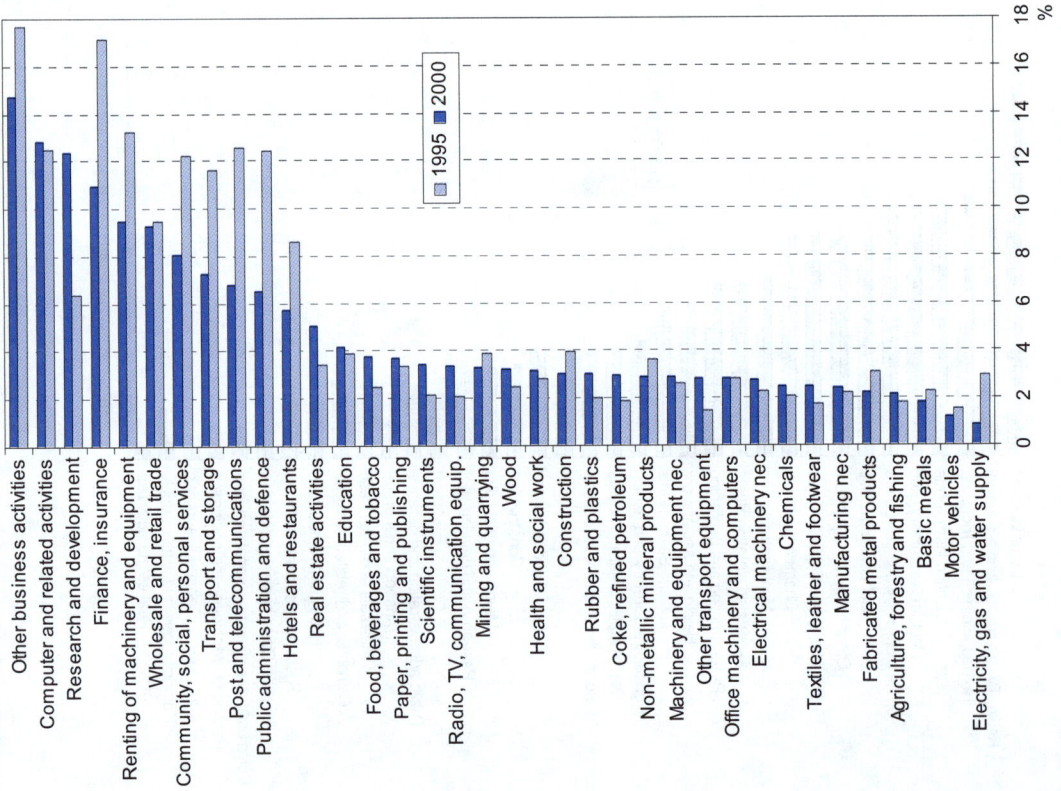

Slovak Rep. - Growth of employment 1995-2000

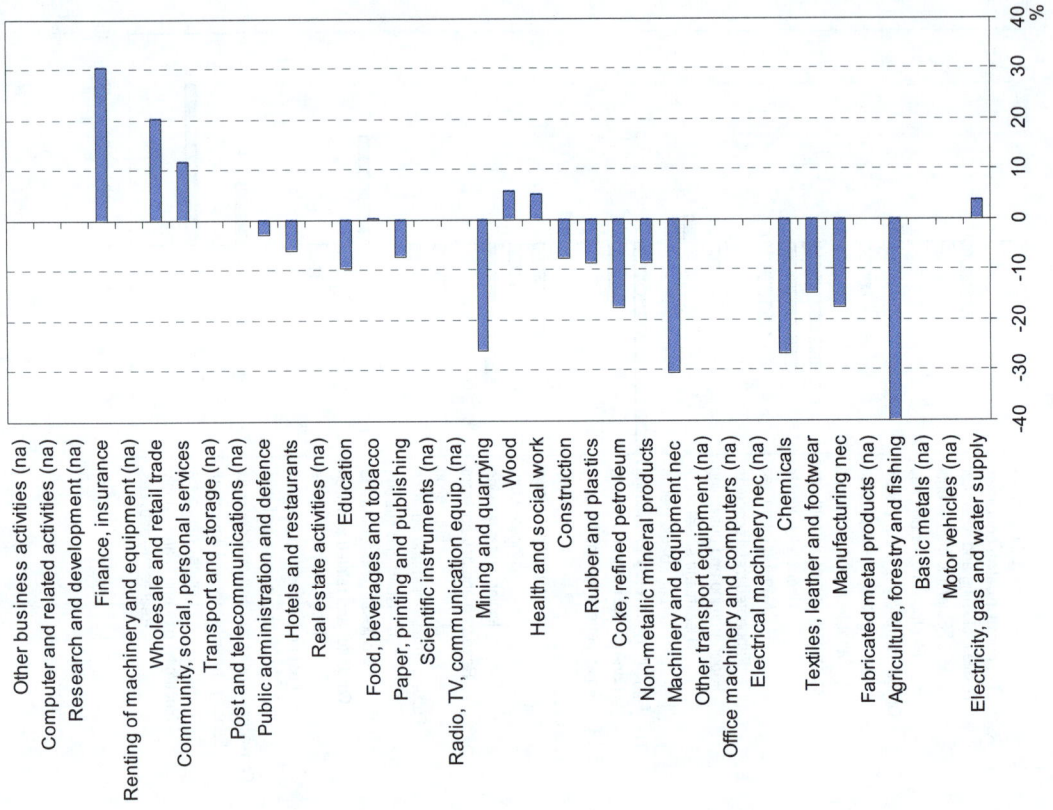

Source: OECD, Input-Output database. *StatLink:* http://dx.doi.org/10.1787/757277370635

Source: OECD, STAN database. *StatLink:* http://dx.doi.org/10.1787/145407851005

OFFSHORING AND EMPLOYMENT: TRENDS AND IMPACTS – ISBN-978-92-64-030923-3 – © OECD 2007

Spain - Index of outsourcing of goods abroad by the goods and service industries

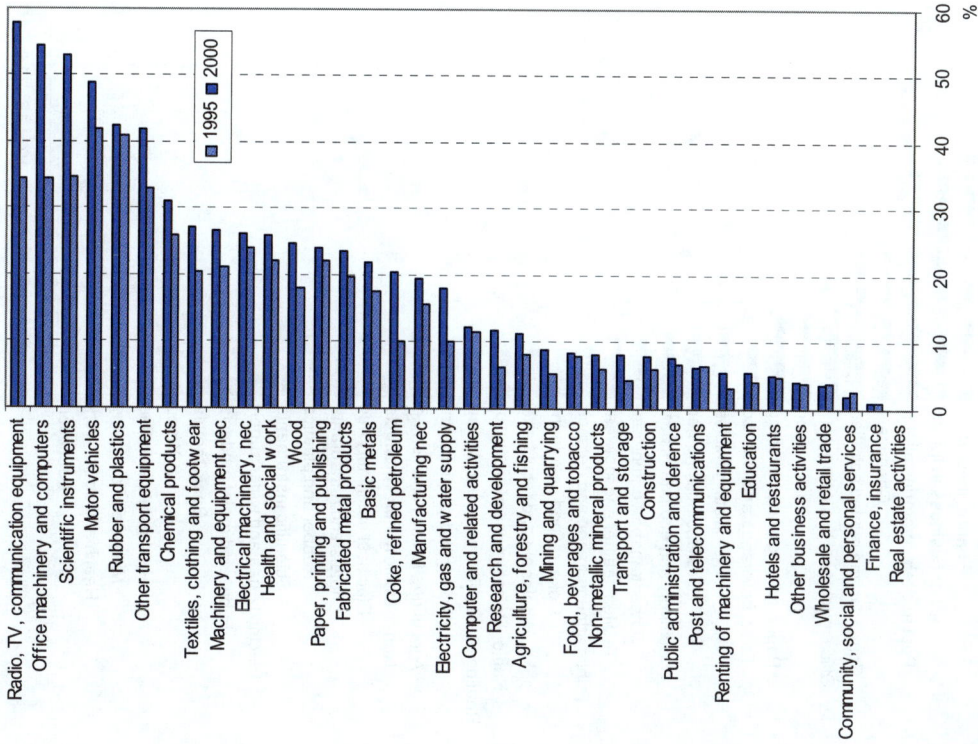

Legend: 1995 | 2000

Categories (left to right):
Radio, TV, communication equipment
Office machinery and computers
Scientific instruments
Motor vehicles
Rubber and plastics
Other transport equipment
Chemical products
Textiles, clothing and footwear
Machinery and equipment nec
Electrical machinery, nec
Health and social work
Wood
Paper, printing and publishing
Fabricated metal products
Basic metals
Coke, refined petroleum
Manufacturing nec
Electricity, gas and water supply
Computer and related activities
Research and development
Agriculture, forestry and fishing
Mining and quarrying
Food, beverages and tobacco
Non-metallic mineral products
Transport and storage
Construction
Public administration and defence
Post and telecommunications
Renting of machinery and equipment
Education
Hotels and restaurants
Other business activities
Wholesale and retail trade
Community, social and personal services
Finance, insurance
Real estate activities

Source: OECD, Input-Output database. *StatLink:* http://dx.doi.org/10.1787/38441084854

Spain - Growth of employment 1995-2000

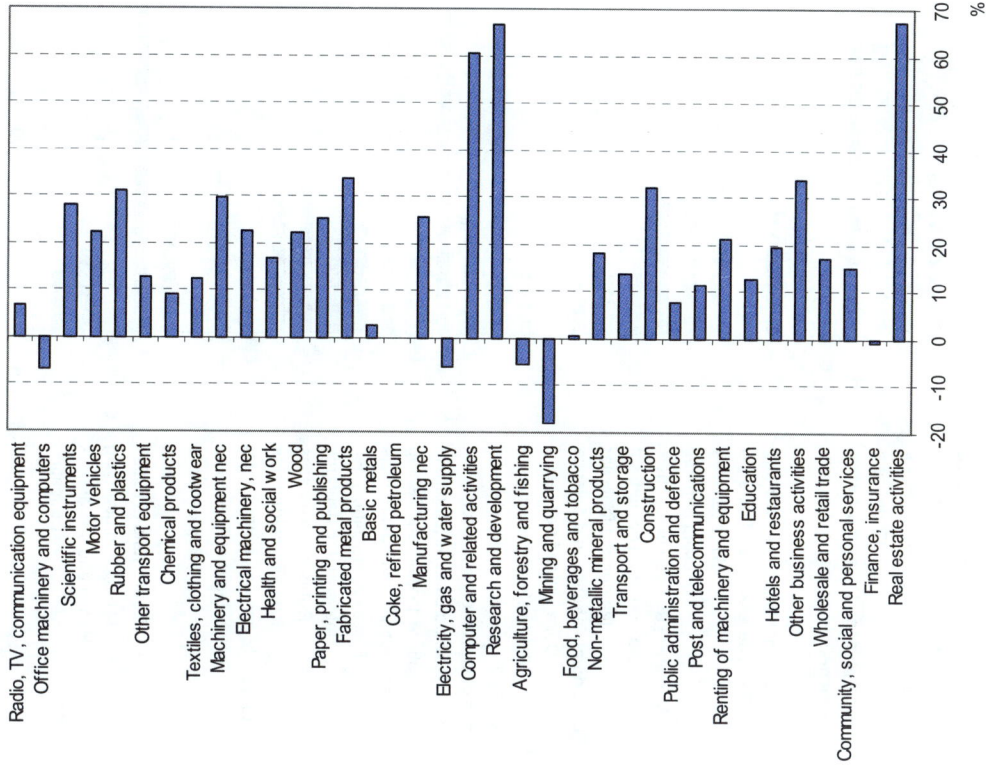

Source: OECD, STAN database. *StatLink:* http://dx.doi.org/10.1787/77075800340

Spain - Index of outsourcing of services abroad by the goods and service industries

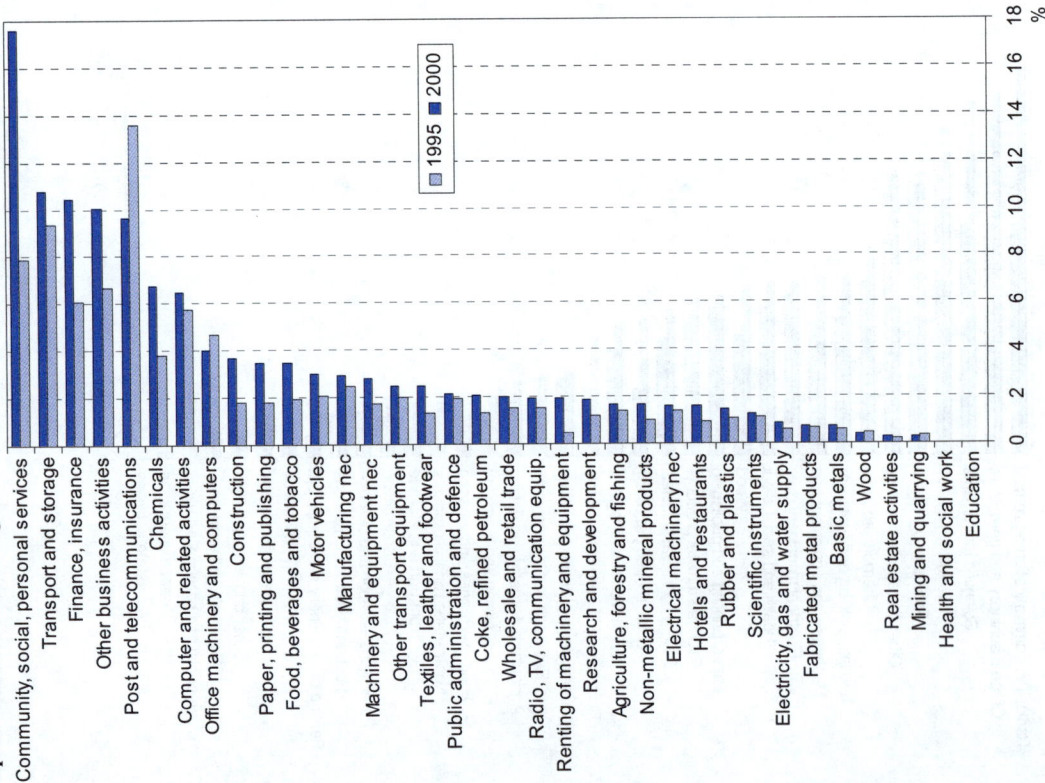

Source: OECD, Input-Output database. *StatLink:* http://dx.doi.org/10.1787/605558374434

Spain - Growth of employment 1995-2000

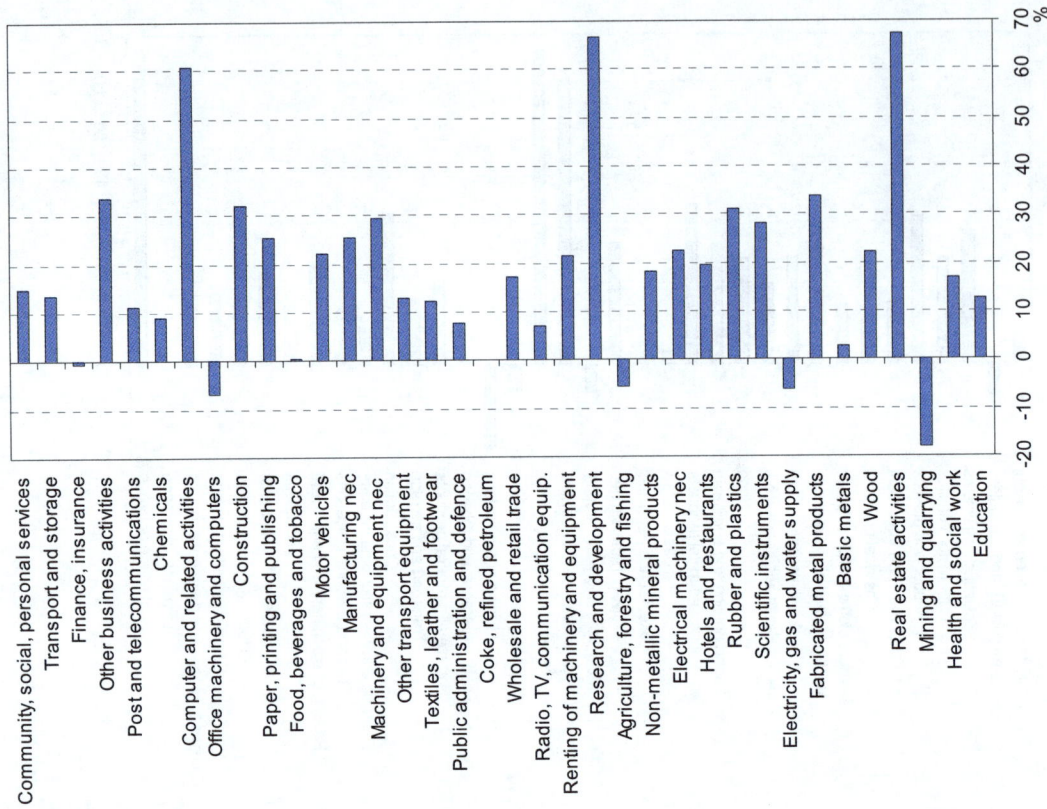

Source: OECD, STAN database. *StatLink:* http://dx.doi.org/10.1787/200675464080

Sweden - Index of outsourcing of goods abroad by the goods and service industries

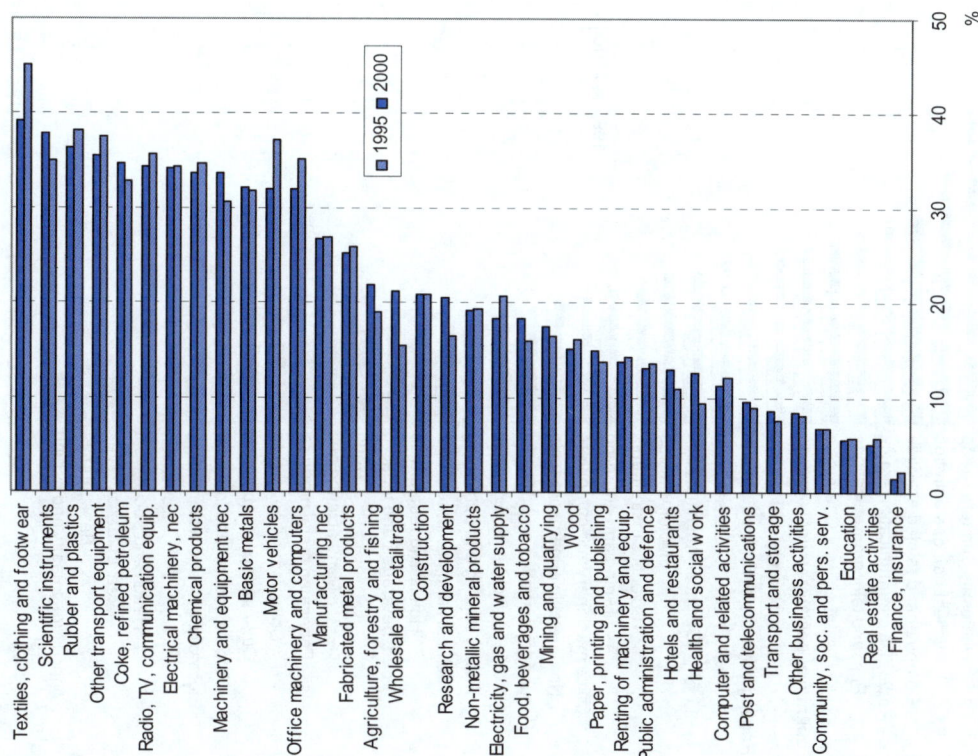

Legend: 1995 | 2000

Sweden - Growth of employment 1995-2000

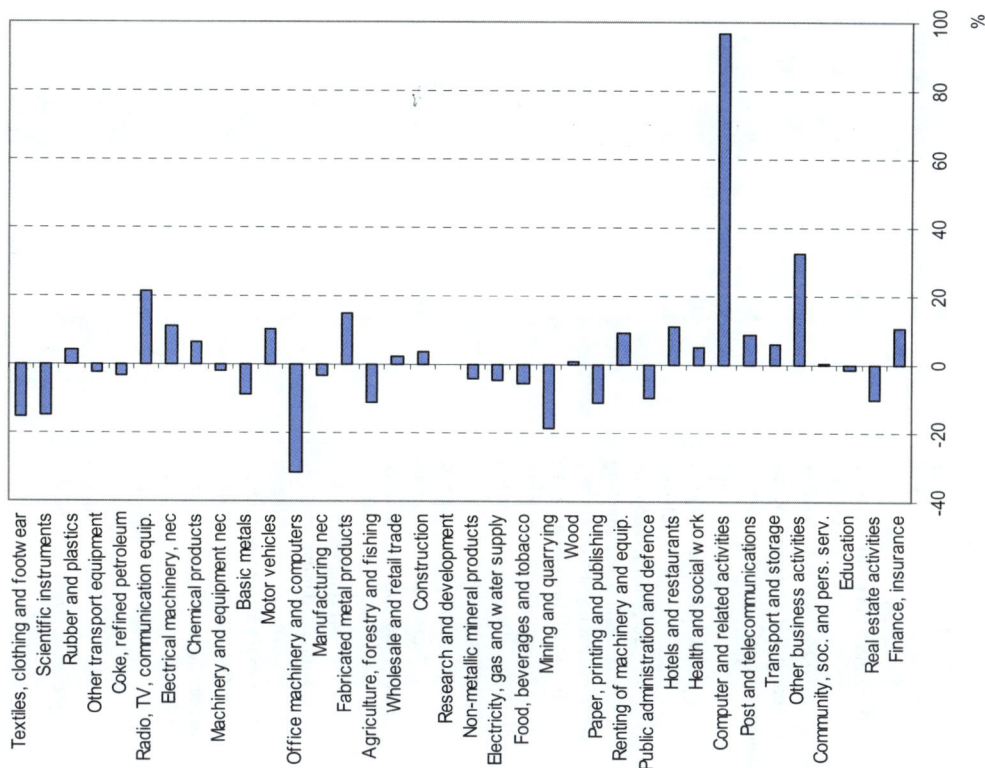

Source: OECD, Input-Output database. *StatLink:* http://dx.doi.org/10.1787/027618610615

Source: OECD, STAN database. *StatLink:* http://dx.doi.org/10.1787/445312316434

Sweden - Index of outsourcing of services abroad by the goods and service industries

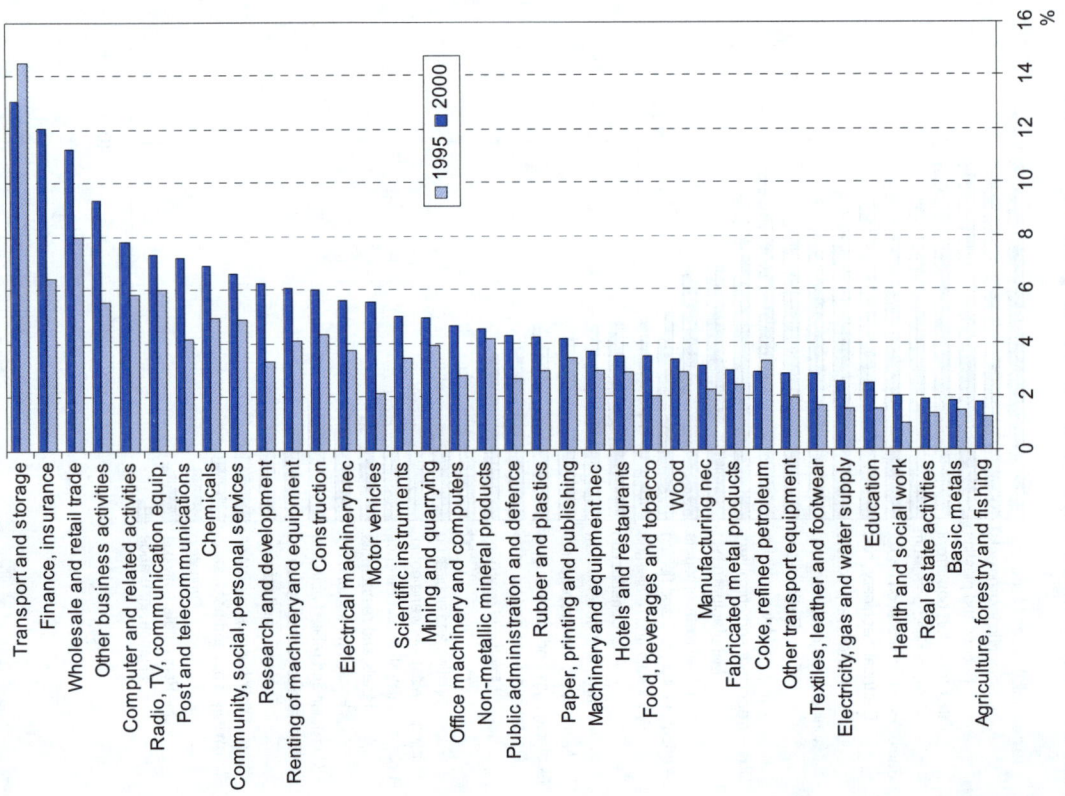

Source: OECD, Input-Output database. *StatLink:* http://dx.doi.org/10.1787/816735623550

Sweden - Growth of employment 1995-2000

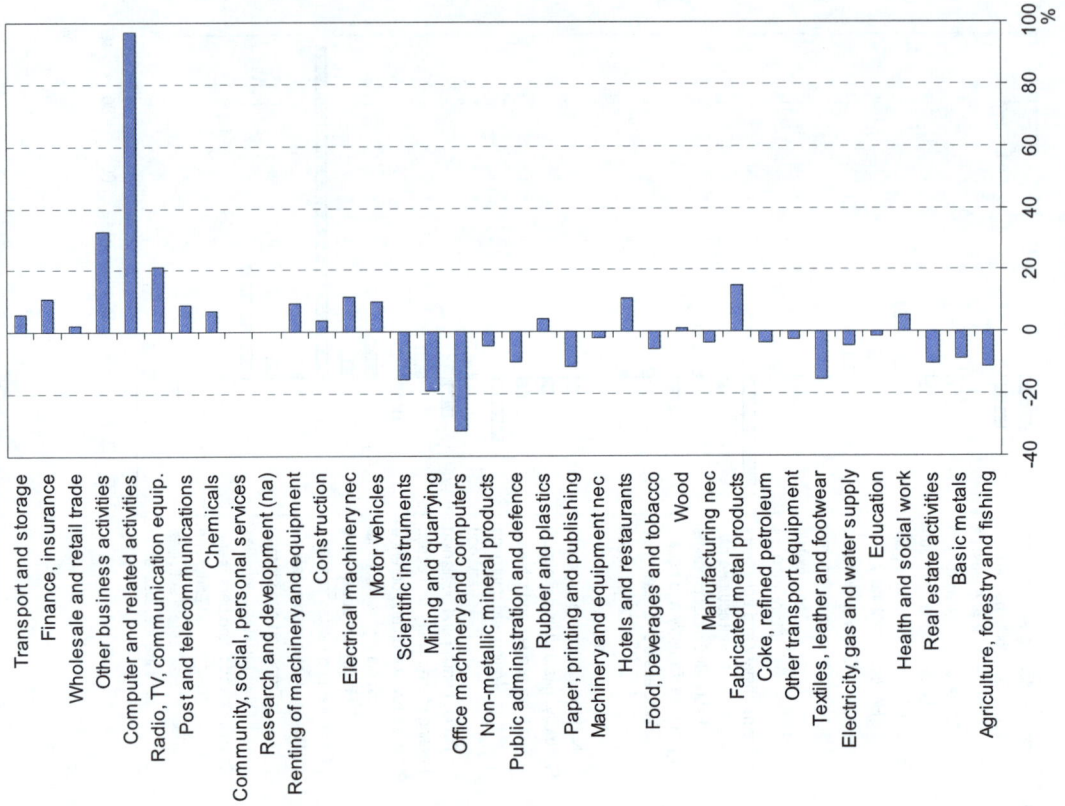

Source: OECD, STAN database. *StatLink:* http://dx.doi.org/10.1787/402527034746

UK - Growth of employment 1995-2000

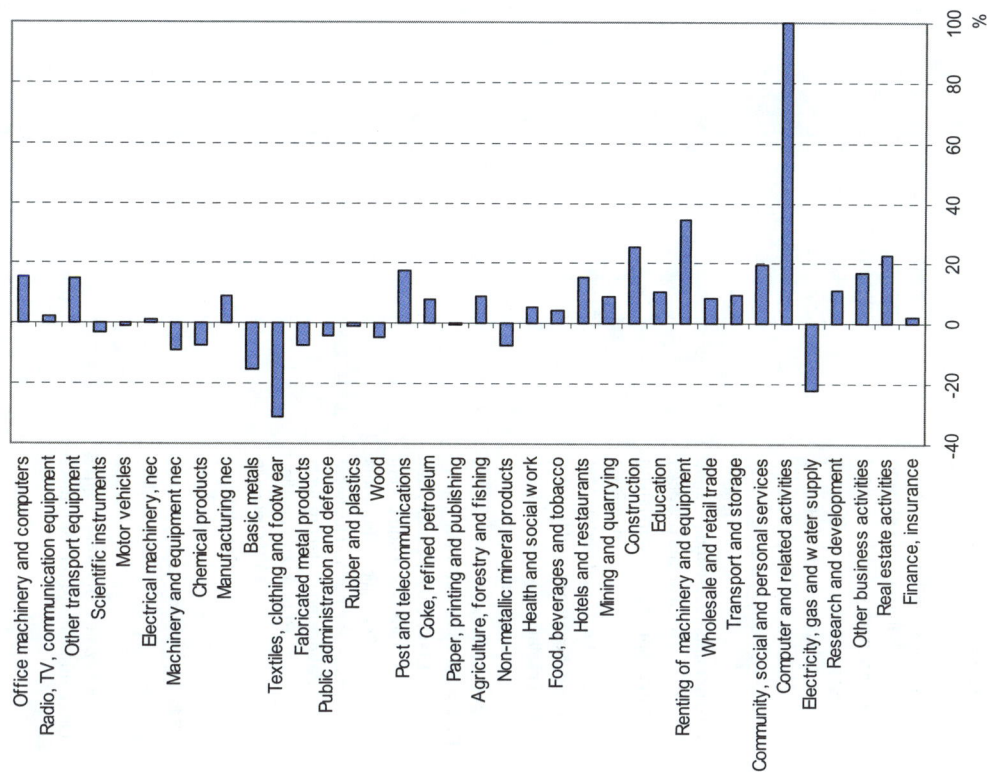

Source: OECD, STAN database. *StatLink:* http://dx.doi.org/10.1787/162483606373

UK - Index of outsourcing of goods abroad by the goods and service industries

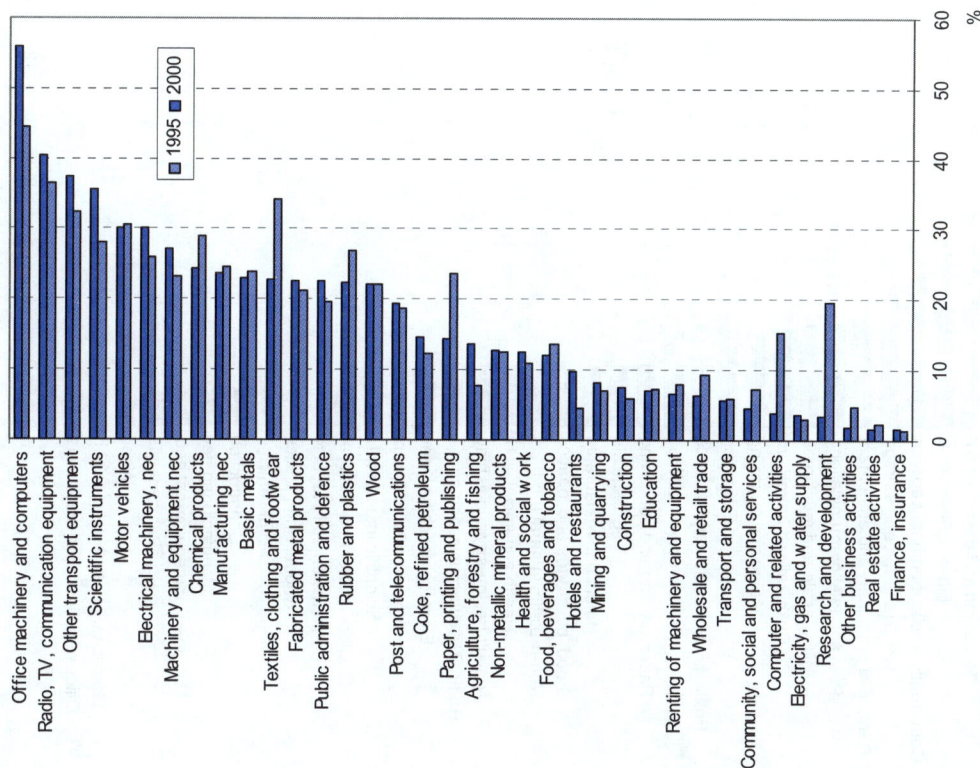

Source: OECD, Input-Output database. *StatLink:* http://dx.doi.org/10.1787/665144632586

UK – Index of outsourcing of services abroad by the goods and service industries

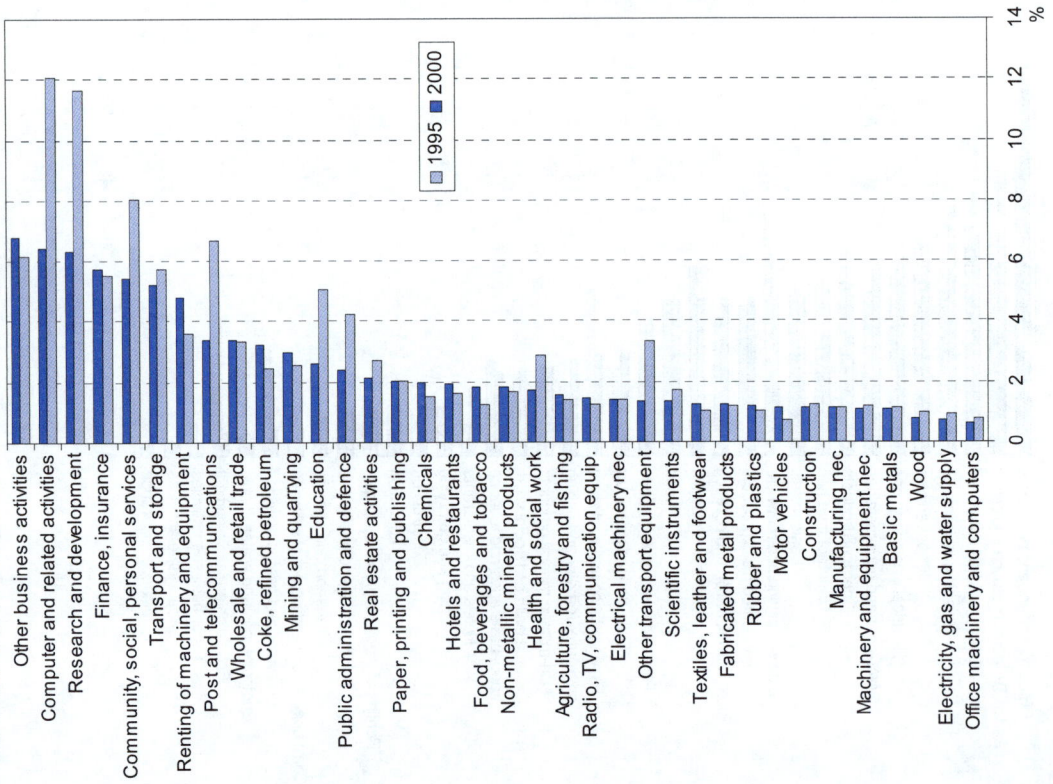

Source: OECD, Input-Output database. *StatLink:* http://dx.doi.org/10.1787/375755807774

UK – Growth of employment 1995-2000

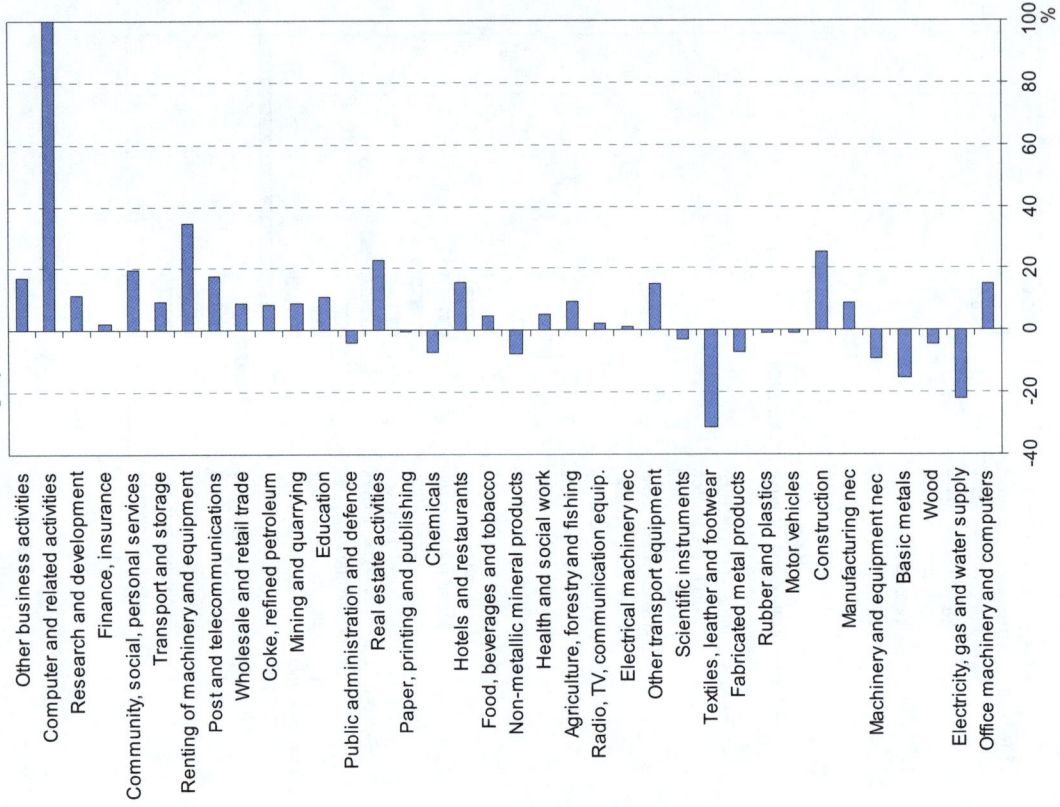

Source: OECD, STAN database. *StatLink:* http://dx.doi.org/10.1787/852633575457

Annex 4

Evolution of employment qualifications in the European Union countries, the United States and Japan

- **Skill level of employment in EU countries, 1997 and 2004**
- **Trends in employment by level of skills in industries with highest outsourcing index in 2000**

Table 1. Skill level[1] of employment in EU countries, 1997 and 2004

		Total*			Manufacturing			Services		
		1997	2004	Growth	1997	2004	Growth	1997	2004	Growth
Austria	Total employment	3 609	3 654	1.2	743	674	-9.4	2 028	2 235	10.2
	High-skilled	1 121	1 421	26.8	146	213	45.6	778	996	28.1
	Low-skilled	649	581	-10.4	206	155	-25.1	333	342	2.8
	Other	1 839	1 651	-10.2	391	306	-21.6	918	897	-2.3
Belgium	Total employment	3 838	4 144	8.0	758	723	-4.6	2 278	2 557	12.3
	High-skilled	1 546	1 779	15.1	194	213	9.8	1 140	1 312	15.1
	Low-skilled	656	740	12.9	259	272	4.8	303	351	15.8
	Other	1 637	1 625	-0.7	304	238	-21.9	836	894	7.0
Denmark	Total employment	2 675	2 742	2.5	502	434	-13.4	1 697	1 833	8.0
	High-skilled	988	1 178	19.2	118	138	17.3	752	900	19.8
	Low-skilled	536	493	-8.0	183	133	-27.0	278	292	5.0
	Other	1 150	1 071	-6.9	201	162	-19.2	667	640	-4.0
Finland	Total employment	2 120	2 384	12.4	423	445	5.3	1 253	1 514	20.8
	High-skilled	886	1 022	15.4	131	166	26.2	636	723	13.7
	Low-skilled	355	413	16.5	123	134	9.0	185	238	28.6
	Other	879	949	7.9	169	145	-13.8	432	553	27.9
France	Total employment	21 958	24 175	10.1	4 110	4 099	-0.3	12 547	14 324	14.2
	High-skilled	8 025	9 448	17.7	1 106	1 241	12.2	5 768	6 801	17.9
	Low-skilled	4 094	4 573	11.7	1 571	1 535	-2.3	1 739	2 012	15.7
	Other	9 838	10 154	3.2	1 432	1 322	-7.7	5 039	5 511	9.4
Germany	Total employment	35 299	35 463	0.5	8 423	8 201	-2.6	18 734	20 576	9.8
	High-skilled	13 735	14 878	8.3	2 321	2 415	4.0	8 657	9 938	14.8
	Low-skilled	5 756	5 286	-8.2	1 968	1 828	-7.1	2 526	2 606	3.2
	Other	15 808	15 299	-3.2	4 133	3 957	-4.3	7 550	8 032	6.4
Greece	Total employment	3 853	4 331	12.4	559	570	2.0	1 901	2 388	25.6
	High-skilled	1 115	1 454	30.4	82	100	22.2	894	1 171	31.1
	Low-skilled	511	606	18.7	137	146	6.4	259	300	16.1
	Other	2 228	2 271	1.9	339	323	-4.7	749	917	22.4
Ireland	Total employment	1 373	1 836	33.7	262	280	6.9	756	1 107	46.4
	High-skilled	409	762	86.3	64	94	46.7	294	498	69.6
	Low-skilled	245	302	23.4	71	89	26.1	102	143	39.9
	Other	720	773	7.4	127	97	-23.8	360	466	29.4
Italy	Total employment	20 032	22 438	12.0	4 500	4 901	8.9	10 629	12 839	20.8
	High-skilled	4 999	9 027	80.6	547	1 127	105.9	3 734	6 670	78.6
	Low-skilled	3 689	4 111	11.5	1 362	1 498	10.0	1 403	1 748	24.6
	Other	11 345	9 299	-18.0	2 590	2 276	-12.2	5 492	4 422	-19.5
Luxembourg	Total employment	169	186	10.3	22	18	-17.4	100	109	9.4
	High-skilled	65	85	31.4	5	5	5.1	45	58	29.4
	Low-skilled	33	37	12.5	9	7	-15.2	14	15	6.4
	Other	72	65	-9.8	9	6	-31.3	41	36	-11.5
Netherlands	Total employment	7 186	8 101	12.7	1 074	1 046	-2.6	4 400	5 348	21.5
	High-skilled	3 310	3 917	18.3	327	342	4.3	2 256	2 765	22.5
	Low-skilled	1 034	1 202	16.3	311	314	1.0	576	725	26.0
	Other	2 842	2 982	4.9	436	391	-10.3	1 568	1 858	18.5
Portugal	Total employment	4 523	5 125	13.3	947	1 004	6.0	2 111	2 425	14.9
	High-skilled	1 134	1 365	20.4	124	161	30.3	832	949	14.0
	Low-skilled	803	1 056	31.4	234	296	26.2	331	399	20.6
	Other	2 586	2 704	4.6	589	546	-7.2	947	1 077	13.7
Spain	Total employment	13 191	17 866	35.4	2 489	3 035	21.9	6 974	9 769	40.1
	High-skilled	3 853	5 586	45.0	461	656	42.2	2 873	4 062	41.4
	Low-skilled	3 193	4 413	38.2	922	1 127	22.2	1 299	1 786	37.5
	Other	6 144	7 867	28.0	1 106	1 252	13.2	2 802	3 921	39.9
Sweden	Total employment	3 917	4 311	10.1	753	684	-9.2	2 570	2 984	16.1
	High-skilled	1 593	1 902	19.4	216	219	1.2	1 176	1 430	21.7
	Low-skilled	638	674	5.6	282	273	-3.3	291	347	19.1
	Other	1 686	1 734	2.9	255	192	-24.7	1 103	1 207	9.4
United Kingdom	Total employment	26 744	27 929	4.4	5 002	3 774	-24.6	17 222	19 211	11.6
	High-skilled	10 478	11 372	8.5	1 555	1 375	-11.6	7 596	8 461	11.4
	Low-skilled	4 298	4 900	14.0	1 544	1 219	-21.1	2 197	3 010	37.0
	Other	11 969	11 657	-2.6	1 903	1 180	-38.0	7 428	7 740	4.2

1. High-skilled: ISCO 1, 2 and 3 ; low-skilled: ISCO 8 and 9.

* Includes agriculture and mining.

Source: EU Labour Force Survey.

Table 2. Trends in employment by level of skills in industries with highest outsourcing index in 2000

Country	Industry	NACE	Total employment		High-skilled		Low-skilled		Other		Growth 1997-2004 (%)			
			1997	2004	1997	2004	1997	2004	1997	2004	Total	High-skilled	Low-skilled	Other
Germany	Other transport equipment	35	162	176	58	62	18	18	86	96	8.8	6.8	1.5	11.7
	Computers	30	138	75	92	49	9	5	38	21	-45.6	-46.2	-45.3	-44.3
	Textiles and clothing	17-19	403	272	78	54	97	73	228	145	-32.5	-31.2	-24.4	-36.4
	Radio, TV, communication equipment, electronic comp.	32	217	259	102	126	31	31	84	102	19.2	23.9	0.0	20.6
	Basic metals	27	445	265	88	60	148	92	208	113	-40.5	-32.6	-37.6	-45.9
	Rubber and plastics	25	319	343	76	80	141	161	101	103	7.5	4.2	13.6	1.6
	Chemical products (including pharmaceuticals)	24	626	626	254	278	219	188	153	160	0.1	9.6	-13.9	4.5
	Other manufacturing industries	36	450	332	63	47	72	49	315	236	-26.1	-24.8	-32.1	-25.0
	Machinery and equipment n.e.c.	29	1184	1119	424	407	150	132	610	580	-5.5	-4.1	-12.1	-4.9
	Instruments	33	272	317	90	113	32	32	149	171	16.6	25.2	1.0	14.8
	Motor vehicles	34	762	1034	196	318	190	228	375	488	35.7	61.9	19.9	30.1
France	Computers	30	40	24	30	19	4	1	6	4	-40.1	-36.2	-74.1	-35.0
	Basic metals	27	138	129	34	34	59	58	45	37	-6.0	-1.3	-1.4	-15.8
	Textiles and clothing	17-19	315	194	32	39	211	101	71	54	-38.5	22.0	-52.4	-24.6
	Rubber and plastics	25	208	241	51	64	106	132	51	45	15.7	24.2	25.4	-12.7
	Other transport equipment	35	153	140	64	72	30	20	60	47	-8.5	13.3	-31.4	-20.4
	Radio, TV, communication equipment, electronic comp.	32	138	131	63	82	42	30	32	19	-4.8	29.8	-28.8	-41.8
	Motor vehicles	34	309	338	81	107	100	111	127	120	9.5	32.4	10.6	-6.0
	Chemical products (including pharmaceuticals)	24	308	316	137	149	104	106	67	61	2.5	9.2	1.2	-9.1
	Electrical machinery n.e.c.	31	162	141	61	47	62	55	39	39	-13.0	-22.7	-11.4	-0.6
	Instruments	33	147	133	76	77	35	27	36	28	-9.6	1.9	-21.3	-22.4
United Kingdom	Computers	30	140	88	76	58	26	11	38	20	-37.2	-24.6	-59.2	-47.6
	Radio, TV, communication equipment, electronic comp.	32	164	95	57	44	63	27	44	24	-42.0	-23.0	-56.5	-45.9
	Other transport equipment	35	232	206	80	84	43	35	110	87	-11.4	5.2	-17.6	-21.1
	Instruments	33	147	126	72	66	28	28	48	32	-14.2	-7.7	2.4	-33.6
	Motor vehicles	34	307	265	79	76	115	97	114	92	-13.8	-4.0	-15.2	-19.2
	Electrical machinery n.e.c.	31	235	168	83	65	70	50	82	53	-28.7	-22.0	-29.2	-35.2
	Machinery and equipment n.e.c.	29	475	356	157	131	115	91	204	134	-25.1	-16.9	-20.8	-34.0
	Chemical products (including pharmaceuticals)	24	350	282	160	157	103	89	88	37	-19.4	-2.2	-13.2	-58.3
	Other manufacturing industries	36	243	195	59	49	74	69	110	78	-19.6	-17.1	-6.4	-29.7
	Basic metals	27	167	104	42	24	58	44	67	35	-37.8	-43.8	-22.9	-46.9

Source: EU Labour Force Survey.

Annex 5

Responses of member countries to the OECD questionnaire

A5.1 The questionnaire

The questionnaire was made up of four parts:

- A. General policy linked to offshoring.
- B. Measures intended to prevent offshoring.
- C. Measures to improve the employment market and promote innovation.
- D. Measures designed to revive economic activity.

A. General policy linked to offshoring (relocation abroad)

1. Does your country have a special policy in relation to offshoring?

Yes	No
❑	❑

2. If "yes", could you outline below the most significant measures taken by your country in this context?

To the question as to whether or not there is a particular policy with regard to offshoring, all the countries have replied "no". In any case, there is no policy that is overtly favorable or overtly unfavorable to offshoring. Conversely, there are many measures in force which have either a direct or indirect impact on offshoring, and which are mentioned in the following parts of the questionnaire. However, these measures have been taken independently without making any reference to offshoring.

B. Measures intended to prevent offshoring

		Yes	No
B.1.	Reduce government support to enterprises relocating their R&D activities or a significant part of their production abroad	❑	❑
B.2.	Exclude offshoring enterprises from public procurement	❑	❑
B.3.	Apply special value-added tax (VAT) to imports of products suspected of being linked to offshoring activities (so that the consumer prices are the same as those of products made by domestic enterprises)	❑	❑
B.4.	Apply penalties to enterprises relocating abroad the R&D or production activities of strategic sectors or sectors linked to national security	❑	❑
B.5.	Other (please specify):	❑	❑

Table 1. Country responses to Part B of the questionnaire

Country	B1		B2		B3		B4	
	Yes	No	Yes	No	Yes	No	Yes	No
Austria		X		X		X		X
Canada		X		X		X		X
Czech Republic		X		X		X		X
Germany		X		X		X		X
Hungary								
Luxembourg		X		X		X		X
Norway		X		X		X		X
Poland	X			X		X		X
Sweden		X		X		X		X
Italy [1]		X		X		X		X
Switzerland		X		X		X		X
United Kingdom		X		X		X		X
United States		X		X		X		X
France		X		X		X		X
Australia	X			X		X		X
Spain	X	X		X		X		X
Finland	X[2]			X		X		X
Portugal		X		X		X		X
Belgium		X[3]		X		X		X

1. Answers have not been provided for topics which are outside the remit of the Tax Policy Department (Ministry of Economy and Finance), which agreed to respond.

2. The legislation implementing pertinent EU acts constitutes a right for the granting authorities to discontinue payment of subsidies to an enterprise in relation to an investment project if there are changes in its implementation that deviate from its intended targets. Further, if conditions agreed upon in a project are not met, the granting authority may request repayment of the subsidy. This can involve *i.e.* cases of relocating entire enterprise activity whilst a condition for employing a given number of people at a given site has been established when granting the subsidy

3. Tax incentives for the employment of researchers must be repaid in the event the employment is terminated. However, this measure does not apply to firms that offshore their activities.

Poland indicates that government aid is reduced for businesses which offshore their R&D activities or a substantial part of their production.

In principle the UK does not take any measure to find companies that offshore their R&D activities abroad. Simply, the businesses which do less R&D to the UK deprive themselves of some of the tax credits for R&D.

As regards the possibility of debarring those businesses which offshore from government procurement, no countries state that such policies are in force in their countries. However, some press accounts have indicated that such measures exist in certain cases but these might concern the regional authorities, something that has not been officially confirmed. The other countries do not mention any policy envisaged to prevent offshoring.

C. Measures to improve the labour market and promote innovation

		Yes	No
C.1.	Apply tax credits or tax reductions to enterprises located in regions with high unemployment	❑	❑
C.2.	Reduce labour costs through:		
	a.　　　　Direct subsidies	❑	❑
	b.　　　　Tax credit	❑	❑
	c.　　　　Reductions in social charges	❑	❑
C.3.	Improve labour flexibility in terms of:		
	a.　　　　Working hours	❑	❑
	b.　　　　Part-time work	❑	❑
	c.　　　　Labour mobility	❑	❑
	d.　　　　Recruitment and laying off of employees	❑	❑
	e.　　　　Other (please specify)	❑	❑
C.4.	Reinforce enterprise competitiveness through:		
	a.　　　　Direct or indirect R&D support	❑	❑
	b.　　　　Policies to create clusters (*e.g.* for R&D and innovation, by establishing close links with R&D centres and universities).	❑	❑
C.5.	Establishment of partnerships between enterprises and local communities	❑	❑
C.6.	Reinforce the competitiveness of local subcontractors (mainly SMEs)	❑	❑
C.7.	Improve relationships between order-placing enterprises and local subcontracting enterprises	❑	❑
C.8.	Develop ways of anticipating enterprises' decisions in respect of offshoring (warning systems)	❑	❑
C.9.	Other (please specify)	❑	❑

Table 2. Country responses to Part C of the questionnaire

Country	C1	C2 a	C2 b	C2 c	C3 a	C3 b	C3 c	C3 d	C4 a	C4 b	C5	C6	C7	C8	C9
Austria	No	No	No	No	No (1)	No (1)	No (1)	No (1)	Yes	Yes	Yes	–	No	No	–
Canada	No	No	No	No	No (2)	No (2)	No (2)	No (2)	No (2)	No (2)	No (2)	No (2)	No	No	–
Czech Rep.	Yes	Yes	No	No	No	No	No	Yes	Yes	Yes	Yes	Yes	No	No	–
Germany	No	No	No	Yes	Yes	Yes	Yes	Yes	Yes	Yes	Yes	–	–	No	–
Hungary	Yes (3)	Yes (4)	No	Yes (5)	No (6)	Yes (7)	Yes (8)	No	Yes (9)	Yes (10)	Yes (11)	Yes (12)	Yes (13)	No	–
Luxembourg	No	No	No	No	Yes	Yes	No	No	Yes	Yes	Yes	Yes	No	Yes	–
Norway	No	No (14)	No	No	No	No	No	No	No	No	–	–	–	No	–
Poland	Yes	Yes	No	No	No	No	No	Yes	Yes	Yes	No	Yes	No	No	–
Sweden	No	No	No	No	No	No	No	No	No	No	No	No	No	No	–
Switzerland	Yes	No	No	No	Yes (15)	Yes (15)	Yes (15)	Yes (15)	Yes	Yes	Yes	Yes	Yes	No	–
UK	No (16)	No	No	No	No (17)	No (17)	No (17)	No (17)	No (18)	No (18)	No (19)	No (20)	No (21)	No	–
USA	Yes	Yes	Yes	Yes	No	No	No	No	Yes	Yes	Yes	Yes	No	No	–
France	Yes (22)	Yes (23)	Yes (24)	Yes (25)	Yes (26)	Yes (27)	Yes (28)	Yes (29)	Yes (30)	Yes (31)	Yes (32)	Yes (33)	No	Yes (34)	–
Australia	No	No	No	No	Yes	Yes	Yes	Yes	Yes	Yes	No	Yes	No	No	–
Spain	No	No	No	No	No	No	No	No	Yes	Yes	No	Yes	No	No	–
Finland	No	No	No	No	Yes	No	Yes	No	Yes	Yes	No	No	No	No	–
Portugal	Yes (35)	No	Yes (36)	No	No (37)	No (37)	No (37)	No (37)	Yes (38)	Yes (38)	No	Yes (39)	No	Yes (40)	Yes (41), (42)
Italy	Yes (43)	No	Yes (44)	Yes (45)	Yes (46)	Yes (46)	Yes (46)	Yes (47)	Yes (48)	Yes (49)	No	No	No	No	n/a
Belgium	Yes (50)	Yes (50)	Yes (50)	Yes (50)	Yes (50)	Yes (50)	No	No	Yes (50)	Yes (50)	Yes (50)	No	No	No	–

Source: EU Labour Force Survey.

Table 2 notes:

1.   The Austrian regulatory framework for the labour market foresees a considerable degree of flexibility with regard to the problems raised by the question; however, none of the measures was introduced explicitly to reduce the pressure of offshoring but rather within a general framework to modernize the regulatory framework of the economy.

2.   Please note that these measures are in place in Canada but were not implemented in the context of offshoring.

3.   Conditions to be eligible for development tax benefit are eased for priority regions (the prescribed minimum value of investment and the employment criterion are lower and have recently been reduced).

4.   The given proportion of labour-related costs (50-60 %) may be refunded by the *Labour Market Fund* to the enterprise that creates jobs through investment to high value added activities.

5.   Social charges have recently been reduced (in a targeted way) to help employment of:

—   Young entrants to labour market.

—   Young mothers

—   Registered unemployed over 50 years.

Proportioning the lump-sum health contribution to working hours, making part-time work more favourable.

Gradually decreasing, and then eliminating (in 2006) the lump-sum health contribution.

6.   No recent changes; basic framework:

Working hours: maximum 12 hours/day or 48 hours/week. Within the given time-frame, working hours can be freely distributed, but a minimum of 4 hours/day is required.

7.   State support can be applied for (when hiring unemployed) + see C.2.c.

8.   State support to promote distance work and labour force rent (Ministry of Labour).

The employer has to refund part of the commuter's costs.

In addition: government-sponsored training for the unemployed, young entrants to labour market and other groups "in a difficult situation".

9.   Corporate tax: deduction of direct expenses related to R&D from the tax base.

The National Development Plan's Economic Competitiveness Operational Program (ECOP), 3rd priority:

—   Creating new jobs through the development of entrepreneurs' research infrastructure.

—   Supporting innovation at the level of SMEs.

—   Supporting technology and knowledge-intensive start-ups, and innovation activity of spin-offs (at micro-enterprise level).

Domestic programmes: setting up innovation funds within Corvinus Rt. (in preparation). Form of support: capital increase (buying ownership).

10.   ECOP 1.1.3/B: expanding the spectrum and raising the quality of services provided by cluster management to cluster members (launched in September 2005).

11.   OECD's Corporate Social Responsibility guideline is observed by large corporations.

12. ECOP 1.1.3.: for raising the number of local subcontractors (SMEs), and improving their competitiveness.

Domestic programme: within the framework of the state-owned Hungarian Development Bank's Supplier and Investor Co., reinforcing the integration of industrial suppliers, aid is form of capital increase.

13. Suppliers' credit programme for SMEs (through the Hungarian Development Bank): loans with favourable interest rates.

14. Employers pay a lower social security contribution on gross salary payments to employees resident in sparsely populated regions in Norway. The aim of the measure is to stimulate employment and settlement in these areas. The measure favours employment of persons resident in these sparsely populated areas as opposed to persons resident in more central parts of Norway. The lower tax rates apply automatically on the basis of fixed and objective criteria. Originally, the decisive factor was solely the place of residence of the employee. As from 1999 minor sector restrictions were introduced and from 2004 certain additional thresholds were introduced, reducing the efficiency of the measure. There are no criteria linked to the nationality or to the size of the offshore activities of the enterprises.

15. Switzerland's flexible labour market policy is not directly linked to offshoring.

16. There are various programmes to help enterprises in regions with high unemployment. Some are tax related *e.g.* Enterprise Zone Capital Allowances that offer accelerated allowances to business in Enterprise Zones. Others involve grants or loans *e.g.* Selective Finance for Investment in England (SFIE) to encourage investment in assisted areas that wouldn't have gone ahead without government assistance or the Phoenix Fund to encourage enterprise in and by disadvantaged communities.

17. The UK looks to establish a fair, flexible labour market that protects employees' rights. We recognise the need for balance: protecting workers without imposing an unnecessary burden on business. The UK has a wide range of working patterns: 26 % work part time, 22% work flexibly and around 4/5ths of employers provide at least one flexible time arrangement.

Working hours: the UK sees it as important to retain flexibility on working hours, leaving this as a matter for individual choice and business competitiveness. Surveys have found that 7 out of 10 workers did not want to reduce their hours if it meant a cut in pay.

Encourage labour flexibility: the UK seeks to encourage flexibility through tax policy – tax credits for families and children – encouraging people to work rather than depend on benefits.

18. The UK promotes high value business activity through a variety of channels including: R&D tax reliefs against corporation tax, support for Higher Education networks and a Technology Programme to encourage collaborative R&D and knowledge transfer.

19. There are various national mechanisms to encourage links, especially between businesses and educational institutions:

   – Knowledge Transfer Networks (KTNs): Promote and accelerate the transfer of knowledge between the science, engineering and technology base on the one hand and industry on the other. KTNs offer networking opportunities for business, academic or research organizations working in similar fields or sectors.

   – Collaborative R&D: Assists the industry and research communities to work together on R&D projects in strategically important areas of science, engineering and technology. It also primes the flow of the latest knowledge and thinking from the UK's science, engineering and technology base to business.

   – Knowledge Transfer Partnerships: Can help a business to develop and grow by accessing knowledge and expertise in the UK's universities, colleges and research organisations.

   In addition, there are also local schemes by Regional Development Agencies (RDAs) to encourage links with their regions.

20.   Whilst there aren't programmes specifically targeted at subcontractors, there are a range of national programmes to help smaller firms, which will include many subcontractors, improve their competitiveness. These include:

— Support to Implement Best Business Practices (SIBBP). Puts small and medium sized businesses in touch with advisers who can help them evaluate their competitive position and define practical ways to enhance it.

— The Manufacturing Advisory Service gives manufacturers in every region direct access to practical advice and support from manufacturing experts.

— The Small Firm Loan Guarantee (SFLG) can guarantee loans from the banks and other small financial institutions for small firms that have viable business proposals but who have tried and failed to obtain a conventional loan because of lack of security.

— The Grant for Research and Development provides grants to help individuals and small and medium-sized businesses develop innovative products and processes.

Again, RDAs also run local schemes.

21.   There currenlty are not any national programmes targeted in this area; however, some RDAs do have schemes along these lines.

22.   Business tax credit.

23.   50% of personnel costs of businesses that relocate are covered.

24.   Competitiveness cluster measures, research jobs.

25.   Competitiveness cluster measures, reduction of labour costs of low wages, exemptions targeting urban zero-tax areas, urban renewal areas and rural renewal areas.

26.   Greater flexibility in the application of the 35-hour work week.

27.   Employment bonus, part-time work, 2006 Budget Act.

28.   Mobility tax credit, 2006 Budget Act, UNEDIC mobility bonus.

29.   New employment contract (*Contrat nouvelle embauche*).

30.   Research tax credit, clusters of competitiveness, Industrial Innovation Agency.

31.   2005 Budget Act.

32.   Clusters of competitiveness.

33.   SME Pact, Industrial Innovation Agency → 25% of funds channelled to SMEs.

34.   Interministerial Mission on Economic Change – MIME → DATAR.

35.   It is a "general policy", the main goal of which is to increase both regional development and employment (see "supplementary information").

36.   It is a "general policy", the main goal of which is to develop employment, and above all the employment of young people (see "supplementary information").

37.   The Portuguese regulatory framework for the labour market provides a considerable degree of flexibility with regard to the problems raised by the question; however, none of the measures was introduced explicitly to reduce the pressure of offshoring, but rather as part of an overall effort to improve the regulatory environment of the economy.

38.   The Technological Plan promotes high-value business activities in a variety of ways including: R&D tax relief on corporation tax, support for higher-education networks and a technology programme to encourage collaborative R&D and knowledge transfer.

39.   System of incentives to improve the dynamism and modernisation of industry as a whole (support for corporate mergers and acquisitions); programmes of advice and training for micro to small enterprises; employer-driven programmes (stimulating contracts and new-job creation for technical workers). Please note that these measures are in force but were not implemented in the context of offshoring.

40.   The Agency for Integrated Intervention for Enterprise Restructuring (AGIIRE) is implementing a warning system aimed at anticipating the decisions of businesses to restructure, resolving their difficulties and ensuring the success of new jobs (see "supplementary information").

41.   Centres for Fast and Personalised Intervention (NIRP) set up to provide local support for workers affected by restructuring processes, by rapidly seeking tailor made solutions whereby the workers can find new jobs and keep their social protection.

42.   The new law aims to speed up liquidation procedures and promote fresh starts, enabling enterprises to recover, and ultimately restore their solvency, so as to make the economy healthier.

43.   Yes. There have been examples in the past (*i.e.* KL.488/92) Further measures could be implemented subject to the finalization of the budget law 2007 and may require EC endorsement/approval.

44.   Yes. Among others, L. 446/97 (art. 11 known as "IRAO Assunzioni") provided for tax incentives for recruitment.

45.   The possibility of reducing charges (known as "Cuneo fiscale") is, at the time of writing, undergoing parliamentary scrutiny within the framework of the budget law 2007.

46.   Labour flexibility is at the core of the so-called "Biagi law" (n.30/2003), which provides for all the items listed above and is currently undergoing revision.

47.   Yes (measures are in force to facilitate traineeship under full recognition of social security guarantees).

48.   Yes. Among others, the so-called "Techno-tremonti" provision (DI n 269/2003) provided for a tax credit in favour of R&D-related investments.

49.   Yes. Among others, DI n. 35/2005 (so-called "on competitiveness" provides for the full deductibility of donations in favours of universities and research centres.

50.   Measures that do not explicitly target firms engaged in offshoring.

D. Measures designed to revive economic activity

			Yes	No
D.1.	Identify enterprises that have offshored some of their activities and develop incentives to encourage them to create jobs in their country of origin		❏	❏
D.2.	In order to reduce the cost advantage of activities relocated abroad, promote:			
	a.	Innovative activities with the object of increasing labour productivity	❏	❏
	b.	New sectors and higher value added activities	❏	❏
	c.	Creation of new firms, particularly SMEs in the high-tech sector	❏	❏
	d.	Others (please specify)	❏	❏
D.3.	Provide incentives to facilitate the repatriation of activities to the country of origin		❏	❏
D.4.	Promote special education and training programmes for people who have lost their jobs owing to offshoring to help them find new jobs		❏	❏

Table 3. Country responses to Part D of the questionnaire

Country	D1	D2			D3	D4
		a	b	c		
Austria	No	No (1)	No (1)	No (1)	No	No (1)
Canada	No	No (2)	No (2)	No	No	No
Czech Rep.	No	Yes	Yes	Yes	No	No
Germany	No	Yes	Yes	Yes	No	Yes
Hungary	No	Yes (3)	Yes (3)	Yes (3)	No (4)	Yes (5)
Luxembourg	No	Yes	Yes	Yes	No	No
Norway	No	No	No	No	No	No
Poland	No	No	No	No	No	No
Sweden	No	No	No	No	No	No
Switzerland	No	Yes	Yes	Yes	No	Yes
United Kingdom	No	No (6)	No (6)	No (6)	No	No (7)
United States	No	No	No	No	No	Yes
France	Yes (8)	Yes (9)	Yes (10)	Yes (11)	Yes (12)	Yes (13)
Australia	No	No	No	No	No	No
Spain	No	Yes	No	Yes	No	Yes
Finland	No	Yes	Yes	Yes	No	Yes
Portugal	No	Yes (14)	Yes (14)	Yes (14)	No	Yes (15)
Italy	No	No	No	No	No	No
Belgium	No	No (16)	Yes (17)	Yes (17)	No	No (18)

Ttable 3 notes:

1. Such activities do exist, however not particularly in response to the threat of offshoring, but as part of an overall programme to improve the structure of the economy.

2. Please note that these measures are in place in Canada, but were not implemented in the context of offshoring.

3. Compare C.4 through C.9.

4. However, there are **direct incentives** to boost investments (including FDI) through the ECOP (co-financed by the EU); special incentive packages for investors, and **indirect incentives** through various tax advantages (such as development tax relief); supplier development programme, one-stop-shop.

5. Government-sponsored training for the unemployed.

6. D2: Promote innovation, higher value added activities and new firms, especially in high-tech sectors.

   The UK government provides funding for (often hi-tech) start-ups through for example Enterprise Capital Funds. In addition, the measures mentioned under C4 are also designed to encourage innovation.

7. D4: Special training/help with finding new jobs for people who have lost their jobs as a result of offshoring.

   RDAs will take the lead whenever there is a large loss of jobs in any area whether as a result of offshoring or not. They would first work with the enterprise concerned to examine potential alternatives, and when these are not found, then with agencies such as JobCentre Plus to identify short and longer-term solutions. There is a comprehensive package of support for those facing redundancy, including the Rapid Response Service, which tailors post-redundancy solutions to the needs of the local economy and labour markets. In addition there is a Rapid Response Action Fund to pay for one-off support *e.g.* training to address individual barriers to re-employment.

8. MIME, business tax credit.

9. TIC tax credit for SMEs.

10. Clusters of competitiveness, Industrial Innovation Agency.

11. "Innovative Young Enterprises" status, OSEO.

12. Tax credit, relocation, return of researchers.

13. Personalised redeployment agreement instituted on 1 July 2005 for workers made redundant.

14. Such measures do exist, although not specifically in response to the threat of offshoring; they are part of a programme to improve structural adjustment of the economy.

15. There are no measures specifically designed to encourage repatriation of activities moved offshore. However, Portugal does have tax incentives aimed at fostering job creation at home and encouraging R&D.

16. There is an overall policy of supporting innovation, but no specific measures in terms of either labour productivity or offshoring.

17. Measures that do not explicitly target firms engaged in offshoring.

18. There are, however, special assistance measures for workers affected by collective redundancies (see Section 5.3.6) which are often linked to offshoring.

A5.2. Supplementary information concerning certain countries

A.5.2.1. United States

Department of the Treasury
Office of Public Affairs

January 13, 2005

Guidance on repatriation of foreign earnings under the American Jobs Creation Act

Overview:

The Treasury Department and IRS today announced the first in a series of notices that will provide detailed guidance for U.S. companies planning to repatriate earnings from overseas subsidiaries subject to the temporary reduced tax rate available under the American Jobs Creation Act (AJCA). The notice released today gives guidance to companies on how to satisfy the domestic reinvestment plan requirement and on the kinds of investments in the United States for which the repatriated funds may be used under this provision.

Background:

Internal Revenue Code Section 965, enacted as part of the AJCA in October 2004, is a temporary provision that allows U.S. companies to repatriate earnings from their foreign subsidiaries at a reduced tax rate provided that the specified conditions and restrictions are satisfied. Section 965 provides that U.S. companies may elect, for one taxable year, an 85% dividends received deduction for eligible dividends from their foreign subsidiaries.

Section 965 contains several limitations on the repatriated dividends that are eligible for the reduced tax rate. One such requirement is that the repatriated funds must be invested by the company in the United States pursuant to a domestic reinvestment plan approved by company management before the funds are repatriated. Today's notice focuses on this requirement and provides detailed guidance to assist companies in satisfying this requirement.

How it works:

- Under the new law, for one year only, companies that repatriate earnings from foreign subsidiaries to the United States and meet the specified requirements are subject to a reduced tax rate on the repatriated earnings.

- Before repatriating the earnings, the company must have a domestic reinvestment plan for such earnings that is approved by the company's CEO or President and is subsequently approved by its board of directors.

- There are limits on what constitutes an investment in the United States as required under this provision.

Domestic reinvestment plan

The domestic reinvestment plan must be approved by the company's president, CEO, or comparable official before the dividend is paid. The plan must also be approved subsequently by the company's board of directors, management committee, executive committee, or similar body.

The plan must describe specific anticipated investments in the United States. There is no required form or template that must be used for the plan. The plan must describe the anticipated U.S. investments in reasonable detail and specificity.

The plan must state a reasonable time period during which the company anticipates completing the investments. The plan may provide for alternative investments to be made if the principal investments specified cannot be made. The plan must state the total dollar amount for each principal investment.

Permitted investments

Section 965 identifies types of U.S. investments for which repatriated funds may be used under a domestic reinvestment plan.

Today's notice provides guidance on the following U.S. investments:

- Hiring and training workers
- Infrastructure and capital investments
- Research and development
- Financial stabilization for the purposes of U.S. job retention or creation
    - o This would include debt repayment and the funding of qualified benefit plan obligations
- Certain acquisitions of business entities with U.S. assets
- Advertising and marketing
- Acquisition of rights to intangible property, such as patent rights

Expenditures that are not permitted investments

Some expenditures do not constitute investments for which repatriated funds may be used under a domestic reinvestment plan.

Today's notice provides guidance on the following non-permitted investments:

- Executive compensation
- Inter-company transactions
- Dividends and other shareholder distributions
- Stock redemptions
- Portfolio investments
- Debt instruments
- Tax payments

Neither the list of permitted investments nor the list of non-permitted investments is exhaustive.

Administrative guidance

The election to apply the Section 965 repatriation provision is made by attaching an election form or statement to the tax return for the year.

Information must be reported to the IRS annually regarding investments made under a domestic reinvestment plan.

A "safe harbour", based on a showing of progress toward completion of the planned U.S. investments, may be used to establish that the domestic reinvestment plan requirement has been satisfied.

Questions and answers

When is the provision effective?

The provision generally applies to the first taxable year beginning on or after the October 22, 2004 enactment (which means 2005 for calendar-year taxpayers). Alternatively, the provision could be applied to the preceding taxable year (which means 2004 for calendar-year taxpayers).A quel taux précis de dégrèvement fiscal les entreprises ont-elles droit sur les bénéfices qu'elles rapatrient de l'étranger ?

Exactly what is the tax reduction to companies on the foreign earnings they repatriate?

The U.S. company is permitted to deduct 85% of the repatriated dividends. If the company is subject to the 35% corporate tax rate on the other 15% of the repatriated amount, that represents effectively a 5.25% tax rate on the total repatriated dividend.

Do firms have to use the tax break in 2005 or could they save it and use it in 2006 or in later years?

The provision applies only for the year specified and cannot be used in later years.

Are companies required to use the exact funds they repatriate to make the required U.S. investment?

No, companies are not required to trace or segregate the repatriated funds. Companies simply must demonstrate that an amount equal to the amount of repatriated funds is invested under the domestic reinvestment plan.

Do the investments have to be completed in a specific time frame? Do they have to be completed in the same year that the company takes the tax break?

No, there is no specific time limit for making the investments. Investments may be completed in a tax year after the year in which the funds are repatriated. The domestic reinvestment plan must state a reasonable time period anticipated for completion of the investments.

Does payment of tort liabilities qualify as a permitted use of repatriated funds ?

Today's notice provides general guidance on the domestic investment of repatriated funds and provides specific guidance on several categories of permitted and non-permitted investments. The investments addressed in the guidance are illustrative and the guidance is not intended to provide an exhaustive list. The notice does not specifically address expenditures for tort liabilities. The notice does provide general guidance that expenditure for financial stabilization for domestic job retention or creation is a permitted use, which could encompass payments to satisfy a company's outstanding liabilities.

A.5.2.2. United Kingdom

The United Kingdom has not introduced any measures to directly either encourage or discourage offshoring.

However, there has been considerable analysis of offshoring and the appropriate policy response, which was set out in the DTI's "Trade and Investment White Paper: Making globalisation a force for good" (July 2004) and accompanying DTI Economics Paper Number 10, "Liberalisation and globalisation: Maximising the benefits of international trade and investment". The main principles are:

- Decisions on location must be commercial ones, for companies to take.

- But encourage companies to take decisions carefully, weighing risks and costs against benefits.

- Encourage companies to consult with their employees.

- Need to work in partnership with developing countries to encourage observance of core labour standard.

Governments need to respond by facilitating adjustment by: helping people improve their skills, companies to improve their performance and to help people The British government also recognises the need to adjust to and take advantage of the opportunities generated by change and has a range of policies to facilitate such adjustment. There are many factors driving changes, of which offshoring is one. So whilst these policies were not directly introduced in response to offshoring, they can affect its impact.

Community competence

On the issue of whether EU Community competence applies, the UK's opinion is that there are very few areas where it could be said that Community legislation may not have a role or may not restrict Member States' ability to take action. Of particular relevance will be Community State Aid rules, although rules on employment, R&D, regional policies and employment could be relevant to the various areas.

A.5.2.3. Sweden

Swedish policy aims to promote structural development, as it will help to improve international competitiveness, national economic growth and living standards. The main view on globalisation and international trade is that it is favourable to society as a whole in the long run. Sweden is vigorously pursuing open, simple and fair conditions for international trade and investment.

However, the effects of globalisation increase the need for flexibility in the labour market, in business as well as for individuals. No policy, though, is particularly related to offshoring.

Labour market policy has three principal tasks:

- To channel work to the unemployed and labour to employees (sic).

- To take measures against shortage occupations and bottlenecks.

- To take initiatives to help those who have difficulty obtaining work.

The government is taking steps to equip people seeking work to meet the needs of the labour market and to facilitate labour force mobility so as to avoid shortages of labour occurring, either locally or regionally. No labour market programmes are targeted specifically to workers displaced due to international trade or outsourcing. Labour market programmes are offered to people that meet the general requirements.

The aim of the Swedish business development policy is to promote sustainable economic growth and higher employment through more enterprises and expanding businesses. Greater economic activity in larger numbers of expanding companies is vital for promoting growth, both in Sweden and Europe. To achieve the overall objective of business development policy, the government is working with the following sub-goals:

- Access to capital – Making use of, and developing ideas, with high growth potential through supplementary funding.

- Entrepreneurship, information, advice and skills development – Helping to develop skills and create favourable conditions for business development and enterprise.

- Simple and better regulations, permits and supervision – Ensuring good basic conditions and a simple regulatory framework for enterprise.

- Well-functioning markets – promoting effective competition, for the benefit of consumers.

- Research and development – Increasing the knowledge and skills needed to encourage innovation, growth and modernisation, within the business sector.

- Business intelligence, evaluation and statistics – By refining available data, creating the conditions for developing business development and innovation policy.

A.5.2.4. France

In France, many debates, studies and publications have recently been devoted to offshoring abroad. A number of measures have also been proposed by experts and politicians. Nonetheless, the main policy effort has to do with the creation of "clusters of competitiveness" with the ultimate objective of strengthening the potential for competition of French businesses and regions and encouraging businesses to keep their activities in France.

Measures relating directly to offshoring

- **Creation of a business tax credit:** This measure seeks to avert offshoring by helping to preserve business activity in areas of France exposed to offshoring and industrial restructuring. The tax credit amounts to a thousand euros per employee, over a three-year period (up to a maximum of EUR 100 000 over three years per enterprise). Among the goals of the credit is to assist employment areas that are having a difficult time adjusting. The decrees stipulating the employment areas eligible for the business tax credit written into the 2005 Budget Act were signed on 12 May 2005. The employment areas in which businesses are eligible for the tax credit are selected annually on the following basis:

  o Amongst areas in which the unemployment rate is two percentage points above the national average and the rate of dependent industrial employment is at least 10%, the **20 areas** in which dependent employment has grown the least over a four-year period.

  o Employment areas in which "ongoing industrial restructuring threatens to have a serious impact on the employment situation"; for 2005, this applies to **15 areas**.

- **Creation of a corporate profit tax credit for firms that bring their operations back to France:** This measure seeks to foster relocation. Its aim is to prompt firms that have shifted all or part of their operations out of the European Economic Area between 1 January 1999 and 22 September 2004 to relocate them in France between 1 January 2005 and 3 December 2006. Personnel costs corresponding to jobs brought back to France will be covered by the government – the first year at a rate of 50%, declining gradually over a five-year period.

Measures helping to steer businesses towards production less subject to being moved offshore

- **Institution of clusters of competitiveness to foster synergy between businesses and research** [following the meeting on 12 July 2005 of the Interministerial Committee for Land-Use Planning and Development (CIADT)]: This measure seeks to create a potential for innovation. A cluster of competitiveness is defined as a combination, in any given geographical area, of businesses, training centres and research units committed to innovative joint projects and having the critical mass needed for international visibility. These clusters, defined geographically and assigned labels (in progress), will enjoy profit tax exemptions as well as relief on business tax contributions and property tax on developed land. Exemptions will be granted for 50% of social security contributions in respect of employees engaged in research and innovation activities, according to size.

- **Creation of the Industrial Innovation Agency (AII):** The Agency's mission is to support major industrial programmes that generate research and development, with co-financing from industrial firms and in compliance with European regulations. The AII became operational in the second half of 2005.

  By basing the definition of its priorities and its action on an analysis of the strengths and weaknesses of French industry, the AII's mission will be to support major innovative programmes (industrial projects receiving aid will last between five and ten years), drawing on large enterprises and on capabilities (human resources, research potential, infrastructure) developed in connection with certain clusters of competitiveness. The AII will co-finance projects in the form of advances repayable if successful, so as to limit the risk incurred by the industrial firm, or as subsidies, the workings of which have not yet been determined.

Prospective analysis

- **Ongoing reform of the Interministerial Committee for Land-Use Planning and Competitiveness (CIACT):** This is the former Interministerial Committee for Land-Use Planning and Development (CIADT). The new committee should help to enhance government anticipation of and assistance with major transformations in industrial and service activities. These transformations may represent an opportunity, or on the contrary a threat to the country's competitiveness and the development of businesses, employment and territories. Here the CIACT will look to assistance from the Delegation for Land-Use Planning and Regional Action (DATAR), merged with the Interministerial Mission on Economic Transformations (MIME), and on a interministerial centre for forecasting and anticipation of economic transformations, which is being created.

A.5.2.5. Portugal

In Portugal, there are many policy measures in force which have either a direct or indirect impact on offshoring, but none of them is specifically related to offshoring. Policy measures are generally aimed at promoting structural adjustment and improving the business environment and the competitiveness of the economy as a whole.

Some of the measures that can indirectly reduce pressure for offshoring, or revive economic activity after offshoring, are related to restructuring processes, qualification of human resources, employment and labour market policies, namely, those implemented under the National Plan for Growth and Employment (**PNACE**). One of the priority areas of **PNACE** is aimed at preventing and managing predictable restructuring processes, where relocations abroad are included, meeting two main goals:

- To adopt a proactive and co-ordinated attitude (prediction), operating at local level in an inter-institutional proximity, promoting competitiveness and respecting market rules.

- To strengthen qualifications and promote the skills required to meet new professional market needs, as well as to improve mechanisms to create self-employment and, in general, all social policy instruments and those designed to promote geographic mobility.

To this end, the main policy instruments included in the PNACE are as follows:

- **The Agency for Integrated Intervention for Enterprise Restructuring Processes (AGIIRE)** is working towards the following goals: i) to identify companies carrying out restructuring operations; ii) to assist companies in their restructuring processes so that they can contribute to the modernisation and improvement of the entrepreneurial environment, and to long-run sustainable employment; iii) to co-ordinate government intervention in respect of firms undergoing restructuring processes and to facilitate corporate recoveries; iv) to monitor corporate recoveries and avoid tax evasion; v) to monitor processes resulting in the cessation of business activities, minimising their social costs.

  AGIIRE is implementing a warning system aimed at anticipating firms' decisions in respect of restructuring processes, resolving difficulties and promoting the success of new opportunities that arise.

- **Centres for Fast and Personalised Intervention (NIRP)** seek to provide local support for workers affected by restructuring processes, through rapid application of policy measures with custom-tailored solutions to help them find new jobs and social protection, which include the creation of Mobile Employment Centres.

  The Centres, which are set up in proximity to companies that are restructuring, begin by taking stock of the situation and ascertaining the resources available. Two examples of presently active NIRPs are those dealing with i) the LEAR Corporation and ii) ALCOA - Fujikura Portugal, SA.

The main **employment policy** measures concerned with the instruments referred to above are:

- **The FACE Programme** lends support for redeploying the labour force of companies operating in industries undergoing restructuring or modernisation processes and that have great importance in regional terms.

- **Advising and training programmes** are in force for micro and small firms, such as REDE and GERIR, based on a concept of "training through action", which includes identification of the problems facing firms, special training and support to create jobs for skilled young graduates, and assistance in designing and implementing plans for change and modernisation.

- **The Employers' Programme** promotes contracts and new job creation for technical staff.

- **The system of incentives to improve the dynamism and modernisation of industry as a whole** specifically targets corporate mergers and acquisitions and the creation of an M&A market capable of revitalising the least dynamic business practices. It encourages firms to attain critical mass, vis-à-vis globalisation procedures, and fosters a return to competitiveness of firms that have suffered severe financial setbacks.

- **The extrajudicial conciliation procedure** advocates flexible agreements between companies and their creditors, compatible with the firms' recovery.

- **The PRASD Programme** seeks out sustainable solutions, driven by the need to prompt changes in traditional economic growth models at a regional level, including the adoption of preventive measures against local decline.

- **The Dínamo Programme** aims to enhance productivity in the textile, clothing and leather industries through a series of reforms in the following areas: marketing, internationalisation, occupational skills, innovation and R&D.

A number of other measures that can indirectly counteract the offshoring trend, or revive economic activity after offshoring, are related to **taxation.** Issues concerning the relocation of individuals and enterprises for tax purposes, as well as the use of preferential or zero taxation countries, regions, territories or jurisdictions, are in fact of concern to the Portuguese authorities. Therefore, although it cannot be said that there is a "special policy in relation to offshoring" in the strictest sense of the term, a whole series of deterrents or penalties have been instituted from a long-term perspective to fight such practices and in particular, in most recent years, to comply with the recommendations and measures implemented by the European Union and OECD, Portugal being a member of both institutions.

These measures are construed around the definition of a **list of specified countries**, territories and regimes considered as "tax havens" or subject to clearly more favourable taxation regimes (the so-called "black list"). This list is reproduced in Ministerial Order No. 150/2004 of 13 February and covers 83 countries or jurisdictions.

Examples of tax measures taken in respect of "offshoring" activities or practices (non-comprehensive list):

Measures involving corporate income tax (IRC)

Example:

- Payments to non-resident entities subject to a preferential tax system — being considered as such those entities located in a country or territory included in the officially approved list — may not be allowed as deductible for the purpose of determining taxable profit in Portugal (see Article 59 of the IRC Code).

- Allocation to resident partners of profits from non-resident companies subject to a preferential tax system (see Article 60 of the IRC Code).

- Harsher tax treatment in respect of thin-capitalisation or "transfer pricing" practices between specially related entities (see Articles 58 and 62 of the IRC Code and Ministerial Order No. 1446-C/2001 of 21 December).

Measures involving personal income tax (IRS)

Example:

- Any person possessing Portuguese nationality who relocates his tax residence in a country, territory or region cited on the aforementioned list may be deemed resident in Portugal in the year during which such relocation occurs and in the four subsequent years (see Article 16 of the IRS Code).

Measures involving taxation of immovable property (IMI and IMT codes)

Example:

- For immovable property owned by entities having their fiscal domicile in a country, territory or region covered by the above-mentioned list, the annual tax rate is 5%, as compared with rates ranging from 0.2% to 0.8% for other taxable immovable property (see Article 112 of the IMI Code).

- The same applies to the tax rate levied on the acquisition of housing, in which case – in contrast to the exemption and reduced rate system in force for residents (maximum tax rate of 6%) – the applicable rate is 15%, regardless of the property's purchase price (see Article 17 of the IMT Code).

Measures involving the Tax Incentive Act

Example:

- Enterprises with investment projects located in a country or region cited on the aforementioned list are not allowed to benefit from conventional tax incentives under Portuguese domestic law.

- Considering the tax exemption for capital gains obtained from the transfer against payment of corporate rights and other securities held by non-residents, such gains may be taxed in case of entities having their domicile in countries and jurisdictions covered by the above-mentioned list (see Article 26 of the Statute above referred to).

Similarly, the temporary exemption benefit in respect of rental property subject to the "conditional leasing" regime, as well as immovable property acquired for owner-occupied housing or for renting for a similar purpose shall not apply (see Articles 41 and 42 of the aforementioned Act).

A.5.2.6. Belgium

In Belgium, there is no register of firms that have transferred activities abroad, which makes it difficult to introduce a specific policy on offshoring. The only information available in this context relates to collective redundancies, which have to be reported under the so-called "Renault" Act (passed after the closure of the Renault factory in Vilvoorde in 1998). But the Belgian authorities sill pay close attention to offshoring, particularly because of the high proportion of foreign firms in the country.

At the same time, Belgium has been introducing policies to attract foreign firms and encourage multinationals to keep their subsidiaries in Belgium. Until recently, the most significant instrument used in this context was the tax status granted to co-ordination centres. However, because this status will shortly be removed, the federal government has introduced a notional interest deduction on equity in order to replace it.

There is also a "Safeguarding Competitiveness Act", which provides a framework for centralised collective pay bargaining. This Act defines a wage norm that aims to limit wage increases to the average rise in the three main neighbouring countries (France, Germany, Netherlands). The implicit goal is to combat offshoring.

A.5.2.7. European Union

While the problem of relocation abroad is not part of European policy, two measures taken in 2004 could have an indirect effect. The first one increases, from the current five years to seven years in 2006, the time frame during which a business benefiting from a subsidy from European funds for its establishment and the development of its activities in a given region may not allow this investment to deteriorate nor cease production, under penalty of having to pay back the EU funding thus received.

Under the second measure, an entrepreneur who has failed, in a given State, to refund the EU aid claimed from him following the relocation of a productive activity within a Member State or another Member State, shall be ineligible for other EU aid for the purpose of making another investment. For this purpose, provision has been made for the exchange of information and very close co-operation between the Commission and the appropriate authorities of the member countries.

A more recent proposal involves creation of a European Globalisation Adjustment Fund (EGF) which would help workers who lose their jobs as a result of international restructuring and offshoring to get back into the labour market. The fund will begin with only 500 million euros. It will be outside the European Union's multi-year budget and will have no pre-determined endowment. Having no budget appropriation of its own, the Fund will be financed with under-utilised appropriations from other lines of the Community budget. Only certain actions are to be eligible for assistance from the Fund, such as training and redeployment, while others, such as social protection allowances for those made jobless, will be excluded. According to the Commission, funding will be available only if offshoring-induced restructuring causes at least one thousand employees of the same company to lose their jobs.

Bibliography

Abowd, J.M., J. Haltiwanger and J. Lane (2004), "Integrated Longitudinal Employee-Employer Data for the United States." Urban Institute, 31 January, *www.urban.org/UploadedPDF/1000615_Integrated_LED.pdf.*

Abrahamsson, M., D. Andersson and S. Brege (2003), *From a Trend to a Strategic Decision: Outsourcing*, magazine number 5 (in Swedish).

Agrawal, V. and D. Farrell (2003), "Who Wins from Offshoring?", *McKinsey Quarterly* no. 4 *(www.mckinseyquarterly.com).*

Amiti, M. and S.J. Wei (2006), "Service Offshoring and Productivity: Evidence from the United States", *National Bureau of Economic Research Working Paper,* No. 11926.

Amiti, Mary and Shang-Jin Wei (2004a), "Fear of Service Outsourcing: Is It Justified?", *NBER Working Paper* # 10808, September 2004, *http://papers.nber.org/papers/w10808.*

Amiti, Mary and Shang-Jin Wei (2004b), "Services Outsourcing, Production and Employment: Evidence from the US", *IMF Working Paper.*

Arthuis, J. (1993), *Les délocalisations et l'emploi*, Les Éditions d'organisation, Paris.

Arthuis, J. (1993), *Rapport d'information sur les délocalisations hors du territoire national des activités industrielles et de service*, fait au nom de la Commission des finances, du contrôle budgétaire et des comptes économiques de la nation, Sénat.

Atkinson, R.D. (2004), "Understanding the Offshoring Challenge", policy report, Progressive Policy Institute, *www.ppionline.org.*

Aubert, P. and P. Sillard (2005), "Délocalisations et réductions d'effectifs dans l'industrie française", *Série des documents de travail de la Direction des Études et Synthèses Économiques,* INSEE, France.

Auer, P., G. Besse and D. Méda (2006), "Offshoring and the Internationalisation of Employment: A Challenge for Fair Globalisation", International Labour Organisation, International Institute for Labour Studies, Geneva.

Aussilloux, V. and M.-L. Cheval (2002), "Les investissements directs français à l'étranger et l'emploi en France", *Économie et Prévision*, no. 152-153, janvier-mars, pp. 171-188.

Baily, Martin N. and D. Farrell (2004), "Exploding the Myths of Offshoring", *The McKinsey Quarterly Web Exclusive*, July 2004, *www.mckinseyquarterly.com.*

Baily, M.N. and D. Farrell (2004), "Exploring the Myths of Offshoring", *McKinsey on Economics*, *The McKinsey Quarterly*, June.

Baily, M.N. and R.Z. Lawrence (2005), "Don't Blame Trade for US Job Losses", *The McKinsey Quarterly*, No. 1, June.

Baldwin, J.R. and W.M. Brown (2004), "Head Office Employment and Foreign Multinationals in Canadian Manufacturing Firms, 1973-1999", Micro-economic Analysis Division, Statistics Canada, 18-F R.H. Coats Building, Ottawa K1A OT6, Work in progress: Draft: 2004-04-15.

Barba Navaretti, G. and D. Castellani (2004), "Investments Abroad and Performance at Home – Evidence from Italian Multinationals", *NBER Working Paper*, January.

Bardhan, A.D. and D. Jaffee (2004), "On Intra-Firm Trade and Multinationals: Foreign Outsourcing and Offshoring in Manufacturing" in M. Graham and R. Solow (eds.), *The Role of Foreign Direct Investment and Multinational Corporations in Economic Development*, draft, 7 April, *http://www.brookings.edu/pge/offshoring_Bardhan.pdf*.

Baumol, W., A. Blinder and E. Wolff (2003), *Downsizing in America: Reality, Causes and Consequences*, New York, Russell Sage Foundation.

Bender, S., C. Dustmann, D. Margolis and C. Meghir (2002), "Worker Displacement in France and Germany", in Kuhn, P.J. (ed.) *Losing Work, Moving on: International Perspectives on Worker Displacement*, Kalamazoo, Michigan, W.E. Upjohn Institute for Employment Research.

Benedetto, G., J. Haltiwanger, J. Lane and K. McKinney (2004), "Using Worker Flows to Measure Firm Dynamics", Urban Institute, May, *www.urban.org/UploadedPDF/411014_worker_flows.pdf*.

Bernard, P., H. Spinnewyn, B. Van den Cruyce, H. Van Sebroeck and P. Vandenhove (1998), "Délocalisation, Mondialisation, un rapport d'actualisation pour la Belgique", Bureau fédéral du plan, *http://www.plan.be/fr/pub/other/OPDE1998/OPDE1998fr.pdf*

Bhagwati, J., A. Panagariya and T.N. Srinivasan (2004), "The Muddles Over Outsourcing", *Journal of Economic Perspectives*, Vol. 18 (Fall), pp. 93-114.

Biswas, D. (2003), "Offshore Outsourcing: Is It the TCO Slasher It Promised to Be?", *Information Age*, October/November 2003, p. 21, *www.acs.org.au/infoage.html*, accessed December 2003.

Bivens, L.J. (2005), "Truth and Consequences of Offshoring", *Briefing Paper* #155, Economic Policy Institute, *www.epi.org/content.cfm/bp155*.

Blanchflower, D. and S. Burgess (1996), "Job Creation and Job Destruction in Great Britain in the 1980s", *CEP Discussion Papers*.

Blinder, A.S. (2006), "Offshoring: The Next Industrial Revolution?", *Foreign Affairs*, 85:2, 113-128.

Bonnaz, H., N. Courtot and D. Nivat (1994), "Le contenu en emplois des échanges industriels de la France avec les pays en développement", *Économie et Statistique*, no. 279-280.

Borga, M. and R.S. Lipsey (2004), "Factor Prices and Factor Substitution in U.S. Firms' Manufacturing Affiliates Abroad", *National Bureau of Economic Research Working Paper* #10442, April, *http://papers.nber.org/papers/w10442*.

Brainard, L. and R.E. Litan (2004), "'Offshoring' Service Jobs: Bane or Boon – And What to Do?" *Policy Brief* #132, The Brookings Institution, Washington, D.C., April, *www.brookings.edu/comm/policybriefs/pb132.pdf*.

Bronfenbrenner, K. and S. Luce (2004), "The Changing Nature of Corporate Global Restructuring: The Impact of Production Shifts on Jobs in the U.S., China, and Around the Globe", prepared for the U.S.-China Economic and Security Review Commission.

Brown, Sharon P. (2004), "Mass layoff statistics and domestic and overseas relocations", presented at the Brookings Institution Data Workshop on Offshoring, Washington, DC, June, *www.brook.edu/pge/20040622_brown.ppt.*

Chena, Y. J. Ishikawab and Z. Yuc (2004), "Trade Liberalization and Strategic Outsourcing", *Journal of International Economics* 63, 419-436, *www.elsevier.com/locate/econbase.*

Conseil des Impôts, "La Concurrence fiscale et l'entreprise", vingt-deuxième rapport au Président de la République.

Corbett, M.F. (2002), *The Global Outsourcing Market 2002*, Corbett & Associates, New York, *www.corbettassociates.com*, accessed January 2004.

Cortes, O. and S. Jean (1997), "La concurrence des pays émergents menace-t-elle le travail des non-qualifiés en Europe ? Une analyse prospective par un modèle d'équilibre général calculable", in J. Melo et P. Guillaumont (eds).

Criscuolo C. and M. Leaver (2005), "Offshore Outsourcing and Productivity", *mimeo.*

Deloitte Research (2003), "The Cusp of a Revolution: How Offshoring will Transform the Financial Services Industry", *www.deloitte.com/dtt/cda/doc/content/The-Cusp-of-a-revolution-2003.pdf.*

De Melo, J. and P. Guillaumont (eds.) (1997), *Commerce Nord-Sud, migration et délocalisation : conséquences pour les salaires et l'emploi*, Economica, Paris.

Deardorff, Alan (2005), "A Trade Theorist's Take on Skilled-Labor Outsourcing" in *International Review of Economics & Finance*, Vol. 14, Issue 3, Elsevier, *www.sciencedirect.com.*

DREE (1994), "Échanges internationaux, délocalisations, emploi", *Notes Bleues de Bercy.*

Drezner, D.W. (2004), "The Outsourcing Bogeyman", *Foreign Affairs*, May/June, *www.foreignaffairs.org/20040501faessay83301-p0/daniel-w-drezner/the-outsourcing-bogeyman.html.*

Drumetz, F. (2004), "La délocalisation", *Bulletin de la Banque de France*, no. 132, pp. 27-42, December.

DTI White Paper (2004), "Making Globalization a Force for Good", United Kingdom Department of Trade and Industry.

Egger, H. and P. Egger (2002), "International Outsourcing and the Productivity of Low-skilled Labour in the EU", April.

Egger, H. and P. Egger (2004), "Outsourcing and Trade in a Spatial World", *CESifo Working Paper* No. 1349, Category 7: Trade Policy, December, *www.ssrn.com*.

Egger, H. and P. Egger (2005), "Labor Market Effects of Outsourcing under Industrial Interdependence" in *International Review of Economics & Finance*, Vol. 14, Issue 3, Elsevier, *www.sciencedirect.com*

Egger, P. M. Pfaffermayer and A. Weber (2003), "Sectoral Adjustment of Employment: The Impact of Outsourcing and Trade at the Micro Level", IZA DP No. 921, November, Forschungsinstitut zur Zukunft der Arbeit.

Egger, P. *et al.* (2001), "The International Fragmentation of Austrian Manufacturing: The Effects of Outsourcing on Productivity and Wages", *North American Journal of Economics and Finance*, Vol. 12, Issue 3.

Ekholm, K. and K. Hakkala (2005), "The Effect of Offshoring on Labor Demand: Evidence from Sweden", *Working Paper No. 654*, Research Institute of Industrial Economics, IUI Stockholm.

European Commission (2004), "Globalisation and Labour Markets: A European Perspective", *Employment in Europe*.

European Commission (2005), "Restructuring and Employment: Anticipating and Accompanying Restructuring in Order to Develop Employment – the Role of the European Union", 120 final, Brussels.

European Foundation for the Improvement of Living and Working Conditions (2005), "Restructuring and Employment in the EU: Concepts, Measurement and Evidence".

Falk, M. and Y. Wolfmayer (2005), "The Impact of International Outsourcing on Employment: Empirical Evidence from EU Countries", *Austrian Institute of Economic Research Paper*, WIFO.

Feenstra, R.C. and G.H. Hanson (2004), "Ownership and Control in Outsourcing to China: Estimating the Property-Rights Theory of the Firm", *National Bureau of Economic Research Working Paper* # 10198, January, *http://papers.nber.org/papers/w10198*.

Feenstra, R.C. and G.H. Hanson (1996), "Globalization, Outsourcing, and Wage Inequality", *American Economic Review,* 86, pp. 240-45.

Feenstra, R.C. and G.H. Hanson (1999), "The Impact of Outsourcing and High-Technology Capital on Wages: Estimates for the United States, 1979-1990", *The Quarterly Journal of Economics, 114, pp. 907-41.*

Fontagné, L. and J.-H. Lorenzi (2005), Désindustrialisation – Délocalisations", *Rapport du Conseil d'Analyse Économique*, no. 55, Paris, 127 p.

Forrester Research (2002), "3.3 Million U.S. Services Jobs To Go Offshore", by J.C. McCarthy with A. Dash, H. Liddell, C.F. Ross and B.D. Temkin, *Trends*, 11 November.

Gaffard, J.-L. (2005), "Attractivité, délocalisations et concurrence fiscale", *Revue de l'OFCE*, Observatoire Français des Conjonctures Économiques, Presses de Sciences Po.

Garner, A.C. (2004), "Offshoring in the Service Sector: Economic Impact and Policy Issues", *Federal Reserve Bank of Kansas City Economic Review*, Third Quarter, *www.kansascityfed.org/PUBLICAT/ECONREV/Pdf/3Q04garn.pdf.*

Gave, F. (1995), "Le calcul usuel des effets du commerce international sur l'emploi: des principes fondamentalement erronés ? ", *Revue française d'économie* no. 19.

Geischecker, I. (2002), "Outsourcing and the Demand for Low-skilled Labour in German Manufacturing: New Evidence", DIW-Berlin, October, German Institute for Economic Research, Berlin, *www.diw.de.*

Geischecker, I. and H. Görg (2004), "International Outsourcing and Wages: Winners and Losers", *Nottingham University Business School Working Paper Series*, Notthingham, United Kingdom.

Gerstenberger, B. and R.A. Roehrl (2006), "Service Jobs on the Move: Offshore Outsourcing of Business Related Services", in P. Auer, G. Besse and D. Méda (eds.), *Offshoring and the Internationalisation of Employment: A Challenge for Fair Globalisation*, International Labour Organisation, International Institute for Labour Studies, Geneva.

Girma, S. and H. Görg (2002), "Outsourcing, Foreign Ownership and Productivity: Evidence from UK Establishment Level Data", Leverhulme Centre for Research on Globalisation and Economic Policy, School of Economics, University of Nottingham.

Global Insight (USA), Inc. (2004), "Summary: The Impact of Offshore IT Software and Services Outsourcing on the US Economy and the IT Industry", sponsored by Information Technology Association of America, March.

Global Insight (USA), Inc (2004), "The Impact of Offshore IT Software and Services Outsourcing on the US Economy and the IT Industry", sponsored by Information Technology Association of America, March.

Görg, H. and A. Hanley (2005), "International Outsourcing and Productivity: Evidence from the Irish Electronics Industry", *North American Journal of Economics and Finance*, Vol. 16, Issue 2.

Görg, H. and A. Hanley (2003), "International Outsourcing and Productivity: Evidence from Plant Level Data", *Globalization, Productivity and Technology*, University of Nottingham.

Görg, H. and A. Hanley (2003), "International Outsourcing and Productivity: Evidence from Plant Level Data", Research Paper 2003/20, Leverhulme Centre for Research on Globalisation and Economic Policy, School of Economics, University of Nottingham, United Kingdom.

Görg, H. and A. Hanley (2003), "Does Outsourcing Increase Profitability?", Nottingham University Business School Working Paper Series, no. 01/2003, Nottingham, United Kingdom.

Görg, H., A. Hanley and E. Strobl (2004), "Outsourcing, Foreign Ownership, Exporting and Productivity: An Empirical Investigation with Plan level Data", Leverhulme Centre for Research on Globalisation and Economic Policy, paper 2004/08, Nottingham, United Kingdom, *www.nottingham.ac.uk/economics/leverhulme/research_papers/04_08.pdf.*

Görg, H. and A. Hanley (2005), "The Labor Demand Effets of International Outsourcing: Evidence from Plant-level Panel Data" in *International Review of Economics and Finance*, Vol. 14, Issue 3, Elsevier, *www.sciencedirect.com.*

Görzig, B. and Andreas Stephan (2002), "Outsourcing and Firm-level Performance", *DIW Berlin Discussion Paper* 309, German Institute for Economic Research, DIW, Berlin.

Gregori, T., "Outsourcing and Service Employment Growth in Italy", Dipartimento di Scienze Economiche Estatistiche, Università degli Studi di Trieste.

Grignon, F. (2004), "Délocalisations: pour un néo-colbertisme européen", *Rapport d'information*, Paris, Sénat.

Grossman, G. M., Princeton University (2004), "Offshoring and Outsourcing: Lessons from the Theory of the Firm", Conference of Federal Reserve Bank of Philadelphia, 2004, *Background Papers:* 1, 2.

Grossman, G. and Rossi-Hansberg, E. (2006), "The Rise of Offshoring: It's Not Wine for Cloth Anymore", Paper presented at Kansas Fed's Jackson Hole Conference for Central Bankers, *http://www.kc.frb.org/.*

Hamilton, J. and K.D. Singh (2003), "Offshore Outsourcing: A Global Trend", Powerpoint presentation, Wipro Technologies, January.

Hatem, F. (2004), "Délocalisations : déclin ou nouveau modèle de spécialisation", *Geoéconomie*, no. 31, pp. 119-149.

Head, K. and J. Ries (2002), "Offshore Production and Skill Upgrading by Japanese Manufacturing Firms", *Journal of International Economics* 58, 81-105, *www.elsevier.com/locate/econbase.*

Hertveldt, B., C. Kegels, B. Michel, B. Van den Cruyce, J. Verlinden, and F Verschueren (2005), "Déterminants de la localisation internationale, avec application aux secteurs Agoria", *Working Paper 16-05*, Bureau fédéral du Plan.

Hijzen, A., H. Görg and R.C. Hine (2005), "International Outsourcing and the Skill Structure of Labour Demand in the United Kingdom", *Economic Journal* 2005, 115(502), pp. 118-132.

Huws, U., S. Dahlmann and J. Flecker (2004), « European Foundation for the Improvement of Living and Working Conditions, "Outsourcing of ICT and Related Services in the EU: A Status Report », Luxembourg, Office for Official Publications of the European Communities, available at: *www.emcc.eurofound.eu.int/content/source/tn04048s.html.*

ITPS (2003), Relocation of Headquarters, Possible Motives (in Swedish).

Jackson, J.K. (2004), "Outsourcing and Insourcing Jobs in the U.S. Economy: Evidence Based on Foreign Investment Data", *Congressional Research Report for Congress* (Order Code RL32461), 2 July.

Jean, S. (2001), "Les effets de la mondialisation sur l'emploi dans les pays industrialisés : un survol de la littérature existante", DSTI/EAS/IND/SWP(2001)7, Groupe de travail sur les statistiques, Directorate for Science, Technology and Industry, OECD.

Jensen, J.B. and L.G. Kletzer, "Tradable Services: Understanding the Scope and Impact of Services Offshoring", Presentation, undated, *www.iie.com/publications/wp/wp05-9.pdf.*

Jones, R., H. Kierzkowski and C. Lurong (2005), "What Does Evidence Tell US About Fragmentation and Outsourcing?" in *International Review of Economics & Finance*, Vol. 14, Issue 3, Elsevier, *www.sciencedirect.com.*

Kakabadse, A. and N. Kakabadse (2002), "Trends in Outsourcing: Contrasting USA and Europe", *European Management Journal*, Vol. 20, No. 2, pp. 189-198.

Kirkegaard, J.F. (2004), "Outsourcing – Stains on the White Collar? » *IIE Working Paper*, Institute for International Economics, Washington, D.C., *www.iie.com/publications/papers/kirkegaard0204.pdf*, accessed June 2004.

Kirkegaard, J. (2006), "Offshoring and Offshore Outsourcing: Extent and Impact of Labour Markets in Origin and Recipient Countries" IIE, Washington, D.C.

Kleinert, J. (2003), "Growing Trade in Intermediate Goods: Outsourcing, Global Sourcing or Increasing Importance of MNE Networks?", *Review of International Economics* 11(3), 464-482.

Konings, J. (2003), "Are Wage Cost Differentials Driving Delocalisation? A Comparative Analysis between High and Low Income Countries Using Firm Level Data", Working Paper no. 134/2003, LICOS Centre for Transition Economics, Katholieke Universiteit, Leuven, Belgique.

Konings, J. and A. Murphy (2005), "Do Multinational Enterprises Relocate Employment to Low Wage Regions? Evidence from European Multinationals", version révisée du CEPR Working Paper no. 2972, LICOS Centre for Transition Economics, Université Catholique, Louvain, Belgium.

Kroll, C.A. (2005), "State and Metropolitan Area Impacts of the Offshore Outsourcing of Business Services and IT", Fisher Center for Real Estate & Urban Economics, Fisher Center Working Papers: Paper 293.

Lauré, M. (1993), "Les délocalisations : enjeux et stratégies des pays développés", *Futuribles*, mai.

Lawrence, R.Z., Harvard University, "Is Offshoring Deindustrializing America? Short- and Long-Run Perspectives", Conference of Federal Reserve Bank of Philadelphia, December 2004.

Letournel, J.-L. (2004), "Les délocalisations d'activités tertiaires dans le monde et en France", *DP Analyses économiques*, no. 55, novembre.

Levine, L. (2004), "Offshoring (a.k.a. Offshore Outsourcing) and Job Insecurity Among U.S. Workers", *Congressional Research Service Report for Congress* (Order Code RL32292), June 18, *http://hutchison.senate.gov/RL32292.pdf.*

Levine, L. (2004), "Unemployment Through Layoffs: What are the Underlying Reasons?", *Congressional Research Service Report for Congress* (Order Code RL30799), 25 June.

Liu, B. J, and A. C. Tung (2004), "Export Outsourcing and Foreign Direct Investment: Evidence from Taiwanese Exporting Firms", *Dynamics, Economic Growth, and International Trade,* conference paper.

Lorentowicz, A., D. Marin and A. Raubold (2002), "Ownership, Capital or Outsourcing: What Drives German Investment to Eastern Europe?", *Discussion Paper* 02-03, May, Department of Economics, University of Munich, Volkswirtschaftliche Fakultät Ludwig-Maximilians-Universität München, *http://epub.ub.uni-muenchen.de.*

Mann, C. (2003), "Globalization of IT Services and White Collar Jobs: The Next Wave of Productivity Growth", Institute for International Economics, *International Economics Policy Brief* #PB03-11, December, *www.iie.com/publications/pb/pb03-11.pdf*

Mankiw, G. and P. Swagel (2005), "The Politics and Economics of Offshore Outsourcing", *Working Paper American Enterprise Institute for Public Policy.*

Markusen, J. (2005), "Modeling the Offshoring of White-Collar Services: from Comparative Advantage to the New Theories of Trade and FDI", *NBER Working Paper 11827.*

Mataloni, Jr., R.J., (2004), "A Note on Patterns of Production and Employment by U.S. Multinational Companies", U.S. Bureau of Economic Analysis, *Survey of Current Business* 84(3), March: 52-56, *http://www.bea.gov/bea/ARTICLES/2004/03March/0304MNC.pdf*

Mathieu, C. and H. Sterdyniak (1994), "L'émergence de l'Asie en développement menace-t-elle l'emploi en France ?", *Revue de l'OFCE*, no. 48, janvier, pp. 55-106.

McCarthy, J.C. (2004), "Near-term Growth of Offshoring Accelerating", *Trends*, Forrester Research, 14 May.

McKinsey Global Institute (2003), "Offshoring: Is It a Win-Win Game?", McKinsey & Company, Inc., San Francisco, August, *www.mckinsey.com/knowledge/mgi*, accessed January 2004.

McKinsey Global Institute (2004), "Can Germany Win from Offshoring?", McKinsey & Co., Washington, D.C.

McKinsey Global Institute (2005), "How Offshoring of Services Could Benefit France".

Miller, A. and P. Codling (2003), *The Offshore Services Report* 2003, Ovum Holway, February, *www.ovum.com/go/content/HAE.htm.*

Moran, N. (2003), "Global Outsourcing: Looking for Savings on Distant Horizons", *Financial Times*, 2 July.

National Academy of Public Administration (2006), "Off-Shoring: An Elusive Phenomenon", *www.napawash.org/Pubs/Off-ShoringJan06.pdf.*

OECD (2006), "Globalisation and Inflation in the OECD Economies", (ECO/CPE/WP1(2006)14), OECD Economics Department.

Office of Senator Joseph I. Lieberman (2004), "Data Dearth in Offshore Outsourcing: Policymaking Requires Facts", December, *www.lieberman.senate.gov/newsroom/whitepapers/Offshoredata.pdf.*

Office of Senator Joseph I. Lieberman (2004), "Offshore Outsourcing and America's Competitive Edge: Losing Out in the High Technology R&D and Services Sectors", 11 May, *www.lieberman.senate.gov/newsroom/whitepapers/Offshoring.pdf.*

Olsen, K.B. (2006), "Productivity Impacts of Offshoring and Outsourcing: A Review", *DSTI Working Paper 2006/1,* Directorate for Science, Technology and Industry, OECD, Paris.

Parker, A. (2004), "Two-speed Europe: Why 1 Million Jobs Will Move Offshore", *Trends*, Forrester Research, August.

Ramioul, M. and S. Kirschenhofer, EMCC (2005), "Offshore Outsourcing of Business Services", Dublin, European Foundation for the Improvement of Living and Working Conditions, available at: *www.emcc.eurofound.eu.int/content/source/tn5001a.html.*

Revenga, A. (1992), "Exporting Jobs? The Impact of Import Competition on Employment and Wages in US Manufacturing", *Quarterly Journal of Economics*, vol. 107, no. 1.

Sachwald, F. (2004), "Délocalisations : une déstruction créatrice ?", *Sociétal* no. 44.

Samuelson, P.A. (2004), "Where Ricardo and Mill Rebut and Confirm Arguments of Mainstream Economists Supporting Globalization", *Journal of Economic Perspectives* 18 (Summer), 135-46.

Schultze, C.L. (2004), "Offshoring, Import Competition and the Jobless Recovery", *Policy Brief* #136, The Brookings Institution, August, *www.brookings.edu/comm/policybriefs/pb136.htm.*

SIF (2004), Jobs Being Relocated? (in Swedish).

Strauss-Kahn, V. (2003), "The Role of Globalization in the Within-Industry Shift Away from Unskilled Workers in France", *NBER Working Papers* no. 9716, May.

Swenson, D.L. (2004), "Overseas Assembly and Country Sourcing Choices", *National Bureau of Economic Research Working Paper* # 10697, August, *http://papers.nber.org/papers/w10697.*

Swenson, D.L. (2004), "Entry Costs and Outsourcing Decisions: Evidence from the US Overseas Assembly Provision", *North American Journal of Economics and Finance*, 15, 267-286.

The Economist (2003), "Re-locating the Back Office – Offshoring – The Benefits of Offshoring", 13 December.

U.S. Government Accountability Office (2006), Report to Congressional Committees, "Offshoring: U.S. Semiconductor and Software Industries Increasingly Produce in China and India", U.S. General Accounting Office (GAO-06-423), September, *www.gao.gov/cgi-bin/getrpt?GAO-06-423.*

U.S. Government Accountability Office (2004), "International Trade: Current Government Data Provide Limited Insight into Offshoring of Services", U.S. General Accounting Office (GAO-04-932), September, *www.gao.gov/cgi-bin/getrpt?GAO-04-932.*

UNCTAD and Roland Berger Strategy Consultants (2004), "Services Offshoring Takes Off in Europe – In Search of Improved Competitiveness", Summary Report, UNCTAD, Geneva.

U.S. Department of Labor, Bureau of Labor Statistics (2004), "Extended Mass Layoffs Associated with Domestic and Overseas Relations, First Quarter 2004", *Bureau of Labor Statistics News Release* USDL 04-1038, 10 June, *www.bls.gov/news.release/pdf/reloc.pdf.*

Van Long, N.(2005), "Outsourcing and Technology Spillovers", *International Review of Economics & Finance*, vol. 14, issue 3, Elsevier, *www.sciencedirect.com.*

Vimont, C. and F. Farhi (1997), "Concurrence internationale et balance en emplois : les échanges de produits industriels", *Economica*, 211 p.

Villemus, P. (2005), "Délocalisations : aurons-nous encore des emplois demain ?" Editions Seuil.

van Welsum, D. (2004), "In Search of 'Offshoring': Evidence from US Imports of Services", Birkbeck Economics Working Paper 2004, no. 2, Birkbeck College, London, *www.econ.bbk.ac.uk/wp/eco/ecoup.htm.*

van Welsum, D. and X. Reif (2005), "The Share of Employment Potentially Affected by Offshoring: An Empirical Investigation", DSTI/ICCP/IE(2005)8/FINAL, Directorate for Science, Technology and Industry, OECD, Paris.

van Welsum, D. and G. Vickery (2005), "Potential Offshoring of ICT-intensive Using Occupations", DSTI/ICCP/IE(2004)19/FINAL, Directorate for Science, Technology and Industry, Paris; available at: *www.oecd.org/sti/offshoring.*

WTO (2005), Offshoring: "More Fears and Hopes than Facts?", in *World Trade Report 2005.*

LES ÉDITIONS DE L'OCDE, 2, rue André-Pascal, 75775 PARIS CEDEX 16
IMPRIMÉ EN FRANCE
(70 2007 01 1 P) ISBN 978-92-64-03092-3 – n° 55561 2007